PRESERVING THE WHITE MAN'S REPUBLIC

A NATION DIVIDED: STUDIES IN THE CIVIL WAR ERA
ORVILLE VERNON BURTON AND ELIZABETH R. VARON, *EDITORS*

PRESERVING THE WHITE MAN'S REPUBLIC

JACKSONIAN DEMOCRACY, RACE,
AND THE TRANSFORMATION
OF AMERICAN CONSERVATISM

Joshua A. Lynn

University of Virginia Press
Charlottesville and London

University of Virginia Press
© 2019 by the Rector and Visitors of the University of Virginia
All rights reserved
Printed in the United States of America on acid-free paper

First published 2019
First paperback edition published 2022
ISBN 978-0-8139-4850-8 (paper)

1 3 5 7 9 8 6 4 2

The Library of Congress has cataloged the hardcover edition as follows:

Names: Lynn, Joshua A., 1985– author.
Title: Preserving the white man's republic : Jacksonian democracy, race, and the transformation of American conservatism / Joshua A. Lynn.
Description: Charlottesville : University of Virginia Press, 2019. | Includes bibliographical references and index. | Identifiers: LCCN 2018052877 (print) | LCCN 2018053359 (ebook) | ISBN 9780813942513 (ebook) | ISBN 9780813942506 (cloth : alk. paper)
Subjects: LCSH: United States—Politics and government—1845–1861. | Conservatism—United States—History—19th century. | Populism—United States—History—19th century. | States' rights (American politics)—History—19th century. | Democratic Party (U.S.)—History—19th century. | White supremacy movements—United States—History—19th century. | United States—Race relations—History—19th century.
Classification: LCC E415.7 (ebook) | LCC E 415.7 .L96 2019 (print) | DDC 320.97309/034—dc23
LC record available at https://lccn.loc.gov/2018052877

Cover photo: *Inauguration of James Buchanan, President of the United States, at the East Front of the U.S. Capitol*, 1857, photograph by John Wood. (Library of Congress, Manuscript Division, Montgomery C. Meigs Papers)

To Darlene and Kevin

CONTENTS

Acknowledgments ix

Introduction
Conserving the Happy Republic 1

One
The Northern Men and Their *National* Principle:
Jacksonian Ideology, Popular Sovereignty,
and White Men's Democracy, 1847–1854 11

Two
Conservatism and Fanaticism:
The Political Ideology of the Democracy
before the Civil War 34

Three
Resisting Realignment:
Democrats Respond to Partisan
and Racial Disorder, 1854–1855 68

Four
Welcoming Realignment:
Democrats, Old Whigs, and
the Conservative Diaspora 96

Five
Doughface Triumphant:
James Buchanan's Manly Conservatism
and the Election of 1856 119

Six
The Other Douglas Debates:
Democrats Debate White Supremacy
and Popular Sovereignty 146

Conclusion
American Democracy,
American Conservatism 175

Notes 181

Bibliography 225

Index 259

ACKNOWLEDGMENTS

WHEN STEPHEN A. DOUGLAS published a treatise that only caused him trouble, an opponent gloated that he had "fallen into the snare of 'writing a book' the very thing that ancient malice prayed that an 'enemy' might do." Thanks to friends and colleagues, I hope to avoid the Little Giant's fate.

I am grateful to extraordinary teachers, including Ray Glenboski at Millbrook Junior High School and Jennifer Cox at Stanhope Elmore High School; at Marshall University, Chuck Bailey, Robert Behrman, Timothy Burbery, Lee Erickson, Dan Holbrook, Charles Lloyd, Carlos López, Montserrat Miller, Bill Palmer, Robert Sawrey, Barry Sharpe, Chris White, and especially Donna Spindel and Jamie Warner; at the University of North Carolina at Chapel Hill, Vicki Behrens, Fitz Brundage, Jerma Jackson, Louise McReynolds, Lou Pérez, and John Wood Sweet.

The members of my dissertation committee at UNC guided the first iteration of this book, and their influence should be obvious. Laura Edwards often understood my arguments before I did. It will require several more books to fully address her questions and live up to the expectations she has set for my work, but I take comfort knowing she will continue to guide me along the way. Bill Barney always challenged me, and always in my best interests. Anticipating his critiques has made me more fully aware of my assumptions as a historian. Mike Lienesch honed my approach to political thought and equipped me to do more than just history. He made sure I play with ideas in a responsible way. Working with Joe Glatthaar was one of the great pleasures of UNC. He taught me how to teach. His zeal for his students and their scholarship, electric classroom presence, and friendship enhanced my graduate experience.

Whether I went into his office obstinate, panicked, or flummoxed, Harry L. Watson responded with unfailing good cheer and soft-spoken reassurance. My adviser once wrote that "contemporary political historians have grown up in the school of hard knocks." Yet Harry teaches his students to see this as an opportunity to be creative with their scholarship rather than close ranks or stubbornly stand athwart historiography. This is a book neither of us anticipated when I first became his student, and I hope I have justified his indulgence and encouragement. I will be fortunate if the sensitivity with which Harry approaches the past echoes in my scholarship, in my classrooms, and throughout my career. I thank him for taking a chance on me when I applied to be his student and for a subsequent decade of his generous mentorship and his friendship.

Nicole Etcheson and Matt Mason showed a collegiality as formidable as their scholarship by graciously reading the manuscript multiple times and helping me improve it dramatically. With such scholarly guidance, all remaining errors are attributable to my stubbornness. Dick Holway at University of Virginia Press was a joy to work with, and I am grateful for his enthusiasm from the beginning.

I wrote this book in Chapel Hill, North Carolina, LeRoy, Michigan, and Prattville, Alabama. I finished it in New Haven, Connecticut. The Yale Center for the Study of Representative Institutions and the MacMillan Center for International and Area Studies at Yale University were the most nurturing of scholarly homes. Michelle Zacks welcomed me into the family of Yale's Gilder Lehrman Center for the Study of Slavery, Abolition, and Resistance. Remarkable students in my seminars at Yale on Jacksonian Democracy, nineteenth-century popular politics, and American conservatism clarified my thinking and refined my arguments. I learned a lot from them.

Steven B. Smith became an indispensable friend and mentor. He showed me how to think about the history of ideas in new ways. He also initiated me into the mysteries of New Haven pizza. I can't thank Steven enough for looking after me at a pivotal stage in my scholarly development and launching me on my career with so much kindness and camaraderie. He also made my time in New Haven a lot more fun. I look forward to many more cigars at the Owl Shop.

I put the final touches on this book in my new home in Richmond, Kentucky. I thank my new colleagues in the Department of History, Philosophy, and Religious Studies at Eastern Kentucky University for their warm welcome.

I thank my friends and fellow scholars: Christina Carroll, Robert Colby, Greg Collins, Adam Domby, Brian Fennessy, Joey Fink, Jen Kosmin, Mordechai Levy-Eichel, Liz Lundeen, Ashley Mays, Dwight Mears, Sari Niedzwiecki, Brad Proctor, Joe Rizzo, Paul Turner, Tyler Will, Tim Williams, David Williard, Alison Wood, and Nic Wood. Shannon Eaves, Jeff Erbig, Robert Richard, Rob Shapard, and Zachary Smith deserve special thanks for reading and commenting on drafts. Shannon and Rob did the most to jumpstart this project in our writing group. Their writing improved mine.

I hope that Tom Goldstein and Elizabeth Smith know how much their friendship means to me. From making me dinner as I soldiered through comps to forgiving my dog for destroying their furniture, they are the best friends. My friend and fencing partner Patrick Kent is a kindred soul. Robert, Emily, and Brian made Chapel Hill my home.

David R. Woodward at Marshall University provided me with an example of a historian that I will always strive to emulate. My model academic is my friend Richard I. Lester, who has been my mentor longer than all the others. Harvey Curtis Fenimore Jr., Henry Lynn, and Jerry Stilp talked to me about history a long time ago, and I have never stopped wanting to talk about it since. In addition to all the other ways in which they shaped me, Patrick Henry Lynn and Joan Toomey Lynn first turned my attention to the past. Although I never met her, Betty Irene Holmes unquestionably shaped me as well. I'm told I have her laugh.

The William L. Clements Library at the University of Michigan, the Virginia Historical Society, the Institute for Humane Studies at George Mason University, the Jack Miller Center, the Graduate School at the University of North Carolina at Chapel Hill, the UNC-CH Center for the Study of the American South, the UNC-CH Department of History, the Yale Center for the Study of Representative Institutions, and the MacMillan Center at Yale supported my research and writing. The UNC-CH Writing Center and UNC Correctional Education are special programs. I am grateful to have had the opportunity to teach for them and to learn from them. A version of chapter 5 appeared in the *Journal of the Civil War Era* 8, no. 4 (Dec. 2018), published by UNC Press. Some material also appeared in the *Muster* blog (Sept. 13, 2016) of the *Journal of the Civil War Era* and in the *Tennessee Historical Quarterly* 76, no. 3 (Fall 2017).

My dog Rupert was my companion for sixteen years, from my freshman year of high school in Millbrook, Alabama, through readying this book for publication at Yale. He more than kept his promise. Rupert's love is matched only by that of my parents, to whom this book is dedicated.

PRESERVING THE WHITE MAN'S REPUBLIC

INTRODUCTION

Conserving the Happy Republic

> To make us love our country, our country ought to be lovely.
> —Edmund Burke, 1790

IN APRIL 1856 the steamer *Arago* deposited valuable cargo in New York City—the next president of the republic. A warm homecoming greeted James Buchanan. The "Old Public Functionary" had commenced his political career decades earlier opposing the Democratic Madison administration. Attuned to political shifts, he abandoned his father's stale Federalism for Andrew Jackson's populist coalition in the 1820s. Now the sanctimonious old bachelor and savvy partisan stood poised to inherit Old Hickory's mantle. An observant Jacksonian, Buchanan genuflected before the self-governing masses welcoming him home from a diplomatic assignment. He answered the cheering throng, "I have been for years abroad in a foreign land, and I like the noise of the democracy!" "If you could feel how despotism looks on; how jealous the despotic powers of the world are of our glorious institutions," he purred, "you would cherish the Constitution and Union to your hearts." Buchanan's praise doubled as admonition. The specter of "arbitrary power" haunted not only the Old World, he hinted, and Americans ought not be complacent about their exceptional republic.[1] Accepting the Democracy's presidential nomination two months later, Buchanan referenced the "dark spirit of despotism and bigotry" rampant in the United States—a domestic form of arbitrary power signaling something awry in the republic.[2]

The Happy Republic

Americans in the mid-nineteenth century were proud of their progressive republic. Democrats in particular congratulated themselves for the contrast between their nation's "happy millions enjoying the blessings of a free government" and the "bloated and festering systems of the Old World."³ "Our country, fellow-citizens, under democratic rule, has prospered beyond all former example of human greatness," beamed a New Yorker in 1858, and "our people are now, through the kind interposition of Divine Providence, every where prosperous and happy."⁴ Indiana's Democratic governor celebrated "our happy republic" and claimed that nowhere else could be found "a political confederation more free, and better adapted, in its practical operations, to raise the whole human family to the highest attainable condition of virtue, freedom, knowledge, political equality, prosperity and safety."⁵

Jacksonian Democrats credited their principles for the unprecedented degree of popular participation characterizing their happy republic. The recognition that "the *people* are capable of self government," gloated an Alabamian, was a "startling principle which amazed the sovereigns of the old world." But it was the basis for "the great democratic Republic of America."⁶ What many historians rightly deem an exclusionary polity was the most democratic yet realized, in which all white men were designated equally the nation's sovereigns. Alongside egalitarianism and majoritarianism, Jacksonians advocated what today would be considered a classically liberal credo regarding the uninfringeable rights of white male individuals and the negative beneficence of the limited state. Taken together, republican equality, majoritarian democracy, and liberal antistatism were meant to elevate the individual by removing constraints on the free exercise of his power, making him, Democrats maintained, the fillip of progress nationally and worldwide.

Democrats had forged this revolutionary political order by enshrining a modern conception of rights as equal, natural, and racially defined. They overturned older understandings of society, by which one's obligations and rights were calibrated relative to others on a sliding scale of social hierarchy. A spectrum of rights existed in colonial and early republican America, when economic and household status determined political privilege. The American Revolution loosened the bonds of this deferential society. The followers of Thomas Jefferson and Andrew Jackson then burst them asunder by reversing the equation whereby social standing predicated political power, starting instead with the premise of equal political rights for *all white men* by virtue of their whiteness and manhood. Impermeable racial boundaries supplanted social gradation, placing white men on a base level of political equality, from which more radical Jacksonians like the Loco-Focos spun out notions of socioeconomic equality. Thus did Democrats discard an organic model of society dating from antiquity for Enlightenment egalitarianism, natural rights, and racial essentialism.⁷

Although Democrats proclaimed rights to be "natural," their rights-bearing individual was not a universal abstraction. He was a white man, making Democrats' happy republic a *white man's republic*. This historically contingent individualism also made their happy republic a fragile one. If, as Democrats contended, individual rights derived from nature, their extension to new groups would be unnatural and corrosive of rights already achieved. In the late 1840s and 1850s, so-called fanatical reformers, especially slavery's opponents, threatened to push progress too far by empowering marginalized Americans. James Buchanan's 1856 campaign biography decreed that "the peace, prosperity, and safety of twenty millions of the happiest, freest, and most advanced white men, with their noble structure of republican government . . . should not be sacrificed—nay, not even jeopardized for the supposed interests of three millions of the African race."[8] Expanding rights, Democrats worried, would resurrect a social order in which their own rights were relative.

Alarmed by the precariousness of the racial equilibrium, Democrats no longer aspired to enlarge democracy but to *conserve* it exclusively for white men. The party previously decried for its radicalism manifested a reflexive conservatism in the 1850s, when they perceived a new generation of reformers seeking coercive state power to enforce gender and racial equality. Additional tinkering, Democrats concluded, would only harm America's already exceptional republic. Maligned then and now as the Slave Power's white supremacist stooge, the late antebellum "Democracy," as the party was commonly known, was still committed to democracy. To preserve their progressive, racially pure republic, Democrats renounced neither democracy nor Enlightenment liberalism. "The great conservative democratic party"[9] instead reimagined democracy as a tool for conserving white men's individual rights and equality, reinventing American conservatism in the process.

The Noise of the Democracy: Rhetoric, Ideology, and Culture

James Buchanan told his boisterous well-wishers that, after his errand among Old World tyrants, he savored the "noise of the democracy." If, like Buchanan, we listen to the Democracy's noise, we will discern the conservative shift in their partisan ideology in the late 1840s and 1850s. Antebellum Americans took political rhetoric seriously. Bemoaning his party's defeat in Pennsylvania's 1847 election, a Whig told his Democratic ("Locofoco") friend that he would have run a stronger campaign by paying attention to what his opponents actually said. He regretted not having "raked from the oblivion to which Locofocoism would now willingly consign them, every Locofoco speech, every Locofoco Banner, every Locofoco song," whereupon he would "have blazoned them to the eye & reiterated them in the ears of the honest rank & file until I have stamped upon the forehead of Locofocoism the deep and demining fraud in characters too indelible for even time to obliterate."[10] I also rake, blazon, and reiterate what Democrats said, read, and sang to comprehend their ideas, albeit without the goal of promoting Whiggery.

Acknowledging that "folks think a senator should be a *talking machine*," a congressman counseled circumspection to a colleague.[11] Fortunately, few heeded this advice, and in their gasconade, antebellum Americans intended not to prevaricate but to expound their beliefs. An array of print sources—speeches, banners, and songs—broadcast political principles and cultural values. While recent scholarship stresses the conventions of print culture and cultural practices as unifying partisan rituals, texts and rites were secondary to the ideas they transmitted.[12] When Democrats distributed speeches and pamphlets in "Stronghold[s] of Negroism" or regions "strongly tinctured with modern whiggery," it was "to furnish speakers and writers with the material for defence or assault."[13] "We are confident, if the pending issues are properly discussed before the people, that the time-honored principles of the Democratic party will be sustained at the polls," a party committee implored Kentuckian Joseph Holt in 1855. Holt was a sought-after speaker during the 1856 presidential canvass. In Louisville, he informed his wife, "I spoke 2½ hours, much longer than was prudent or kind to the audience." "I found my clothes almost as wet as if I had been plunged in the river," he recounted, "& in despite of all precautions I took cold." His wife pleaded prudence, but his party beseeched.[14] Democrats needed ideological proselytizers in a contest the stakes of which transcended the spoils of patronage.

Although historians now recognize the Civil War era as riven by ideological sparring over sectionalism, race, and slavery, the Democracy rarely figures as protagonist. Studying ideology reoriented the political history of the period away from politicians blundering into an unnecessary war to analyses of genuine and decisive moral and political disagreements over race and slavery. This bevy of scholarship prioritizes actors with sectional visions—antislavery northerners and proslavery southerners. Compared to antislavery Republicans and to its own earlier history, the 1850s Democracy appears bereft of its Jacksonian verve, impelled only by partisan inertia. Roy F. Nichols's 1948 assessment of the party as "old and faction-scarred, institutionalized, and no longer spurred by pristine enthusiasm" stands unchallenged.[15]

The prevailing historical view, inaugurated by Arthur Schlesinger Jr. and reenergized by Sean Wilentz and Jonathan H. Earle, holds that the racist, reactionary, and prosouthern Democracy of the 1850s ceased to be the party of Jacksonian Democracy. True Jacksonians abandoned the party for the antislavery Free Soil and Republican Parties. Many of these historians find something worthwhile in Jacksonian Democracy and would insulate it from a party beholden to the "Slave Power" and its northern "Doughfaces." Denunciations of the Democracy as undemocratic also evince a reluctance to acknowledge that democracy can coexist with white male supremacy and that white supremacy can be a substantive ideology. The Democratic Party, accordingly, was undemocratic *because* it was racist and proslavery, with the party's support attributed to undemocratic manipulation and the opiate of race baiting. Given a meaningful democratic choice, the people would have preferred Abraham Lincoln's Republicans to Stephen A. Douglas's Democrats.[16]

Democrats nonetheless persisted in calling their party "the Democracy," because they continued to conflate their principles and practices with democratic self-governance itself.[17] Their white male supremacy and their hostility to antislavery and other "fanatical" reformism were not cynical means to hoodwink white men into betraying their interests. These stances resonated with much of the electorate, keeping the Democracy in power and competitive throughout the decade. Many Jacksonians did desert their party. Those Democrats whose interpretation of Jacksonian producerism and egalitarianism propelled them into antislavery ranks to advance the rights of *all* laborers have been extensively chronicled. Yet those whose Jacksonianism made them hunker down in their ancestral party to defend white men's equality have received scant attention. The house of Jackson was capacious. Those who remained in the party were just as Jacksonian as those who left. Their ideology synthesized democracy, equality, *and* white male supremacy. White men nationwide identified with the Democracy's racial and gender assumptions. Not only could democracy and white supremacy coincide, they necessitated one another for these Americans. Democrats in the 1850s were still Jacksonians, and they were still democrats, even as they rebranded themselves as a conservative party dedicated to preserving racial and gender inequality in the white man's republic. The reciprocity between self-government and white male supremacy reminds us that democracy is not inherently progressive. It is often conservative.[18]

Racial democracy united white men from the slave states and the free states. While the Democracy fractured in 1860, its endurance as an intersectional institution in an age of sectionalism testifies to the nationality of its worldview. Contention over slavery precipitated a partisan realignment in interbellum America. The Democracy trudged along as established parties collapsed and new ones coalesced between the Mexican War and the Civil War. I focus on those who stayed in the party. Most accounts examine only northern Democrats, assuming sectional differentiation and a shallow democratic political culture in the slave states. Southern Democrats appear only as the Slave Power, which demanded sycophantic northern Doughfaces sabotage democracy to perpetuate slavery. Historians largely agree with a critic's 1858 rendering of the Democracy as "the slaveholders of the South on the one hand and the demagogues and office seekers of the North on the other." This study goes beyond Doughface and Slave Power caricatures by reevaluating both northern *and* southern Democrats as more than proslavery allies of convenience. Northern Democrats cannot be understood apart from southern Democrats, with whom they shared a partisan cultural identity that often outranked any sectional affinity felt toward fellow northerners outside their party. National in scope and ideologically vibrant, the party knitted together white men across the country to protect the racial and gender hierarchies upon which their identities as democratically self-governing white men were based.[19]

The interbellum era was a discrete period in the Democracy's ideological development. The 1850s witnessed the breakdown of the second party system and the eclipse of its divisive economic disputes. Territorial acquisition after the Mexican War made the moral impasse over slavery and its expansion paramount in politics for the next decade. Drawing on Jacksonian teachings, Democrats responded to the antislavery movement and related reformism with "popular sovereignty." As party doctrine from 1848 to 1860, popular sovereignty provided coherence and continuity to Democratic thought during the interwar period. With popular sovereignty, Democrats recommended that white men in the territories democratically determine whether to permit slavery. Devolving decision making, Democrats promised, would exert a conservative influence, as white men could be trusted to use democracy to preserve the racial and gender order from which they benefited. Local democracy rested at the heart of Democrats' conservatism and informed their approach to other fraught moral and cultural issues such as temperance and nativism. Committed to popular sovereignty and officially indifferent to the morality of slavery, the party shed its most avowedly antislavery membership, reinforcing its conservative cast.

Haranguing voters on the hustings about popular sovereignty, Democrats were not just proposing public policy. They were also explicating political philosophy. Rather than scrutinize individuals' political thought, we can recapture the *political thought of a party*, found not in the arid texts of elite political theorists, themselves a rarity in this era, but in newspapers, speeches, cartoons, songs, and private writings authored by Democrats from all walks of life and all regions. Democrats were partisans and government officials. Yet, like other antebellum Americans, they imbued electioneering and policy making with theoretical heft, peppering bland debates with talk of rights, equality, and self-government.[20] Exalting politics to the plane of first principles backfired, however, when party platforms could not subsequently be compromised. The invocation of rights and equality on the stump, moreover, often jarred with reality. Rhetoric about equal natural rights obscured socioeconomic disparities among white men and the way that rights operated in law and local custom.[21] By steeping policy in Enlightenment thought, Democrats crafted a compelling worldview for white men. The repeated failures of that worldview point to the problems politicians created for themselves by posing as political theorists. When mapping a political party's philosophy, we cannot expect intellectual rigor. The inconsistencies themselves are historically significant.

Just as important is the messy cultural context that hindered the straightforward realization of ideological visions. Synthesizing *ideology* and *culture* enmeshes political principles in the quotidian concerns of daily life, nestling politics within wider histories of race, gender, sexuality, and the household. Democrats' appropriation of conservatism occurred at the intersection of political thought with cultural constructions of race and gender. Democratic manhood, for example, complemented their understanding of political economy and the state. While slave states and free states diverged culturally before the Civil War, northern and southern Democrats' common partisan culture encompassed shared templates of manhood, whiteness, and domesticity. Democrats enacted gender and structured their households in ways distinct from other parties. They sought to conserve their party's normative cultural assumptions in the 1850s. Appreciating that race, gender, and sexuality were also the stuff of partisan politics and that competing conceptions of the family were just as much components of a party's platform as a position on the tariff explains why all antebellum Americans found the stakes of politics so high.[22]

Conserving the White Man's Republic

Juxtaposing published texts and unpublished manuscripts grounds political theory in this cultural setting, allowing us to historicize the Democracy's variant of conservatism, a political ideology uniquely conditioned by context. Conservatism has been defined as a preference for the "familiar," a "disposition," according to theorist Michael Oakeshott, "to delight in what is present rather than what was or what may be." For other theorists, it entails systematic, timeless principles. But context still matters. Samuel P. Huntington, who classified conservatism as an "ideology" in opposition to Oakeshott's "disposition," clarified that it is a "positional" ideology dependent upon the specific present it is enlisted to defend. The late-eighteenth-century thinker Edmund Burke, often regarded as the source for whatever principles characterize conservatism, emphasized that "circumstances . . . give in reality to every political principle its distinguishing color and discriminating effect."[23]

Changed circumstances meant that interbellum Democrats were no longer the rabble-rousers denounced by their conservative opponents in the 1820s and 1830s. Historian and Democrat George Bancroft watched from London as the Revolutions of 1848 convulsed the Continent. He found that "all Europe has its eyes turned towards us." "The world has entered in a new era," Bancroft effused, "with America openly in the lead among the nations; & the sovereigns know it." Yet Bancroft was not referring to revolutionaries finding inspiration in the American republic but to "the lovers of order [who] now look to the United States." Bancroft told Lewis Cass, the Democrats' 1848 presidential nominee, that "it is while all Europe is full of anxiety, that you will be called to preside over the happy republic, whose only danger is in the pride of its exuberant prosperity." Democrats' happy republic, long resisted by European and even American conservatives as an unsteady siren of democracy, suddenly modeled stability.[24]

Before returning to the United States to claim the presidency in 1856, James Buchanan dined with exiled leaders of those failed revolutions. The luminaries at the 1854 London dinner party included Hungary's Lajos Kossuth, Italy's Giuseppe Garibaldi and Giuseppe Mazzini, and Russian socialist Aleksandr Herzen. A ribald old flirt, Buchanan inquired of the host's wife "if she was not afraid the combustible materials around her would explode & blow us all up." "They are very able & agreeable men," Buchanan relayed to the secretary of state, and "should the revolutionary spirit again break out in Europe, which they all anticipate within a brief period, they are sensible of the necessity of confining it within more rational limits than in 1848." Buchanan judged that "Kossuth's views upon this subject are quite reasonable," as he was "against Socialism, Fourierism & all other isms inconsistent with liberty & order." Six years earlier Bancroft had suggested that monarchs besieged by these men look to the United States. Buchanan recommended Europe's liberals and radicals do likewise. Both conservatives and revolutionaries could turn to the happy republic, a synthesis of "liberty & order."[25]

Even as they adopted a conservative disposition to maintain order in their republic, Democrats' stand was principled, because their happy republic was the culmination of Jacksonian Democracy. To conserve their progressive republic, as well as the race and gender relations that buttressed it, Democrats relied on democracy, hardly a typical conservative panacea. Rather than a romanticized nation-state, aristocratic elites, or the clergy, Democrats expected local majorities of white men to instill social order. While heady Democrats touted their party's "great principles of liberty and equality" and its "respect for the universal rights of man,"[26] their liberal individual was not a neutral construct. *He* was the white master of female and black dependents. Democrats argued that self-rule would stabilize society, because white men would not undermine the racial and gender inequality that generated their democratic equality. The democratic process projected their household mastery into political power over all women and Americans of color. Democracy was an assertion of white manhood. Because he would uphold the racial and gender prerogatives that empowered him, the progressive, self-governing individual was simultaneously the conservative bulwark of the status quo, with the intermingling of "liberty & order" in his person a microcosm of their reciprocity within the republic. Thus were democracy, liberal individualism, egalitarianism, and white supremacy turned toward conservative ends.

The repurposing of Jacksonian Democracy as "the great cause of conservative Democracy"[27] constitutes a homegrown American conservatism. Historians usually locate antebellum conservatism among Federalists, Whigs, and slavery's apologists, who, despite their differences, idealized a hierarchical and organic society over democracy, individualism, natural rights, and modern notions of indelible racial difference.[28] Starved of sources of conservative legitimacy, such as a feudal past, landed aristocracy, established church, or deferential society, philosophical conservatism in the European vein struggled to take root in America's liberal democratic political culture.[29] The germ of an indigenous American conservatism, amenable to modern liberal democracy, is not to be found in the invasive Burkeanism of traditional conservatives skeptical of self-government but among Jacksonian Democrats, who began with the tenets of egalitarian democracy and individualism and nudged them in a conservative direction.

In 1815 James Buchanan, still a callow Federalist youth, had arraigned Democrats as "enemies of social order" and espousers of "wild and visionary theories."[30] Almost forty years later, as that party's presidential nominee, he hailed the Democracy as "the only true conservative party of the Country."[31] That the stodgy James Buchanan became the standard-bearer of Jackson's rough-and-tumble party shows the extent to which the Democracy had assumed a conservative posture by the 1850s. After decades of partisan brawling, Democrats had realized their wild and visionary theories in the brittle concreteness of the white man's republic. Styling themselves conservatives in their quest to preserve this republic, they remained wedded to potentially radical doctrines. White men's democratic self-governance was a novel proposition for safeguarding a regime of racial and gender privilege. The disastrous results of relying on local democracy to defuse questions of slavery and race would eventually vindicate the young Buchanan's distrust of Democrats as guarantors of social order.

In the long run, however, Democrats transformed American conservatism, giving it the buoyancy to carry it into the twentieth and twenty-first centuries. To perpetuate the gender and racial exclusivity of their republic, Democrats updated conservatism by placing it on a uniquely American foundation of local, egalitarian democracy and liberal individualism. Somewhere between John Locke and Barry Goldwater, "liberalism" became "conservative" in the United States, and historians have vexed themselves in pursuit of the turning point.[32] In attempting to conserve white men's democracy, Democrats laid the intellectual groundwork for modern American conservatism. They failed to preserve their happy republic, but they did start conservatism on a new, populist trajectory, one in which democracy is called upon to legitimize inequality, a distinctly American conservatism that endures in our republic today.

ONE

The Northern Men and Their *National* Principle
JACKSONIAN IDEOLOGY, POPULAR SOVEREIGNTY,
AND WHITE MEN'S DEMOCRACY, 1847–1854

> It is better to give time for the councils of moderation to be heard.
> —Lewis Cass, 1846

DEMOCRATS ENTERED the last antebellum decade exultant. The Democratic Polk administration had conquered Mexico, transformed the United States into a continental republic, and implemented decisive economic reforms. By 1849, despite decades of Federalist and Whig obstruction, the party of Jefferson and Jackson had given the American people a political culture sanctifying mass democracy for equal white men, a political economy sundering the national state from the market, and a foreign policy rejecting colonization in favor of conquest, accession, and assimilation into an eclectic federal system. Altogether it was a regime facilitating the unimpeded spread of a white man's republic across space and through time. The victorious Democracy thrilled over its happy republic and looked forward to an era of consolidation under its uncontested stewardship.

Yet new challenges to Jacksonian hegemony arose between the end of the Mexican War and the start of the Civil War. Disputes over slavery in the new national domain imperiled the white man's republic at the moment of its continent-wide consummation. Historians chronicling these events tell a story of ideological antipodes, with the South clamoring for slavery's expansion and the North demanding its proscription. The Democratic Party's compromise solution of "popular sovereignty," which allowed territorial settlers to determine the status of slavery themselves, is often dismissed as a disingenuous bid for southern support by northern "Doughfaces," those "northern men with southern principles." By countenancing the democratically sanctioned spread of both free labor and enslaved labor, Democrats in fact drew from their ideological heritage to articulate a national and conservative response to antislavery "agitation" and related "fanatical" reformism. Inspired by the Jacksonian preference for local self-government under a minimalist state, Democrats proposed that territorial settlers democratically decide the fate of African Americans—the ultimate demonstration of white men's political power. The Democrats who introduced popular sovereignty in the late 1840s turned the radical tenets of Jacksonian Democracy toward the conservation of racial order.

Jacksonian Overture

Democrats considered themselves the nation's natural majority party. "The Democratic has been the dominant and ruling party ever since the formation of the general government," boasted an Alabamian in the 1850s, concluding, "the principles of that party prevailed and now obtain in the country." James Shields, an Irish-born Illinoisan who donned a general's uniform in the Mexican War, similarly gloated in 1852 that "for the last fifty years the history of the democratic party is the political history of this country." Given this ascendancy, a Tennessee Democrat suggested that the people investigate competing parties, in order "to satisfy themselves what party it is upon the administration of whose principles the country has attained its gigantic proportions and unequalled prosperity."[1] Such an inquiry reveals that Jacksonian principles, forged in battles with Whigs during the second party system, conditioned Democrats' reactions to new challenges in the 1850s. Andrew Jackson had primed his party to be wary of any source of power antagonistic to its rightful wielders—the sovereign people. The Old Hero warned that despotic monopolies, whether in the guise of the state, a national bank, or abolitionist fanaticism, usurped white men's democratic power and eroded their equality. Democrats in the interbellum period transferred their animus from the Whiggish Money Power to a new tyranny—fanatical reformers who craved centralized state power to inflict moral reforms on otherwise autonomous white men. Democrats responded to this foe as Jackson had taught them.

Claiming to be a party of principles, Democrats publicized their beliefs at every opportunity. "When I see the measures which are in contest, and the distinctive principles upon which they are based," James Bayard of Delaware asserted, "I know where to place myself." His self-assurance contrasted with "that class of politicians who bellow about democratic principles, without attempting to define them, and who consider *party* as a mere union of *men* to secure power of office."[2] Partisans like Bayard offered up their "Democracy" for inspection when standing for election or grubbing after patronage. A Democrat vying for a postmaster appointment bore the recommendation that "he is undoubtedly qualified & his democracy I believe is undoubted."[3] James Buchanan found Irish Americans immune to Whig electioneering; they were "hard to be blarneyed themselves, especially out of their Democracy." Henry A. Wise of Virginia began and ended his antebellum political career as a Democrat. Accounting for the "wayward political predilections" that diverted him to Whiggery in the interim, he claimed fidelity to the Democracy's principles, if not to the party. Having returned to the fold, Wise explained his consistent beliefs in 1846: "That is my democracy, contradistinguished on the one hand from the *Exclusive* principles which would erect an eminence high enough for *a few* only & which would kick all others down; and from the *mob* principles on the other hand which would kick & keep all down."[4]

Like Wise, Democrats of all ranks willingly submitted to political catechesis. Angling for political advancement while an officer in Mr. Polk's army of occupation in Mexico City, General William J. Worth responded to a query about his politics in 1848. He favored an independent treasury over a national bank, because a bank "must of necessity have within itself, elements dangerous to private and public virtue." A tariff was acceptable, provided it was "for revenue," not for the protection of industry, and was "adjusted to the various *interests* and *rights* of every part of the country."[5] While self-interested, such personal platforms demonstrate how individuals understood their party's ideology. Robert Kyle, the deposed assistant doorkeeper of the Indiana Senate, recited his "Political creed" for the governor in 1852. He rehashed Jacksonian political economy, including "no connexion between Goverment & Banks," "no Swindling Corporations," and "no grants of exclusive charters, and privileges by special Legislation to Banks." Unlike the man who had ousted him, Kyle was a "Democrat of the right stripe."[6]

Fellow Indianan William H. English, in his first congressional bid in 1852, affirmed that "it is the duty of every man, canvassing for an office involving political principles, to state frankly and fairly to the people . . . the line of policy he will pursue." He opposed "all class legislation" and "fostering one branch of industry to the detriment of another." Like Worth and Kyle, English believed that government should ensure "equal and exact justice to all men and all classes of men, no matter of what profession, what religion, or what political faith."[7] In 1843 Levi Woodbury, who had served in Jackson's cabinet, reassured New Hampshire Democrats wary of his party loyalty by expounding his principles, including his "ultra" views concerning corporations. They should not receive "special charters" but should be "regulated under careful general laws," ensuring that "they would, then, not be in any case matters of power or monopoly."[8]

Woodbury's stance on corporations captured Jacksonians' antipathy toward concentrations of power. Democrats prescribed a minimalist state incapable of preferential economic intervention like tariffs. "The people should be left free to pursue whatever course they may deem most conducive to their own happiness and good," English concluded.[9] Guaranteeing white men's equality and liberty could, however, necessitate energetic government to dismantle grasping agglomerations like corporations, humble other nations, and fortify white men's mastery over Americans of color and their rights to enslaved property. Jacksonians' selective use of state power struck some as inconsistent. One wag teased his Democratic friend Jackson Woodward that "since the day that the iron willed Tennessean your illustrious namesake dressed despotism in the garb of Democracy there is very little difference between an Emperor and a President." The consistent goal of a political, economic, and social order purged of despotic power blocs nevertheless impelled Jacksonians. The state was not to be used against white men, but antistatist qualms did not apply to Americans of color. Democrats looked back to monopolies set against white men's equality and independence, whether the Second Bank of the United States, the Supreme Court aiding Native Americans resisting removal, or abolitionists instigating servile insurrection. They remembered that Jackson vanquished them all.[10]

The administration of James K. Polk (1845–1849) continued Jackson's mission of striking down hurdles to white men's progress, whether foreign powers or domestic monopolies. A Virginia congressman running for reelection in 1847 told constituents that, "under the auspices of his Administration, we have introduced, and have in successful operation, the leading and favorite measures of the Democratic party."[11] Like Old Hickory, Polk hankered after territorial expansion in order to create opportunity for white men. Saber-rattling diplomacy helped secure the Oregon Territory, while the administration's most stunning success was the Mexican War. In 1847 New York City's Tammany Hall paid homage to the "handful of brave freemen under the immortal JACKSON" at the Battle of New Orleans as the "high example which led our troops to a succession of victories in Mexico."[12]

At home, Polk oversaw "*a complete reform* in the commercial and financial system," an arena where state-sponsored monopolies always menaced liberty and equality. He revivified the Independent Treasury, or subtreasury, thereby concluding the acrimonious divorce of bank and state initiated by Jackson. A purist regarding federal meddling, he vetoed a river and harbor internal improvements bill favored by midwestern Democrats.[13] The administration also reduced tariff rates, guided by the Jacksonian stricture that a tariff's constitutional purpose was raising revenue, not "selecting favored classes of industry for special protection and encouragement."[14] Vice President George Mifflin Dallas cast the deciding vote for the administration's 1846 Walker Tariff in the Senate. He relished defying industrial interests in his home state of Pennsylvania and having "embittered against me the monopolists every where."[15]

Climactic actions like the vice president's *"Casting Vote"*[16] lent the administration's achievements the ictus of finality. A southern Democrat found "cause of congratulation, that after years of doubtful party conflict," the Democratic "theory of our Government" had triumphed. Going into the presidential election of 1848, he and other Democrats celebrated that ancient impasses seemed "permanently settled." Ohioan William Allen wearied of the decades-old tiff over the tariff, even as it crescendoed in 1846. "The tariff debate is still going on, hot and heavy," he complained to his wife from the Senate, "and I am obliged to pay some attention to it, though it is so old a subject."[17] The Bank had "intellectually descended to the 'tomb of the Capulets,'" eulogized Dallas, and, thanks to the subtreasury, added General Worth, "it is difficult to conceive a state of affairs, to tempt any sane, or excuse any honest man, in the effort to give it vital life again." Even after the Whigs took the presidency in 1849, Rhode Island's Thomas W. Dorr was confident that "the question of a high tariff has been decided forever in the negative." A bank that amassed undemocratic power and a preferential tariff that violated republican equality, along with the rest of Whig political economy, were, Dallas decreed, "obsolete ideas" in national politics after 1848.[18]

As the economic debates between Democrats and Whigs under the second party system lost their immediacy in interbellum America, an enduring dispute seeped into the vacuum. The Democracy owed its existence to the desire to mitigate sectional antagonism over slavery. The party's founders had forged an intersectional coalition to joust over economic agendas instead.[19] Democrats' martial and domestic success in the late 1840s, however, enhanced the political significance of slavery, an issue they had never actually dispelled. In December 1848 Vice President Dallas grumbled to his daughter, "I can't perceive any business of interest in the future of this Session of Congress, except that connected with the Slavery question." In August 1846, soon after the start of the Mexican War, northern congressmen irrespective of party had rallied behind the Wilmot Proviso, a failed legislative rider outlawing slavery in annexed territory. The furor over the proviso indicated that the question of slavery and its expansion could destabilize party politics. "Slavery broke out again in the Senate yesterday, as it probably will, in some way or other, every day during the Session," Dallas pouted at the start of 1849. Little seemed to have changed a decade later—a southern diarist carped in 1859 that "Congress is busy doing nothing but discussing the everlasting slavery question."[20]

Balloting over the Wilmot Proviso shuffled congressmen into southern and northern blocs, raising the possibility of a sectionally driven partisan realignment inimical to the intersectional Democratic and Whig Parties. What President Polk called "that delicate and most dangerous sectional controversy" alarmed party stalwarts, because, as an Indiana Democrat noticed, "This question has now assumed a character far above party."[21] Frustrated Democrats had to weigh antislavery convictions against party loyalty in the presidential election of 1848. The Democracy's nominee, Senator Lewis Cass of Michigan, rejected the Wilmot Proviso to conciliate southerners. "I do not wish to vote upon the question of slavery at all," sighed one antislavery, pro-Cass Michigander.[22] Numerous antislavery Democrats did favor the proviso, and party rupture ensued when many defected and fused with like-minded refugees from other parties in the Free Soil movement. After the election and Cass's defeat, Ohio Democrat turned Free Soiler Benjamin Tappan reported to Senator William Allen that "neither of the old parties" could control the state legislature and that "the Free democracy holds the balance of power." Free Soil's effervescence ensured that Allen, a regular Democrat, lost his seat when the legislature replaced him with an opponent of slavery. Antislavery politicians had exploited the creaking party system by mobilizing outside the major parties.[23]

Antislavery was not the only "politico-moral, one-idea reform"[24] upsetting party regularity in the 1850s. Democrats painted the political landscape as a Boschian triptych in which fiendish abolitionists, nativists, and temperance crusaders flayed men of their autonomy, manhood, and whiteness. Nativism and temperance were not new impulses. The Democratic and Whig Parties had previously subsumed religious and moral concerns into partisan worldviews centered on political economy.[25] Now, however, independent temperance movements fermented in the free states, while the new anti-Catholic and nativist Know-Nothing Party aspired to become the Democracy's national opposition beginning in 1854. Temperance and nativism, like antislavery, confounded party distinctions. In 1853 an Alabamian informed Democratic legislative candidate Bolling Hall that "we would support any good man without regard to old party politics" who supported a "prohibatory law" against alcohol. From Louisiana came accounts of the Know-Nothing "dark lantern crowd" who were "hoodwinking and deceiving" and "exercising a delusive sway over former good, well meaning democrats." A Marylander also worried that nativism, operating independently of "the old party organizations," exerted "a disastrous influence upon the organization of the Democratic party."[26] While recognizing slavery's centrality in politics, Democrats took all opponents seriously.

Democrats refused to narrow their partisan worldview to "one 'Idea,'"[27] whether the Wilmot Proviso, temperance, or nativism. Virginian R. M. T. Hunter resisted such reductionism, asking, "If a representative is with you on political tests, does it matter, so far as the politician is concerned, what are his opinions upon other subjects? If he is with you on the subjects of trade, currency, and the principles of constitutional construction, when they are in issue, does it matter that he differs from you on the doctrine of transubstantiation?" Some Democrats still viewed the old economic disputes as the only legitimate "political tests." James Bayard remained steadfast amid protemperance Know-Nothings' seizure of Delaware in 1854. "The exciting causes amongst the mass of the people *now* are for the most part of a *temporary* character, and I do not wish to embark in the divisions to which they give rise," he reassured a correspondent. When temperance became an independent electoral question in Indiana, a Hoosier Democrat qualified that, although "I am a devoted Temperance man," still, "I love my old party and will vote it whiskey or no whiskey."[28]

Democrats attributed one-idea politics to the splintering of comprehensive, national party platforms. An Ohio Democrat regretted the rise of the "*one-idea*" party," an organization "which discards all the political philosophy of both the great parties, which have directed the policy of the government since its beginning, so that its one idea may reign paramount." This Democrat wanted the unattainable—a return to economic debates in a political context riven by cultural and moral disagreement.[29] Although unable to resuscitate the politics of political economy, Democrats did not despair of entering the 1850s with an encompassing ideology. Which of the "one ideas" would emerge ascendant was an academic concern, as Democrats melded them into a common enemy they designated "fanaticism." Fanaticism replaced Whiggery as Democracy's ideological antithesis, because, like Whiggery before it, fanaticism sought consolidated power to degrade the liberty and equality of self-governing white men. To address new political adversaries with a coherent, national platform, Democrats simply reapplied Jacksonian principles to temperance, nativism, and, most importantly, antislavery.

The Northern Men and Their *National* Principle

Prior to the Mexican War, all federal territory was open or closed to slavery by the 1787 Northwest Ordinance and the 1820 Missouri Compromise. The 1848 Mexican Cession, however, raised the question anew. Some southerners followed John C. Calhoun in denying that any power could ban territorial slavery, while many northerners, such as Pennsylvania Democrat David Wilmot, demanded congressional proscription. Moderate Democrats bemoaned each section's extremism during tense debates lasting from the war's outbreak through the Compromise of 1850. Senator William R. King juxtaposed his "moderation and firmness" against the "fanaticism" of Alabama secessionists like William Lowndes Yancey, who demanded that the South gain the Calhounite position or secede. King sought a solution that would "protect the rights of the South and save the Union" as well as "maintain the ascendancy of the Democratic Party."[30] James Bayard similarly eschewed sectional dogma and backed Henry Clay's compromise proposal in order to disarm "the fanatical madness of men of extremes."[31]

Northern moderates also shunned their section's antislavery shibboleth. A New Yorker in Schoharie County told Senator Stephen A. Douglas that he "now occup[ied] a well defined position as one of the leading *conservative* democrats of this county." His "position," and that of other "N.Y. Conservative Democrats," entailed "the election of Anti-Wilmot-Proviso delegates" to the 1848 national convention.[32] Antislavery absolutism fomented fanaticism in the slave states. "Moderate men of all parties" saw the "danger" of the Wilmot Proviso, argued Congressman Willis A. Gorman. Another Indianan agreed.

While he did not favor slavery's spread, he granted that it was "humiliating to southerners to submit to the adoption of the Wilmot Proviso." If slavery could be arrested in a less confrontational way, he suggested to Gorman, "I can not see the necessity of wrangling about a particular manner of obtaining our wishes."[33] Each section's fanaticism only exacerbated the other. A hollow sectional victory, Democrats throughout the nation pleaded, was not worth inciting the "nullifiers and abolitionists who have been Siamese in their efforts."[34]

One group of northern Democrats denied federal jurisdiction over the question altogether. Designated "non-intervention" or "popular sovereignty," their proposal would prevent Congress from favoring the institution's limitation or growth by allowing white men themselves to decide if they wanted slavery in their territory or future state. Northern Democrats, eager to placate both South and North as the 1848 election approached, propounded the policy. In a speech in Pittsburgh in 1847, Vice President Dallas praised the Polk administration's course on the tariff and the war and vowed to deliver another *"casting vote,"* this time against the Wilmot Proviso. Rather than the congressional restriction of slavery, "the very best thing which can be done," he advised, "will be to let it alone entirely—leaving to the people of the territory to be acquired, the business of settling the matter for themselves." Dallas inaugurated a theme Democrats would echo for a decade when he decided that settlers "have the right, alone, to determine their own institutions."[35]

Daniel Dickinson of New York, inveterate foe of the antislavery movement, offered resolutions in the Senate in December 1847 that insisted that the territorial people, not Congress, possessed power over slavery. "In organizing a territorial government," Dickinson posited, "the principle of self-government upon which our federative system rests will be best promoted . . . by leaving all questions concerning the domestic policy therein to the legislatures chosen by the people thereof." Presidential aspirant Lewis Cass appropriated the doctrine in a public letter to Tennessee Democrat A. O. P. Nicholson the same month. "I am opposed to the exercise of any jurisdiction by Congress over this matter," Cass announced, "and I am in favor of leaving to the people of any territory, which may be hereafter acquired, the right to regulate it for themselves." With Cass's nomination in 1848, the proposal became a Democratic principle.[36]

Despite Cass's defeat, popular sovereignty remained party dogma among northern and southern Democrats for over a decade. The idea was one ingredient in the Compromise of 1850, which effectively delegated authority to settlers by admitting California as a free state and remaining silent on slavery in the territories of Utah and New Mexico. When Senator Stephen A. Douglas of Illinois urged the application of popular sovereignty to the Kansas and Nebraska territories, he invoked the Compromise of 1850 as precedent. Part of the Louisiana Purchase, Kansas and Nebraska had been reserved for freedom by the 1820 Missouri Compromise. To curry southern support, Douglas's 1854 Kansas-Nebraska Act expressly repealed the Missouri Compromise. Alabama congressman Philip Phillips, one of the architects of revocation, later recounted his rationale regarding Kansas and Nebraska: "They must be thrown open to all alike, and this can only be effected by a *repeal of the inhibition in the Act of 1820.*" Douglas and a cadre of southern Democrats secured President Franklin Pierce's approval for making this divisive legislation a party test.[37]

Because popular sovereignty allowed slavery's expansion, antislavery critics pilloried Cass, Douglas, and other northern Democrats as "Doughfaces"—a slur aimed at purportedly proslavery northerners. Yet these men viewed themselves as their party's national conscience. They were northern men who advanced a *national* principle, one that allowed both proslavery and antislavery Americans to democratically compete as equals. For all the turmoil eventually produced by popular sovereignty, Democrats pointed to it as proof of their conservative nationalism. A Bostonian believed that Kansas-Nebraska's enactment would "satisfy the people, and a calm will follow." Even as late as 1856, despite evidence to the contrary, a North Carolina Democrat expected that "the success of its principles will give permanent repose to the country." With its abdication of decision making to "the people," popular sovereignty was, Democrats argued, a *conservative* solution. In its supposed sectional neutrality, moreover, it was a *national* policy.[38]

Democrats intended popular sovereignty to exert a conservative influence by changing the venue in which slavery was contested. Congressional stalemate over territorial slavery stymied the national growth Jacksonians craved. By punting the question to territorial settlers, popular sovereignty would deprive extremists of a national pulpit, gratifying those who "desire[d] to see congress throw aside all fanaticism."[39] Congressional silence would foster a wider social armistice, undercutting the fanatic "who claims that a phrenzied north has a right to sit in judgment upon the affairs of the south, or he who would rouse a maddened south to enter upon a crusade against the north." In 1848

President Polk was willing to accept popular sovereignty, or any *"compromise,"* in order to organize California, which was otherwise hurtling toward "a state of anarchy—and without Government of law." Popular sovereignty would answer the president's plea by breaking the congressional logjam and empowering settlers to oversee their own orderly development.[40]

Popular sovereignty also enabled moderates to claim victory short of their section's hard-line position. "The bill before us grants no favor to any section of the Union," Alabama's Philip Phillips explained of Kansas-Nebraska, and "no one has the right to triumph; no one has cause to complain."[41] Democrats told antislavery northerners that popular sovereignty would yield free territories. Cass argued that the Mexican Cession was climatically "unfit for the production of the great staples, which can alone render slave labor valuable." Allowing nature to shape a free labor economy, Democrats suggested, was less inflammatory than the Wilmot Proviso. Given the climate, Phillips acknowledged, "I was actuated by what I then regarded as a *theoretical right*."[42] Some southerners, however, sought more than a theoretical right by exporting enslaved labor to Kansas. Proslavery expansion, combined with antislavery northerners' belief in the "impracticability of the prosperous subsistence of the two systems of freedom and slavery in the same territory," produced a collision unanticipated by Democrats when they opened the territories to democratic competition.[43]

The immediate effects of popular sovereignty thus seemed anything but conservative. Many northern Democrats' unwillingness to countenance slavery's expansion prompted the 1848 Free Soil revolt. Shortly before his own departure from the Democracy, Pennsylvanian Simon Cameron reflected in 1849 that, "in the North, while all sensible Democrats are willing to let the South alone, there is none who could sustain themselves by even admitting the propriety of an extension of slavery to the territories."[44] "The Nebraska outrage"[45] restarted and made permanent the antislavery exodus with the creation of the Republican Party in 1854. That Kansas-Nebraska overturned a long-standing compromise and substituted a "new fangled doctrine in respect to the Territories," a northern Democrat warned, "would seem to indicate that nothing can ever hereafter be considered *settled* under our Government;—a very alarming thought certainly to conservative minds." A slave-state Democrat fretted over the Union's future: "The alienation of feelings is growing daily & I have almost lost hope that it will even last my day. Indeed the madness of the North, & the general tone of sentiment shakes my confidence in the *durability* of democratic institutions."⁴⁶ Fracturing parties and disregarding precedent, the reputedly conservative policy of popular sovereignty struck many as radical.

Northerners like Cass and Douglas nonetheless used popular sovereignty to posture as conservative nationalists who accorded equality to the free states and slave states. Yet to many northerners, they were "Doughfaces"—"northern men, with southern principles."⁴⁷ A vibrant discourse surrounding Doughfacism existed by the 1850s. The splenetic John Randolph of Roanoke had coined the epithet in 1820 to jeer northern congressmen who added a slave state to the Union by supporting the Missouri Compromise. Randolph hissed, "I knew *these would give way.*—They were scared at their own dough faces—yes, they were scared at their own dough faces!"⁴⁸ Subsequent attacks on such northerners established enduring motifs of Doughfaces as weak and unmanly traitors to free labor society. They were *"servile"* tools who could be "moulded into any shape" by southern masters. One northern newspaper in 1820 called them *"slave-voter[s],"* referencing their willingness to vote in favor of slavery and to their own enslaved status.⁴⁹ Walt Whitman had them mock themselves in verse: "We are all docile dough-faces, / They knead us with the fist, / They, the dashing southern lords, / We labor as they list."⁵⁰

Castigations of Doughfacism swelled in the 1850s when it became synonymous with "certain *Northern Gentlemen*" who denied congressional power over slavery—in other words, the advocates of popular sovereignty.⁵¹ Baffled by arguments for repealing the Missouri Compromise's restriction on slavery's expansion, Free Soil Democrat John Van Buren asked, "Could anything but a desire to buy the South at the Presidential shambles dictate such an outrage?"⁵² While Van Buren claimed that unprincipled northerners were bribing the South, many saw Doughfaces as chattel that southerners purchased for political purposes. Franklin Pierce, for instance, "had been put in office by the Slave Power" and "longed for nothing so much as to signalize his servility to the class to which he owed his honors."⁵³ Free Soiler Joshua R. Giddings, protesting Kansas-Nebraska, resolved that "it is time that this slave trade, now carried on in the bodies of members of Congress, should be prohibited."⁵⁴

Southerners showed more gratitude to their northern men in the 1850s than did Randolph of Roanoke in 1820. Polk comforted his would-have-been successor, telling Cass that "neither yourself nor your friends made secret pledges or wrote inconsistent letters to different sections to defraud the people and secure votes." Fellow northerners denounced Doughfaces for their southern connections. An antislavery Democrat in Centre Sandwich, New Hampshire, complained in 1851 that Doughfaces sounded the alarm of southern secession to cow the North. "If the friends of freedom continue to insist upon no more extension of slavery," he complained, then "southern hotspurs" with their "doughfaces and official sycophants" trotted out the "old *Humbug*" that "*the union is in danger.*"[55] Yet southern allies steeled their Doughfaces by reminding them that their unpopularity stemmed from selflessly treating South and North equally with popular sovereignty. Virginia's Henry Wise commended those who, "in the midst of non-slaveholding passions and prejudices," fought for "popular self-government" and "State rights."[56] Electoral defeat underscored the statesmanship of these "martyrs."[57] "It was for adhering to this non-intervention principle that northern men have been crushed," extolled one pamphlet.[58]

Southern moderates cited these northern men to deflate their own section's extremists. That Doughfaces combatted northern fanaticism guaranteed a Union safe for slavery. After Cass's 1848 nomination, Stephen Douglas relayed that in Alabama "Democrats are well pleased with the nomination & disapprove of the course of Yancey."[59] With allies like Cass, southerners did not need Yancey's quixotic sectionalism. Doughfaces aided Herschel V. Johnson, running for governor of Georgia in 1855, in steering a course "sufficiently sectional to protect the rights of the South and yet sufficiently national . . . to preserve the integrity of the Union." A "sectional party" was unnecessary, Johnson concluded, as "in the ranks of the Northern Democracy are to be found the only reliable friends of the South; and they are many." A fervent southern-rights Democrat like Louisianan John Perkins could concede that "*in the Democratic organization at the north are embraced the truest and most reliable friends of the South,*" even if it "has not entirely escaped the taint of abolitionism."[60]

The Republican Party "stigmatizes those as cowardly and base who stand upon Northern soil to speak for our whole country," lamented a New York Democrat.[61] The party's critics throughout the interbellum period failed to read southern support as an index of northern Democrats' nationalism. "What States in the Union are more conservative than our own?" asked an Indianan in 1852. "If a candidate from a *free State* must be selected by the Slave States," he wondered, "who more likely to command their votes" than a midwesterner like Douglas? The South would look to the Midwest because, "in all questions deeply affecting their 'peculiar institution,' we have done them justice."[62] Robert McLane, following the Kansas-Nebraska debate from a diplomatic post in Shanghai, saw the danger in Doughfaces' sectional balancing act. He told his father Louis McLane, a veteran of Jackson's cabinet, that the bill would embolden the South and that "Douglass, or any other northern man who gives impulse to this wave will be overwhelmed in the south when he hesitates to ride on its summit to the breakers." And if Douglas did satisfy the South, "he will be repudiated by a public sentiment in the north, infinitely more active in its zeal and fanaticism."[63] While the rest of the decade would bear out McLane's prediction, Doughfaces had made themselves the fulcrum of intersectional politics in the short term by using popular sovereignty to build a national alliance of white men in pursuit of principle, not simply power or plunder.

Popular Sovereignty and Jacksonian Democracy

In 1848 two Democrats in Portugal found a more creative medium than party platforms to convey their beliefs. They dispatched Madeira to President Polk and other leading Democrats. Colonel Jefferson Davis received bottles emblazoned with "Buena Vista," the battle at which he was wounded during the Mexican War. "The whole of Mexico," a slogan seized upon by expansionist Democrats, graced those allotted to Secretary of the Treasury Robert J. Walker. The bottles to be enjoyed by Senator Douglas bore the designation "Progressive."[64] Whether ratified in platforms or affixed to bottles of fortified wine, Democrats' ideological pronouncements reveal that they entered the interbellum era animated by Jackson's vision of fostering opportunity for white men through territorial expansion and dispersing consolidated power. Democrats resisted the blurring of party lines when traditional issues lost potency during the 1850s partisan realignment. They argued that a Jacksonian disposition was still needed to protect equality, liberty, and white male supremacy from despotic power, now manifesting itself as fanatical reformism rather than Federalist monocrats or the Whiggish Money Power. Popular sovereignty, by devolving power to local majorities of white men as they expanded geographically, constituted an ideologically Jacksonian response to the politics of the 1850s.[65]

Although opponents spurned popular sovereignty as an opportunistic, if not immoral, attempt to straddle the sectional divide, Democrats regarded it as both a "practical issue" and an "abstract principle."⁶⁶ Lewis Cass's 1847 Nicholson letter set the tone by synthesizing the pragmatic and the principled. "By going back to our true principles, we go back to the road of peace and safety," Cass advised. In the short term, the policy promised "peace and safety" by ending contention in Congress and permitting orderly territorial development. But it did so by appealing to the party and the nation's "true principles."⁶⁷ Democrats constructed a narrative of political history in which Americans, beginning with the Compromise of 1850, repeatedly affirmed popular sovereignty. A critic of Democrats' historical rendition asked, "Have the Compromise Measures of 1850, has the Kansas Nebraska Act of 1854, the resolutions of National Conventions, and the endorsement of a Presidential Candidate metamorphosed a policy into a principle, an expediency into a right?"⁶⁸ One Democrat did just that in a letter to Stephen Douglas in 1854. Murray McConnel, aptly living in Jacksonville, Illinois, reported that "the whigs and free soilers and some of the democrats will be united and are now agitating upon and against the princiles of the Nebraska bill." Still, he reassured the Little Giant, the issue was "so clearly right that if properly presented to the People and *in time* we can triumphantly carry them." McConnel initially wrote "the subject of the Nebraska bill," but crossed out and replaced the word "subject," making the final phrasing read, "the princiles of the Nebraska bill." This Democrat did metamorphose policy into principle.⁶⁹

Democrats rooted territorial popular sovereignty in a larger theoretical tradition descended from "principles as ancient as free government itself."⁷⁰ The theorists of the American Revolution had redefined sovereignty with the radical proposition that the people never relinquished their inherent and absolute power to the state. Seventeenth-century social contract theorists like Thomas Hobbes and John Locke had not anticipated such a departure when they posited a compact through which the people willed their power to the sovereign state when emerging from the state of nature. The American Founders added the radical notion that the government was never sovereign, because the people's sovereignty was inalienable. They collapsed the distinction in Western political thought between "rulers" and "ruled," making the two synonymous in the body of "the people." When founding new governments, Thomas Paine advised in 1776, it was best "that the *elected* might never form to themselves an interest separate from the *electors*." Inspired by a wariness of arbitrary power, the theory of "popular sovereignty" became ensconced in American constitutionalism and political culture.⁷¹

The American Revolution demonstrated that the people possessed the competence and power to regulate slavery, Democrats concluded. Daniel Dickinson, introducing popular sovereignty in Congress in 1847, lectured, "The republican theory teaches that sovereignty resides with the people of a State, and not with its political organization." Those who pressed for congressional jurisdiction, meanwhile, were regurgitating the "doctrine of Lord North," charged Georgia's Alexander H. Stephens, who rammed Kansas-Nebraska through the House.[72] The purpose of the Revolution had been "to assert in arms the principle, that the true basis of government is the consent of the governed," and Kansas-Nebraska, Congressman Phillips argued, was "founded upon the great principle of self-government consecrated by our Revolution."[73]

Having imbibed revolutionary republicanism, Jacksonians conceptualized a stark trade-off between power and liberty, rulers and ruled. Old Hickory had made himself the vehicle of the people's sovereignty against concentrated power. "In your hands is rightfully placed the sovereignty of the country," Jackson imparted to the nation in 1837. He had to slay the Monster Bank, an institution that questioned "whether the people of the United States are to govern."[74] Jacksonians continued to underwrite the people's sovereignty in the 1850s. Kansas-Nebraska was one more validation of the people's capacity for self-governance. In 1854 New York's Aaron Ward held that "the great constitutional issue that is approaching, is not unlike that which accompanied the downfall of the United States Bank." Jackson had relied on the people during that crisis. Ward trusted them now: "I believe the people are capable of self-government, and are willing to trust the citizens of Kansas and Nebraska in organizing governments for themselves." "*Keep it before the people* that the only question involved in the Nebraska issue is; are the popular masses capable of self-government," instructed a Democratic newspaper.[75]

Popular sovereignty also perpetuated Jackson's distinct Unionism. Although Jackson expanded national borders and opposed nullification, he and his party also sanctified the rights of states and of slaveholders. One of Democracy's discontents noted in 1848 that "the South accuses the North of fanaticism," and, indeed, Jacksonians nationwide placed the burden of sectional agitation on the free states. Jackson had raged against the reenergized abolitionist movement of the 1830s, commanding citizens to "frown upon any proceedings within their own borders likely to disturb the tranquility of their political brethren in other portions of the Union." Pacifying southern extremism by silencing antislavery was intrinsic to Jacksonian Unionism.[76]

Popular sovereignty, by prioritizing local self-determination, adhered to the Jacksonian dictum that slavery should be shielded from outside interference. According to a Tennessean, Kansas-Nebraska decreed that "every people, community, or State, should attend to its own business and let its neighbor's alone." "The Democracy of the North," Congressman William H. English chorused, "believe that States and Territories, like individuals, ought to mind their own business."[77]

Tutored in Jackson's faith in the people, interbellum Democrats responded to territorial settlers' demands for self-government. Oregonians' request for organization as a territory stalled due to congressional bickering over slavery. An Ohioan who settled in Oregon implored a Democratic congressman, "With very great anxiety we have been and are yet looking for the extension of the jurisdiction of the U.S. over the territory." Laws were unenforceable, and white settlers were abusing the indigenous population. The new Oregonian pleaded, "Are we not bone of your bone and flesh of your flesh, then why delay to do us the same measure of justice we would have received at home[?]"[78] Stability would come only when the territories' white men were granted democratic equality. When a convention of New Mexicans petitioned for recognition in 1848, one correspondent expressed to a Democratic senator his hope that Congress would "succeed in giving them a government," as "the people themselves ought to know what they want."[79] A southerner defended Stephen Douglas's decision to organize Kansas and Nebraska, as "the matter came up naturally of itself . . . forced upon attention by the people themselves legitimately through petition expressing a want."[80]

"My Dear Douglass," James Shields wrote his former colleague from his new home in Minnesota Territory, "I myself am a squatter now." Shields was one of the many northern Democrats ousted from Congress in the fall of 1854 for supporting Kansas-Nebraska, whereupon the Illinoisan decamped for the West. "I live amongst squatters I know something of their condition," he updated Douglas in 1856. Shields's fellow settlers were "building little cabins to shelter their families, cutting rails making fences, and trying work I say trying to live." "I haul rails every day myself," boasted the former senator. Emigrants desired fairness, which meant minimal federal intrusion. Referencing the troubles brewing in Kansas, Shields forewarned, "The people would do what they did in Oregon, in California, and wherever they were left to themselves. Give them no *rule* and they will make a *rule*. Give them misrule, and even poor squatters will not be content, and you will have to make them content with the bayonet."⁸¹ Popular sovereignty reflected sympathy with territorial settlers' demands to govern themselves, which no self-respecting Jacksonian could ignore.

Yet pragmatic and philosophical concerns over settlers practicing democracy beyond the government's ken pestered Democrats throughout the 1850s. Popular sovereignty did not define the mechanism of democratic decision making. Many northern Democrats wanted territorial legislatures to rule on slavery, while many southerners countered that constitutional conventions on the cusp of statehood should make the momentous decision. The former position would enable emigrants to ban slavery soon after settlement, while the latter would allow slavery's potential entrenchment. Beneath this narrow debate lay a deeper liability—that a democratic decision had to occur at all. Democrats stripped Congress of its discretion, but someone *would* have to decide, and only one side could win. Democrats raised the stakes of fraught moral disputes over slavery by posing as political theorists and reframing the debate as one over democracy. Territorial popular sovereignty and democracy itself, despite being offered as conservative solutions, were unstable as policy and radical as theory. Jacksonians would be unable to recant a doctrine that proved increasingly disruptive, because they made it a test of white men's self-government.⁸²

Popular Sovereignty and White Men's Democracy

Although entranced by the sovereignty of "the people," Democrats would not empower all Americans. When Daniel Dickinson proclaimed that popular sovereignty "would practically acknowledge man's capacity for self-government, and vindicate the integrity of his race," he had in mind a precise definition of the "race" entitled to self-rule.⁸³ Abolitionists, Free Soilers, and Republicans, in contrast, not only opposed slavery, Democrats alleged, but welcomed black political agency. As the stewards of white men's sovereignty, Democrats resisted its extension to others, because, in the racialized worldview of Jacksonians, white men surrendered their sovereignty in proportion to its exercise by people of color. By avowing white men's right to legislate for themselves and all others, popular sovereignty preserved the racial exclusivity of democratic power in the white man's republic.

Territorial popular sovereignty grew out of Jacksonian racial democracy. White supremacy, the defense of slavery, and the ethnic cleansing of Native

Americans ranked alongside the Bank War and mass politics in defining Jacksonian Democracy. Democrats manufactured their radical egalitarianism out of the hard exclusion of Americans of color, a formula scholars have labeled *Herrenvolk* democracy. Jacksonians welcomed "racial modernity" in the early nineteenth century. Along with Enlightenment individualism and democratic majoritarianism, they subscribed to modern notions of racial distinctiveness. They abandoned a graded patriarchal society and environmentalist constructions of race for a conception of white equality resting on an impermeable color line now deemed natural. Jacksonians, whether urban workingmen, southern planters and yeomen, or frontier settlers, shared a political culture premised on racial essentialism. Northern Democrats showed as much solicitude as southerners for racism's leveling effects among white men. A Whig disparaged that party "which, in the nominally Free States, plants its heel on the neck of the abject and powerless negro, and hurls its axe after the flying form of the plundered, homeless, and desolate Indian."[84] The pervasiveness of Jacksonian white supremacy was evident among northern Democrats who later became Free Soilers and Republicans. Many who demanded slavery's proscription did so not out of affinity for African Americans but to engineer a racially pure West.[85]

Even when they shared their culture's racism, the brazenness of antislavery reformers made Democrats fear for the strict correlation of whiteness with political legitimacy. An Ohio Democrat complained in 1849 that Free Soilers in the legislature had "bamboozled" Democrats into voting for "a *Repeal* of the whole Black Code of Ohio!!!" Free states, especially in the Midwest, employed black codes to restrict the movement and rights of African Americans. "A principle of high state Policy laid at the foundation of the Black Laws," explained this Democrat. Yet, "*humbugged* and cheated" by antislavery forces, Ohio Democrats had "vot[ed] contrary to the proffessions and votes of the Party for years past" by repealing restrictions "deeply connected with the future prosperity of Ohio."[86] The political exclusion of African Americans and inclusion of all whites formed the bedrock of Jacksonian Democracy.

Popular sovereignty ratified white male egalitarianism by regarding territorial settlers as equal white men. Although early territorial policy reflected angst over unsupervised, independence-minded westerners, Jeffersonian Republicans had decided against treating emigrants as colonial vassals. Settlers had long insisted on self-government and often exercised significant control on the ground, even over slavery, irrespective of federal oversight.[87] Jacksonians later prioritized inexpensive federal land, Indian removal, and preemption rights for squatters to pursue egalitarian expansion. Kansas-Nebraska took these precedents further as policy by formally devolving more power to settlers.[88] While elevating the issue to a principled contest over white men's democratic equality was politically effective and hewed to Jacksonian intuitions, ideology made for problematic policy, as territories and states had never enjoyed equal standing and were constitutionally distinct. Still, giddy over self-government, Democrats criticized adversaries for disempowering emigrants. "Whether in a State or in a Territory," a correspondent lectured New Hampshire representative Harry Hibbard in 1850, "their rights are the same for they are *Americans* & have the inherent right to form their Government & make their own laws." The opponents of Kansas-Nebraska, cautioned a Democratic newspaper, "would yield to that central power, the Federal Government, the prerogative of making a law for a territory or State—*to bind the people in all time to come.*"[89] In a slaveholding republic, efforts to "bind" white men were troubling indeed.

The advocates of popular sovereignty also agreed with Jefferson and Jackson that racial minorities would be subjugated or otherwise vanish before the tide of white civilization. "Andrew Jackson never occupied a doubtful position upon any question," Oliver Wendell Holmes beamed in 1853, especially that of "Indian warfare" and the expulsion of "savage life" from lands destined for white settlement. Jackson's Indian wars, followed by his and Martin Van Buren's removal policy, expressed the Democratic supposition that white Americans' progress eclipsed other races. Dickinson, proselytizing popular sovereignty, noted that "numerous aboriginal nations have been displaced before the resistless tide of our prevailing arts, arms, and free principles." Dallas, meanwhile, heady with victory over Mexico, prophesized that "the Yankees will in time overrun that portion of their territory; and though there is much Mexican blood upon it, we may look to the period as not more remote" when new states would join the "constellation of our Union." Popular sovereignty hastened racial cleansing, a precursor to the political equality of both white men and of nascent states in America's unfurling federal system.[90]

Stephen Douglas warned that popular sovereignty's detractors would derail this destiny by denying "that those of our fellow citizens who emigrated to the shores of the Pacific and to our other territories, were as capable of self-government as their neighbors and kindred whom they left behind." Antislavery fanatics belittled white men's ability to govern themselves and to oversee supposedly inferior races. Explaining the Compromise of 1850 to a skeptical Chicago audience, Douglas defended the application of white self-rule to the question of slavery: "If they have the requisite intelligence and honesty to be intrusted with the enactment of laws for the government of white men, I know of no reason why they should not be deemed competent to legislate for the negro."[91] Doubting white men's democratic prowess insulted them and suggested a higher threshold of governance for America's population of color, perhaps even that of allowing them to rule themselves.

Popular sovereignty forestalled black political agency by reinforcing all white men's mastery over Americans of color at home and in politics. Cass used his Nicholson letter to unite southern and northern patriarchs against fanatical meddling in their households. Congressional interference with territorial slavery undercut white southerners' lordship over their white and enslaved "families." Cass made southerners' plight relatable to northerners, asking, "What would be thought if Congress should undertake to prescribe the terms of marriage in New York, or to regulate the authority of parents over their children in Pennsylvania?"[92] Democrats' defense of domestic mastery resonated with northern men, especially those wary of the market economy's subversion of traditional household patriarchy. "When the US sells me a farm & I move onto it," snapped a New Englander, "Congress has no more power over me or my farm, than it has over the person & farm of any other man whether that farm & myself are in Missouri or Oregon."[93] Popular sovereignty magnified white men's power over dependents at home into democratic power over women and racial others throughout the republic.

The racial absolutism of *Herrenvolk* democracy only functioned when *all* white men could partake of popular sovereignty. The Kansas-Nebraska Act, by permitting white southerners to force enslaved southerners into the territories, "obliterates unjust distinctions" between white settlers from the North and South, cheered a Democrat in St. Louis.[94] Jacksonians instinctively hated all such distinctions among white men. Democrats likewise railed against Whig senator John M. Clayton's nativist amendment to Kansas-Nebraska refusing political rights to unnaturalized immigrants in the territories. Nativism endangered more than the Democracy's electoral strength by penalizing Irish and German supporters—it undermined white male equality itself. Indiana's governor urged a congressman considering Kansas-Nebraska to "give all the white men of every nation" who "settle there the absolute right to select their own law making, without any restriction as to Birth Education or property."

The "same spirit of popular distrust" that opposed popular sovereignty over slavery, contended Dickinson in 1848, also looked "with holy horror upon the naturalization of foreigners." Inhibiting white immigrants from voting on slavery would "enslave one race, lest they should tolerate a system which holds in bondage another." The stakes of denying any white men power over slavery was *their* enslavement.[95]

Withholding self-rule from white men, whether southern or northern, native or foreign-born, or living in territories as opposed to states, entailed slavery's degradation. In the political culture of the white man's republic, the rhetorical trope of slavery referred to the forfeiture of the political prerogatives incident to whiteness and manhood. Democrats often referred to Republicans as "Black" Republicans. Connecticut Democrat Isaac Chadbourne condensed the epithet when he fumed that "the Blacks contend that Congress must be the guardians of the people for the reason the people are not competent to manage their own affairs." A North Carolinian explained that the Republican Party "seeks at the same time to deprive the white men of the Territories of the right of self-government, and to put negroes on a level with them."[96] Preventing white men from governing enslaved Americans degraded them to that very status. "Have they not attempted to enslave the posterity of the whites, in the territories, by denying the people the rights of self-government . . . ?" asked a Democratic pamphlet. An editorial posed the alternatives: "No Slavery in Kansas—Popular Sovereignty there."[97] "Popular Sovereignty" precluded "Slavery" for white men, the only type of slavery Democrats would not tolerate.

In 1854 Senator Salmon P. Chase told his predecessor William Allen that he looked forward to "a reorganization of parties." Chase decreed that "the old democratic organization" had "fulfilled its mission when the Ind^t. Treasury was established on the Ruins of the Slave Power." Although Chase had never been a Democrat, he possessed Jacksonian sensibilities in matters of political economy, and he hoped to fuse Jacksonianism with antislavery. With the Bank War settled and the question of slavery's expansion ascendant at the end of the Mexican War, Chase had cast his lot with the Free Soilers, who rewarded him with Allen's Senate seat in 1849. After the 1854 Kansas-Nebraska Act, Chase anticipated further realignment. "There must be as heretofore a Democratic Party & a Conservative Party under some name," he told Allen. The new Democratic Party he hoped for was not the current one dominated by the Slave Power and its Doughface acolytes. It would instead be "a really progressive earnestly resolute democracy, suited to the times," meaning it would oppose slavery.[98]

Chase, like many Americans, thought in terms of a two-party system pitting progress against conservatism. He agreed that Jacksonian economic thought was a progressive force. In choosing to be a Free Soiler and later a Republican, however, he had concluded that the Democracy's proslavery stance snuffed out its progressive ethos. One stalwart Democrat disagreed. Fellow Ohioan William M. Corry maintained in 1852 that the Democracy was yet America's progressive party and was destined to play a pivotal role in world affairs. He divined the outcome of the halting realignment: "The Whigs and the Democrats will decompose and recompose:—the former making their organisation under the name of a Union party; and the latter calling themselves Progressive democrats." "There is no question upon which side the strength will be," this progressive Democrat asserted.[99]

While Democrats like Corry vowed to remain agents of progress, many took advantage of the 1850s realignment to blend progressivism and conservatism. By the end of the Mexican War, Democrats had created an unprecedentedly free and equal democratic polity for white men. Yet they anticipated that fanaticism would erase the racial inequality antecedent to white democracy. Democrats resolved to conserve the progress already achieved. Egalitarian democracy, geographical expansion, racial essentialism, and the limited state were not simply the fruits of progressive reform. They could also be, Democrats theorized, sources of social order. The Democracy intended to become America's progressive *and* conservative party in the 1850s. To do so, Democrats would not have to become votaries of the Slave Power, as Salmon Chase characterized them. Nor would they have to restrain the ructious democracy they had already unleashed. With popular sovereignty, Democrats prescribed a hearty dose of democracy as a conservative means of preserving the white man's republic.

TWO

Conservatism and Fanaticism
THE POLITICAL IDEOLOGY OF THE DEMOCRACY BEFORE THE CIVIL WAR

> Of all the political parties which have arisen in this or any other country, there has not been another, in the formation and history of which, there have been such exclusive regard and devotion to the maintenance of human rights, and the happiness and welfare of the masses of the people.
> —Martin Van Buren, 1856

Jonathan S. Wilcox's diary presents a caricature of Yankee stolidity. The entries capture the deliberate rhythms of his life as a farmer and merchant, Christian, and Democrat in Madison, Connecticut. Terse notations record the day's weather and the agricultural tasks it permitted. Weekly entries on the Sabbath attest to Wilcox's religious devotion. The less frequent, but no less regular, tides of American democracy also flow into the diary. Wilcox was a staunch party man, and he attended the various county and state nominating conventions that punctuated the life of a partisan. As with farming, these events merited brief mention—"I attended a county convention of the Democrats I was President of the convention" as noteworthy as "I this day planted Potatoes!!" Wilcox structured his life around the predictability of raising and marketing his crop, worshipping his God, and observing the electoral calendar. There was little that disturbed his equanimity enough to provoke sustained reflection.[1]

Wilcox did indulge occasional loquacity on Sundays, when his uprightness extended to appraisals of the day's sermons, those delivered "in the a m" and "in the pm." After the usual notation, "I attended church all day," follow his assessments of the preachers' efforts. The morning sermon for July 31, 1859, on "the sins of omission," he judged "pretty good." Wilcox was less charitable to the evening sermon, when the pastor "preach'd what I call socialist doctrine *That is*—he wanted all men to be made equal in every respect." Wilcox's livelihood, faith, and politics usually coexisted. Occasionally, however, a dissonant note, such as socialist claptrap about equality, prompted him to forgo his usual parsimony, allowing us to glimpse the assumptions undergirding his worldview.[2]

The catharsis of writing restored this New England burgher's self-assurance after a similar incident in April 1860. In an unusually long entry Wilcox stewed over an antislavery "Political harangue" masquerading as a sermon, an act that he deemed a "desecration of the Pulpit & of the Sabbath." Wilcox confronted the preacher afterward: "I said to him that I had one request to ask him, and that was—If he wished to give Madison people a Political Lecture and would do it on a week day—we would hear it—But I did not want him to do it on the Sabbath." In a moment of self-doubt, he wondered if "I shold be concerned—for what I said, as 7/8 of the people present—agree with the Preacher in Politics and I do not." "I am a Democrat," he yelled into his diary, his confidence restored, "and believe that each state in the Union of states have a perfect right to make their own municipal Laws as suits themselves." This Democrat refused to tolerate an attack on his party's beliefs that feigned sanction from a higher authority. The matter so ruffled Wilcox that he refused to "go to church in the PM as I did not want to hear him any more such Preaching on the Sabbath."[3]

Wilcox reacted to this antislavery preacher chastening the slave states as he would have bristled at dictation leveled at him personally, because he understood his rights and mastery as bound up with the self-rule of white men in the South. Questioning any white men's ability to govern themselves was a threat to *all* white men. The white male individual lay at the heart of Democrats' political ideology. Democrats built their notions of progress, social order, and, ultimately, the Good Society around this raced and gendered individual. Enjoying mastery at home and treated as an equal sovereign in public, the individual was simultaneously the salient of social progress and the redoubt of social order. Reflecting the individual's dual role, Democrats described their political beliefs in multiple ways. The New Hampshire Democracy received praise in 1852 for being "ever conservative to preserve the good of our polity, and ever progressive to adopt a well-based experiment." James L. Orr reassured fellow South Carolinians in 1855 that they had allies among Doughfaces, alternately labeling them "conservative men at the North" and "liberal men from the North."[4] That Democrats in the 1850s identified themselves by seemingly jarring terms showed that they intensified their devotion to progressive and liberal precepts even as they bent them in a conservative direction. Beset with new challenges, Democrats attempted to conserve what had been progressive, if not even radical—a nation premised on mass democracy and liberal toleration of individual diversity.

Democrats juxtaposed their democratic conservatism against a primeval foe they termed fanaticism. Their diverse enemies were facets of this ideological monolith. The hydra of fanaticism presented itself as "Free-Loveism, Spiritualism"; "Millerism, Mesmerism, Mormonism"; "know nothingism, Dowism, abolitionism"; "Wilmot *proviso-ism*";[5] "transcendentalism"; "anti-Foreignism"; "Native-Americanism"; "Fanny Wrightism, Agrarianism";[6] "higher-lawism"; "Puritanism"; "communism and socialism"; "Church burning Nativism"; "Sectionalism, Maine Law-ism, Woman's Rights-ism, and every other ism that can be conceived of."[7] Infatuated with their *isms*, "Grahamites and Fourierites"; "Dorrites"; "anti-renters";[8] "the agrarian and leveler"; "small editors, little speakers on low stumps, writers of bad novels and forgotten poems, preachers of Pantheism"; and other "mad-brained fanatics, and visionary reformers"[9] sowed disorder in pursuit of perfectionist hobbies. Democrats unearthed a common foundation for this "modern Babel" with its "many conflicting *isms*."[10] After accounting for variations, the dross that remained was the fanatical tendency to employ the state to impose restrictive moral codes on independent white men, degrading their democratic autonomy and mastery. Individual mastery and fanatical degradation were the ideological antipodes orienting Democrats' mental universe.

The "strange medley of united fanaticisms"[11] intruded upon Democrats' harmonious worldview. Democrats valued the *progress* that resulted from individuals and communities democratically governing themselves, while fanatics resorted to centralized state power to impose reforms. Basing progress on the individual demanded *liberal* toleration of white men's diversity, which, in turn, spawned an inclusive *nationalism*. Fanatical bigotry sacrificed this diversity for uniformity. The Democratic individual was a raced and gendered being—abstract individualism took concrete form in the master of black and female dependents. He secured the boundaries of the white man's republic by his maintenance of racial and gender hierarchies at home. Individual mastery engendered *conservatism*. Fanatics ignored the racial and gender basis of individualism, subsequently degrading white men and the white man's republic by encouraging female and black political agency. Democrats did not abandon their Jacksonian progressivism in the 1850s. But by newly emphasizing that the individual energy that catalyzed progress also exerted a soothing conservatism, they fused their progressive past with the conservative posture that present exigencies demanded.

Progressive Individualism, or Fanatical Centralization

Democrats in the late 1840s and 1850s were enamored of the progressive dispensation in which they lived. Whether Young Americans, Old Fogies, or southern states' rights extremists, all Democrats hailed discovery, industrial progress, and geographical expansion. Democrats even lionized progress seemingly antithetical to Jefferson's agrarian vision. Vice President George M. Dallas, visiting Pittsburgh in 1847, pointed skyward to the "dark and almost fixed cloud of coal smoke" as testament to the "rising prosperity, and wealth, and importance of the 'Iron City.'" Democrats anticipated the march of progress, even unto perfection. In 1847 a Virginia congressman welcomed the "general peace" and "continuous amelioration of humanity" that Democratic free trade policy would inaugurate through the eradication of "illiberal restrictions, ancient prejudices, and venerated errors."[12] Democrats attributed this progress to their party's "benign principles,"[13] especially their theory of individualism. As opposed to foisting reforms on individuals through a centralized state, Democrats would "remove impediments from national progress," freeing up individuals for their own pursuits.[14] Recognizing the right of sovereign individuals and autonomous communities to rule themselves under a limited state made progress compatible with liberty and order. These "great principles of progressive Democracy" enabled the "full expression of the energies and capacity of this great and progressive people."[15]

Senator James Shields of Illinois enumerated his party's central beliefs in 1852: "national progress, territorial extension, the constitutional independence of the States, and the political liberty of the individual." Individual liberty anteceded the others: the "cardinal principle of that party—the cherished principle of every liberal heart—is its sacred regard for the natural and political rights of individuals." Democrats defined individual liberty expansively. Shields demanded "freedom of action in all cases where the act is not prejudicial to others."[16] Individual liberty also required an unshackled mind so that each white man could decide for himself, especially concerning personal morality. "It ought to be our pride and boast," maintained an Alabamian, "that there never has been and never can be in this country any organization of society to awe the mind from an investigation of what claims to be established creeds."[17] An outgrowth of individualism was self-determination for political communities composed of autonomous white men. A Massachusetts Democrat lauded the individual's "free exercise of his wisdom in domestic control," as well as the "right of every town, of those 'little democracies,' . . . to manage their own municipal matters in their own way."[18]

Unrestrained individuals and self-governing political communities were the engines of progress. "Human imagination has never conceived a system," effused Virginian Robert M. T. Hunter, as that predicated on "the principle of voluntary action, in both individuals and societies." Hunter looked to Jefferson, who "proposed to allow the largest liberty of individual action, which was compatible with the peace and order of the whole." "Free and equal competition" among individuals and among states provided "so powerful a spur to human progress, and so great an impulse to human energy." American advancement, according to James L. Orr, "has been attained by aggregating individual industry and energy." "Man," he instructed graduates at Furman University, "individual man, has made these brilliant achievements."[19]

Their reliance on "the sovereign people,"[20] who "have in their own hands the destiny of their country," reflected Democrats' devotion to the theory of popular sovereignty inherited from the American Revolution. A Democrat in Mobile countered nativists by arguing that an immigrant could not help but be cowed by this American innovation: "He soon finds that the people here are the *sovereigns*, and he leads a virtuous and industrious life to win their confidence and merit their esteem."[21] A Virginian could not understand how anyone could mock the militia, composed as it was of "men whom the constitution makes the chief depository of political power, and pronounces capable and worthy to control the complex and splendid machinery of our government."[22] Putting theory into practice, Democrats empowered the people to rule themselves. They were proud of white men's unprecedented franchise, by the 1850s a fait accompli. Voting was the moment when the people's sovereignty emerged out of abstraction to operate as a mechanism of routine governance, when the individual "exercise[d] the high prerogative of a freeman in reality—in other words, to be his own representative." Men retained sovereignty even after electing representatives, moreover, as "in this great Republic of ours, private citizens are the sovereigns."[23]

The assumption that power resided with the people transcended Fourth of July bluster—it shaped Democratic culture and policy. A correspondent told Senator Stephen A. Douglas that "I have some claim to your attention . . . I am one of the Sovreigns." Douglas and his party took their sovereigns seriously. Upon his 1851 inauguration, Governor William H. Ross lent his support to a convention to revise Delaware's constitution. He was content to follow the people in this matter, because "the will of the people is the sovereign power" and "should control the action of their agents" such as himself.[24] Virginia Democrat John Y. Mason, one such officeholding "agent," reclaimed his sovereignty only *after* leaving the cabinet in 1849. A friend reflected that "we have both returned to private life, & [are] both therefore *Sovereigns*." Democrats acknowledged the sovereignty of the people most dramatically by allowing territorial settlers to legislate on slavery, a specific policy distilled from the larger political theory and also labeled "popular sovereignty." In 1858 Douglas, the policy's most vocal proponent, received news of an "immense meeting" in Ohio, at which "at least *twelve hundred popular sovereigns* sent up their shouts of gladness" for the Little Giant to hear.[25]

The linkage of popular sovereignty and national progress testified to Democrats' positive view of human nature. Several historians have grounded Democratic antistatism in their pessimism regarding individuals' self-interestedness—Democrats would disempower the state, lest individuals use it for corrupt purposes. In his inaugural editorial for the *Democratic Review* in 1837, John L. O'Sullivan had admonished, "All government is evil, and the parent of evil." He also imparted to American politics the memorable dictum "The best government is that which governs least." Yet Democrats could hardly have been so optimistic about democracy if man was inherently debased. O'Sullivan, for instance, although suspicious of the state, trusted the people, declaring, "We have an abiding confidence in the virtue, intelligence, and full capacity for self-government, of the great mass of our people." "Democracy is the cause of Humanity. It has faith in human nature," he trumpeted. This praise echoed in the 1850s. A New Yorker claimed in 1854 that his party "believes the people may be safely entrusted with power, and that man is advancing to a state of greater perfectibility, and that even ancient laws may be modified to meet the progressive spirit of the age."[26]

While Democrats reveled in progress, they were alienated from some contemporary intellectual currents, especially reformism they perceived as infringing on individual rights and democratic self-governance. Ohio's George Pugh found that beneath the age's "material prosperity" festered the spiritual rot of fanaticism. Fanatical reformism promised social strife, not orderly progress. When transfixed by fanaticism, Pugh observed, "we look for something vast, and intricate, and new, some panacea," including antislavery agitation, temperance, and nativism. In a speech inveighing against the "insanity of the times," Illinois congressman Samuel S. Marshall observed that "we believe ourselves to be the most intelligent and enlightened people that the sun shines on." "And yet," he lamented, there was "no folly so great, no theory in religion, morals, or politics, so wild and visionary, that it will not find numerous and zealous advocates among our people." The fanatical disposition donned multiple guises, including religious persecution and superstition, its oldest variants, alongside recent experimentation with communalism, "woman's rights conventions," and "free-love societies." Modern America was restless because its people were smitten with "wild and crazy theories."[27]

Democrats thus insisted that individuals pursue perfection without state aid, lest perfectionism generate governmental fanaticism. According to a Massachusetts Democrat, there was a "madness which fanaticism always arouses in the human heart."[28] A Tennessean found the seeds of fanaticism in individuals' disregard for parts of the Constitution, such as the fugitive slave clause, that guarded the rights of other white men—"they begin by resisting it *in their hearts*," acts that could escalate into "open warfare against both the Constitution and Law of Congress." In reference to the antislavery movement, R. M. T. Hunter complained that "the debates and action of Congress were sought to be perverted to the creation of a moral machinery for the destruction of the institutions of some of the States."[29] Access to the government's "moral machinery" metastasized individuals' perfectionism into state fanaticism when they used governmental power to force the unwilling into their procrustean utopias. Leaving every man and community to their own perfectionist strivings would instead kindle national progress. Congressman Marshall advised "every people to attend to the correction of their own evils and their own laws, and leave other communities the right and privilege of doing the same thing for themselves." According to another midwesterner, all "should be left free to arive at full perfection, without the influences of a great overshadowing, central, consolidated government."[30] Their desire that all white men have equal opportunity to chase perfection, not revulsion at human nature, informed Democrats' antistatism.

Fanatics sought reforms through undemocratic state power because they despaired of white men's ability to exercise popular sovereignty. Politics was a cosmic showdown between "two opposite views of government."[31] Democrats' "theory of local self-government" preserved liberty, unlike "the meddling theory of government."[32] Fanaticism was the latest reincarnation of Democrats' ancient enemy—"the Federal, or Whig philosophy."[33] Federalists and Whigs, recounted Lewis Cass, had "doubted the capacity of men for self-government."[34] The hubris that they knew better than the people impelled Tories, Federalists, Whigs, and their fanatical heirs in the 1850s. The modern fanatical impulse created a society in which "each of us bewails the necessity of reformation in every body except himself; and pursuing this benevolent design, we have enacted laws for the regulation of social as well as political duties." Fanatical government would supplant individuals' democratic power. The *Democratic Review* cautioned against the "concession or surrender of power, belonging to the people in their organic functions, in their capacities as sovereigns." The state should be starved of power: "We would say, Reserve as much as is possible to the sovereigns, the people."[35]

Democrats feared that the state's growth would prove inevitable once its moral machinery was accepted as a tool of reform. Energetic government translated philanthropy into tyranny. A Democratic newspaper cheered President Pierce's 1854 veto of the "Insane Bill," which would have charged Congress with caring for "the indigent insane of the different States." Assuming custody over one class of Americans, state paternalism would know no bounds. The reform would "empower the federal government to take under its protection the indigent who are not insane." There would be no "limit or restraint to the charitable impulses of Congress," with the state becoming "a husband to the widow and a father to the fatherless." In their version of this slippery slope mind-set, southerners dreaded the state becoming master of their slaves, harking back to Nathaniel Macon, the Old Republican who had foretold that "if Congress can make canals, they can with more propriety emancipate." Like republicans of the Revolutionary era, Democrats knew that governmental power accreted over time. Eventually the state would even usurp white men's household mastery.[36]

State power was only one of the purportedly disproportionate means upon which fanatics relied. They also employed "inflammatory addresses made to the passions" rather than to reason. They were "base enough to attempt to obtain political power by catering to morbid sentimentality."[37] A short distance separated impassioned politics from violence, whereupon "missionaries of blood" would introduce "the guillotines of reckless politicians" to the United

States.[38] The "personal worshipers and particular fannatical followers" of antislavery congressman Joshua R. Giddings, for example, "would destroy the Union itself if they could by that course accomplish their fiendish purpose."[39] Democrats recognized that political ideas had consequences and ought to be handled cautiously. When Winfield Scott ran for president in 1852, Democrats remembered that nativist riots in Philadelphia in 1844 had been "the legitimate consequences of his views" on immigrants and Catholics.[40] In 1859 John Brown led an antislavery uprising of "armed men, incited to the wildest excesses by the dangerous teachings of a false philanthropy." In the aftermath, Virginia's governor Henry A. Wise notified an abolitionist that Brown's "attempt was a natural consequence of your sympathy."[41]

That fanatics like Brown, consumed by "a rabid fanaticism, that loses the substance in grasping the shadow,"[42] failed to calibrate their means to their ends yielded outsized and unintended consequences. Eschewing practical politics for "baseless abstraction[s],"[43] fanatics exacerbated the social ills they would alleviate. A conservative Whig supporting the Democrats griped about this "distempered and unmeaning philanthropy," which longed for "the cure of one evil by the creation of ten thousand."[44] Those "boastful philanthropies and philosophies" and those "machineries to be engrafted upon legislation" then in vogue, explained an Ohioan, would only "be successful, . . . because they include and foster the very disease which they profess to extirpate."[45] Antislavery fanatics would always be able to rail against slavery, Democrats charged, as their crusading ensured its continuance. "But for the rashness and inconsiderate zeal of outside agitators," claimed a Marylander in 1852, "the progress of emancipation would have been much greater." James Henry Hammond enthused over "the happy results of this abolition discussion," which had prompted a "re-examination and explosion of the false theories of religion, philanthropy and political economy" by which slavery was previously considered "an evil."[46] Thanks to abolitionists, southerners claimed, they now saw the institution for what it really was—a positive good.

Democrats' critiques grew out of a tradition of antifanaticism in Western political thought. Many European political theorists, having witnessed the Continent's religious wars and England's seventeenth-century Puritan despotism, denounced overly enthusiastic politics. "Enthusiasm," according to David Hume, was "founded on strong spirits, and a presumptuous boldness of character." Dire consequences resulted when passion "rises to that height as to inspire the deluded fanatic with the opinion of divine illuminations, and with a contempt for the common rules of reason, morality, and prudence." In the ecstasy of self-righteousness, fanatics could not help but trample upon others. Voltaire's 1741 play *Fanaticism* featured Mahomet, a caricature of religious extremism, who is rebuked by another character for "hav[ing] the nerve to think you can mold the world to your whims and order people to think like you do, even as you bring them nothing but carnage and fear." Antifanaticism energized the Enlightenment as theorists enshrined reason and natural law, as well as a social contract that limited the state and protected individual rights, to defuse impassioned politics.[47]

Enlightenment thinkers blamed fanaticism for casting society into perpetual flux. Democrats agreed. Fanaticism comprised a mode of conducting politics without defining a normative social order as an ultimate goal.[48] "Abolition will not stop" and "run-mad fanaticism" would never desist, because there was always one more reform to agitate in pursuit of unattainable utopias.[49] Fanatics were "those who cannot let well enough alone," as they hurried "from one subject of excitement to another, from one hatred to another, from one persecution to another."[50] "Phrenzied fanaticism," in its "nervous haste to discuss new topics before old ones are understood," could not be glutted.[51] During the Civil War, former president James Buchanan delivered the epitaph for the fanatical 1850s: "Fanaticism never stops to reason. Driven by honest impulse, it rushes on to its object without regard to interposing obstacles." "This spirit of interference with what we may choose to consider the domestic evils of other nations," he moralized, "has in former periods covered the earth with blood."[52]

Liberal Toleration, or Fanatical Bigotry

Jonathan S. Wilcox was a devout man, and his diary registers approval of evangelical reforms, such as temperance and the colonization of African Americans. The tempo of his trade regularly took Wilcox from Connecticut to New York to market goods, and he attended services while traveling. We can imagine an impish, even voyeuristic, urge propelling him to "Henry Ward Beechers church in Brooklyn" in February 1854. "Had I not have known that it was a church and the pastor a professed preacher of Christ," he recollected, "I should have thought that I had been in a political caucus." Wilcox resolved not to "desecrate another Sabbath ever in hearing such a libelious & seditious harrange." Mixing the temporal and the spiritual struck

Wilcox as indecorous. His revulsion was indicative of the Democracy's aversion to a symbiotic church and state. Religious extremism fueled many fanatical political crusades, Democrats maintained, including those aimed at Catholicism, slavery, and alcohol. Zealots like Beecher, who, according to Virginia's Henry Wise, "bray a political religion and religious politics," manifested a trait common to all fanatics—bigoted intolerance.[53] Fanatical bigotry injected schismatic proscription and inquisitional persecution into politics. An intolerant state, under the sway of "politico-religious fanaticism,"[54] would excommunicate white men from the body politic.

Democrats contrasted fanatics' "bigotry and intollerance" with their own liberal toleration. Alabamian Clement C. Clay abjured "that intolerance, which, in some countries, has proven a bloody scourge, and is, in all, the chief bane of social concord."[55] In 1852 Whig presidential candidate Winfield Scott's nativist baggage epitomized such illiberality. Democrats appraised him as "a man of envious spirit, narrow and malignant feelings, and intolerant and proscriptive nature." Scott's statesmanship paled next to that of Andrew Jackson, given "the generous and liberal principles which signalized his political creed, [which] would never have permitted that he should give his agency to encourage a spirit of civil and religious intolerance."[56] Democrats called themselves and their principles "liberal" to denote their acceptance of white men's diversity. Following Jackson's lead, broad-minded Democrats tolerated much that other Americans considered social, political, or moral evils, including white men's ethnic and religious diversity, tippling in addition to teetotaling, enslavement alongside freedom.

Intolerant fanaticism degraded white men because it acted on its bigotry through improper means—legal coercion, rather than moral suasion. Democrats believed that reformers should appeal to white men as equals, allowing them to choose to modify their behavior. Indulging intolerance set a disturbing precedent—according to a Catholic member of the Democracy, "In a Government like ours, the rights of no class, however humble they may be, can be assailed without endangering the rights of all."[57] When bigots used the state's moral machinery to discriminate against one group of white men, such as Catholics, they invalidated the equality of all white men. Individuals exercised autonomy when adopting a new moral code, but it was an affront to self-rule and individual manhood when the state imposed a minority's religious or moral scruples. The political campaign against alcohol was, accordingly, "intemperate in its temperance," as governmental regulation "enthrones a legal inquisition in place of moral suasion."[58] Democrats' toleration complemented their antistatism; the state ought to be both small and amoral.

Many Democrats went further and attacked bigotry not only on the part of the state but also within society. Toleration, they argued, was a fundamental American value. Private bigotry easily spilled into politics. "Intolerance lies dormant in the breast," awaiting the opportune moment for bigots "to stimulate this feeling for political objects."[59] Democrats wanted to avoid the amplification of personal intolerance through the state. "Next to a bigot in religion, a bigot in politics is perhaps the bitterest and the worst," preached a Democratic pamphlet, "but when, as in the present instance, political bigotry is nearly allied to religious bigotry, there is difficulty in discriminating between the two." Democrats demanded an inclusive society in addition to a neutral state. They would not tolerate intolerance in the white man's republic.[60]

Northerners could privately oppose slavery, many Democrats conceded, provided they publicly honor slaveholders' rights. Franklin Pierce, a campaign pamphlet noted, "spoke of slavery as all conservative northern men speak of it"—as an "evil" that "we must endure."[61] Georgian Howell Cobb, playing the exotic southerner, denied to a New England audience that "my purpose in addressing you would be to convert you into advocates of the peculiar institutions of my own section of the country." Cobb reassured them that "I come not to invite you to the adoption of our local institutions," although he did "come with the constitution of our common country in my hands, to ask you to abide by its obligations." Refusing to treat "the abstract question of slavery," he invoked only constitutional right. The question was "not whether slavery is right or wrong" but "what says the constitution?" The answer was that northerners had to tolerate slavery.[62]

Northern Democrats shared Cobb's aversion to the "self-righteous idea that one man is called upon to be the conscience-keeper of another." When righteousness wedded itself to "the strong arm of the law," then "the convincing argument of the philanthropist, and the persuasive appeals of good men . . . are thrown aside for the more effective weapon of legislative power."[63] An Indianan acknowledged that "I have always in sentiment, been opposed to Slavery." But he specified that he "never proposed any other means than moral suasion for its eradication."[64] New Yorker Rufus W. Peckham commiserated with southern secession after the election of a Republican president in 1860, commenting to his son that "I love the pharisees or the bigots of the present day no better than those of olden time." Peckham did "not feel it a sin to be honest & to do unto others as I would they should do unto me."[65] Toleration had to be mutual and unbegrudging, so that all white men could enjoy it. A South Carolinian turned the tables by telling Yankees that northern abolition had occurred only by southern forbearance. "We believed you were the best judges of your own interest," he explained, and "we had no right under our system of government to enter your State and either advocate or oppose emancipation."[66]

The sop to southerners—that northerners could privately detest slavery provided they remained politically neutral—did not go far enough for all Democrats. Some northerners cheered slavery as a positive good. An Alabamian expressed satisfaction that New York's Charles O'Conor "made a telling speech, in which he took the bull by the horns, and declared that negro slavery is right and not wrong."[67] A Democrat in Minnesota Territory attributed Americans' role as "the chosen people of God, commissioned to work out the salvation of mankind," to the economic benefits of enslaved labor. National prosperity originated in the South, where "the labor of the inferior negro race, is directed by the superior intellect of the white man, on a better system of servile labor, a more humane system, than has ever existed." Democrats' racism led them to designate slavery the most efficient regime for the coexistence of unequal races.[68] "Abolitionists," on the contrary, "with their false and heartless sympathies," hypocritically "claim equal rights for a race that is void of means necessary to its own continued existence." Those genuinely concerned with the plight of the enslaved, Democrats clarified, knew that allowing slavery to spread would enhance their well-being.[69]

Along with slaveholders and free laborers, Democrats also tolerated abstainers and partakers. Many Democrats approved of shaping a temperate citizenry through moral suasion, and some sanctioned temperance legislation. Even when the "Whig Main [sic] Law-Abolition Ticket" trounced the Connecticut Democracy in 1854, Jonathan Wilcox solaced himself with the "hope they will make a good law to stop ardent spirits from being sold at all in any way."[70] But protemperance Democrats had to balance hostility toward alcohol with wariness of state power. Democrats were reluctant to join the temperance movement so long as reformers advanced coercive legislation such as Maine's infamous 1851 prohibitory statute. One prohibitionist complained that the Democracy would maintain the allegiance of those "who only *occasionally* taste it—or who *never* taste it, but don't approve of restraints,

& the principle of the Maine Law." Many Democrats supported the movement's ends but not its means. As an Ohio Democrat queried, "Shall we use the sovereign power of the State . . . to compel the performance of what is esteemed a private moral duty[?]"[71]

Even short of legislative endorsement, temperance abridged white men's moral prerogative. A manuscript speech in the papers of Alabama Democrat Sydenham Moore protests against personally pledging oneself to temperance: "Now this tying a man up not to commit an act in itself indifferent, is such a restraint upon his freedom of action, as in a large proportion of cases, will make [him] restless & dissatisfied." Like other fanatical nostrums, the temperance pledge had unintended consequences, being "productive of more injury than benefit." Treating "an act in itself indifferent" as an evil and conforming one's behavior to that arbitrary standard "leads in too many cases to hypocrisy." Sydenham Moore adhered to this teaching. When he learned that his overseer imbibed, he told the man that he preferred a lieutenant "who will not go off on frolics or frolic at home. And while in liquor injure & abuse my negroes." He counseled moderation but did not exact abstention and offered to keep the man on for another season.[72]

Fanaticism encouraged hypocrisy not only by insisting that individuals fit themselves to the contours of another's morality but also, Democrats believed, because fanatics were themselves insincere. "A man who mearly refrains from drinking liquor, with a smack of hypocracy about it, & a bloat in every other vice, cannot correct over a timperate dram drinker, who is timperet in all things," groused an Indiana Democrat. Fanatics feigned moral purity to seize power. Our Connecticut diarist impugned Republicans' sincerity: "They do not care a Pin for the Negroe if they can carry their point so as to Elect an anti Slavery President and get the advantage of 15 Slave States."[73] Their "pretended sympathy for the slave," alleged a Pennsylvanian, amounted to nothing more than "hypocritical pretense." Democrats suspected that even when the fanatical rank and file were truly devoted, demagogic leaders manipulated their sentimentality to win office.[74] According to a modern philosopher, "When we criticize someone for being fanatical or hypocritical, we are passing judgment on his mode of commitment, and at most only very indirectly on the credal content of his particular world view." Fanaticism was a mode of acquiring power, not an ideological prescription for meaningful reform. Fanatics' zeal, whether genuine or contrived, was not a basis for social order.[75]

Democrats espoused toleration most stridently through anticlericalism and calls for the "absolute and unqualified divorce of Church and State, religion and politics."[76] Democrats were not irreverent, and they often foregrounded their own religious beliefs. The party no longer trucked with the deists, atheists, and iconoclasts who had moved on Jacksonianism's fringes in the 1820s and 1830s. A Democratic organization in New York, for instance, avowed in 1860, "We believe all power emanates from God, by whom it is entrusted to individuals and communities to be exercised by them for the general welfare." Yet, while many Democrats in the 1850s professed Christianity, they snarled at preachers who dared to enter politics, thereby hewing to what historian Arthur M. Schlesinger Jr. labels the "republican anticlericalism" of Jefferson and Jackson. Democrats had long been suspicious of religiously inspired political beliefs that infringed on white men's moral and political autonomy.[77]

In response to nativist and anti-Catholic proscription, Democrats championed religious and ethnic diversity. Not all Democrats were models of toleration. Channeling his Puritan forebears, Jonathan Wilcox exhibited contempt toward popery. He crowed that, while viewing a Catholic procession, "some few like myself did not bow down to this Idol." But most Democrats regarded toleration as conducive to social progress. Levi Woodbury believed that constitutions should be amended cautiously. But he wanted New Hampshire's charter purged of its religious test in 1850, explaining, "I am willing, when a provision like this becomes hostile to the tolerant spirit of the age and a more enlightened public opinion, to expunge it at once."[78] European immigrants, welcomed by the party's "broad, just and liberal platform in favor of naturalization," were valued for their economic and cultural contributions to the nation. Celebrating religious and ethnic difference meshed with the party's belief that unimpeded individualism was a progressive force.[79]

Religious toleration was an imperative for Democrats. Lewis Cass, commonly dismissed as an Old Fogy by the 1850s, proved a Young American in his belief that citizens carried their uniquely American freedom of conscience abroad. "MAN HAS A RIGHT TO WORSHIP GOD UNRESTRAINED BY HUMAN LAWS," he boomed, and he wanted the United States to enforce this principle worldwide. A newspaper seconded Cass's expansive notions: "Intolerance is all wrong and wicked by whomsoever exercised. It is the mission of this country to unloose the fetters upon religious freedom everywhere." New York's Catholic archbishop John Hughes thought such a notion invited fanaticism. Cass's contention that other governments "must give way to the individual, provided that individual be an American," would obligate the United States to defend American religious fanatics, such as "Mormon[s]" and "Millerite[s]," abroad.[80] Archbishop Hughes's criticism notwithstanding, Democrats were just as fervent in their promotion of America's Catholic minority. Proclaiming, "I am a Democrat and a Catholic" in 1856, John Kelly, Congress's only adherent of that faith, responded to hackneyed assertions that his coreligionists were unrepublican. Catholics always voted Democratic, proving their republicanism. President Pierce, additionally, named Catholic James Campbell as postmaster general and dispatched August Belmont, a foreign-born Jew, as a diplomat to The Hague, appointments that stoked nativist, anti-Catholic, and anti-Semitic ire.[81]

Democrats protested the union of church and state, not simply to protect religious minorities but as another concentration of power that trespassed on the people's sovereignty. A Methodist clergyman evidenced his Democracy by opposing an antislavery proposal under consideration by his denomination. "The New Testament contains no particular form of Government," the Reverend Henry Slicer remonstrated, and "it has left it with the people to enact such a form as they may judge most expedient." The belief that "God has prescribed the form and principles of government," expounded Stephen Douglas, "would annihilate the fundamental principle upon which our political system rests . . . that the people had an inherent right to establish such Constitution and laws for the government of themselves." A self-governing people followed their own dictates, not those of a deity and its oracles.[82]

Religious toleration deflated fanaticism. Democrats recycled John Locke's seventeenth-century solution to religious conflict by pronouncing that one had to tolerate in order to be tolerated. "If the Law of Toleration were once so settled," Locke pleaded, "that all Churches were obliged to lay down Toleration as the Foundation of their own Liberty," then the "endless Hatreds, Rapines, and Slaughters" heretofore blighting history would cease. State neutrality was salutary. A Democrat in 1850 similarly hoped that the government should, "if true to republican principles, shield all in their religious tenets . . . and protect all in their pursuits and worship, however different."[83] R. M. T. Hunter invoked Locke and held that it was "far better to pursue the present practice; tolerate all religions, and have each church free to pursue its mission in its own way." Otherwise, fanatics, in "unprotestantizing Protestantism itself, and returning to the practices of the darkest ages of religious bigotry and persecution," would prompt Catholics to become the enemies they were painted to be, before they moved against other denominations such as Quakers. Intolerant fanatics would engender the evils they persecuted by placing the nation on the slippery slope of "sectarian jealousy."[84]

The meddling cleric was Democrats' archetypal fanatic. A Know-Nothing publication grumbled about a Democratic leader who "flare[s] up with a fierce spirit and hot indignation to devour some black-coat who presumes to touch ever so tenderly on some political measure in his pulpit discussions."[85] Democrats did indeed rage against "political preacher[s]," "partizan priests," and "Sunday political sermons."[86] Their contest with these "fossils of the twelfth century, dug up and stamped anew," was a continuation of the Enlightenment struggle against "Priest craft" and "Jesuitism."[87] Clerical opposition validated one's Democracy. Surveying the outcry over the Kansas-Nebraska Act, one Democrat unfriendly to the Little Giant mused, "If the fools do not quit burning Douglas in efegy and the Priest do not let him alone they will make him President" and "will learn me to love him." "The Democracy of this country has always been opposed in every important crisis by the clergy," declaimed another Democrat, as "every quarter of a century . . . they get frightened from their propriety, seize all the thunders of Sinai, and hurl them upon the Democratic party." Such denunciation signaled that the party marched on the side of progress.[88]

Party leaders in the 1850s emulated Andrew Jackson's contempt for clerics. Douglas obscured the moral issue of slavery's expansion by turning clerical opposition to Kansas-Nebraska into a debate over the involvement of preachers in politics. Douglas accused them of false philanthropy, charging that their objections did not reflect antislavery conviction but their fear that popular sovereignty diminished their own pretensions to "divinely-constituted power." Granting the clergy political authority risked transforming the state into a moral machinery, with "the representatives of the people converted into machines in the hands of an all-controlling priesthood." Although he had been an early ally of the persecuted Church of Jesus Christ of Latter-day Saints, Douglas also exulted over having defied "the Mormon prophet," who had announced "that it was the decree of heaven" that the Little Giant should suffer electoral defeat. The people had rebuffed clerical intercession by reelecting Douglas.[89] Buchanan also censured a group of divines requesting his repentance for Bleeding Kansas. After thanking them for praying for his administration, the president retorted that "genuine philanthropy" required that they look to their own meddling, not his sins, as the source of "sectional excitement."[90]

Anticlericalism also pervaded the party's grassroots. Jeptha Garrigus, a staunch old Hoosier Jacksonian, complained to a representative that "they have elected a chaplain To both houses" of Congress, which he deemed "a very wrong act." "Pay for your own preaching if you Want to have it," he growled. A visitor to Utah Territory juxtaposed Brigham Young's opulent palace and gardens, akin to those of an Oriental despot, with the "greater portion of the masses [who] are ignorant, deluded, well meaning fanatical people," hoodwinked by "shrewd, unprincipled" theocrats.[91] Democrats' relationship with the clergy was one of eternal enmity. During the Kansas-Nebraska debate, one Democrat wrote Douglas that he had "expected the opposition of these *Black coated clergymen*," which he thought "fortunate for I never knew them right in my life on any political subject." "I never had a very great respect for that class of our citizens any way," he concluded.[92]

National Diversity, or Fanatical Uniformity

Religious fanatics' inability to peer beyond the horizons of their brittle morality unsuited them for leadership of a heterogeneous and unfolding empire of liberty. So too did their ally, the sectionalist, falter as a steward of American exceptionalism. National statesmanship meant nurturing geographical variation and cultural intermingling. Voters learned that 1852 presidential candidate Franklin Pierce's character was neither "narrow nor sectional," but "liberal, enlarged, and national."[93] 1856 vice presidential candidate John C. Breckinridge, likewise, was "a statesman of the most enlarged and comprehensive policy; the friend of freedom and of the oppressed everywhere."[94] Senator Andrew Pickens Butler offered a different assessment of his Republican colleague Charles Sumner when he reproached, "I had known many who came into the Senate of the United States, reeking with prejudices from home, who afterwards had the courage to lift themselves above the temporary influences which had controlled them." Sumner's intolerance of slavery, born of chauvinistic sectionalism, compromised the national scope of his statesmanship. The South Carolinian added rhetorical blows to the physical ones from which Sumner was then convalescing, sneering, "I supposed that a man who had read history could not be a bigot."[95]

Sumner's bigoted provincialism contrasted with Democrats' eclectic nationalism. Governor Henry A. Wise of Virginia always thumped his chest over his nationalism; yet, like any conscientious slaveholder, he added caveats.

He denounced "*nationality* in opposition to democracy or State rights . . . all that sort of *federal nationality* which would *consolidate us into one centralized position.*" Wise instead preferred "the *nationality of democracy* . . . which maintains State rights and State equality," a nationality he claimed to "honor and cherish and glory in!" Democrats, especially those anxious over vested interests such as slavery or toleration for their church, rejected state consolidation and the uniformity that accompanied it, but they did not dispense with nationalism. Rather, they equated American nationality with diversity, articulating a loose-fitting nationalism fostered not by the nation-state but by their party. Fanatics, in contrast, would straiten diversity into stifling uniformity by exacting adherence to moral and sectional dreams. Democrats' regard for the autonomous individual and toleration of his variations led them to condone competing socioeconomic regimes and jarring ethnic, religious, and regional folkways. The Democracy cultivated the national loyalty of white men by promising that, while it controlled the state, the government would be one that tolerated their diversity and maintained their equality across the continent.[96]

Social and cultural variation was Democrats' prescription for orderly national growth. They updated the pluralism of James Madison, who had opted for a geographically broadcast and internally discordant republic in which antagonistic interests checked despotism, and projected it onto an unprecedented continental canvas. Self-governing individuals and communities would develop along their own trajectories, buffered from the tampering of others and themselves unable to overreach, a blueprint for social order amid expansion that historian Robert H. Wiebe refers to as "parallelism."[97] The Democratic governor of California, a state owing its existence to his party's gleeful expansionism, advised that "the only way to secure the peace and tranquility of the republic, is for each to abstain from intermeddling with the affairs of its neighbor." Toleration was requisite among individuals and among sections; according to a New York Democrat, "The free exercise of the rights of citizens in other sections of the Union is necessary for the preservation of our own."[98] Tolerating diversity ensured the "unlimited extension" of Democrats' "benign system of federative self-government," enlarging what Franklin Pierce praised as "a confederation so vast and so varied, both in numbers and in territorial extent, in habits and in interests."[99]

Diversity inhibited a consolidated state from instilling fanatical uniformity and effacing differences among white men and among sections. A Connecticut

Democrat lectured that "the great and varied interests of the Union have proved a safeguard to itself and a benefit to mankind." Stephen Douglas warned that a Republican rival's dictum that the nation must "become *all* one thing or *all* the other" regarding slavery harbingered "uniformity in the local laws and domestic institutions," which was "destructive of State rights, of State sovereignty, of personal liberty and personal freedom."[100] Where Douglas recommended a variety of inferior roles for African Americans to occupy at the discretion of white men, an Arkansas Democrat endorsed ethnic diversity among equal white men through immigration as an obstacle to fanaticism. "The greater the diversity of interests confided to the care of the Union," he reasoned, "the less danger is there of its subversion by any one of them."[101] Democrats' baroque republic, splayed over a vast expanse, guaranteed that no single *ism* could compel conformity to its visions.

To encourage diversity and forestall uniformity, Democrats countenanced slavery's expansion. The federal government did not need to turn the territories into a preserve for either slavery or freedom. It was unhelpful, objected a Massachusetts Democrat, to approach territorial settlement as "a sort of proclaimed steeple-chase . . . between the Northern and the Southern States." Territorial popular sovereignty would defuse controversy and hinder the onset of hated uniformity, especially if fraught decisions were never actually made (the doctrine's fatal flaw was that eventually the people would have to choose).[102] National economic progress, moreover, depended on regional economic specialization. A Minnesota Democrat defended the South because "commercial prosperity" required "variety in unity, combining north, south, east and west, consisting of free white labor where it flourishes in temperate climes, and forced dark labor in the tropics."[103]

Democrats contended that only their party incubated national diversity because, by the late 1850s, only their membership approximated the nation itself. A delegate surveying the 1856 national convention gushed over "this vast assemblage, from all—not sections; there are no sections (cheers)—but latitudes and longitudes (applause) of the republic."[104] Whigs and Know-Nothings splintered over slavery, while the Republican Party was born exclusively northern, innovations that Democrats blamed on a burgeoning "spirit of sectional hate" and a tendency to "organize political parties on geographical lines."[105] The Democracy, however, could ritualistically conflate itself with the nation because it contained northerners and southerners. Intersectional commingling produced a national partisan ideology. Because delegates "from the cold regions of the

North, others from the sultry clime of the South" drafted the party's 1856 platform, it contained neither "religious bigotry" directed at northern immigrants nor "hypocritical negro-fanaticism" aimed at white southerners.[106]

A Whig pamphlet joked that "it is really too bad to have these Southerners prowling about New England, over-hearing the Democracy there as they spread themselves on the subject of slavery," hinting that northern Democrats conveyed different messages to southerners and northerners.[107] Slave-state Democrats did regularly canvass the free states on behalf of northern colleagues. One southerner "prowling about New England" assured listeners that he "promulgate[d] the same political sentiments which I proclaim to my own honored constituency in South Carolina." He elaborated, "I am here to demonstrate the great fact that the Democratic party—differing from all other parties in that respect—is national in its principles, and its members, whether hailing from the North or South, speaking amidst the frigid hills of New England or on the sunny plains of the South, can safely publish the same doctrines." Northern Democrats could boast likewise. A partisan noticed that the Little Giant's speeches in Memphis and New Orleans "breathed the same Democracy, that he gave to the People of Illinois," as "he did not speak to suit two Localities, but he proclaimed the same doctrine that will go all over the nation."[108]

Democrats could "everywhere speak the same language"[109] because they reduced nationality to a common component—the autonomous white man. Stripped of regional identity, white men were interchangeable, which made the party's proselytizers fungible on the stump. The individual was the locus of American nationality, around which emanated concentric loyalties—to family, community, religion, state, section, and, ultimately, nation. Historian David M. Potter cautions against reducing the Civil War to a trade-off between nationalism and sectionalism. Antebellum Americans held multiple loyalties, and national allegiance could draw strength from parochial identities. Because of their interchangeable individual, Democrats did not hold regionalism and nationalism in antagonism. Akin to the party's principles, which were not fixed geographically, Democrats were not concerned whether a white man was a southerner or a northerner, a slaveholder or a Roman Catholic—all possessed the same rights and, ideally, tolerated one another.[110]

Beginning with the individual white man, Democrats channeled local fealty toward national ends. Henry Wise reassured Indiana Democrats that he would "know no sections in administering the powers and duties of our Federative system; that as a Virginian, as an American, as a Democrat," and "as a Southern man and a slaveholder," he would shield all Americans against "inequality" and "injustice." By respecting the equality of individuals, despite their variation, the Democracy funneled white men's loyalty through the stratifications of household, community, state, and section to the nation. Governor Joseph A. Wright of Indiana used an address before an agricultural society to both promote flax cultivation and theorize on American identity. Regard for the individual strengthened the nation by making him the unit of progress in his community, with the result that "by the form and structure of our government, the little local communities at home, from school districts to townships, counties, and State, are all made, as it were, part and parcel of the machinery that moves and regulates the action of our republic." The recognition that diverse individuals were the nation's sovereigns at all levels comprised "the strength and beauty of our form of Government."[111]

Democrats made their party and its ideas, not the state, responsible for generating national sentiment. James Buchanan complimented Wright's discourse, in which "the principles of the Democratic party are traced back to their fountain." With its partisan ideology, long consisting of states' rights, constitutional "strict construction," and, more recently, territorial popular sovereignty, the Democracy worked toward a political order that balanced individual and state equality with nationality.[112] According to an Ohioan, "Our fathers established a Union of States diverse in local institutions, and separately sovereign, but nevertheless compacted into one Nation." Other countries privy to America's feat, claimed New York's Elijah Ward, "naturally desire the benefits of a government that give[s] such evidence of prosperity and stability, affords such protection to person and property, and leaves the people in such unrestricted enjoyment of social and political liberty."[113] Democrats told white men that, with their party at the helm, nationalism need not subsume individualism or localism.

The normative nationality of the Democracy would gently swaddle all Americans. Sectional actors, seeking to impose an idealized image of their region upon the nation, were not alone in advancing ideological visions. Democrats also limned a Good Society. "We shall present the glorious spectacle," regaled Marylander Reverdy Johnson, "of an enlightened people, harmonious and powerful in our very contrasts, living under State governments adequate to all our local wants, and under a general government subjected to all the restraints which freedom requires." Virginia's R. M. T. Hunter, after painting a portrait of national tranquility, opined before a northern audience, "And upon what reposed this grand scheme of human happiness? It rested on the faith felt by our people that they would continue to live under the Constitution, and the equal laws which it enjoined, in the confidence they reposed in the sense of justice and mutual affection of each other." Neither atomization nor fanatical uniformity but mutual affection despite diversity characterized Democrats' happy republic.[114]

Nationalism nurtured by an antistatist party, not a centralized nation-state, accounts for the exceptionalism and fragility of the American Union before the Civil War. Democratic nationalism skirted two extremes. Some defenders of slavery, particularly adherents of John C. Calhoun, theorized the Union as an arena of jostling factions in which minorities, specifically the slave states, wielded vetoes over national policy. Many Democrats spurned this model, as it stunted the development of what one proslavery northerner called "an all-embracing, an all-cherishing nationality."[115] Yet, in articulating an "all-embracing" nationality, Democrats did not melt down heterogeneity to a *völkisch* reduction in the crucible of European Romantic nationalism. American identity, as Democrats understood it, was not based on signifiers of nineteenth-century nationhood such as ethnicity, ancestral territory, or common folkways. Nor was it inculcated by the nation-state. Democrats would contain the state but facilitate nationalism—what President Pierce defined as "the minimum of Federal government compatible with the maintenance of national unity."[116] Democratic nationalism, premised on individual and local diversity, was uniquely inclusive, but also bluntly exclusionary. Even though Democrats railed against arbitrary uniformity, they circumscribed their own national vista with unyielding demarcations of race and gender.

Conservative Mastery, or Fanatical Degradation

Faced with the fanatical ambition to hem white men's diversity into a narrow nationality, Democrats relied on the "sober second thought of the people" to inoculate the republic against the "delirium tremens of fanaticism."[117] Democrats applauded the democratic people's innate conservatism. "I do not believe that fanaticism is to be rampant, in this enlightened day," ruminated a Maine Democrat, as "the second sober thought of the people will take the place of the unnatural excitement which, seems to pass, over the political and social circles, as a whirlwind, only to deform and make hateful."[118] The nation's silent majority of self-governing individuals would rebuke fanatics, because

Democrats' vaunted individual was not a theoretical abstraction but a historically contingent raced and gendered being. By sanctifying their mastery over black and female dependents, Democrats empowered white men to preserve racial and gender order. The concept of *mastery* rooted political legitimacy in the governance of household dependents. Fanaticism corroded this autonomy by undermining domestic hierarchies. A white man's *degradation* at home presaged the degradation of the white man's republic itself. Democrats made individualism the conservative bulwark of the republic by making equal white men masters at home and in politics.[119]

An ominous undercurrent of violence pulsed behind even mundane transactions in the interbellum Senate. In 1856 Alabamian Clement Claiborne Clay launched a tirade against John P. Hale of New Hampshire. Hale would neither join him in debate, Clay charged, nor meet him in a violent test of honor. Instead, Senator Hale "soils the carpet upon which he treads" and "skulks behind petticoats, on the plea of non-combatancy, for protection." Clay was impugning Hale's manhood. More than cowardice accounted for his unmanliness—Hale's political beliefs invalidated his masculinity. Hale's politics, particularly his "tender conscience" for enslaved Americans, led to his "debasement or degradation." He was an effeminate fanatic, while Clay and fellow Democrats were manly conservatives.[120]

Hale's unmanliness was attributable to fanatical *degradation*, a term with precise meaning in the white man's republic. Degradation was the forfeiture of one's manly autonomy, both personally and politically. Fanatical political traits, such as undue passion, zealous reformism, or blind obedience, showed a dearth of independence as a man and of republican virtue as a statesman. One could, for example, be "enslaved by party necessity."[121] The man possessing "native dignity of original manhood," Clay had imparted earlier to students at the University of Alabama, is "not the slave of passion, or prejudice, or self-interest, or party, or public opinion."[122] The notion of being "enslaved" to one's politics indicates the stakes of degradation. The political degradation of a statesman and the racial degradation of a white man were reciprocal.

Fanatics degraded themselves as white men by succumbing to "misplaced and sickly sentiment."[123] Such men acted on their politics like impassioned women. An 1856 pamphlet noted that the Republican presidential candidate would "be wafted to the White House, on the prayers of the devout, the tears and smiles of woman, and the sympathies of the humane."[124] Rather than strengthening the Union, effeminate fanatics chased "a will-o'-the-wisp, an intangibility, a theory." After emasculating themselves, fanatics seduced other white men to the same fate, "whining with all the pathos of the sentimental lady's sonnet to the dying frog, in the hope of cheating unsuspecting people into prostituting their privileges."[125] They sapped other men's manhood and whiteness by enslaving them to their moral *diktats*. According to Thomas L. Clingman, the foes of slavery "intensely hate whatever is honorable and manly in the human character, and nothing would be more gratifying to them than to see the southern men and women whom they have so long vilified degraded to the level of the negroes."[126] All white men faced gender and racial debasement. A southern Democrat noted that nativism "tends to degrade the naturalized citizen." A northern Democrat detected a threat to both slaveholders and immigrants, with Republicans and Know-Nothings each "unit[ing] to place a class of persons in a condition of pupilage."[127]

By undercutting household mastery, fanatics targeted white men's autonomy at its source. Opponents infuriated by Vice President Dallas's tie-breaking vote for the Tariff of 1846 assaulted his manly form and physical home by "burning him in effigy, and insulting the ladies of his family by placards upon his door."[128] Democrats reserved questions such as temperance, religion, and slaveholding for heads of household. The Know-Nothing Party, however, "under pretext of sanctimonious purity invades the private domicil, the home that is every man's castle."[129] In Massachusetts, "the sanctity of the domestic hearth is violated" by the Know-Nothing legislature's infringements upon "freedom of conscience."[130] Penalties against Catholics, charged a Pennsylvania Democrat, would discourage men from marrying them, allowing Know-Nothings to "set themselves up to control the most sacred relation of society." Samuel Tilden warned that a proposed temperance law in New York "invades the rightful domain of the individual judgment and conscience, and takes a step backward toward that barbarian age when the wages of labor, the prices of commodities, a man's food and clothing, were dictated to him by a government calling itself paternal."[131] Democrats had no qualms with paternalism provided its objects were African Americans and women, not white men.

Democrats sought to cordon off their conception of the patriarchal household from "this meddling philanthropy."[132] They envisioned a hierarchical, organic family unit under the tutelage of a white head of household. Antebellum parties propounded competing domestic ideologies. The Democracy as a party did not ascribe to the ideology of separate spheres and privatization accompanying the Market Revolution. They anchored mastery in the pre-bourgeois corporate household of the free states and the plantation household of the slave states, whereby white men derived their public power from domestic patriarchy. Superintending inequality at home, patriarchs mingled in public as equals. "When we happen to meet in the common Territories, to make new homes and neighborhoods there," Henry Wise counseled, "all we have to do is to respect each other's equal right."[133]

Egalitarianism and liberal individualism conditioned white men's interactions in public, while conservative organicism shaped household relations, creating parallel regimes of rights. White men's rights were equal and natural. All other Americans' rights and duties were relative. Democrats would realize, however, that blending Enlightenment liberalism with conservative organicism was self-defeating. Critics cried that all rights, even those of African Americans, were absolute and natural or that all rights, even those of white men, were relational. Democrats refused to recognize white men as dependents, regardless of class or household status, as dependency was raced and gendered. This egalitarian patriarchy that Democrats seemingly harked back to was actually a modern—and unstable—innovation in that it aligned with the demands of *Herrenvolk* democracy and racial modernity.[134]

Fanaticism weakened this idealized patriarchal order. Virginia conservative Muscoe R. H. Garnett blamed an impersonal manufacturing economy and fanatical ideologies for domestic chaos in the free states. Fanaticism, Garnett found, "invades the interior of the family; it destroys the unity of married life" and "divide[s] the household into separate interests." A privatized, feminized sphere empowered women and impinged on men's household authority. Fanatics' "socialist philanthropy" abolished gender hierarchy in marriage as well as parental authority, with the state usurping the patriarch as caretaker of children.[135] Northern fanaticism could also infiltrate plantation households. Slaveholders subsumed enslaved laborers into their domestic ideal. Alabama senator Benjamin Fitzpatrick, for instance, wrote his absent wife that "the boys all send love to you" and "so do all the negroes." He grouped the "negro children" on his plantation near Wetumpka in his "family." Abolitionism, by attacking slavery, represented one more fanatical assault on patriarchal domesticity.[136]

The *isms* fomented household mutiny. Lewis Cass fretted over the "pseudo reformers [who] are entering our domestic circles, and striving to break up our family organizations."[137] In Portage County, Ohio, "eighteen thousand 'freeman' [*sic*] assembled to listen to the Champion of Negro Worshipers (S. P. Chase)." The meeting raised money to purchase fugitive slaves, "two young wenches that were about being returned to Slavery."[138] Even worse than encouraging runaways was antislavery fanaticism's logical terminus in violent insurrection. In the Virginia House of Delegates, a Democrat lambasted the "hireling emissaries" of fanaticism who were "circulating incendiary documents, breathing into the ear of the slave sentiments whose aim is insurrection, rapine, and murder."[139] Republicans, claimed Rufus W. Peckham, the patriarch of a Democratic family in Albany, New York, "would be delighted with a servile war in the South." At the start of the Civil War, one member of the Peckham clan tried to dissuade another from joining the military, protesting that he was "not for warring against women & children nor against institutions that are guaranteed by the constitution of my country."[140] Democrats told all white men, whether southern or northern, that they had an interest in preserving each other's household hierarchies.

Democrats accordingly vowed to protect white men nationwide as masters of their small worlds. The son of Virginia Democrat John Y. Mason resolved to leave his patronage position after the 1849 accession of a Whig presidential administration. He told his father, "I will resign this slave's position, & settle at days-neck on a portion of your farm say 50 or 100 acres, with one or two good negroes." Rather than submit to the degradation of being Whigs' patronage slave, he would ennoble himself into a master of chattel slaves. Slaveholding was not the only demonstration of mastery, even if it was the most elegant. A Virginian in Missouri reflected on the state's population of "German Emigrants." Germans in Missouri "do very well until they get too *fat, saucy & 40 acres of land*, then they become 'Lords of creation,' [and] whip their *wives*." "If not kind husbands," at least "they always vote the right way." The Pennsylvania political operative John W. Forney explained that immigrants merely wanted to escape "persecution" and "worship God as did our fathers of old, in their hour of travail, 'under their own vine and fig-tree, with none to molest or make them afraid.'" Germans in Missouri and all foreign-born white men, Democrats boasted, "vote[d] the right way" by supporting the party that gave them license to be "Lords of creation."[141]

Complete mastery entailed control over thought, conscience, and morality in addition to household dependents. Fanaticism, however, manacled white men's moral and mental faculties. Withholding territorial popular sovereignty meant not only "that their hands shall be tied up," but that "their minds shall be enslaved."¹⁴² "Confidence in mans capacity for self government will be shaken," conjectured a Democrat in Autaugaville, Alabama, if Know-Nothings "humbugged" the "unsuspecting" into becoming "fit subjects for the superstitions of Mahomet or Jos[eph] Smith." Know-Nothings' ritualistic oaths dulled independent thought, prompting a Connecticut Democrat to wonder, "Is that obligation a proper one for a freeman to take?"¹⁴³ "Let it be your stern resolution through life to 'Know Nothing,'" converts to the order were allegedly admonished. Stephen Douglas mocked this willful ignorance: "*They did not know* that the obligations and principles of their society were at war with the genius of our whole republican system."¹⁴⁴

Judge A. A. Coleman of Alabama effused instead over a "mind habituated to patient and correct thinking—developing thereby its nerve and muscle grappling the realities of life in its given orbit, and gaining the mastery." He continued: "The ardent restless spirit of our people has but little communion with the abject prostration of intellect which makes men crouch before his fellow submitting his reason and conscience to the *will* of another." "The separation, absolute and complete, of Church and State" was likewise emancipatory, declared an Arkansas Democrat, as it "has done much to unfetter the conscience by removing an odious code of restrictions upon its exercise." A man with a mind of "mastery" and an unrestricted conscience did not submit to another's moral code but avowed his manhood by instilling his own morality at home.¹⁴⁵

The mentally and politically autonomous white man exerted a conservative influence in American democracy. Former New York governor Horatio Seymour explained how democratic agency at the local level honed individual mastery: "He learns that the performance of his duty as a citizen is the best corrective for the evils of society, and is not led to place a vague, unfounded dependence upon legislative wisdom or inspirations." Assertive individualism made self-governing white men the antidote to fanatical statism. Another Democratic governor challenged his state's legislators to rely on "individual enterprise," not the state, for internal improvements: "Let us, as individuals, arouse our slumbering energies, gird on our manhood and strength, and by individual labor and individual contribution, link together the different sections of our State."¹⁴⁶

Democrats ensured local democracy would be a conservative force by making it an affirmation of equal white manhood. The devolution of political power, Horatio Seymour explained, "not only secures good government for each locality, but it also brings home to each individual a sense of his rights and responsibilities; it elevates his character as a man." "The principle of local and distributed jurisdiction," he exulted, "not only makes good government, but it also makes good manhood." Individuals enacted whiteness and manhood when democratically deciding the fate of other Americans. The democratic process translated their mastery at home into ostensibly equal political power over women and Americans of color throughout the republic. As Andrew Jackson had rationalized his faith in the people, "If they have no higher or better motives to govern them, they will at least perceive that their own interest requires them to be just to others, as they hope to receive justice at their hands."[147] White men would be just to one another by acknowledging each other's equal mastery. They could also be trusted to preserve, not subvert, the unjust racial and gender order that underwrote this equality. Thus was egalitarian democracy made conservative in the white man's republic.

Democrats both chuckled in condescension and recoiled with horror when anyone other than white men engaged in politics. Alabama Democrat Matthew Powers Blue learned of such an occurrence in New York City from his brother Albert, who recounted that "Miss Lucy Stone, Miss Antoinette Brown, Mrs. Bloomer and all the other notorious Infidels, Abolishonists and Bloomers, held a sort of preparatory meeting at Our Establishment last night, to the 'Grand Woman's Rights convention.'" None other than "Wm Lloyd Garrison (the old slick headed thief) presided over the meeting." The women's transgression of gender roles troubled Albert. "The husbands of a good many of them sat in the 'back-ground' and sanctioned everything that was done and said," while he "thought that those who had children had better be at home attending to them." The politicized Lucy Stone was "very little above a common strumpet." "To me it was a very disgusting sight," he concluded, as "they looked like so many fools sitting around the table voting." Such occurrences signaled that white men had surrendered their mastery. As Blue noted, women in politics shunted their husbands into the background or even burdened them with domestic chores.[148] The Jacksonian republic rested on an uncompromising correlation whereby white male mastery and political legitimacy stemmed from others' marginalization. Enmeshing women and African Americans in household hierarchies was the precondition of white men's political power.

Politics was necessarily a male preserve for Democrats. Speaking at a women's academy jubilee, Daniel Dickinson bemoaned those "ambitious and clamorous few" who were "preparing their minds and adjusting their costume for making more hasty and enlarged strides in pursuit of their *lost rights*." Caleb Cushing interrupted his remarks in Newburyport, Massachusetts, to observe that "some ladies have honored me with their presence here to-night." He returned the compliment by informing them that "good taste forbids me to address them specially" and marveling that "dry" legal topics interested them.[149] Democrats rhetorically forced women out of the political sphere, and they could do so with derision. A congressional veteran offered advice to a new senator in 1848—he should not be disappointed if "the lobbies may not be crowd[ed] with ladies" when he spoke. Women attended Congress as a social outing only when the heavyweights Webster and Calhoun performed. Some women agreed that their gender precluded politics. Indianan Charlotte Nantz confided to Congressman William H. English that "I am happy that the heavy responsibility of legislation rests not on shoulders so weak as womans."[150]

Fanatics, meanwhile, seemed to encourage women in politics. "What tender women!" exclaimed a Democratic newspaper, after reporting that "women were present and took part" at an "abolition, anti-Nebraska meeting at Boston."[151] Although cultural conventions limited women's formal political agency across the partisan spectrum, the Democratic Party was most opposed to their participation. For Democrats, politically involved women could only be fanatics beyond the pale of political legitimacy. The daughter of abolitionist Gerrit Smith, for instance, shared her father's radicalism, as evidenced by her "full Bloomer costume." The Whig and Republican Parties were more receptive to female participation, and evangelical and antislavery reformism depended upon women's mobilization. Democrats were reacting to changed circumstances—the gradual acceptance of women's political agency by the fanatical opposition.[152]

Antislavery petitions, by fusing female political agency and abolitionism, particularly perturbed Democrats. Alabama's William Lowndes Yancey seethed that "our representatives were daily and constantly insulted by the most insulting petitions from women, and children, and preachers and men, to take from us our clearly defined constitutional rights." Disfranchised Americans practiced politics through petitions, and southerners expected northern Democrats to resist antislavery appeals "from men, women and children, [which] poured into Congress, session after session."[153] An Indianan writing to Congressman John Givan Davis wanted to avoid association with such radicals, apologizing, "I do not wish you to think me a womans rights woman."

A Virginian submitting a petition on behalf of a widow who lost her husband in John Brown's raid also distanced herself from fanatical women. She reassured Governor Wise that she did "not covet the reputation of the *strong minded* women of the North." Wise did not answer and passed the plea off to his wife.[154]

Democrats also barred African Americans from political spaces. James Buchanan, serving as minister to the Court of St. James's, recounted the opening of Parliament to his niece: "What struck me most forcibly was the appearance in the Diplomatic Box of a full blooded black negro as the Representative of his Imperial Majesty of Hayti." A correspondent of Stephen Douglas, after visiting Brazil, commented in 1848 on the novelty of there being "no distinction, political nor social, between the black and the white."[155] Fanatics received blame for similar transgressions in the United States. An Illinois Democrat complained about the "rank abolitionist" who ran the local post office—the man "called an indignation meeting in November last because I would not let a negro have the use of the school house to give a lecture against the motives of the democratic party and abuse its *leading men*."[156]

By conflating African Americans' entrance into the body politic with sexual violation of white bodies, Democrats conveyed the stakes of black political agency. Douglas's correspondent who had been to Brazil related, "I have seen in the Imperial Senate [illegible] woolly headed Senator, and a fair Portuguese maiden," implying both debased politics and illicit sexuality. He predicted that the country would become "the abode of a mongrel race."[157] Frederick Douglass regularly served as Democrats' personification of political and sexual amalgamation. Debating Abraham Lincoln in 1858, Stephen Douglas claimed that at a political gathering he had glimpsed a carriage driven by a white man, with Frederick Douglass sitting inside with the man's wife. Douglas chastised "Black Republicans" for believing "that the negro ought to be on a social equality with your wives and daughters, and ride in a carriage with your wife, whilst you drive the team." The white fanatic who had invited Douglass into the political sphere welcomed his own degradation, his household mastery usurped by a black man now sexually proximal to his wife. Stephen placed Frederick's carriage "on the outside of the crowd," consigning him to political liminality.[158] Degraded fanatics, however, would encourage Douglass and other African Americans to move from the margins into politics proper.

Frederick Douglass's sexualized political incursion exemplified the adulteration of the republic that would ensue with the political mixing of female and

Figure 1. "The Great Republican Reform Party, Calling on Their Candidate," 1856. Fanatics make demands of a compliant John C. Frémont, the 1856 Republican presidential candidate. (Library of Congress, Prints and Photographs Division, LC-DIG-pga-04866)

male, black and white. Democrats bawled about "wanton orgies of fanaticism" and intimated sexual impropriety when they fussed over the composition of fanatical meetings, which made no "distinction of sex, color, sect, or party."[159] Horace Greeley was charged with having "assisted at public meetings of blacks and whites in the city of New York, where both God and the Constitution have been reviled" and with supporting "woman's rights" and "free love."[160] A cartoon portrayed the 1856 Republican presidential candidate pandering to his diverse fanatical constituencies (fig. 1). Along with fanatics crying for "an equal division of Property" and vegetarianism, a white woman (who looks suspiciously like William Lloyd Garrison in women's clothes) invites John C. Frémont to "our Free Love association, where the shackles of marriage are not tolerated & perfect freedom exist in love matters." Playing on the candidate's name, she promises, "You will, be sure to Enjoy yourself, for we are all Freemounters." This scandalous woman is standing near a black man, a fellow fanatic, who is demanding black racial supremacy. Placing black and white political actors together led to political—and sexual—amalgamation, an erosion of the strict equivalency of whiteness and mastery in the white man's republic.

Black political actors disconcerted Democrats, who configured mastery and degradation in zero-sum terms. Echoing sentiments that earlier inspired Indian removal, an Arkansas Democrat in 1855 wondered, "What millions of civilized people will it require to fill the void which their extermination must make," referring to what he assumed to be the inevitable disappearance of western Indians. His solution was for European immigrants to settle the West, thereby giving the foreign-born a stake in *Herrenvolk* democracy.[161] The trade-off between the rights of Native Americans and of naturalized Americans was absolute. Any challenge to white supremacy and slavery marked one as a fanatical proponent of racial equality, of "negro-fanaticism," "Niggerism," *"woollyism,"* "negrophilism," and, correspondingly, of white enslavement.[162] The "Black Republican party" bore a fitting name, "because, while it is devoted to the elevation of the negroes, it ignores, disregards, and contemns the rights of white men."[163] According to a Catholic immigrant in the Democratic Party, the "Abolition Know-nothing party" favored "enslaving and disfranchising the *Irishman*, the *Dutchman*, and all persons born in foreign countries, and freeing the *negro* and enfranchising him." Democrats told Americans they had to choose either black slavery or *"white slavery"*—there was no middle ground.[164]

Virginia conservative Robert Mercer Taliaferro Hunter laughed that Federalists had once believed that Jeffersonian individualism would usher in "the destruction of the necessary establishments of the Government, an era of radicalism, a sort of wild, Democratic saturnalia." The republic had not descended to this nadir under Jefferson or Jackson. Nor would it under Pierce and Buchanan, because the 1850s Democracy leavened its progressivism with conservatism. A Tennessean designated the Democracy "the party of conservatism," praising it for "advocating a wise progress in the science of free government" and for "conserving the great principles which lie at the foundation of our system."[165] Democrats in the 1850s simply perpetuated their ancient faith. "Democracy is based upon eternal principles," rhapsodized a campaign pamphlet, continuing, "it is the conservator of humanity, in its progressive steps."[166] The party was simultaneously progressive and conservative, because the individual at the heart of Democratic ideology was the agent of both liberty and order. Democrats diverged with traditional European and American conservatives who distrusted individualism and democracy. They instead argued that white men policing racial and gender borders at home and through the democratic process provided a stable foundation for their republic's steady advancement.

It required only a change of emphasis to bend seemingly progressive ideas toward conservative ends. Democrats took the abstract individual of liberal social contract theory, at times a revolutionary force in the modern era, and made him a tangible, raced and gendered entity. Yet the liberal individual had never been neutral; he had always been a historically contingent being, a fact compromising equality in polities based on consent theory and legal systems premised on contract and individual rights.[167] The social contract allowed political man to emerge out of the state of nature and inaugurate a regime of rights under a minimalist state, a liberating notion for some in the seventeenth century. Yet for all its radical possibilities, it was still a means for achieving social stability. Theorists such as Hobbes and Locke resorted to contract not to atomize society through individual license but to create a consensual regime that stanched religious fanaticism and social unrest. Democrats in the 1850s feared that fanaticism would make life "solitary, poor, nasty, brutish, and short" in their republic.[168] They intensified their commitment to majoritarian democracy, racial absolutism, the limited state, and liberal individualism—an otherwise modern cocktail of potentially subversive doctrines—in order to solidify a social order in which political legitimacy rested solely with white men. The result was an enduring American synthesis as Democrats affirmed the conservatism of liberalism.

THREE

Resisting Realignment

DEMOCRATS RESPOND TO PARTISAN
AND RACIAL DISORDER, 1854–1855

> We have fallen upon times that try men's common sense, if not their souls.
> Old parties have been breaking up, new parties are being formed.
> —Democracy of Boston and Suffolk, Massachusetts, 1855

THE PARTISAN realignment took a toll on Democratic unity in the mid-1850s. The party struggled to splint itself together after the 1848 presidential election and the debates over the Compromise of 1850. After inheriting the Democracy in its "disorganized state" upon his 1852 election, President Franklin Pierce succeeded in uniting Democrats only in shared anger by doling out patronage to both rebellious Free Soil Democrats and southern-rights Democrats who had opposed the compromise.[1] "The disorganization of both parties here is complete," one senator fumed, and "the administration is divided & held in general contempt."[2] The Kansas-Nebraska Act, introduced in January and passed in May 1854, compounded the discord. Democratic "Hards," who had opposed Free Soil and favored the compromise, demanded that Free Soilers and the party's "Softs," party regulars more forgiving of antislavery defectors, support the legislation as a "test."[3] William L. Marcy, Pierce's secretary of state and a leader of the New York Softshells, received panicked queries over "what this Nebraska business means" from back home, where Daniel Dickinson's Hardshells were using the legislation to purge the party.[4] Attorney General Caleb Cushing, meanwhile, monitored Democratic disaffection throughout the nation, especially in Missouri, where the old Jacksonian Thomas Hart Benton opposed Kansas-Nebraska in his anti–Slave Power insurgency. "Bentonism" joined the already formidable inventory of *isms*.[5]

Many Democrats failed the test and bolted to the anti-Nebraska coalitions that congealed into the antislavery Republican Party. Complicating matters, a Michigander reported that "a new party, the Know Nothings, has sprung into existence and appears to carry every thing before it." The addition of nativism and anti-Catholicism to the political upheaval over slavery "produces a queer state of things."[6] Temperance campaigns also intensified throughout the free states. Southerners looked askance at the North's burgeoning fanaticism. A Georgian predicted that the "Whigs, Anti Nebraska Democrats, Free Soilers & Abolitionists, will unite, and endeavour to crush out what remains of democracy in the Free States." It was not long, however, before the realignment spread south. A Missourian ascertained that "the new element introduced into our politics, the 'Know Nothings,' disturbs all calculations."[7]

Although their opposition varied by locale, Democrats formulated a consistent ideological response by targeting fanaticism, the common denominator of antislavery, temperance, and nativism. Democrats proved that they remained a national party by deploying similar rhetoric throughout the country. The realignment's causes and the inevitability of its outcome—a new two-party system arraying Democrats against Republicans—continue to provoke debate. Historians who emphasize ideological contestation over slavery argue for the ease of the Republican ascendancy over the Know-Nothings.[8] Those who examine ethnic and religious determinants of partisanship instead conclude that nativism and temperance were a viable basis for opposition to the Democracy.[9] Most Democrats in the 1850s did regard antislavery as ringleader of the *isms*, agreeing with Virginian R. M. T. Hunter that slavery was the "question which more than any other disturbs the harmony of the Union."[10] Nonetheless, Democrats could not anticipate the realignment's outcome and took both antislavery and nativism seriously. They did so by blending them into a single fanatical philosophy against which they counterpoised their conservatism.

In 1855 a political veteran harrumphed that, back in his day, there were "none of your hard-shells soft shells, Old Hunkers & Barn burners."[11] Meeting the fanatical menace demanded party unity. Attorney General Cushing, speaking for the Pierce administration, forbade fusion between "democrats and freesoilers" back home in Massachusetts. "Backslidings" and "defections," Cushing warned, "may prejudice or embarrass the onward progress of the republic."[12] The fruits of "fusion"[13] flummoxed Democrats. Political taxonomists catalogued an evolving menagerie of partisan hybrids, including "States Rights Nebraska Whig[s]," "Free Soil*ish* Whigs,"[14] "Democratic

Know Nothing[s]," "union Democrat[s]," "Temperance Democrats,"[15] "regular Abolition Whig[s]," *"abolition know-nothings,"* and "whig quasi abolitionism."[16] The relentless realignment spawned these mutations. The blurring of party lines through defection and fusion disconcerted those Americans who took comfort in strict delineations not only between parties but between races. Partisan cross-pollination evoked more taboo mixtures.

Democrats compared partisan irregularity to racial amalgamation, with the buckling of parties prefacing the breaching of racial and gender barriers. Partisan boundaries *were* racial boundaries for Democrats. Observing the first phase of the realignment in 1848, a Virginian proudly concluded that it was Whigs, not Democrats, who were likely to join the "Amalgamation Abolitionists."[17] Democrats cringed when wobbly partisans fused with fanatics, as when one renegade "threw himself into the arms of Black Republicanism"[18] or when they consorted with a "secret conclave" of Know-Nothings, "with its heterogeneous materials."[19] Joining a "Hivmaphrodite party" such as the Know-Nothings was "an act of prostitution and treason."[20] Abandoning the party of white male supremacy was to endorse fanatical racial doctrines, interracial politics, and racial mixing more broadly. Democrats used the sexualized rhetoric of racial amalgamation to shore up party loyalty because they worried that the realignment's "strange amalgamation & general confusion"[21] would not confine itself to parties but would spread to the republic's racial and gender hierarchies.

In the free states and in the slave states, Democrats turned to the politics of slavery, race, and sexuality in the realignment elections of 1854 and 1855 to argue that only their party would preserve the purity of the white man's republic. In Indiana's state election in 1854, Democrats faced an anti-Nebraska movement, Know-Nothings, a temperance effort, and a politically assertive clergy. Virginia Democrats faced the Know-Nothings in their 1855 gubernatorial canvass. In both elections, Democrats relied on analogous arguments because they were defending the rights of all white men from the same fanatical conspiracy. Reacting to unique partisan alignments in each state, Indiana and Virginia Democrats constructed a nationally shared conservative and white supremacist ideology.

"A Conglomeration of Antagonisms" in Indiana

The Democracy dominated Indiana politics under the second party system. Initially willing to ban territorial slavery after the Mexican War, the party terminated its Free Soil flirtation after ratifying the Compromise of 1850. In 1854, moreover, it embraced Kansas-Nebraska and popular sovereignty. The resilient Indiana Democracy typifies free-state Democrats' conservative trajectory in response to antislavery "agitation." Multiple fanatical impulses vied to poach Indiana Democrats from their party in the 1854 realignment election. Kansas-Nebraska emboldened antislavery Indianans, while temperance and nativism coursed through the electorate. What the state's leading Democratic newspaper observed of temperance was also true of antislavery and nativism—it did "not accommodate itself to existing party organizations." A Democrat in Indianapolis expected the opposition to wage a "guerialla fight—adapting their issues to the particular locality—and its whims and isms."[22] Like other northern Democrats, Hoosiers tapped into inherited beliefs to address disparate foes and preserve party identity. They envisioned the election as one more Jacksonian showdown between the people and undemocratic power, an ideological confrontation between the conservative guarantors of self-government and the fanatics who would disempower white men, empower the state, and invite African Americans into politics.

In late 1853 temperance became the first *ism* to declare itself. "The issue next election," one Democrat pronounced, "will be the Maine Law."[23] A state convention in Indianapolis in January 1854 called for legislation, resembling Maine's 1851 statute, "prohibiting the manufacture and sale, as a beverage, of intoxicating drinks."[24] Although Democrats expected "some confusion in our Party in consequence of the agitation of the temperance question,"[25] its impact was unclear. Temperance was variously deemed the campaign's defining issue, a purely local affair, or a disingenuous "whig trap to catch Democrats" and "resucitate the almost expiring Whig party."[26] Temperance donned more sinister vestments when the state's Methodist clergy rallied behind it. "The Methodist church . . . especially the clergy have embarked," announced one Democrat. The quarrel over legislated temperance became part of Democrats' timeless "struggle for the people against the encroachments of the clergy on their rights."[27] The issue activated the instinctive revulsion felt when a cleric "enters into political contests" and "wield[s] his Maker's name for his own purposes and designs."[28] Indiana Democrats praised Stephen Douglas's pamphlet chastising clerics opposed to Kansas-Nebraska, and one suggested circulating "a few *Bushels* of those to great advantage" throughout the state.[29]

Although anxious of reprisal, a shadowy informant provided Congressman John G. Davis with inside knowledge of the "*mysterious under current*, that is said to have dispersed itself throughout this state." "It is found in every *township* in this congressional district," and, he confided, "if you *knew* its strenght it would *astonish* you, & if you knew the number of *Democrats* connected with it, it would *startle* you." Davis ought to "beware of invoking to your aid *Irish votes*." The Know-Nothings had made their melodramatic appearance in Indiana. Their native-born and Protestant chauvinism prompted many Democrats to associate them with temperance and the politicized clergy. These polarizing moral and cultural forces attained newfound salience during the realignment. During the second party system, ethnocultural issues had been subordinate to positions on political economy as indicators of party identity. Democrats now feared that nativism and temperance would divide their party, as these topics no longer respected party lines.[30]

To this "conglomeration of antagonisms,"[31] Stephen Douglas added a combustible federal question. Many Indiana Democrats were leery of Kansas-Nebraska. Indianans generally favored a homestead bill to spur westward expansion, and Hoosier Democrats did not welcome a measure that would pit white settlers against slavery. Democratic congressmen John G. Davis and William H. English, running for reelection, received conflicting assessments of the bill's popularity back home. In Davis's congressional district, Absalom Sappenfield confirmed that "Democrats in his neighborhood are for the bill," while Peter Swain "says he is opposed to the bill and all his neighbours."[32] One supporter cautioned English against voting for the bill, as midwesterners would not tolerate an "additional foot of Slave Territory to come into the Union." Davis, on the other hand, learned that the bill enjoyed enough popularity to "make it, in a short time, a party test."[33]

Democrats also had to consider Kansas-Nebraska's implications for party factionalism. National divisions spilled into the state, with Governor Joseph A. Wright aligned with the president and Senator Jesse D. Bright, disgruntled over Pierce's patronage disbursement, leading the state's Hards. Congressman Davis worked closely with Wright, while Congressman English was Bright's confidant. Both factions eventually converged on the issue, as did most of the state's Democratic congressmen, including Davis and English.[34] Disgruntled Democrats could, nonetheless, use the measure to challenge rivals. Dr. William R. Nofsinger was rumored to oppose Kansas-Nebraska in order to unseat Davis. Such men, critics claimed, would take any position for the sake of ambition: "If he can get a party strong enough will make no difference what you call it, anti Nebraska anti Liquor Whig abolition or prohibition he would take the track."[35]

Some wondered if Governor Wright, sympathetic to temperance and the Methodist Church, and with his power based in the more antislavery northern part of the state, would become a rallying point for insurgents. Wright agreed with Davis that, as a political measure, Kansas-Nebraska was "ill advised." But he also conceded that the underlying "principle is right."[36] The previous year, Wright had delivered a disquisition on political economy to an agricultural society in Livonia. In a paean to localism, he praised "the great truth that, under our government, man, *in his individual capacity*, is entrusted with rights and privileges which, when properly used, enable him to aid in advancing the welfare of the community in which he lives." Wright found in the Kansas-Nebraska Act a similar "great principle, and this is the right of the people, every where, North & South, to make their own form & structure of government." He approved the legislation despite the political risk, because it complemented his Democracy. Still, attuned to the political climate, he advised Davis to "make no speech on the Nebraska Bill."[37]

Wright's endorsement stemmed from his "westernism." Situated in a region that softened sectional distinctions, midwestern Democrats believed they possessed a special appreciation for the Union. White upland southerners, whose folkways and political culture oriented them toward southern society, settled much of the lower Old Northwest. Early in 1854 Wright paid an official visit to Governor Lazarus Powell of Kentucky. Later in the year, he once again crossed the Ohio River, this time to marry a Kentuckian.[38] Midwesterners boasted of their cultural and economic ties to the slave states. They ritualistically enacted this fraternity when they campaigned with southerners. Prominent Mississippi valley Democrats, including Governor Powell and John C. Breckinridge of Kentucky, Stephen Douglas, and Ohio's George E. Pugh, for example, were the advertised guests at a "Grand Rally" in Indianapolis.[39]

The doctrine of popular sovereignty intersected with Wright's midwestern brand of Unionism. "Indiana, as a central State, has always maintained a high conservative position" on slavery, he reflected.[40] When visiting Kentucky, he extolled "the great center and heart of this nation," which already "theoretically and practically carry out the doctrine of non-intervention, each State attending to its own municipal affairs."[41] Kansas-Nebraska was the means by which the entire country could adopt western values through refusing to pass judgment on slavery, replicating on a national scale the Midwest's harmonizing of North and South. In 1856, when Bleeding Kansas made intersectional amiability difficult, Wright publicly refused to intercede on behalf of antislavery settlers: "Indiana, as a state, has wisely selected her own domestic policy. She is willing to give her neighbor the same right, and to suppose them capable of choosing and deciding for themselves."[42]

"Some tenderfooted democrats,"[43] like those who encouraged Wright to support temperance and oppose Kanas-Nebraska, recommended co-opting the new issues. Alarmed over how many Democrats were "diseased with reference to a new secret association," one partisan pleaded, "The safe course for all Democrats everry where is to go into this no nothing association."[44] Another wanted to "engraft the Temperance platform, with the glorious principles of Democracy," while many worried that demanding adherence to Kansas-Nebraska would drive Democrats out of the party.[45] An attack on Methodists troubled a Democrat in Jeffersonville. He urged English to *"take occasion to repudiate the sentiments avowed by Robinson in regard to the Methodist Clergy"* in order to placate Democrats of that confession. Taking a definitive stand on any of these questions would only alienate. As one Democrat elegantly summarized, "Politicks here are in a Snarl."[46]

The Party of "Slavery Drunkenness, & Infidelity"

One of Democracy's foes imposed order on Indiana's political snarl by dividing the state into two coalitions. "The friends of the Nebraska bill go for the Extension of Slavery—against religion & Temperance," he explained, while "the Anti Nebraska Party, go, against Slavery . . . , against Drunkenness, & for the Protection of Religion." The Democracy was the party of *"Slavery Drunkenness, & Infidelity."*[47] This description may have possessed literal truth—the opposition charged that one of the Democracy's "Nebraska & Anti Maine Law" legislative candidates had been "drunk in Indianapolis the greater part of the Session of 52 & 3, lying on benches on the public streets so stupid that he was not capable of attending any of his Legislative duties." But this demarcation was also ideological.[48] Democrats likewise detected two ideological camps in Indiana—conservatism and fanaticism. They positively framed their approval of popular sovereignty, imbibers' prerogative, and religious freedom—*"Slavery Drunkenness, & Infidelity"*—as a defense of self-government and white male mastery.

Democrats ideologically merged their enemies, but sometimes the fanatics did the work themselves. Bemused Democrats watched the *isms* parasitize each other. "The opponents of the Nebraska bill are busy secretly and stealthily circulating petitions," discovered one Democrat. The petitions were "found either in the hands of open abolitionists or rampant Whigs." The venue for circulating these petitions, moreover, was "the county 'Temperance Convention.'"[49] One of Davis's correspondents verified that an individual deserved to be stripped of patronage for being an *"abolitionist, Anti Nebraska, Now Knuthing* School Teacher."[50] Some fanatics were even more ecumenical. One editor was "a violent opponent of President Pierce, and the administration[,] a strong advocate for the repeal of the Nebraska bill, A main [sic] Law advocate, a strong abolitionist," and, for good measure, was "also Native American[,] a violent opponent to Catholicism."[51]

The opposition unified themselves when they convened in Indianapolis in July to form the "People's Party." Similar movements occurred across the free states as critics of Kansas-Nebraska allied with other elements. These coalitions were the genesis of the Republican Party.[52] Indiana Democrats denounced "the specious humbug of a 'People's Convention'"[53] because "the people were not there."[54] In attendance at "the Ism Convention" were "disaffected Democrats, Freesoil Whigs, Maine Law men, Know Nothings, Freesoilers and Bible Burning Garri[sonian]-Abolitionists,"[55] sanctified by "clergymen who were on the stand, sitting in the prominent places."[56] Democrats theorized as to what fueled this "Medley Convention."[57] For some, the answer was simple: hatred of Democracy. One delegate "admitted that the Convention *was* an Abolition Convention." "They had come up here," he quipped, "to abolish the Democratic platform and all who stood upon it."[58]

While Democrats agreed that cynical opposition to their party melded the groups, many isolated opposition to slavery and Kansas-Nebraska as the impetus of the People's Party. By the summer, with the state Democratic Party committed to the bill, Democrats began to trumpet its animating principle—popular sovereignty—thereby redefining the election as one between the champions and denigrators of self-government. The party's state organ at first tepidly defended the legislation by rebutting arguments that it abrogated the Missouri Compromise. Yet the *Indiana Daily State Sentinel* eventually turned to the ideological offensive to uphold "the right of the people of the States to govern themselves."[59] Average Democrats contributed to the construction of this ideology when, along with Governor Wright, they evaluated Kansas-Nebraska alongside their cherished assumptions. The old Jacksonian Jeptha Garrigus affirmed that "it certainly will be right to let the people deside wheathan tgay will have slaves or not." One Democrat recounted to Davis that he fought back against the "Abolitionist[s] [who] are raving about the Nebraska question" by "tak[ing] the ground to leave it to the Citizens of the Terrytory to decide." "They call the Bill a democratic measure," he concluded, which it was, owing to its appropriation by such grassroots Democrats.[60]

With the dispute over Kansas-Nebraska ennobled into a contest over self-rule, Democrats viewed the measure's opponents as united with the other *isms* in disdain for the sovereign people. For a party pledged "to resist all aggressions upon the doctrine of self government," this rivalry was not new—fanaticism was naught but the primordial nemesis Federalism. "Aristocracy is the innate and inexorable enemy and active antagonist of republicanism," according to the state Democratic convention, "and has . . . always attempted and been willing to coalesce with any faction, to wed with any popular heresy, and to court any *ism* or vagrant party organization."[61] The irascible Garrigus vowed "to assist in giving to Tories one more defeat" in 1854. He assured Davis that "if I am abel I am bound to take the stump this summer," because "whilst I live I am bound to fite whiggery let it come In what shape it will."[62] The names of their opponents had changed, but Indiana Democrats were still vindicating Jefferson's and Jackson's faith in the self-governing masses.

Democrats accordingly presented their opposition to temperance as a defense of popular democracy and individual autonomy. Because many Indiana Democrats supported temperance and even governmental regulation, the party could not risk estranging its own abstainers. Democrats tried to remain noncommittal by proposing a separate referendum on the issue. A nonbinding referendum would allow protemperance Democrats to register their preference and still vote for the party's nominees. When the state temperance convention instead called on Indianans to vote for candidates who expressly backed prohibition, the Democracy postured as the only party that trusted the people. Democrats chided, "We were not aware that the people are so utterly dependent—that they cannot vote upon a simple question of this sort." "We have a better opinion of the people generally," they grandstanded.[63] Prohibitory legislation also undercut individual autonomy. Temperance could be laudable, but its legislative imposition coerced individual morality. "While we are in favor of the cause of Temperance as a great moral question," the Jennings County convention clarified, "we deprecate the course pursued by some to make this great moral a political one."[64] In a typical conservative critique of one-idea fanaticism, Democrats believed that legislation against an acknowledged "moral and social evil" would "result in the infliction of greater ones."⁶⁵ Even teetotaling Democrats blanched at the governmental despotism promised by a "law which will sanction the entry of private residences of our citizens, and invade the sacred precincts of home life."⁶⁶

Know-Nothings and the clergy came in for comparable indictments of undemocratic tendencies. Know-Nothings were "illiberal" and "anti-republican and Anti-American."⁶⁷ Their intended proscription of immigrants would create unequal classes, while their dictation as to who was suitable for office based on religion was "preventive of a free and true expression of the voice of the people at the ballot-box."⁶⁸ The clergy also insulted democracy, because "no minister has a right to dictate to the members of his church how they shall vote."⁶⁹ A correspondent told English that "the principle of non-intervention on the subject of Slavery, embraced in the Nebraska bill is decidedly popular with us at present." He wondered, however, "how long it may continue so, should the Methodist ministry, in their sovereign care for the welfare [of] mankind, think fit to make a crusade against it."⁷⁰ The clerics' "sovereign care" jarred with the sovereignty of the people.

The Northern Politics of Slavery and Race

Those individuals "benumbed and degraded by the unhallowed influence of superstitious priest craft"⁷¹ were self-governing neither as republicans nor as men. When individuals succumbed to fanaticism, they forfeited whiteness in addition to manhood, both prerequisites of political legitimacy in the white man's republic. White men's disempowerment redounded to the benefit of black political actors. Novel political movements, arising out of the confusion of the realignment, suggested to Democrats the racial mixture that would flourish as fanatics broke down partisan boundaries. Indiana Democrats deployed the sexualized politics of slavery and race to impugn fanatics as unsound on white supremacy and to keep their own membership in line. Political instinct in the slave states led partisans to regularly disparage one another as unreliable protectors of slavery, making the "politics of slavery" the default transcript of southern political culture. In an antebellum precursor to the twentieth-century southernization of American politics, northern Democrats practiced their own *northern* politics of slavery, skewering opponents as enemies of the South, antislavery extremists, and, most egregious, racial egalitarians and amalgamationists. Suspected antislavery proclivities could prove just as fatal in free-state politics.⁷²

Indiana Democrats dealt harshly with "deserters."[73] The Democracy of the sixth congressional district, for instance, excommunicated J. W. Peaslee, James Ritchey, Jacob P. Chapman, and Lucian Barbour for "political treasons" and "union with the enemies of the Democratic party."[74] The fourth congressional district passed over its usual nominee because he had "been for some time past tending towards his ancient and our present political enemies—especially the Abolitionists and Free Soilers."[75] Kansas-Nebraska and popular sovereignty, much as Stephen Douglas had intended nationally, became a party test in Indiana. One Hoosier Democrat predicted that Douglas's "wholesale denunciation of the opponents of this bill as 'abolitionists' and 'nigger' sympathizers will avail him but little," as "people are not to be frightened from their propriety by such epithets now-a-days."[76] Yet its ubiquity attested to the resonance of this line of attack. In the minds of Indiana Democrats, a slight distance separated a skeptic of their policies from a rabid abolitionist. Eschewing nuance, they described "anti-Nebraska meetings" as having "assumed, a deep abolition type."[77] Democrat Peter Swain, who claimed that his neighborhood opposed Kansas-Nebraska, "talks very much like an abolitionist." Another group of Democrats complained about "our Abolition P.M." and demanded the postmaster's removal "as soon as possible."[78]

The mutual recrimination of factional infighting could play out in the idiom of the politics of slavery. J. O. Jones, a Democrat who rejected Kansas-Nebraska, later testified that Congressman John G. Davis *"was at heart against the measure"* but had backed the bill to secure reelection. Jones took umbrage at Davis's "unblushing effrontery in denouncing as Abolitionists, Sectionalists, and Disunionists, all who now entertain the same opinions he formerly did."[79] Davis, however, had experienced firsthand the danger of leaving himself vulnerable to the politics of slavery. Dr. Nofsinger, who considered running against Davis as an opponent of Kansas-Nebraska, reminded the congressman that "a few years ago they denounced you as a free soiler, because you were opposed to some of the features of the fugitive slave law." Now, Nofsinger whined, the party was using the latest proslavery measure to "test each man's democracy." Davis had learned the necessity of avoiding antislavery stigma, so that he was safe in 1854 when his party was "denouncing every body as abolitionists" who did not support Kansas-Nebraska.[80]

The politics of slavery and race pervaded the culture of the entire free-state Democracy. An Illinois Democrat told Douglas to expect opposition to Kansas-Nebraska from "whigs and free soilers and some of the democrats." In assessing a potential congressional candidate, he worried that "the People have an impression that he is half an abolitionist" and that the man's "family are the rankest abolitionist[s] I know of." "One of his brothers," for example, was "smart in a negro speech."[81] Such misgivings weakened one's electoral prospects, leading Democrats to lob similar accusations even at intraparty rivals. Caleb Cushing, who refused to countenance fusion in Massachusetts, found himself charged with complicity in President Pierce's appointment of Free Soilers. A fellow Democrat branded this accomplished Doughface "an Abolition agitator."[82] It was not uncommon for even New England Democrats to have to prove their proslavery bona fides, as Edmund Burke in New Hampshire did when he vouched, "I have never been an abolitionist or Wilmot provisoist."[83]

Although their political culture primed them to appease the South, northern Democrats did not recognize theirs as a proslavery party. Rather, their course reflected their self-appointed role as intersectional mediators. Jeptha Garrigus appropriated the castigation "Doughface," exclaiming, "I am a northern man with southern Principels." "I do not believe the north have any right to meddle with the subject of Slavery," he sermonized, and "the South have just as much right to go north and steal horses, as the north have to go south and steal Negroes."[84] In an exchange between Congressmen Joshua R. Giddings and Samuel S. Cox, both from neighboring Ohio, the Republican presented Cox with a dilemma. He could either condone reopening the international slave trade, proving his was a "pro-slavery party," or he could demur, risking retribution from fellow Democrats. Cox skirted the snare by responding that his "party is neither a pro-slavery party nor an anti-slavery party." The Democracy, instead, "leaves that subject to the people to deal with as they may think proper." Democrats were, nevertheless, hardly neutral on white supremacy, and Cox concluded the debate by charging that Giddings favored "negro equality with the white man."[85]

Fanatics like Giddings would engender this equality because they did not respect white men's sole claim to self-governance. All varieties of fanaticism, not just the antislavery strain, degraded white manhood and equality. Indiana Democrats drew from *Herrenvolk* democracy to argue that *all* white men were equal, because *all* persons of color were inferior. Yet Know-Nothings "seem to take it for granted that an Irishman or a German is a new species of human creation in the United States."[86] Former congressman W. W. Wick reassured English that the preservation of white male mastery would resonate with German Americans. Antislavery Germans would cooperate with the Democracy, because, although "they abhor the Nebraska bill," they "still more abhor to have their whiskey and lager beer stopped."[87] Democrats solidified a bond among white men by offering them white racial privilege and self-determination, whether in regard to alcohol consumption or territorial slavery.

Once the popular sovereignty of white men was vitiated, it was a small step to the elevation of black political actors. An article reprinted in the *Indiana Daily State Sentinel* compared the fanatical denial of white men's ability to govern African Americans in the territories with Know-Nothings' efforts to "reduce to the condition of a degraded caste, hundreds and thousands of their white fellow citizens." The movements shared an impulse: "The two manias of the day are aiming to raise with one hand the negro, and with the other to strike down men of the same race as ourselves." Once the idea took hold that territorial settlers could not be trusted to govern African Americans and that immigrants could not govern themselves, then Americans would be ready to send Frederick Douglass to Congress.[88] This denouement made sense to Democrats, as an ironclad inverse relationship existed between white men's democratic equality and everyone else's subordination.

Fanatics upset this equilibrium, Democrats rationalized, because the aspersion of white men's aptitude for self-government led to the enfranchisement of African Americans. Democrats heard rumors of "Yankee tramping lecturers"[89] traversing Indiana at the behest of the opposition. These "emissaries from this land of Blue Laws, intolerance, and abolition fanaticism [who] are now perambulating"[90] the state presumed to instruct Indianans, as "they regard the people of Indiana as little children, incapable of making laws themselves."[91] Just as fanatics would deprive white men in Kansas of the right to set their own racial policies, condescending New England fanatics were dictating to white Indianans. Many of these political missionaries hailed from Connecticut, "one of the States which are held up to the people of Indiana as models." In that state, African Americans could vote, while illiterate white men were disfranchised.[92] The same would happen in Indiana if the People's Party won the election—Hoosiers would watch helplessly as "an honest white man whose education has been neglected must stand back whilst Cuffee walks up and casts his vote."[93]

It was not just fanatics' policies that degraded white men. For Democrats, the partisan realignment itself bespoke a breakdown of gender and racial order, one that fanatics hastened. Enticing members away from the Democracy, fanatics weakened the party of white supremacy. In consenting to fusion and fanatics' racial doctrines, white men violated racial boundaries and relinquished whiteness, becoming, in the eyes of Democrats, racially mixed or black men. The hapless William Nofsinger, who finally received the "nomination of the fusion convention," was dubbed "DR. NOFFSINGER, the *mongrel* candidate for Treasurer of State."[94] "The *white nigger* Hull," meanwhile, "addressed a large crowd at the Court House," where he attacked good Democrats such as W. W. Wick and the editors of the *Sentinel*.[95] When Congressman English ran for reelection in 1856, he charged that a Republican not only "talked flippantly about '*letting the Union slide*'" but also admitted that "he was not prepared to decide whether the negro or the white was the superior race; that whichever was the superior would, in time, absorb the other." This Republican "left the solution of the question to be determined by time—thus seeming to contemplate and approve the horrible doctrine of amalgamation."[96]

The trope of racial amalgamation conveyed Democrats' horror over deteriorating party loyalty—traitors to Democracy were traitors to white male supremacy. Fusion was a political transgression tantamount to the most taboo form of racial mixture—interracial sex. An Indianan lamented the "defection" of fellow Democrats who joined antislavery politicians; he designated the resulting "Fusion Ticket" the "mongrel Ticket."[97] Because fanatics enabled black political actors and were themselves men denuded of whiteness, "fusion" with them yielded the political equivalent of racially mixed offspring. The state People's Party convention was referred to as the "Speckled" or "spotted" convention,[98] while an "Abolition Mongrel Convention" met in the sixth congressional district.[99] The campaign wearied Senator Jesse Bright. He told his colleague Robert M. T. Hunter of Virginia that he would rather be attending to their joint land speculation than dealing with "the mongrel mixed up political Canvass going on here now." With their condemnations of racially intermingled politics and the political "amalgamation of all the odds and ends that hate Democracy,"[100] Democrats were forecasting actual racial amalgamation. In Indiana and the Midwest, the politics of slavery and race was about more than mollifying the South to preserve party and Union. It was about securing white supremacy at home.

Virginia and the South

An exultant supporter congratulated English on his reelection "in spite of disintegrated Whigery Know nothing ism Free Soil ism Main [*sic*] Liquor

Law ism and vilest Abolitionism." Most Indiana Democrats could not gloat, as the opposition swept Indiana and the free states in the fall of 1854. In a near electoral eclipse, the northern Democracy lost more than two-thirds of its House seats, including that of John G. Davis. Indiana congressman Thomas A. Hendricks, also turned out of office, consoled Davis: "Our defeat is so general and overwhelming that we have no cause for personal mortification."[101] Democrats turned to the slave states to blunt the fanaticism unloosed in the North. Lewis Cass surmised that the Democracy faced "a new element of difficulty" in "the strange party, which has swept the West, and I suspect is about to sweep the South." Still, Cass affirmed, "My faith in our old party principles is as strong as ever, and I am full of confidence, that the Democracy will again resume its ascendancy."[102]

National attention fixed on Virginia, where one observer agreed with Cass that "the Know Nothings I fear are to be troublesome."[103] Virginia's 1855 campaign began as the free states' 1854 fall elections ended. The gubernatorial race pitted Democrats against a vibrant Know-Nothing Party. The Old Dominion, home of Jefferson and Madison, occupied a venerable place in Democratic mythology. The coordination between Martin Van Buren's Albany Regency and Thomas F. Ritchie's Richmond Junto in the 1820s cemented a New York–Virginia backbone for the Jacksonian coalition that became the *National Democracy*. Van Buren had proposed a union of "the planters of the South and the plain Republicans of the North" to mitigate the centrifugal effects of slavery and sectionalism. Although byzantine factionalism desiccated the Empire State Democracy by the 1850s, Virginia remained steady. Under the second party system, Virginians had experienced decades of evenly matched partisan competition in a democratic political culture, even before their 1851 constitution formalized full democracy for white men. Given Virginia's preeminence within the Democracy and the Union, and the deference shown it as the arbiter of southern opinion, a Democrat contemplating the election could only gasp, "Think of the calamity of loosing the old dominion."[104]

While typically the majority party, the Virginia Democracy never enjoyed hegemony, even after Whiggery's collapse. Enduring opposition, including briefly the Know-Nothings, precluded complacency. Like Indianans in their realignment election, Virginia Democrats ideologically distinguished themselves from their new foe. Virginia's May election was the first in the slave states in 1855, making it a trial run for the rest of the South and for the 1856 presidential race. Virginians taught other Democrats, especially southerners, how to acclimate to the realignment by offering white men a binary choice, rooted in Jacksonian ideology, between white male autonomy and racial degradation. Before a national audience, moreover, Virginia Democrats appealed to white men in the slave states *and* in the free states. As the state's leading Democratic newspaper put it, "The Democratic party of the Union look to the Democracy of Virginia . . . to arrest the tide of fanaticism and corruption which threatens to overwhelm the country."[105]

Factionalism did afflict the Virginia Democracy, without crippling it. Southern-rights Democrats took their cues from Senator Robert Mercer Taliaferro Hunter, a protégé of Calhoun. Hunter's gadfly was Henry A. Wise, a maverick reformer who was the Democracy's gubernatorial candidate in 1855. Hunter dryly acknowledged to Wise that his "impulsive nature and the energy with which you pursue whatever you have in view" had the potential to spark animosity between them.[106] Wise's nomination, with the acquiescence of Hunter's clique, thereby signaled that, at least temporarily, Virginia Democrats had turned from states' rights, proslavery "particularism" toward a national orientation. A fellow southern-rights Democrat stressed to Hunter the necessity for action, for "if we . . . beat this movement in Virginia I feel that our institutions will be sound." More than slavery or control of the state party was at stake; so too was leadership of the slave states and of the National Democracy. This adviser stressed that "to get the South straight Know Nothingism must be overcome," counseling Hunter, "You had better take your part in this canvass, at least in a National point of view."[107] The election was not Virginians' alone.

Despite Hunter's exertions, and doubtless to his chagrin, Henry A. Wise embodied the campaign. He drew on his gubernatorial victory for the rest of the decade to cultivate a reputation as an intersectional harmonizer, often at the expense of states' rights and proslavery orthodoxy. Both leaders, in fact, while being routinely touted for the presidency themselves, were veteran seekers after that southern chimera—the "sound and reliable Northern or free State men" who would "keep down the slavery agitation." Hunter had entertained the possibility of running on a ticket with Stephen A. Douglas in 1852.[108] Wise, that same year, swung Virginia's delegation at the Baltimore convention behind his close friend James Buchanan. Three years later, as he followed the gubernatorial race from his diplomatic post in London, Buchanan related that he was "most anxious about the result of the Virginia election; and this both for the cause and the man who represents it."[109]

Contemporaries regarded the gubernatorial election as a turning point in southern—and national—politics, as it would decide whether Know-Nothingism could bloom outside of its northern hothouses or if it was an invasive species ill-suited to southern climes. If the party could take Virginia, it could spread southward and become the national successor to the Whigs. Virginia Democrats moved to prevent this by painting Know-Nothings as untrustworthy stewards of slavery, prompting several historians to conclude that the politics of slavery shaped the campaign. Yet Wise and his party derided Know-Nothingism as far more than "abolitionism in disguise." The American Party, even in the South, was avowedly nativist and anti-Catholic.[110] Virginia Democrats, like those in Indiana, framed the election as a plebiscite on the rights of white men, regardless of religion, ethnicity, or nativity. Even when they did excoriate the party for its shakiness on slavery, theirs was not a uniquely southern strategy, as northerners depended upon similar ploys to fight fanaticism. Virginia Democrats, along with southerners following the Old Dominion's lead, refined their party's national and conservative ideology as they assailed Know-Nothingism on grounds that resounded among white men nationwide.

The Politics of Slavery in Virginia

Know-Nothing political culture alarmed established parties. The American Party originated as a secret order in the urban North, its "Know-Nothing" cognomen stemming from adherents' professed ignorance concerning their organization. The movement shocked Whigs and Democrats by initially electing candidates who never publicly campaigned. "Sam," the party's personification as Uncle Sam's youthful nephew, "sprung forth fully armed" onto the political landscape "like Minerva from the brain of Jove."[111] Although much of their mystery had dissipated by 1855 in their institutionalization as a political party, Know-Nothings still seemed illegitimate to many traditional partisans. Democrats reacted to Sam's southern foray by falling back on the politics of slavery. Yet Know-Nothings were more than just the allies of northern abolitionists, as Virginia Whigs had been, Democrats warned. The organization also muddled partisan and racial peripheries in the South and provided a template for enslaved southerners to resist their bondage. Know-Nothing fanaticism, in short, facilitated black political agency and racial amalgamation.

As they had previously done with Whigs, Virginia Democrats railed against Know-Nothings' alleged connections with antislavery fanatics in the free states. Attachment to unreliable northerners meant political doom in the South. Know-Nothings' northern affiliates consequently came under scrutiny. The American Party was "born among the abolition and corruption of the North," where the party was "turning out of office the conservative men, and placing in their stead the rankest Freesoilers."[112] Know-Nothingism and antislavery shared a geographical and ideological provenance. As Wise howled at Know-Nothings heckling him during a speech in Washington, DC, "You have joined in the war of the Abolitionists on the institutions of Virginia." An Alabama Democrat summarized the campaigns against Know-Nothings in 1855 and 1856: "Last year it was 'Sam & Sambo'—This year it is 'Sambo & Sam.'"[113]

The interracial alliance connoted by Sam and Sambo led Democrats to portray fusion with the American Party as racial amalgamation. According to Democratic newspapers, the Know-Nothing ticket, composed of disreputable Whigs and "*fishy* Democrats," was an "amalgamation ticket."[114] As in Indiana, Democrats treated party blending as racial adulteration. Speculating on the nature of "old Sam's children," the *Richmond Enquirer* offered various alternatives: "an abortion," a "premature" birth that "won't live," or, alternately, "It will be black, others think it will be mulatto." It could even "be white on one side of its face, and black on the other," with the ability to "turn one side or the other North, or South, as it suits." Sam's progeny would, regardless, be a monstrous birth.[115] The Know-Nothings' "hybrid ticket" was a "mermaid ticket," a reference to P. T. Barnum's zoological oddity.[116] Political fusion with Know-Nothings confounded the lines separating races and even species. These appeals resonated in a culture increasingly reliant on "scientific" racial taxonomy.

Democrats used this imagery to forestall defections, with the result that the "Democratic papers of the State manifest a zeal and ability in their assaults on the mongrel ticket."[117] The anticipated amalgamation was not merely metaphorical. The North offered a negative referent, as Massachusetts Know-Nothings "have taken the first step toward practical amalgamation by placing negro and white children in their common schools upon terms of equality."[118] The presence of the *"foul, demoralizing, debasing, filthy thing, that has got into Virginia pastures from the Northern pig-sty"* would, incidentally, purify the party. It would peel off unsteady Democrats and other "impure ingredients that before had an accidental place in the Democratic mass," leaving a "pure lump of genuine Democracy, cleansed and refined."[119] Ideologically—and racially—unsullied, the Democratic Party would confront an opponent with "no cohesive power at the South but an amalgamating hatred of Democracy."[120]

Know-Nothings imperiled white supremacy even more overtly by sanctioning black politics. The organization's secrecy and rituals, what one Mississippian mocked as "the signs, and grips, and passwords, and squalls, and oaths, and flag-fribble of the order," struck many as illegitimate.[121] Indianans had already noticed this unrepublican behavior. Hoosiers believed that "our enemies are working in the dark" and that "our defeat was owing to the secret conclave & the methodist church they all met in cornfields & Reveires [sic, Reveries] on monday night before the Election."[122] Know-Nothings were "those who strike in the dark," "modern Jacobins" who fomented revolution in secret.[123] A Democrat in Madison Court House, Virginia, kept Congressman Paulus Powell "apprize[d] . . . of their contemplated movements." Know-Nothings were reportedly planning a nocturnal nominating convention in Charlottesville. Politics conducted surreptitiously, under cover of darkness, suggested illicit goals and unrepublican reluctance to undergo public scrutiny. These practices evoked something even more dire to white southerners.[124]

Virginians equated white fanatics' political style with black politics. Historians have been hard at work expanding the borders of "the political" in antebellum America by uncovering the often overlooked ways in which African Americans, including enslaved southerners, engaged in politics, notwithstanding exclusion from the formal political sphere. White southerners were fully aware of at least some of the covert means by which slaves practiced politics.[125] Belying the comforting illusion that slavery abnegated civil and political agency, slaveholders understood their "property" as political actors and were unnerved when white and black political practices converged. Because Know-Nothings "exist somewhere in the dark," Wise explained, "their blows can't be guarded against, for they strike, not like freemen, bold, bravely for rights." Know-Nothings did not act like republican freemen but like subversive slaves. According to a Tennessee Democrat, Know-Nothings recruited "converts in your secret hiding places, in your dark cellars, in your unfrequented garrets, in your caves, or the lonely glens of the mountain."[126] When Democrats referred to a Know-Nothing as a "secret agitator, muffling his face, and treading the dark alley to the back door of his midnight conventicle," in order to "gather recruits by whispers" and indulge his "desire to retire in secret, and by secret means to propagate a political thought, or word, or deed,"[127] the parallel was not lost on white southerners who had long dreaded clandestine gatherings as preludes to insurrection.

Know-Nothings acted like slaves. But enslaved southerners also seemed to emulate Know-Nothings. Democrats nurtured a suspicion of "Know-Nothingism being productive of a spirit of imitation among our slave population." Slaveholders imagined "blacks, who are forming themselves into similar societies, and banding together under solemn oaths of secrecy."[128] They fantasized about vicious white men, especially mendicant Yankees, skulking about the countryside, sowing insurrection. In 1855 both northern and indigenous Know-Nothing "emissaries" were "nightly prowling about our doors."[129] Several Louisianans congratulated a former Democratic congressman for exposing that Know-Nothings furthered the "disguised movements of Abolitionist [sic] of the North who . . . are *secretly* and insidiously working a 'subterranean passage' to undermine the cherished institutions of the South." Whether Know-Nothings took their cues from slaves or slaves followed the Know-Nothing script, the consonance between white and black politics, practiced beyond the ken of formal institutions and reliable white men's oversight, risked fired barns and slit throats. Wise privately agonized to a northern ally over the thought of "Sam with a dark lantern among the negroes."[130]

The Politics of Religious Liberty in Virginia

A Kentuckian impressed with the new party cautioned his Virginia relative, Congressman John Letcher, against engaging the Know-Nothings, lest Letcher hazard reelection. "As you dont know any thing about them," he admonished, *"let them alone."* Before his gubernatorial nomination in December 1854, Henry Wise hypothesized that he could avoid conflict with the American Party, as he was "a native, a protestant. . . . This may satisfy them." These Democrats, however, chose to challenge the Know-Nothings,[131] "to strike so fast and thick at 'Sam' that he was kept on the defensive all the time." Wise "would make no committals to or compromises with any sect or party organization except that of the good old Democratic party."[132] He also forbade equivocation by others, asking, *"Is it not time that candidates for Congress as well as for the Govr. place were called on to declare whether they are tainted with Know Nothingism or not, whether they are contented with Democracy*[?]*"*[133] As

Indiana Democrats had done with Kansas-Nebraska, Wise made antinativism an ideological test for his party.

Although Know-Nothings supposedly endangered slavery and invited enslaved insurrection, Virginia Democrats made the party's nativism and anti-Catholicism the fulcrum of the campaign. Before his nomination, Wise released a lengthy encyclical condemning the order. Many southern Know-Nothings resented their characterization as intolerant, proscriptive bigots. One critic called Wise "a thorough Know-Nothing, so far as a knowledge of the principles of that order are concerned." Their exaggerations notwithstanding, Democrats were instinctively bristling at the American Party's open enmity toward Catholics and the foreign-born and their intention to politically handicap white men.[134] At the same time, Democrats laughed off Know-Nothing fearmongering, as Virginia lacked a sizable immigrant population; at 3 percent in 1850, it was less than that of Indiana and other northern states.[135] This response did not tarnish southerners' sincere antinativism. Justifying his animus to the American Party, a South Carolinian reflected, "Personally, its provisions . . . would never reach me. I am not a foreigner; nor am I a Roman Catholic." "But," he reckoned, "I am a Free-man. That I can only be, while the land in which I live is free."[136] By contending for the rights of these groups, despite their slight presence in the South, Democrats were defending white men throughout the Union.

Citing its hostility toward religious liberty, the separation of church and state, and immigration, Virginia Democrats charged that the American Party was "against Americanism itself." "Imposing civil incapacitations on account of religious opinions" amounted to an unconstitutional and un-American calumny upon the Founders, some of whom were Catholic and foreign-born.[137] Know-Nothings would usher in "the worst union which could be devised, [that] of church and state" and would impinge upon the "liberty of conscience."[138] Virginians drew on their party's anticlericalism to demand official toleration for all sects. Protestants who wanted to restrict the political rights of Catholics exhibited the very narrow-mindedness they credited to the Catholic Church. "How can this bigotry be subdued by bigotry . . . ?" Wise asked. Frenzied Protestants would merely "out-Jesuit the Jesuits," he answered.[139] Similar to other fanatics, Know-Nothings were intolerant and hypocritical in their quest to realize a religiously inspired agenda through the state's moral machinery.

The most eloquent proponents of religious liberty in antebellum America were southern Democrats. Former Alabama congressman Philip Phillips issued a strong exposition of Democratic anticlericalism during his state's 1855 election. He indicted Know-Nothings for violating the "Separation of Church and State, [the] eternal divorce between civil and ecclesiastical jurisdiction," which characterized America's "model of a republican government." A Tennessean claimed that Know-Nothingism, with its "adulterous union of Church and State," was "nothing but mere, sheer, bigoted intolerance, and that of the most malignant type," worthy of the ancient Puritans. Most of the slave states held elections later in 1855, and, Phillips ventured, "the South, always conservative, always jealous of power," would follow "Virginia, the oldest of the sisters," in preserving the "principle of religious equality and freedom."[140]

The Democracy's southern supporters repudiated Know-Nothingism as alien to their section and its values. They perceived the American Party as the leading edge of a Yankee onslaught. "That '*ism*' is the worst of all," Wise sputtered at Alabama Democrat J. L. M. Curry, "a cunning devise to subject slave-holders to the sign of passive obedience & non-resistance to a Dark Lantern Priest craft oligarchy of N. England!!" The Mississippi author and Methodist preacher Augustus Baldwin Longstreet likewise spurned the American Party, asserting, "The thing has no southern feature." Its "avowed aims," he expounded, were to attack Catholics and "oppose foreigners," and, while "fighting under an anti-Catholic flag, they killed nobody but Democrats." It was unfortunate, Longstreet observed, that the party was "hissing, bleating, and coughing down such men as Wise and Douglas," thereby linking the most prominent Democrat from each section in their national contest with the order.[141]

Southern Democrats had their own reason to resist the union of temporal and spiritual authority, as slaveholding stood foremost among the rights endangered by religious reformers. In the late eighteenth and early nineteenth centuries, elite white men in the South had interpreted evangelical Protestantism as a threat. They converted only when evangelicalism could be used to sacralize their household mastery.[142] Even more menacing than a congregation curbing one's mastery was the government doing so in the guise of religion. Phillips argued that once Americans accepted that religion "forms 'an element of our political system,'" as Know-Nothings claimed, then "we should soon be called upon to submit our consciences to Congressional dictation." This warning echoed Phillips's earlier protest against congressional dictation regarding territorial slavery as an author of Kansas-Nebraska.[143] For a speaker at a barbecue in Tennessee, antislavery agitation and the national

Know-Nothing Party's religious intolerance were each "an invasion of the rights of the States." He made the connection between religious liberty and slaveholders' rights: "There is not a man in Tennessee who will say that any other State has a right to interfere with our rights of property. Then I ask, Are not our religious rights more sacred . . . ?"[144] Southerners' aversion to "religious and political fanaticism"[145] dovetailed with their desire to protect slaveholding as a state right and as an inviolable individual right.

There was, additionally, a distinctly Virginian reason to bid defiance to "proscription, bigotry and intolerance."[146] After reading an address R. M. T. Hunter delivered at Petersburg, a Virginian compared the senator to Thomas Jefferson. He gushed, "If the Apostle of Liberty desired to perpetuate his fame by directing it to be inscribed on his tomb that he was the author of the 'Act for establishing Religious Freedom,' so might you rest the immortality of your name upon the delivery of this speech."[147] Virginia Democrats wrapped themselves in the mantle of "Jefferson the Free Thinker."[148] They applauded their state's tradition of religious disestablishment and toleration, exemplified in the Virginia Statute for Religious Freedom and embodied by the Sage of Monticello. The American Party's "venom of intolerance," in contrast, contradicted "the native generosity of the Virginia character" and blemished the reputation of the man who founded the Democracy.[149]

Virginia Democrats, and those throughout the slave states, were happy to share Jefferson's legacy with Irish Catholics, because Irish Americans appeared willing to defend slavery and white supremacy. Native-born Protestants fueled fanaticism in the free states, while "Irishmen have vindicated the Constitution and law against the fiendish clamor of raging and gnashing hell-hound mobs of native Abolitionists." Southern Democrats praised the Irish militia regiment that helped secure the enslaved fugitive Anthony Burns from an abolitionist crowd in Boston in order to dispatch him to the South in 1854.[150] An Old Whig in Maryland friendly to the Democracy took a pragmatic view of Catholics. Unlike northern Protestants, the Catholic Church, he noted, "does not hold it to be morally or religiously wrong to hold slaves, but on the contrary, by precept and example teaches it to be religiously and morally right to hold them." "We of the South," he concluded, can "confidently rely for the maintenance of our Constitutional rights upon the Catholic of Massachusetts, as upon the Catholic of Louisianna or Maryland." 1850s Democrats updated Van Buren and Ritchie's alliance to include the slaveholders of the South and the Catholic immigrants of the North. By defending freedom of conscience and extending white racial status to immigrants, slaveholders forged a mutually beneficial intersectional alliance.[151]

Rechristened the "Democratic and Anti-Know Nothing party of Alabama," the Democracy in Philip Phillips's state ratified this intersectional bargain in its platform. At its January 1856 convention in Montgomery, the party reduced its creed to two essential "principles": "the perfect equality of privileges—civil, religious and political—of every citizen of our country, without reference to the place of his birth" and "the unqualified right of the people of the slave-holding States to the protection of their property in the States, [and] in the Territories."[152] White southerners wedded a genuine concern for freedom of conscience and immigrants' rights to a defense of slavery. "Are not the religious and political rights of a *native-born* Roman Catholic citizen as dear to him as is the right . . . to hold and enjoy their slave property . . . ?" inquired a Kentucky congressman, adding, "Are not the rights of a naturalized citizen . . . as sacred as either of the rights above-mentioned?"[153] This was more than a sectional quid pro quo between northern immigrants and southern slaveholders—it was the distillation of a worldview prizing self-determination for *all* white men.

The National Politics of Fanaticism, Slavery, and Race

Democrats conjured Jefferson with care. While his legacy was useful to censure Know-Nothings for trespassing against "liberty of conscience," many white southerners had no patience with other notions ascribed to Virginia's Apostle of Liberty. Indeed, the extent to which even northern Democrats disowned Jefferson reinforced the party's proslavery image.[154] Indiana senator John Pettit, for instance, speaking in favor of Kansas-Nebraska, roused national ire in early 1854 for "fearlessly" renouncing Jefferson's dictum that "all men are created equal" as a "self-evident lie." Pettit wanted no one to think that he was the equal of African Americans. Only a year after Hunter found himself compared to Jefferson, he arraigned "that cardinal political maxim, that all men were created equal" as one of "those doctrines upon which" the opponents of slavery were "agitating the public mind and seeking to subvert the social system of the South."[155] Democrats invoked Jefferson to protest only one type of enslavement—their own.

Know-Nothings, although unsound on chattel slavery, seemed to promote just this type of enslavement. These fanatics first degraded themselves by forfeiting mental and moral autonomy. By their "passive obedience" to their hierarchical organization and "by their test oath [they] enslave themselves."[156] In Washington County in southwest Virginia, related a Democratic newspaper, "they already boasted to have captured and bound and fettered, by oaths and pledges, a majority of the *freemen* of the county."[157] Know-Nothings then jeopardized the republican equality of other white men by sorting them into unequal classes. "If you proscribe the Catholic for his religion," Hunter explained, "you refuse him the equal privileges of a citizen, and stamp upon him the brand of inferiority." Wise elaborated, "If we let foreigners be naturalized and don't extend to them equality of privileges, we set up classes and distinctions of persons wholly opposed to Republicanism."[158] The civil and political inequality of white men offended Jacksonians' egalitarianism, leading Democrats to conclude that they were confronting an "*exclusive*, if not an aristocratic feeling" redolent of Federalism.[159]

Denying white men equal political rights nullified the zero-sum racial absolutism of *Herrenvolk* democracy. Withholding rights from white men meant granting them to African Americans, and Know-Nothings would do both. Hunter pointed to Massachusetts, controlled by Know-Nothings, during a speech in Richmond. "Whilst she is so anxious to free the African slave in the South," he observed, "she is engaged in a scheme to proscribe and degrade; yes, sirs, and to enslave . . . all that portion of her own white laborers who are foreign born." Even the liberty of white "native-born laborer[s]" was precarious, Hunter intimated. A Tennessean saw the result of imposing duties on immigrants without according them rights: "When war comes he shall fight our battles, but he shall not rise much above the manumitted slave in his rights."[160] Virginian James Lawson Kemper, campaigning in 1856, denigrated the Know-Nothing presidential candidate for alleged antislavery views. The fact that "he who now pronounces a Dutchman unworthy of Citizenship in this country, supported a petition asking that Free-negro foreigners should be naturalized as citizens of the Union" highlighted fanatics' undue regard for African Americans at the expense of fellow white men.[161]

For Senator Hunter, the deeper fanatical impulse, of which Know-Nothingism was one facet, portended white slavery. Rather than connecting abolitionism and Know-Nothingism, he compared abolitionism with socialism before an audience in Poughkeepsie, New York, in 1856. Abolitionists undermined property in man, while the "socialist sect" attacked private property more generally, endangering the North's free labor economy.[162] Other

Democrats also linked Europe's *"Red republicans"* with America's *"Black republicans."*[163] Northern laborers, Hunter explained, possessed property in their labor, so that abolishing property rights would leave a worker unable to "sell his labor in the highest market." This slaveholding patrician, in his first time speaking outside the South, postured as free labor's ally. Hunter's argument that slavery and hired labor each constituted examples of "hold[ing] property in man" came close to analogizing white northern workers with slaves, a trap into which other haughty planters fell. Hunter nonetheless wove a national defense of white manhood against fanaticism by "endeavoring to show that the application of these principles would be revolutionary in any system of society."[164] The legislative meddling of abolitionists, Know-Nothings, and socialists, Democrats warned, would all lead to white men's enslavement.

Wise's advocacy of white men's democracy was more sincere. He had honed his egalitarianism by demanding the "white basis" for legislative representation during Virginia's 1850–1851 constitutional convention. Although an Eastern Shore planter, Wise chafed at the diluted political power of white men west of the Blue Ridge. Western Virginians later advanced Wise for the gubernatorial nomination, according to a resident of the Shenandoah Valley, because of "the noble stand he took in the late convention in favor of the white basis." Historian Craig M. Simpson holds that a calculating Wise bartered democracy for westerners' loyalty to slavery.[165] Wise's career, however, testified to his reverence for individually autonomous and democratically equal white men. Unlike Hunter's backhanded dismissal of workingmen, Wise honored "the dignity of mechanic labor," a profession "upon which every civilization depends." His heterodox hobbies, including public education, economic diversification, and statewide internal improvements, were meant to make Jacksonian equality a reality. These convictions spurred Wise to clothe himself in homespun and barnstorm the state in his unprecedentedly democratic campaign.[166]

Kenneth Rayner, a leader of the American Party in North Carolina, called Wise's widely circulated missive a *"pronunciamento* against the so-called order of 'Know-Nothings,' not only in Virginia, but throughout the Union."[167] Crafting a national response was Wise's intention. Wise's texts brought wayward Democrats back to the fold in Arkansas, and one supplicant requested additional aid from Virginia against the "political party that has very recently sprung into existence."[168] During his canvass, Wise addressed the entire South and nation, because Democrats everywhere faced the same fanatical foe. He juxtaposed Democrats' conservatism with fanaticism, which included "Unitarianism, Universalism, Fourierism, Millerism, Mormonism—all the odds and ends of isms."[169] A northern senator reminded Wise of his "promise": "that if the sword was placed in your hands as Gov you would use it if necessary not only on the Northern fanatics but upon ones at home also." Wise concurred that enemies were "now in our camp, south, north, east and west," continuing, "I rejoice that you and thousands of other honest and earnest men approve of my remedies against them."[170]

The Democrats of the free states, where most Catholics and immigrants lived, were not alone in combating nativist fanaticism. White southerners, likewise, did not meet abolitionist fanaticism on their own. Former Virginia congressman Richard K. Meade related to Hunter that midwestern Democrats such as Stephen Douglas and Jesse Bright had offered to provide "their opinions of this party & its ultimate tendencies" and to "give their views in relation to the designs of the Know Nothings of the North." Virginians welcomed the cooperation of northerners experienced in sparring with Know-Nothingism. As Meade counseled Hunter, "I am fearful of the result of our elections. If upon the authority of these gentlemen . . . we could show their affiliations with the abolitionists, the party would at once be driven to the wall."[171] Know-Nothings' "ultimate tendencies," whether defined as the proscription of immigrants or of slaveholders, dismayed northerners and southerners alike.

Douglas went to Virginia in 1855 to share his "authority" on Know-Nothing fanaticism. He told a Richmond crowd that midwestern Democrats had already grappled with "a combination of Abolitionists, Whigs, Know Nothings and anti-Liquor men," all united by antipathy to "the great Nebraska principle, and against the Democratic party sustaining it." Know-Nothings in particular "substituted, in a government where the individual and the people are sovereign, a conflicting sovereignty and a different and dangerous authority."[172] The previous year, Douglas had visited Indianapolis to confront antislavery fanaticism. He accused slavery's opponents of thwarting white men's self-government by doubting the truism that "if they (the people of the Territories) can legislate for all else, why not for niggers?" Douglas delivered the refrain that he could say the same thing in the slave states or the free states because Democrats "speak only the truth, and that is applicable everywhere."[173] The truth that Democrats peddled, whether in Richmond or Indianapolis, the South or the Midwest, was that only their party would ensure that democracy continued the purview of *all* white men and *only* white men.

Wise's election in May, Virginia diplomat A. Dudley Mann recognized, would "be every where hailed by the democracy" as "a great triumph." Heartened Democrats in other southern states vowed to "stand by the side of the proud old Commonwealth" in their contests against the new party. Know-Nothings went down to defeat across the slave states in 1855.[174] Following their success, North Carolina Democrats invited Virginia congressman Charles James Faulkner to a "Grand Anti Know Nothing Festival" in Granville County. Northerners also savored the southern rout of Know-Nothingism. Joseph Wright, after his party electorally recovered in 1855, bragged to his new gubernatorial counterpart, "Our State is side by side with Virginia. . . . Indiana is safe for the National Democracy of 1856." He conveyed to Wise his "hope that I shall have the pleasure of witnessing your inauguration."[175] Democrats rejoiced over their decisive national victory in Virginia. New Yorkers saw Tammany Hall illuminated, while Philadelphians heard one hundred guns chortle self-congratulation.[176] A dinner party in Dubuque, meanwhile, offered three toasts to Wise's presidential prospects. Even the embattled Franklin Pierce expressed relief, realizing that "the result of the election in Virginia has put a new face upon the prospects of the Democratic party—the only party which carries no dark lantern & gives its time honored banner to the breeze."[177]

Yet fanaticism still stalked the land after the realignment elections of 1854 and 1855. In September 1855, Whig Edward Everett wished to disclose to Wise the "reasons why not only his efforts, but those of all the leading spirits of conservatism, are well nigh powerless amid the hosts of political huckstering rascals" in Massachusetts. But the Virginia election did provide a brief respite from the ravaging effects of the partisan realignment. Even as late as 1858, when the party was suffering from the sectional fissures that would eventually consume it, Senator George W. Jones of Iowa reminisced with Wise about "the wonderful triumph which elevated you to your present position & which was the death-blow to Know Nothingism in Virginia, if not in the whole South & the Union itself every where."[178]

FOUR

Welcoming Realignment
DEMOCRATS, OLD WHIGS, AND
THE CONSERVATIVE DIASPORA

> It is quite impossible that you should become Know Nothings or Free
> Soilers; & you have no place to go except to the Democratic party, which
> has now become the only true conservative party of the Country.
> —James Buchanan to a Whig, 1856

ROBERT C. WINTHROP shared Edward Everett's dread of fanaticism in Massachusetts. Scion of a hoary New England conservatism, he protested against the living entombment of his party in the wake of the *isms*. Observing the 1850s partisan realignment from Boston, the necropolis of Whiggery, Winthrop defied the prevailing wisdom that his party was dead, grousing, "The democracy—I will do them the justice to say—never listen to these idle rumors about their danger of dying, and we might well borrow a leaf out of their book." Just as Caleb Cushing had forbidden Democrats' fusion with Free Soilers in Massachusetts, Winthrop refused to entertain Whigs' fusion with Republicans in 1855. He reminded fellow Old Whigs of their principles. Hailing from a "CONSTITUTIONAL PARTY" and a "party of LAW AND ORDER," Whigs would never condescend to "rush wildly into the promiscuous ranks of a one-idea party, in order to promote some grand result connected with human liberty." Wary of Republicanism, Winthrop still fell short of endorsing Democracy. Yet his disdain for antislavery fanaticism possessed important similarities with Democrats' conservatism, which explains why many Old Whigs, including eventually Winthrop, voted for Democrats.[1]

The uncertain course of politically homeless Old Whigs exacerbated the realignment's confusion. Informing a southern correspondent of the collapse of Whiggery and the ascendancy of "a combination of Know-Nothings &

Freesoilers" in Massachusetts, Everett announced that "conservative men have been silenced,—or ceased to be conservative."² Whigs like Everett and Winthrop labored to perpetuate their party's conservatism. A vigorous contest ensued as multiple parties courted former Whigs, hoping to profit from their conservative, Unionist reputation. Republicans, Know-Nothings, and Democrats all craved designation as the true "conservative" party destined to purify the republic and preserve the Union. Some Whigs joined the Know-Nothings, whether because they held nativist beliefs or because they aspired to overtake that party as a vehicle for Whiggery. The most persistent clung to their rump party or continued it in the guise of "Opposition" Parties, especially in the Upper South. While scholarship has traced the Whig diaspora into the Know-Nothing and Republican Parties, less attention has been paid to those who repressed bitter memories to pursue a tactical alliance with Democrats.³

Conservative Whigs fled their faltering party for the Democracy throughout the early 1850s. In the slave states, many were dissatisfied with President Zachary Taylor and the 1852 nomination of Winfield Scott, both deemed insufficiently prosouthern. "Far better will it be for the national men of our party," concluded one southern Whig after Scott's nomination, "that a *conservative Democrat* be elected." Bipartisan backing for the Compromise of 1850 on the part of southern Whigs and northern Democrats hinted at convergence. When a pro-compromise Union party failed to solidify, southern Whigs drifted into the Democracy. In 1854 southern Whigs again allied with Democrats to pass the Kansas-Nebraska Act.⁴ The antislavery stance of northern Conscience Whigs precluded rapprochement with southern Whigs and also estranged northern conservatives. Cotton Whigs, epitomized by the New England devotees of Daniel Webster, and Silver Grays following the lead of New York's Millard Fillmore accepted compromise on slavery as the price of Union. In 1852 Webster grumbled that "the [h]*oi polloi* of the Whig party, especially in the north and east, were . . . fast sinking into the slough of freesoilism and abolitionism." Uneasy with the fanaticism enervating their party and with the new antislavery and nativist movements seducing their compatriots, many conservative Whigs found a home in the Democracy.⁵

Democracy crowed over Whiggery's death throes like a carrion bird. Democrats resisted realignment when the question was of maintaining their party, but they welcomed it to deprive Whigs of theirs. They intended to expedite the Whig Party's demise and appropriate its conservative patina. Through mourning the death of influential Old Whigs, the Whig Party, and the second party system itself, Democrats worked to convince Whigs that their party was dead and that so too were the issues over which they had previously tussled. Whigs and Democrats could now ally as conservatives and nationalists against fanaticism. Democrats also appealed to Whigs as fellow white men who shared a stake in defending their republic against fanatics who fostered female and black political agency. While Democrats proclaimed a conservative concordance with Whigs, they did not coalesce ideologically. That Democrats and Whigs remained philosophically distinct despite their cooperation underscores the novelty of Democrats' redefinition of American conservatism.

Eulogizing the Second Party System

After attending a colleague's funeral in 1848, Michigan senator Alpheus Felch reported to his wife that "we have had an unusual number of deaths in Congress the present year." He tallied "nine members of the present congress [who] have died since the 4th March of last year," which amounted to "a much larger number than usual for the same length of time." Political deaths burdened the nation. Felch explained, "All members of Congress who die here are buried at the public expense, at a cost near a thousand Dollars." "The pay of the member," moreover, "is also always given for the whole session, notwithstand his death may occur soon after its commencement."[6] The costly expiration of numerous political leaders vexed Americans in the interbellum era. Politicians employed the eldritch imagery of death and mourning to interpret more than the departure of these elder statesmen. After Vice President William Rufus King died in office in 1853, a eulogizing senator imbued his passing with larger significance: "Those to whom our people have been long accustomed to look . . . are falling fast around us." "It is an anxious thing to feel their loss," he continued, "at a period like this, pregnant with change, and teeming, perhaps, with great and strange events." When Democrats and Whigs lamented the death of individual statesmen, they were also grieving over the death of their conservative political order.[7]

Democrats and fellow conservatives elegized the death of Jacksonian two-party politics to forge unity amid the "political anarchy" of the 1850s. They envisioned "the conservative men of the country of all shades of opinion, and of all old party alliances" uniting to redeem the Union from sectionalism and fanaticism.[8] Democrats were not simply gloating over the death of their nemesis. They mourned the likes of Henry Clay and Daniel Webster to argue that the Whig Party had died, along with the political culture that had legitimized partisan opposition. In their eulogies of deceased parties and statesmen, conservative Democrats and their Whig allies selectively remembered past political battles in order to enshrine a standard of partisan competition that denied legitimacy to upstart sectional and fanatical coalitions. Democrats absorbed "disintegrated Whigery" into their party to confirm that Whiggery was dead and to make the cause of American conservatism their own, allowing them to triumph over their new foes as they had prevailed over their ancient one.[9]

"The Whig party is dead" sounded a Democratic refrain in the 1850s. James Buchanan, stumping for Franklin Pierce against Winfield Scott, unfavorably compared the Whig nominee to Henry Clay, asserting that "Mr. Clay . . . was the very essence, the life and soul of Whiggery." If Clay was the "life and soul of Whiggery," then Whiggery was dead as early as 1852.[10] A Whig newspaper in Boston acknowledged that the nomination of the purportedly antislavery Scott troubled conservative Whigs—*"It fell like a funeral pall upon their spirits."*[11] Pierce and the Democracy, in comparison, were the true heirs to Clay's Unionism. A Maryland Whig explained that "the conservative spirit of the country was aroused, the Whig candidate was distrusted, and the Democratic party achieved an overwhelming triumph." In an obituary address for his Senate colleague who died in 1856, James A. Bayard of Delaware noted that John M. Clayton was "a cherished leader of one of the great political parties of the country whilst its national organization was maintained."[12] Clayton's demise paralleled that of the national Whig Party, leaving Democrats the sole national force in politics.

Many Whigs concurred, although not all conceded that their party was totally extinct. Whigs already suffered from an acute morbidness, burdened with the memory that "twice have the Whigs carried the Presidential election, and on both occasions . . . they were called upon to mourn the death of their President." Rufus Choate of Massachusetts was unwilling to admit his party's death but granted that the question of "whether we are dead, as reported in the newspapers, or, if not, whether we shall fall upon our own swords and die even so, will be a debate possessing the interest of novelty at least."[13] A Kentuckian despaired of Whiggery's "resurrection," despite "every effort to resuscitate the old party."[14] The ubiquitous inquests of political coroners primed Americans to grieve the passing of the Whig Party, a conclusion that Democrats encouraged.

The most compelling evidence Democrats marshaled was that prominent Old Whigs were indeed dead. During an 1848 yellow fever outbreak in New Orleans that seemed to afflict only Whigs, a Democrat blustered that "Democrats dont die so easily."[15] Death was, nonetheless, bipartisan. Jacksonian America's surplus of statesmen thinned between the Mexican War and the Civil War. Presidents Polk and Taylor, Vice President King, and Senator Clayton, in addition to the "immortal triumvirate" of Webster, Calhoun, and Clay, died in the late 1840s and 1850s. A Whig congressman marveled that "death has so often invaded" Congress and that "even the executive mansion is not unfrequently invaded by the King of Terrors."[16] This gloom accentuated those relics of the Age of Jackson who stubbornly endured. Chief Justice Roger B. Taney, for example, although "yet living, . . . already ranked with his illustrious predecessors." His longevity, and perhaps his cadaveresque countenance, prompted William Lowndes Yancey to depict the jurist in 1860 as "trembling upon the very verge of the grave, for years kept merely alive by the pure spirit of patriotic duty."[17]

Democrats brandished their connections to these lamented statesmen to win over living Whigs. A bipartisan political past was an electoral asset for conservatives. One of Franklin Pierce's campaign biographies boasted that he had served alongside the "intellectual giants of the land." These included, in bipartisan pairings, "Calhoun and Webster, Buchanan and Clay, Woodbury and Choate, Grundy and Crittenden, Wright and Southard, Walker and Preston, Rives and Benton."[18] When the party split in 1860, both Democratic nominees claimed Clay's imprimatur. Voters learned of Stephen Douglas's role in the Compromise of 1850 and that "Mr. Clay subsequently bore honorable testimony to the ability, fairness, and patriotism displayed by Mr. Douglas." John C. Breckinridge, meanwhile, traced his initial electoral success in a Whig district to "Henry Clay, who abjured his politics to pay a just tribute to the worth and ability of the gallant young Kentuckian."[19] Democrats were not simply energizing their partisan base in the 1850s. They were also taking advantage of the realignment to broaden their electoral appeal.

Through rhetorical necromancy, Democrats and Whigs resurrected the great statesmen. They channeled the spirits of deceased Whigs to bolster the Democracy against fanatics claiming Whiggish antecedents. One pamphlet shouted, "MR. CLAY SPEAKS," and encouraged readers to "HEAR HIM" endorse James Buchanan for president in 1856. In 1858 James B. Clay, son of the Great Compromiser, decried the "use which has been attempted to be made of the name of my father . . . since his death, for partizan and party purposes." His indignation had not prevented him from drawing on his father's memory to justify his approval of the 1856 Democratic ticket and his subsequent support for the Buchanan administration.[20] Virginia Democrat James Lawson Kemper conjured Clay's apparition to attack Know-Nothings, exclaiming, "Ah! if the great-hearted Clay could once more walk the earth in the plenitude of his pride! How would his lofty spirit chafe under the unmanly surrender of his party and his cause to the ignoble control" of Know-Nothings.[21]

Douglas summoned the specter of Clay to curry favor with Illinois Whigs in his 1858 senatorial reelection campaign. Abraham Lincoln's political career and the Republican Party, Douglas cried, were built atop Clay's grave. "Clay was dead, and although the sod was not yet green on his grave," Douglas charged, "this man undertook to bring into disrepute those great Compromise measures of 1850, with which Clay and Webster were identified." "After the death of Clay and Webster," it was easy for the Whig Party "to have its throat cut from ear to ear" by Lincoln in his effort to "Abolitionize the Whig party, by dissolving it, [and] transferring the members into the Abolition camp." Douglas convinced Democrats at least; one southern admirer of the Little Giant gushed, "I had often heard it said that when Randolph Calhoun Clay and Webster died that Patriotism and unflinching integrity were gone but Sir in your present campaing against, Lincoln . . . you have shown yourself a patriot gentleman and a Loyal Democrat."[22]

To confront fanaticism together, Democrats and Whigs interred the issues they fought over in the 1830s and 1840s. James Lawson Kemper concluded that "the very questions which heretofore divided the old parties are known to be dead forever. . . . The old issues are buried too deep for any man's resurrecting arm to reach them." James B. Clay extended the metaphor; he equated ghoulishly unearthing such topics with wielding "weapons dragged from the tomb." Previous debates, an erstwhile Whig in Alabama contended, focused on "mere measures of Governmental policy," while current disputes touched on "fundamental and vital principles."[23] Slavery, Democrats agreed, was "the living question now before the country."[24] With politics centered on slavery, disunion, and fanatical reformism, Whigs ought to affiliate with Democrats rather than continue in opposition on moribund matters like internal improvements or the subtreasury.

Having trivialized the old issues, Democrats recalled their enmity with the Whig Party as the heroic age of American politics. Conservatives remembered

Jacksonian political battles as high-minded parties dueling over economic platforms, while according each other legitimacy and refusing to pander to sectionalism and slavery. This account was sanitized. The politics of slavery had regularly intruded into the second party system, and the concept of a legitimate opposition had hardly been sacrosanct.[25] But this reimagined party rivalry fostered reconciliation. Democrats recited past instances of bipartisan compromise as models for how Whigs should act in the present. With the Compromise of 1850, two southern Democrats reminisced in 1852, "men laid aside old party distinctions. The great and illustrious of the land—Clay and Cass, Webster and Dickinson, and many others who had fought each other for years upon questions of policy—gathered together, shoulder to shoulder, like brothers."[26] Whereas a Democrat in 1848 had scoffed, "Who ever heard of Whig principles[?]"[27] Democrats in the 1850s announced their preference for Whiggery over Know-Nothingism and Black Republicanism. "Since the death of these great men the whig party has ceased to exist; even its name is forgotten," an Iowa Democrat alleged. But he realized that "still an opposition is left, more bitter and virulent; barbarous and depraved, than ever the whig party professed to be." A New York Democrat likewise complained, "I wish that I could say that we had the Whig party to oppose," because "we never allowed ourselves to apprehend from the old Whig party, any design to subvert our Union or overturn our liberties."[28]

Democrats bestowed posthumous legitimacy on Whigs to discredit the new fanatical parties. R. M. T. Hunter, reacting to Virginia Know-Nothings in 1855, declared, "I prefer the old to the new enemy. The old Whigs were a manly party" that "fought upon principles."[29] Honoring Whigs' manly, principled stands, even if those principles were flawed, allowed Democrats to disparage Know-Nothings, often portrayed as political opportunists whose mysterious organization relied on "secret cabals" and "midnight caucuses."[30] Those Old Whigs who followed leaders such as Millard Fillmore into the American Party would find themselves deceived, for the soul of Whiggery did not inhabit that party, which was "soon to be buried with its bones, and forever to rest under the gravestones which bear the record of its follies."[31] Aaron V. Brown shamed Old Whigs in Tennessee for allowing Know-Nothings to desecrate the memory of their party. He registered "astonishment that no warm and devoted friend has yet come forward to rescue the fame of HUGH LAWSON WHITE, Mr. WEBSTER, and Mr. CLAY, from this bold charge of corruption in the Whig party." It was up to "living Statesmen" to preserve this legacy, and Democrats like him were happy to do it if no one else would.[32]

Republicans, Democrats found, also proved unworthy successors to Whiggery. Conservatives insisted that, even at the height of their rivalry, the two old parties possessed more in common with each other, because they were national and conservative parties, than either did with this new one. One Massachusetts Whig judged that "the basis of the [Republican] organization is reciprocal sectional hate."[33] Whigs, in contrast, were extolled for moderation and Unionism. As a national party, they had never sought the "exclusive benefit of one section of the country to the exclusive detriment of another."[34] John M. Clayton, eulogized both for his individual character and for the party he represented, received praise for the "intense nationality of his feelings." When "the integrity of the Union was involved, he broke those fetters" of partisanship.[35] Democrats hoped that Clayton's example would lead Whigs to join the Democracy. Their alternative was the Republican Party, a "Geographical party" that was fanatical in its antislavery. Gone were the "two great parties" and the nationally inclusive politics they sponsored, when "Webster could address Virginians" and southerners such as "Berrien and Bell and Leigh and Johnson could feel and heighten the inspiration of Faneuil Hall and Bunker Hill."[36]

Whigs accepted their passing with varying degrees of enthusiasm for collaboration with "their ancient foe."[37] Georgian Robert Toombs did not relish working with the Democracy, but he decided such an effort would protect slavery. "There is no safety for our constitutional rights at this time in any other organization," he admitted, "& we must therefore do the best we can with them." The Democracy, unlike the Whigs, remained a viable party. As James B. Clay justified his turn toward Democracy, "We Whigs know well, and to our cost, the wonderful tenacity of the Democratic party."[38] A North Carolinian ascribed the Democracy's tenacity to former Whigs like himself who "went to its aid and were incorporated in its ranks."[39] According to Rufus Choate, "The Whigs of Massachusetts are absolutely glad that they are alive" to make a final stand for the Union against sectionalism and fanaticism. "Would it not be a glorious page on which . . . he should record that their last organic act was to meet the dark wave of this tide of sectionalism," he mused, "to fall, and let our recorded honors thicken on our graves[?]" Supporting the 1856 Democratic presidential ticket was Choate's means of partisan self-immolation.[40]

Clay, Choate, and like-minded Whigs were prescribing a "Good Death" for their party. Historian Drew Gilpin Faust rediscovered the cultural imperative of meeting one's end in an acceptable way in the Civil War era.[41] Political death could also be praiseworthy or ignoble. The rhetoric of decay and dishonorable demise suffused politics. An unlucky politician could "die a most wretched political death" and end up "a mere effete, corrupting political carcass."[42] One ex-Democrat, weary of parties, scorned presidential candidates as no more than "dead corpses," unsuited to lead a "heroic nation of thirty millions of live and electric men." A loyal Democrat likewise condemned a politician who persisted in outdated partisanship: "His very bones are rotten with party selfishness; and when he dies, his poisoned carcass will so putrify the adjacent soil, and so defile with its effluvia the surrounding atmosphere, that none of Gods green grass will ever live above his accursed grave!"[43]

A Pennsylvania Whig turned Democrat chided "those of fanatic zeal [who] habitually denounce with derision, as 'Union savers,' patriotic citizens and statesmen who have resolved to stand by it to the death." The Union, for this Whig, was instead "an incentive to glorious death," a sacrifice incomprehensible to fanatical politicians.[44] The Good Death that Democrats offered Whigs amounted to "political martyrdom"—snuffing out one's partisan existence through a bold stand for principle, whether the Union, slavery, or the "Constitution of their country."[45] One Whig achieved a good political death because "before he died, he became a Democrat, and fully and repeatedly atoned for the wrong he did to Mr. Buchanan."[46] Democrats were eager to grant absolution and hasten the Good Death of Whiggery, leaving them the nation's sole national and conservative party.

A Bipartisan Defense of the White Man's Republic

Stephen Douglas recollected that "the old Whig party and the Democratic party had stood on a common platform so far as this slavery question was concerned." The parties "differed about the bank, the tariff, distribution, the specie circular and the sub-treasury," he reminisced, "but we agreed on this slavery question."[47] Democrats and their Whig allies invented this consensus in order to withhold legitimacy from Republicans and Know-Nothings. Conservatives of both old parties wanted to guard the white man's republic against fanatics who undermined slavery and promoted the political agency of women and African Americans. Safeguarding racial and gender boundaries by engaging in the politics of slavery and race became a basis of cooperation among Democrats and Old Whigs.

The veterans of the second party system were well versed in the politics of slavery and race. Martin Van Buren, who had advised Americans in the 1820s to substitute partisanship for sectionalism, conceded in 1856 that "slavery questions have from the beginning had more or less to do with our political contests." Still, he noted in response to the rise of the Republican Party, these disputes "have never before had the effect of dissolving old party connections and sympathies."[48] While numerous northern Whigs followed their antislavery convictions into the Republican Party, many were nostalgic for working alongside southerners. Conservative Whigs in the North, like Doughface Democrats, were experienced in appeasing southern allies within national parties, and Whigs nationwide had long attacked opponents as weak on race and slavery.[49] In 1852 a Whig pamphlet charged that Franklin Pierce had criticized the Fugitive Slave Act, verifying that he was "thoroughly imbued with anti-slavery sentiment and prejudice, and that he will betray the South and all its vast interests." The Democracy was running a "WOOLLY-HEADED CANDIDATE FOR THE PRESIDENCY." Democrats dismissed this indictment as a "foul and exploded conspiracy of the abolitionists to represent General Pierce as an abolitionist in his views, in order to defeat his election." They countered that southerners should be alarmed by Winfield Scott's antislavery tendencies. While the Democracy was more avowedly racist, with white supremacy a core component of its partisan ideology, the Whig Party knew how to craft political appeals in a racist society.[50]

It was thus reflexive that Old Whigs, like Democrats, reached for the analogy of racial amalgamation to make sense of partisan fluctuations. Senator James Pearce of Maryland believed that Know-Nothings were tainted by working with the "motly alliance" composing the Republican Party. Robert Winthrop similarly feared Whigs falling in line behind the "speckled and motley" "Fusion flag" overtaking Massachusetts.[51] Responding to this same menace, Massachusetts Democrats told Whigs that "temperance, statesmanship, constitution, Union, nationality, law and Gospel are to be all abandoned for negro philanthropy, by the leaders of this 'fusion' movement, who call themselves '*republicans*.'" "The democracy and the Union men of the north" were safer than the *"Black republicans,"* because Democrats' "love of the Union and the white race is stronger than their false philanthropy for the negro."[52]

Democrats predicted racial degradation for those Whigs who did not accept their invitation to join the white man's party. They inflicted this degradation themselves with racial attacks against Whigs considering fusion with antislavery or nativism. Samuel S. Cox told Douglas about the "Fusion Anti Nebraska" movement in Ohio and anticipated that "we can to day, whip the Whigs & Abolitionists clean out—niggers too."⁵³ Such Whigs, as evidenced by their associates, forfeited legitimacy as white political actors. Old Whigs could affiliate with a "compound and motley mixture of Northern Whigs, Free-soilers and Abolitionists,"⁵⁴ "a political conglomerate of all parties, headed by Abolitionism," or they could avoid racial debasement in the Democracy. The latter course guaranteed that a Whig "has preserved a proper self-respect, and has consented to no degrading coalition."⁵⁵

Even before they became Republicans, antislavery Whigs stood accused of blurring racial and gender lines, making their party inhospitable to conservatives. In 1851 William H. Seward reportedly defended a "mob" that, acting on a "higher law," had rescued a fugitive slave. Seward bailed them out of jail and hosted the "motley crowd of men and women, white and black" at his home. "Brothers in breeches and sisters in Bloomers, in part—have been feted, entertained, welcomed, shaken hands with, if not embraced, by" the New York Conscience Whig. This "miserable and degrading exhibition" was a manifestation of what would happen to the body politic when fanatics took power. Just as Seward had done at his home, antislavery fanatics would open the political sphere to "the whole motley group, (negroes and all . . .)."⁵⁶

Democrats and Whigs united in distress at fanatics' political practices, which seemed to portend black political agency. In comparison to the statesmanship of Whigs and Democrats, fanatics did not conduct themselves like white men—their political activities resembled those of enslaved Americans. Know-Nothings' nocturnal conclaves approximated slaves plotting revolt. An Alabama Democrat made this point by striking a contrast with Clay: "He fought long and manfully to the very last, this noblest Roman of them all fought openly, [and] *never stabbed his foe in the dark*."⁵⁷ Another southern Democrat questioned Old Whigs who would trust "twelve hundred millions of your property" to "this Secret and Midnight Junto." The conflation of the figurative danger of white fanatics and the literal danger of black fanatics played on southerners' primal nightmare. Former Whig congressman John Crisfield, referencing Republicans, alerted Marylanders that "the torch of the incendiary is blazing."⁵⁸

Fanatics sanctioned black politics at its most violent, conservatives warned. "Twenty years ago," recalled Democrat Fernando Wood in 1860, "the nation was divided into two parties, . . . each truly national, conservative and patriotic." They eschewed issues "which struck at the homes and the firesides of women and children." Fanaticism, however, now made "negro insurrection" a reality at the South.[59] Conservatives knew that enslaved African Americans were attuned to national politics and took encouragement from Republicans' condemnations of slavery. One southern Whig noted that "we see the effects of this in the increasing restiveness of a part of our population, in the often repeated escapes of our servants from the mildest form of servitude ever known." New England's Rufus Choate asked, "Should we like to see black regiments from the West Indies landing at Charleston or New Orleans to help on emancipation?" The fanatical impulse terminated in racial apocalypse in the conservative mind.[60]

Southern Democrats stoked such anxieties to steer Whigs away from Know-Nothings. During Virginia's 1855 gubernatorial race, the *Richmond Enquirer* asked, "What must be the feeling of every honest Whig to whom this hybrid ticket is presented?" Democrats had faith that "the independent and incorruptible Whigs of Virginia" would "not degrade themselves by the support of the Know Nothing nominees" and their "amalgamation ticket."[61] Southern Whigs dare not work with their former allies, Henry Wise reproached, because "Northern Whigs have become abolitionized." These antislavery Whigs were now Know-Nothings, and the party's secrecy allowed traitorous southerners to conspire with the same antislavery northerners who had already ruined Whiggery as a national force. Surreptitious collusion with Yankees suggested transgressive sexuality for Wise. "Behind the curtain," he insinuated, "these gentlemen can shake hands and honey-fuggle with one another. [Much laughter.] This is what is called conservatism."[62] In contrast to this corrupted "conservatism," the Alabama Democracy praised those "patriotic Whigs" who, "without regard to past political distinctions," resisted Know-Nothings and prevented the "South from being prostrated before the power of Northern fanaticism and misrule."[63]

Northern Democrats similarly deployed racism to discourage Whigs from aiding any party other than the Democracy. During Indiana's 1854 election, the Democratic *Indiana Daily State Sentinel* appealed to "liberal minded Whigs who are unwilling to be transferred to the mongrels." The paper applauded Illinois Whig Usher F. Linder after he "repudiated all connection with the piebald woollies in that State." In 1858 a correspondent reassured Congressman William H. English that "you may expect to hear good news from the old Gibraltar of Whiggery." The Democracy could depend on Harrison County, where Democrats were painting opponents as racial extremists by circulating one Republican candidate's approval of black suffrage and another's declaration that he would vote for an African American over a German American. English's correspondent explained, "I use these remarks to some advantage in my speeches and they will serve to show that the Rep party is fast becoming abolitionized."[64] Such a party, Democrats stressed, was uncongenial for Old Whigs or for any white man, regardless of section, ethnicity, or past partisanship.

In 1858, after years of such bipartisan dalliance, Frederick Douglass mocked what he deemed a contrived consensus on race and slavery. He parodied Fourth of July celebrations at which former Whigs spoke before Democratic gatherings. Rufus Choate "talked gloriously, vain-gloriously, and furiously, for it is no trouble for Mr. Choate to talk." The essence of his rhetorical "whirlwind" was to "seal our lips on the subject of American Slavery for the sake of the Union with the South." Douglass reported that Caleb Cushing, speaking at Tammany Hall, likewise sought to "convert the great celebration of Liberty into a means of making friends for Slavery," while Edward Everett demeaned himself by "his general reprehensible truckling to the dark spirit of Slavery." Even if a truce on slavery had not existed in the early republic, some Old Whigs were seeking one now, an effort Douglass lampooned as disingenuous and immoral. But he could not deny its effectiveness.[65]

Spurious Democracy?

This bipartisan "fraternization" both bemused and troubled Douglass. "The Silver Gray Whig shakes hands with the Hunker Democrat," he elaborated, "the former only differing from the latter in name." Douglass identified the source of this newfound affinity: "Both hate negroes, . . . and upon this hateful basis they are forming a union of hatred." Old antagonists were "rapidly sinking all other questions to nothing, compared with the increasing demands of Slavery."[66] Concern for slavery and the white man's republic facilitated fraternization among Democrats and Whigs. Democracy's detractors in the 1850s, and historians subsequently, have explained away the late antebellum Democracy as a hollow shell of its former Jacksonian self. These critics charged that Democrats renounced egalitarianism for a reactionary and undemocratic defense of slavery. No less an authority than the old Jacksonian Francis P. Blair flayed "the spurious Democracy" from which he departed to become a Republican. Full of southern aristocrats and Whigs, "men who never were Democrats" during Jackson's day, his old party appeared unrecognizable. The jettisoned Jacksonian ethos, borne by men like Blair, came to rest in antislavery politics, culminating in the Republican Party. In taking Jacksonianism out of the party of Jackson, historians further Blair's goal of insulating this intellectual tradition from a conservative organization of proslavery ideologues and their Doughface enablers. To make their case, historians point to the replacement of stalwart Jacksonians like Blair within the party by the Old Whigs whom Douglass attacked.[67]

Douglass and Blair exaggerated the conservative entente. The party of Jefferson and Jackson did not morph into the party of Hamilton and Webster because Democrats and Whigs diverged in their conservatism. When Louisiana Whig Judah P. Benjamin joined the Democracy in 1856, he told his fellow senators, "The democratic platform is identical with that of the old whig party; and, in declaring my adhesion to the former, I but change name, not principle." By "principle," Benjamin meant a broader political sensibility that Democrats and conservative Whigs shared by shunning fanaticism and sectionalism. "Converts from the old whig party," judged an Ohioan, "can never unite with the isms now extant and prefer enrolling themselves with the Democrats."[68] Aversion to *isms* did not, however, entail a common vision of governance and social order. Democrats premised their conservatism on liberal individualism, antistatism, white male egalitarianism, and democratic majoritarianism, all *isms* foreign to the conservative tradition represented by Whiggery. As a party and as a philosophy, Democracy was far from spurious in the 1850s.

Many Jacksonians did leave their party after the Mexican War, convinced of its abandonment of democracy and subservience to the Slave Power. Blair saw through Kansas-Nebraska's democratic facade. Its authors "never meant that the majority rule provided in the law should supplant the weight which the constitutional equality of the South would bring . . . to overcome the masses." Undemocratic and prosouthern, the Democratic Party left Blair; he didn't leave it. Walt Whitman cautioned "free work-people" against his former party "bawling in your ears the easily-spoken words Democracy and the democratic party."⁶⁹ Jacksonians turned Republicans argued that opposition to slavery's expansion represented workingmen's true interests. A Pennsylvania Republican concurred with his former Democratic colleagues that the two old parties once agreed on slavery, only that accord was in favor of territorial slavery's prohibition. The "sham Democracy of to-day," by condoning slavery's growth, reneged on its founders' legacy and would "degrade the freemen of the North to a level with the slave of the South."⁷⁰

Hannibal Hamlin, like his colleague Judah Benjamin, rose before the Senate in 1856 to do what many antebellum Americans found painful—he switched parties. Kansas-Nebraska prompted him to "declare here that I can maintain political associations with no party that insists upon such doctrines." Although he had tried to submerge his differences with the Democracy, he found that "tests are applied by that party with which I have acted to which I cannot submit."⁷¹ Hamlin's course met with mixed reactions back home. Ichabod Cole hoped that he would still "take the stump in Maine for Old Buck" in 1856, even though Hamlin objected to the party's platform. After all, this adviser entreated, Hamlin could overlook the planks he disagreed with and still campaign for James Buchanan, because platforms "have not much binding force after the election."⁷² Others, meanwhile, expressed "gratification" that Hamlin "had openly & boldly thrown off [his] allegiance to the mis-named democratic party, & had refused to follow it in its slimy course in pursuit of southern plunders."⁷³ It was time to slough off "the humbug of 'Popular Sovereignty'"⁷⁴ and differentiate the parties. Hamlin's belief that "the entire and unqualified sovereignty of the Territories is in Congress" contradicted popular sovereignty and drove him from the party. He stumped for himself in 1856 to become Maine's first Republican governor.⁷⁵

For all their histrionics over partisan waffling, Democrats appreciated the realignment's purgative effects. Before Hamlin left the party, his antislavery proclivities prompted one Democrat to alert Attorney General Cushing in 1854 about a dangerous political *"clique"* in Maine—"Hamlin *abolition democrats*" were working with "*abolition* whig[s]" against Kansas-Nebraska. Just as opposition to antislavery fanaticism created common ground for conservatives, opposition to slavery's expansion united antislavery Whigs and Democrats. This Democrat was willing to risk "break[ing] up the democratic party" in Maine to be rid of *"abolitionized," "pseudo* democrats" and to advance popular sovereignty, the "correct and *sound* democratic doctrine."⁷⁶ Another Maine Democrat insisted that a naval yard appointee cut ties with the apostate

Hamlin and with "every Black Republican Know Nothing," lest "he is willing to be charged with treason to his party."[77] Committing to popular sovereignty and excising "Black" Republicans like Hamlin promoted ideological—and racial—purity.

The realignment enhanced organizational and doctrinal clarity. Institutional winnowing occurred as the party shed "deserters," "denationalized democrats," and "parasite freesoilers."[78] An Indianan took a sanguine view of the 1854 election, when northern voters punished Democrats for Kansas-Nebraska, moralizing that "the catastrophe, sad as it is, will unite the *sound* democrats with greater cohesive force than they ever were before."[79] Bidding farewell to unsound Democrats enabled a recommitment to principle. A correspondent advised Stephen Douglas, "The Democracy has at this time new parties to oppose and it behooves us to take every opportunity to let its principles and measures [be] known to the public: and success is certain." In addition to advancing popular sovereignty, Democrats were committed to antinativism. James Buchanan observed in 1855 that "the Know Nothing party has produced one good effect" in Pennsylvania, in that "it has lopped many rotten branches from the Democratic tree." Buchanan would prune nativists and engraft instead "hones[t] & independent Whigs *willing to indorse & maintain the principles of our party.*"[80]

Alliance with "hones[t] & independent Whigs" did not dull Democratic ideology, because those Whigs were expected to *"indorse & maintain"* Democracy. In 1855 Maryland Whig Thomas G. Pratt endeavored to avoid outright "fusion" with the Democratic Party by urging "the conservative citizens of all parties and all sections . . . to unite as one party to preserve the Federal Constitution and Government." Yet Democrats never intended to give up their party—Old Whigs were expected to forsake theirs. Gideon Welles claimed "devotion to the good old cause" and lectured fellow New England Democrat Edmund Burke that the "obliteration of old lanmarks" was "injudicious." While some Whigs hoped "a union party would rise on the fragments of the old," Welles would "lament such an amalgamation in our state." Pratt had desired "a new party," because "mere fusion" would advantage Democrats and their still vibrant party. Underscoring the Democrats' stronger position, Pratt went on to campaign for the Democratic ticket in 1856. Bipartisan rhetoric was an effective overture to Whigs, who had always been less comfortable with partisan fervor, but it was not meant to dampen Democrats' own partisanship.[81]

Opponents cited the corralling of conservatives within the Democracy as evidence of ideological adultery. For one refugee from the party, the Democracy had always been a party of *isms*, but now, "from extreme radicalism, it has gone over to extreme Hunkerism." Whiggery's "transmigration" was to blame. When the Whig Party "died of political marasmus," the Democracy "inherited its legacy of conservatism." The "rollicking, dashing party of the past, full of revolutionary designs," atrophied as it "gathered to itself the conservatism of the North and of the South" and adopted "the specious cry of 'popular sovereignty.'"[82] The renunciation of the party's own fanatical heritage is what some departing Democrats regretted most. Even former Whigs concluded that, in catering to their decomposing party, "the so-called democracy of to-day" had abandoned "the principles of free government" in favor of "classification, caste,"[83] and "THE EXTENSION OF SLAVERY INTO FREE TERRITORIES."[84] A former Illinois Whig attributed this metamorphosis to the entrance of the "old exclusive silk-stocking whiggery" into the Democratic Party. "The plain old democracy" of Illinois backed Republicans, the true Jeffersonians.[85]

Yet Democrats maintained ideological orthodoxy along with organizational integrity. When Buchanan admitted Whigs into the party, it was "upon no other understanding than that they should join the party in principle & in heart."[86] While individual Whigs like Caleb Cushing had converted to Jacksonian Democracy, the Democracy itself held aloof from Whiggery. Republican James Harlan, a former Whig, asserted that members of his old party became Democrats because of shared proslavery sentiments but persevered in their political economy. Yet the Democracy did not become a party of tariffs and internal improvements. As many Democrats and Whigs repeated, these issues were dead. More importantly, Whigs were the ones who converged with Jacksonians, especially on race and slavery. When Whigs became Democrats, it was often because they found Jacksonian precepts like racial absolutism and limited government useful for neutering fanaticism and sustaining racial order. If conservative Whigs and Democrats aligned only on white supremacy, it still signaled the Democracy's enduring Jacksonianism, notwithstanding Whig interlopers.[87]

If their "radical, progressive, *revolutionary*" demeanor had turned "retrogressive and conservative"[88] in the 1850s, Democrats answered that their underlying Jacksonian beliefs had not withered. It was the conservative veneer Democrats placed on their principles that was new. One Democrat noted that

Republicans "charge upon the Democrats—that they are spurious, that they themselves wish to bring the government back to the principles of Washington and Jefferson." "The modern Democracy," he retorted, comprised "children of their sires." While welcoming Whigs represented a broadened rhetorical appeal, there was a simultaneous ideological deepening as Democrats reaffirmed Jacksonian dogma. Although united in rejecting sectionalism and fanaticism, Whigs and Democrats defined nationalism and conservatism differently. Democrats' adherence to liberal individualism and democratic self-governance distinguished their conservatism from Whiggery.[89]

That the Democracy enabled rumbustious self-government had long unsettled conservatives. Democratic editor William Leggett noted in 1835 that there had been "a deal of declamation about our ultraism" and "our Utopianism, Jacobinism, Agrarianism, Fanny Wright-ism, Jack Cade-ism; and a dozen other *isms* imputed to us." Democrats were supposedly "for overthrowing all the cherished institutions of society; for breaking down the foundations of private right, [and] sundering the marriage tie."[90] An 1840 pamphlet arraigned a leading "Loco Foco" for radicalism, citing his "zeal for the rights of man, [which] knows not the bounds of conservatism." Before jumping to the Republicans in the 1850s, Horace Greeley explained his preference for Whiggish "Order" over the Democrats' surfeit of "Liberty." Demagogic Democrats offered only "anarchy or mob-rule," the "worst of despotisms,—it is the rule of thousands of savage tyrants instead of one—it is a carnival of unbridled lust, brutality, and ruffianism." By the late antebellum era, established conservatives had difficulty overlooking Democrats' reputation as overzealous reformers with misplaced confidence in the people.[91]

Democratic territorial policy scared away many conservatives. Expansionism seemed subversive of orderly national development. S. S. Nicholas, a conservative Kentuckian, countered Democrats' contention that "our system may advantageously embrace an indefinite extent of population and territory." "Vigilance committees ruling California with lynch law, the northwest territories governed by martial law, Utah ruled by priest despotism, and civil war in Kansas" were the nation's Manifest Destiny under Democrats.[92] Authentic conservatives, moreover, would not have annulled a long-standing compact like the Missouri Compromise and thrust the nation into turmoil with popular sovereignty. A Pennsylvania Whig questioned the propriety of territorial emigrants governing themselves soon after settlement. Still, a good conservative, he counseled accepting Kansas-Nebraska rather than prolonging political "agitation."⁹³ Some Whigs, however, went beyond pragmatic acquiescence and appropriated popular sovereignty as a conservative measure. Maryland's Reverdy Johnson became one of Stephen Douglas's staunchest defenders. He lionized popular sovereignty as a "great national and conservative doctrine" because, when "the matter was . . . to be referred to the territorial people," it "imputed no censure, moral or political, to any section" and left the question "forever excluded from the halls of Congress."⁹⁴

Despite scattered endorsements, Whiggish discomfort with Democratic doctrine revealed a deeper ideological and cultural divide over majoritarian democracy and popular politics. In 1850 a former Whig congressman pleaded with a delegate to Indiana's constitutional convention to "let the Whigs remain as they have ever been, true men—conservative men—law and order men—Let them resist everything which approaches the *leveling down* system of locofocoism." He objected to Democrats' call for the direct election of judges. "The corrupt tendencies of our own nature" meant that "popular elections" would "tend to corrupt *candidates.*" Self-government was dangerous, because human nature was flawed. This Whig feared his party would capitulate because Democrats had framed their proposal as "a question of trust in the people." Democrats were "always talking of their confidence in the people & their readiness to trust them," which struck him as disingenuous "demagoguism."⁹⁵

Just as Democrats and conservative Whigs diverged over democracy, these fellow Unionists disagreed on nationhood and state power. Whigs and Democrats celebrated the Union and bemoaned sectionalism. Yet Whigs like Edward Everett echoed contemporary European nationalists in their evocations of a mythic nation organically binding individuals to one another in the present and across generations—a polity at odds with Democratic individualism and localism.⁹⁶ Whigs and Democrats also assigned the state different roles in national development. Both parties voiced support for "progress," which for Whigs meant an activist state creating economic opportunity, whereby "Government is regarded as the natural friend and servant of the People," a force to "increase their facilities for intercourse or intelligence." Whigs would construct nationalism with roads and canals.⁹⁷ Democrats, meanwhile, exulted that their "party crushed the financial monster, [and] swept away the cords of that wire work of national improvements—which if they had been fastened upon the country, would have bound down the nation."⁹⁸ Democrats furthered progress by liberating white men from consolidation and uniformity, which during the 1830s and 1840s meant Whiggery.

Democrats whetted their Jacksonianism by transferring their scorn for Whiggish statism to the homogenizing moralism of Republicans and Know-Nothings. Democrats often lumped Whigs and fanatics together as the progeny of primeval Federalism. The "shibboleth" of Federalism, and thence of Whiggery, judged Martin Van Buren, was "an inextinguishable distrust, on the part of numerous and powerful classes, of the capacities and dispositions of the great body of their fellow-citizens."[99] Fanaticism took up this undemocratic standard in the 1850s. Democrats collapsed generational differences when they spoke of the "federal abolition Whig press" in 1854 or warned in 1860 of "the old Federal and now the Black Republican doctrine that the people are not compitent to govern them selves."[100] Approaching 1850s politics as an ideological showdown with fanaticism begotten of Federalism and Whiggery honed Jacksonians' animus toward undemocratic concentrations of power. Some historians argue that Democrats and Whigs' reconciliation on a host of issues before the Civil War enfeebled partisan loyalty. While discrete disputes like state aid to internal improvements lost their potency, the underlying theoretical cleavage persisted. Party identity remained compelling for Democrats, because Federalism, Whiggery, and fanaticism shared an ideological taproot—an undemocratic fondness for an overweening state.[101]

Quarrels over state power stemmed from conflicting assumptions regarding individualism. Whigs wanted to mend human nature through social engineering, circumscribing individuals with moral admonitions, institutional impediments, and state supervision. The Whiggish Good Society consisted of individuals encased within organic units. Hierarchy and mutual obligations within collectivities such as the family or congregation would temper individual passions and foster a harmony of interests. The Anglo-Irish conservative theorist Edmund Burke called these cellular units within the organic body politic "little platoons." "To be attached to the subdivision, to love the little platoon we belong to in society," Burke elaborated, "is the first link in the series by which we proceed toward a love to our country and to mankind." Edward Everett made these platoons responsible for cultivating "civil liberty." The American Founders had bequeathed a progressive nation, but "they dug the foundation deep down to the eternal rock; the town, the school, the militia, the church." "The organized institutions of an enlightened community, institutions of religion, law, education, charity, art," were the nurturing broth of "republican independence."[102]

Proslavery conservatives also praised their peculiar platoons. The partisan vagabond John C. Calhoun called the slave states "an aggregate, in fact, of communities, not of individuals." "Every plantation is a little community" in which "labor and capital" were "perfectly harmonized," contributing to "the harmony, the union, and stability" of southern society. For Robert Toombs, the reciprocal "relation of master and slave" likewise generated "harmony." Even after he began cooperating with the Democrats, this former Whig seconded Burke by dismissing "vague notions of abstract liberty, or natural equality" and specifying that social context conditioned rights. Harmony and order originated in hierarchy, duty, and the recognition that "all individual rights [are] subordinate to the great interests of the whole society."[103]

Unlike Whiggish and proslavery conservatives, Democrats equated social harmony with the interaction of equal white men bearing individual rights. Democrats nested white male republicans in concentric circles of overlapping loyalties, emanating outward from the family to the Union. Their platoons, however, were platforms to power, not receptacles of restraint. Burke cautioned against prioritizing "personal advantage" over the good of one's little platoon.[104] Democrats advanced just such a utilitarian conception, placing platoons in a supporting role to the sovereign individual. Mastery within subsidiary social units like the household was a springboard for white men into politics on terms of equality. The interaction of equal white men in an atomistic social order was more stable than diffusing their power through organic networks of mutual obligations, which attenuated their autonomy and made them ripe for fanatical degradation.

Empowered individuals, an Alabama Democrat explained, engendered order by thinking for themselves and ridding society of "the utopian dreams of visionary philosophers." He discerned the effects of this individualism in "our institutions[,] its component parts possessing elements of discord[,] each acting independently of the other, each sovereign within its sphere, and yet all moving in harmony to the sublime unity of one government."[105] In 1858 a minister recoiled at "that democracy which openly denounces God, and proclaims a state free from every moral restraint." Without Christianity's guidance, he sermonized, "such a race as this is not a human race, but a great machine, . . . where freedom cannot exist and progress is a dream, and life itself but the submission of the soul to the animal."[106] Democrats, rooted in Enlightenment rationalism, not Romanticism or evangelicalism, were untroubled by such a clockwork society.

The individual's place in society constitutes the primary distinction between Whiggish and Democratic conservatism. Democrats adopted a "conservative" disposition in order to preserve the natural rights and equality of white men, concepts alien to traditional conservatism descended from Burke. Whigs and proslavery conservatives were better Burkeans and agreed that organic communities yielded social harmony by hemming in individuals. Yet social organicism assumed a gradation of rights. Democrats were happy to enmesh women and Americans of color in webs of dependency, but organicism applied to white men reminded them of a time before Jackson made whiteness and manhood the signifiers of the rights-bearing individual. Organicism also informed Whigs' nationalism, whereby state-led social development in the name of the collective good superseded individual autonomy and states' rights. Democrats, alternately, favored the replication of their already perfect republic across space, with unencumbered, diverse individuals pursuing their own progress.[107]

Social order achieved through the democratic interaction of sovereign individuals was an innovative conservatism. By the mid-nineteenth century, most American politicians agreed on the merits of democratic self-rule, at least in the abstract. Yet Democrats and traditional conservatives had arrived at that consensus by different routes. American conservatives, with Whigs following the lead of the Federalists, acclimated themselves to democracy and popular, partisan politics after the 1790s in order to survive in a political culture based on popular sovereignty. Recounting his 1831–1832 visit, Alexis de Tocqueville marveled that the theory of popular sovereignty had attained concrete expression in the United States: "In America the sovereignty of the people is not, as with certain nations, a hidden or barren notion; it is acknowledged in custom, celebrated by law." The Democracy had long treated popular sovereignty as more than a "barren notion" by placing it at the heart of their partisan ideology and political culture. Democrats began with the premise of democracy and were loath to restrain it. Forced to accept the Democrats' gambit, conservatives were comfortable "imposing fetters upon the power of the majority," according to a conservative jurist, as "those fetters are the very essence of civil liberty." That the heirs of Jefferson and Jackson were never begrudging in their "democracy" alarmed American conservatives from the 1790s through the 1850s.[108]

When Democrats invited Whigs into their party, they did not adopt their theoretical conservatism or their suspicion of democracy. Rather, Democrats wanted the reputation of Old Whigs to lend rhetorical heft to their redefinition of democracy and individualism as conservative means for preserving their happy republic. Conservative Whigs, in turn, shied away from Democrats' obeisance to the popular will. As the Indiana Whig exercised over an elective judiciary feared, democracy would permit the dark side of human nature to "rush forth with accelerated speed and hightened fury bearing away upon their maddened bosoms all these fine but frail castles that demagogues build upon their *pretended* 'confidence in the people.'"[109] The differences between these collusive conservatives expose the fundamental tension within Democratic political thought. There was something distinctly unconservative, maybe even fanatical, about territorial popular sovereignty specifically and majoritarian democracy generally. Many Democrats, who yearned to be America's conservative party, began to detect whiffs of this theoretical impasse. As would become clear, it was not Democrats' democracy that was spurious but their conservatism.

FIVE

Doughface Triumphant
JAMES BUCHANAN'S MANLY CONSERVATISM
AND THE ELECTION OF 1856

> I have no patience at the distrust of any southern man
> in regard to my course on the subject of Slavery.
> —James Buchanan, 1856

FRESH OFF his gubernatorial victory, Henry A. Wise traded in his homespun to play Democratic kingmaker. The Virginian believed he and his state should choose the party's 1856 presidential nominee. Wise recalled that when northern states fell to Know-Nothing fanaticism, the "indomitable democracy of Virginia, here and nowhere else, turned back the tide of revolution." "If any State could in justice claim the right to have her wishes preferred," Wise concluded, "it was Virginia, in this nomination." Some admirers promoted him for the honor. Senator George W. Jones of Iowa favored Wise's prospects, seeing as he had "already saved the Country from ruin."[1] Virginia Democrats had railed against both antislavery and nativism on behalf of slaveholders, Catholics, and immigrants. They raised the stakes of their state contest by defending all white men against fanaticism. Wise and his fellow Virginians in 1855, along with Indianans in 1854, pioneered Democratic strategy for the 1856 presidential election. Democrats approached these realignment elections as climactic confrontations between conservatism and fanaticism. Wise later connected his gubernatorial race to the presidential campaign and found that "by the position V^a took under my lead in 1855 [and] '56 the Democratic Party triumphed and the Union was saved."[2]

Despite his national notoriety, Wise stayed true to the man whose ambitions he had been advancing for years—James Buchanan of Pennsylvania. Wise and Buchanan shared a close political and "personal" friendship. "I am warmly attached to the man," Buchanan told a correspondent in 1855.[3] The Virginian had led slave-state delegates in balloting for Buchanan at the 1852 national convention. Buchanan appreciated these "exertions in my favor," which, he promised Wise, "shall ever remain deeply engraven on my heart."[4] Although failing to nominate Buchanan, Wise enjoyed playing power broker and, ever adaptable, took credit for Franklin Pierce's eventual nomination. During the canvass, he offered to help Pierce fend off accusations of drunkenness. Wise should know, because Pierce had "never had but one frolic" as a congressman, "and in that," the Virginian reminisced, "I was a partaker."[5] Wise finally succeeded at the 1856 Cincinnati national convention when Buchanan secured the nomination. True to form, Wise "gladly took the responsibility."[6]

James Buchanan led the Democracy to victory in 1856 in what he styled "one of the severest struggles recorded in our history."[7] His party triumphed over Republican John C. Frémont and Know-Nothing Millard Fillmore. In this confusing realignment election, Fillmore also had the backing of a rump convention of the defunct Whig Party, while Frémont received the nomination of the North Americans—nativist northerners who had abandoned the Know-Nothing Party after finding it insufficiently antislavery. Another national party had splintered. Faced with seemingly evanescent, sectional opposition, Democrats designated themselves the Union's sole national and conservative party. This transitional election marked the end of the second American party system and the commencement of institutionalized rivalry between Democrats and Republicans. Yet partisan stability was not apparent at the time. The only consistent element before and after the election was the Democracy, and the party's *national* success was impressive. Although the party would unravel four years later, the election saw the consolidation of Democrats' conservatism nationwide. The party did not, as some historians contend, run distinct campaigns against northern Republicans and predominantly southern Know-Nothings by emphasizing contradictory antislavery and proslavery messages in each section. Democrats' rhetorical timbre may have varied by region, reflecting their embrace of diversity over uniformity, but their underlying conservative and national message sounded throughout the Union.[8]

The Democracy could articulate a nationally consistent message because of the compatibility of its conservative principles with its conservative candidate. Democrats prided themselves on being a party of ideas. At the Cincinnati convention, when the Illinois delegation abandoned Stephen Douglas to make

Buchanan's nomination unanimous, they consoled themselves that the platform included popular sovereignty—the Little Giant's "great principle"—and that the "spirit of the Democratic party resides in its principles more than in its men."[9] Lofty pronouncements notwithstanding, the Democracy was a party of "men and measures."[10] As Douglas himself explained, "Democrats hold that it is not only essential to have sound principles, but to have honest and patriotic men to carry those principles into effect."[11] Democrats conflated principles and men by inscribing their beliefs onto leaders who embodied both philosophical tenets and laudable personal qualities. Buchanan thus had to prove his principles and his manhood in 1856. This meticulous politico flaunted a long history of denouncing fanaticism and catering to southern interests. He interpreted his election as the vindication of the "great conservative Democratic principles immediately involved in the late canvass on which the Constitution & the Union depend."[12] An ideal Democrat, however, had to subscribe to conservative principles *and* exhibit conservative manhood.

Buchanan was a lifelong bachelor, presenting both difficulties and opportunities for his party. Bachelorhood was a liability for any statesman in antebellum America. Buchanan may have advocated the proper principles, but as a man he seemed an unlikely choice to lead Andrew Jackson's aggressively masculine Democracy. Creative Democrats, nonetheless, argued that their candidate's manhood actually enhanced his conservative and national standing, and in doing so they laid bare the gendered assumptions of their party's conservative political culture. By recasting bachelorhood as a signifier of manhood, conservatism, and nationalism, Democrats turned Buchanan into a candidate whose conservative masculinity dovetailed with his conservative principles—the party's principles and the candidate's manhood aligned *because* Buchanan was a bachelor.

The 1856 election politicized the candidates' domestic lives and masculinity, revealing how intrinsic constructions of gender and domesticity were to antebellum political culture. The election was a contest among a bachelor, a husband, and a widower. Reporting on discussions of Buchanan's "celibacy"[13] and Frémont's elopement, the *New York Herald* asked, "What has all this to do with the capacity, public services and real eminence of our distinguished men?" Electioneers were seeking "some advantages of a domestic character—in this struggle to get into the White House." Yet the candidates' personal lives *were* political. In light of Know-Nothings' anti-Catholicism, for example, Frémont's marriage by a Catholic priest, alongside rumors about the Catholic ancestry of Fillmore's deceased wife and the education of his daughter at a convent, represented more than entertaining speculations. Indeed, the *Herald*, which endorsed Frémont, abandoned its principled course and ruled that Buchanan's bachelorhood disqualified him from the presidency.[14]

A Democratic pamphlet notified Pennsylvanians that "whenever he emerged from his quiet home, it was to demand the recognition of all the guarantees of the Constitution to all the States."[15] Buchanan endured scrutiny of his public record and private life, as Americans looked to the "home" from which he "emerged" into the political arena to anticipate whether he would favor free labor or plantation households as president. Political economy and culture produced sectionally distinct conceptions of the household and gender relations in antebellum America, with the archetype of the southern plantation household, a site of economic production using enslaved labor, set against the privatized northern bourgeois household shaped by the separate spheres ideology of the Market Revolution.[16] Answering accusations that their "Doughface" candidate would prioritize the interests of plantation households, Democrats responded that being unmarried and lacking his own family poised Buchanan to be an impartial arbiter among heads of household, especially those competing in the territories.

Democrats conformed the masculinity of their "dried up old bachelor"[17] to their conservative ideology. Newspaperman Murat Halstead predicted that Buchanan's lack of substance would permit his party "to give him, pending the canvass, either a Northern or Southern face, or both at once if it shall be deemed expedient." Buchanan would be able to "combine the radical and conservative sections of the party North and South," while "his great caution . . . will secure to him a large body of the Whigs."[18] For Democrats, this pliability bespoke the amoral neutrality essential to leading a diverse republic. An unattached bachelor, Buchanan's gender and sexuality heightened a Doughface's capacity for intersectional mediation. His bachelorhood signified a naturally conservative temperament—unlike fanatics, he did not submit to his passions in private or in politics. His roots in the early republic, legible on his aged countenance, comforted both loyal Jacksonians and Old Whigs. Unencumbered by his own northern family, furthermore, Buchanan would evenhandedly superintend all families, whether plantation households or those composed of free laborers. Buchanan's unorthodox manhood became the gendered equivalent of popular sovereignty—a consonance between man and principle, candidate and platform.

James Buchanan's Conservative Body

Stumping in Virginia, Henry Wise suggested that Buchanan's masculine vitality stemmed from a bachelor's sexual abstinence. "A man of sound morals," Wise conjectured, "he has conserved himself, and kept his faculties so well by a virtuous life, that he, now at the age of sixty-five, has many years of service still in him." Thus was the elder statesman available to be "called upon at the right time, for his conservatisms." Wise likely drew from health reformers like Sylvester Graham, who preached abstemiousness, dietary and sexual.[19] Buchanan's official campaign biography similarly gloated that "he had been reserved for the occasion" when antislavery and nativist fanaticism, which he had long opposed, "are just now the exciting questions in issue."[20] Buchanan's personal conservatism prolonged his life so that his ideological conservatism could prove useful. He was conservative in politics because he was "conservative" in private life, and the proof of his conservatism was his aged, yet virile, body.

Observers saw that conservatives such as Buchanan were manlier than fanatics, because fanatical degradation, the result of surrendering to the moral dictates of the *isms*, manifested itself physically. Democrats maligned fanatics' manhood by deriding them as "busy-bodies and meddlers" and "political prostitutes." Stephen Douglas ridiculed "all the little Abolition orators, who go around and lecture in the basements of schools and churches."[21] Fanatical women, likewise, "unsexed" themselves by trespassing in the political sphere and "addressing mobs of men in strains of vulgar violence."[22] In fabricating social problems to crusade against, fanatics were "misanthropic spirits"[23]—and they looked it. The *Democratic Review* described an antislavery meeting as composed of "lank-jawed, hungry-eyed men," "snuffy old women," and "sanctimonious, unhappy-looking individuals, in white chokers." Uptight in restrictive clothing, yet impassioned in their reformism, fanatics' physiognomy and even fashion choices betrayed their puritanical politics. Henry Wise's cousin endured one of Senator Henry Wilson's "harangue[s]" on Kansas. The appearance of the Massachusetts Republican's antislavery audience—"some six or eight sleek fellows in white chokers"—as well as the "coarse expression to his face" underscored their degraded self-righteousness.[24]

To contrast fanatics' debauched manhood with Buchanan's manly conservatism, Democrats had to overcome the stigma attached to unmarried men. A newspaper recounted a joke in which a student answered "why the noun bachelor was singular" by responding, "It is so very *singular* they don't get married." Lifelong unmarried men were a marginal group, susceptible to caricature as effeminate fops or hypersexual lechers, neither of which adhered to normative manhood in antebellum America.[25] Massachusetts Democrat Caleb Cushing, who never remarried after his wife's death in 1832, reflected on marriage when he received news of a friend's engagement in 1854. Cushing noted that remaining single could be a liability. Having long "urge[d] such a step" upon his friend, he conceded that "my example has not conformed with my doctrine." Marriage would benefit his friend because, "as the general rule, personal happiness, not less than true usefulness, and respectability, is only to be found in well-chosen matrimonial association."[26] Bachelorhood may not have precluded "personal happiness," but it did endanger one's political "respectability."

Bachelorhood was a political transgression, because republican citizenship presumed marriage and household mastery. Even Cushing mocked a "crusty old bachelor" to elicit laughter in a political speech. Bachelors served as negative foils for republican virtue.[27] Wise, despite his friendship with both Buchanan and Cushing, the latter serving as the Virginian's chief groomsman at his *third* marriage in 1853, turned to coercive state power to redeem bachelors. Unmarried men lacked virtue because they "selfishly evaded . . . the burthens in society of supporting a wife and family of children—the highest duty of a good citizen." The unconventional Virginian supported public education in his state, for which bachelors would bear the brunt of taxation. He queried, "Is there any old bachelor among you, who has no child of his own, who is too mean to support some poor man's daughter as his wife?" To compel them to contribute to the public good, Wise proposed that "rich bachelor[s] . . . should be taxed most of all."[28] During the 1856 canvass, Massachusetts Democrat Benjamin F. Butler jokingly recommended "send[ing] old bachelors to Utah" to combat polygamy.[29] Single men had to be turned into "good citizen[s]," because, as Cushing had observed, "true usefulness" required marriage.

Rebutting the image of bachelors as subpar men and statesmen, Democrats argued that bachelorhood undergirded Buchanan's masculinity and conservatism. Buchanan was not a lecherous old man untempered by feminine domesticity. Rather, his bachelorhood suggested physical self-control and correspondingly conservative politics. By never marrying or fathering children, Buchanan had renounced undiluted passion, whether defined as sexual excess or overzealous politics, both of which hypersexualized fanatics promiscuously indulged. References to "the even tenor of his life," "the spotless purity of his character,"[30] and his reputation as "a man of known caution"[31] had dual meanings: at home and in politics he was conservative. The "hot blood that distends the swollen veins of fanaticism" made reformers as "ardent"[32] in their politics as in their sexual pursuits, which included amalgamation and "free love."[33] Buchanan's sexuality showed that he instead boasted "a mind free from that species of insanity, where passion usurps the place of reason." "His inclinations," one southern Whig concluded, "are generally conservative."[34]

Unlike fanatical men, Buchanan's body projected manhood; his sexual restraint did not make him a stereotypically effeminate bachelor. In a political culture prizing assertive masculinity, lacking virility precluded statesmanship. Supporters thus depicted the portly, white-haired, sixty-five-year-old perpetual officeholder as "muscular," and "in the vigor of health, intellectually and physically."[35] According to the hyperbolic Wise, "Though his head be white as snow . . . he is yet vigorous in mind and body, and is a man of Herculean labor."[36] This portrayal takes on significance given that bachelorhood and advanced age provided easy fodder for critics. Democrats responded that Buchanan's bachelorhood accounted for his virility in old age—abstinence had kept him healthy. Testaments to his health and strength answered the charge that his marital status detracted from his manhood and statesmanship.

Buchanan's sexual and political moderation set an example for the nation's gender norms, which were being flouted by Republican women, especially Jessie Benton Frémont. Jessie Frémont attained celebrity status with the candidacy of her husband John. Republicans practically turned her into a candidate, and antislavery women mobilized for "John and Jessie."[37] Writing from New York City, she observed, "Just here & just now I am quite the fashion—5th Avenue asks itself, 'Have we a Presidentess among us[?]'"[38] Conservative Democrats grimaced. Bemoaning the fact that "the women of the north are certainly making long strides in a political direction," one Texas newspaper applauded "how much more like women the Buchanan and Fillmore ladies behave" when compared with "abolition females" organizing and even stumping for Frémont. Buchanan was stodgily unimpressed. When he modestly reminded his friend John Y. Mason of Virginia that his wife "ought not to think of apartments in the White House until after the election," he sniped that "our 'Jessie' has no doubt but that she will occupy these apartments." Buchanan acknowledged Frémont's unprecedented political incursion, even as he returned her to a domestic role.[39]

While Buchanan's "blameless life"[40] conveyed a conservative political disposition, the Frémonts' domestic life bespoke only fanaticism. Jessie and John had eloped. The Republican candidate's elopement, with no less than the daughter of old Jacksonian Thomas Hart Benton, made him "a bold defiant and unrepenting REBEL against the LAWS OF FILIAL DUTY, the LAWS OF HIS COUNTRY, and the LAW OF GOD."[41] A Democratic speaker scoffed at the Republican platform's denunciation of Mormon polygamy. Americans of all parties condemned Mormons as fanatics. But Republican opposition to Mormons' marital practices, this Democrat believed, was disingenuous, "considering the record of their candidate and ours on the marriage question." This may have been an allusion to the fact that Frémont's mother had left her husband for Frémont's father and that the Republican nominee was born out of wedlock.[42] Given two generations of the Frémonts' transgressive domesticity, Democrats concluded that the Republican's private life presaged fanatical politics. A bachelor, on the other hand, was the furthest thing from an adulterer or polygamist.

Democrats cited Buchanan's restrained sexuality to position him as the proper mean between passionate overindulgence and effeminate subservience. "His tall, commanding figure, his serene and lofty aspect" registered his conservative temperament, both as a man and a politician. A midwestern Democrat captured the correlation of Buchanan's political legitimacy and gender: "He is a man, & a statesman, & I can vote & work for him, for he is a *man*."[43] As in private life, Buchanan avoided political extremes. He was "progressive, not in the spirit of lawlessness, but in harmony with the steady advance of our institutions." At the same time, he was "conservative, not in veneration for antiquated abuses, but in sacred regard for rights which cannot be violated without destroying the fundamental law." Both his "personal character" and his "political orthodoxy" were reassuringly conservative.[44]

James Buchanan's Nonpartisan Body

A Whig defined the choice as between "a ripe and experienced statesmen [*sic*]" and the neophyte Frémont's "untried statesmanship."[45] By subduing his passions and "conserving himself," as Henry Wise put it, Buchanan had reached a respectable old age. His physical longevity harked back to the imagined stability of the early republic, allowing supporters, both Democrat and Whig, to link him to the second party system's heroes, both Whig and Democrat. Buchanan's simultaneously partisan and nonpartisan body intensified

Jacksonian loyalties and enticed leaderless Whigs. Democrats intended their evocations of the early republic, discernible in Buchanan's lengthy career and elderly countenance, to resonate with conservatives of all parties. Buchanan himself counseled unattached Old Whigs: "It is quite impossible that you should become Know Nothings or Free Soilers; & you have no place to go except to the Democratic party, which has now become the only true conservative party of the Country."[46] Buchanan and his party made nonpartisan appeals to "Democrats—Whigs—Conservatives of all parties" a cornerstone of their canvass.[47]

Democrats and Know-Nothings competed for former Whigs, and each party's candidate "aspire[d] to command the conservative army." Know-Nothings attempted to deny Democrats the mantle of conservative Unionism. Millard Fillmore, like Buchanan, was offered to voters as "a national and conservative man."[48] Some Whigs, including Fillmore, drifted into the American Party, irrespective of nativism and anti-Catholicism, to perpetuate Whiggery in a new guise. Ambitious Know-Nothings even hoped to woo Democrats into their conservative coalition. New York congressman Solomon G. Haven, one of Fillmore's advisers, anticipated that the renomination of Franklin Pierce would anger conservative Hunker Democrats. The Pierce administration had alienated many Hardshell Hunkers, especially in New York, by doling out patronage to Softshells and Free Soil Democrats. Haven predicted that "the Hards will not be satisfied" and that failure to secure the nomination of their leader, Daniel Dickinson, "will send them to our side." Buchanan's nomination, however, placated Hunkers. "Not only will he be supported by all true Democrats," Dickinson commended, "but by all conservative Whigs who are unwilling to forsake a national to rally under a sectional standard."[49]

A united Democracy continued to mourn the second party system to court conservative Whigs. In 1856 Democrats bolstered their case by offering Buchanan as a relic of that golden age. Buchanan was one who "yet lives," the "sole survivor" of "that race of giants" that included Jackson, Calhoun, Clay, Webster, and Polk.[50] The Pennsylvania Whig William B. Reed traced Buchanan's legislative history and found him aligned with the pillars of the second party system: "Mr. Buchanan vot[ed] with Clay, and Clayton, and Crittenden, and Rives, and Tallmadge, and White," "BENTON, . . . WEBSTER, and WRIGHT." Given this "consistent record," Reed affirmed that "Mr. Buchanan will make a safe, and moderate, and National President."[51] By connecting him with the titans of Jacksonian politics, Democrats tried to remove Buchanan from contemporary disputes by concluding that, like the deceased sages, he "has outlived detraction." Emulating Washington's dedication to his country, Buchanan "has grown gray in her service."[52] As with his sexual abstinence, installing him in America's political pantheon insulated him from the impassioned fanaticism of the 1850s. Buchanan's stature increased in proportion to how long he outlived the men who had once dwarfed him.

Dead Whigs even vouched for Buchanan from beyond the grave. The sons of Webster and Clay backed Buchanan, and both visited the Keystone State to channel their fathers in his support. James B. Clay conjured an endorsement on behalf of the Great Compromiser, as he shared with Kentucky Whigs, "How it is possible that I, my father's son, can reconcile it to myself to vote for Mr. Buchanan[?]" Clay could not acquiesce in Republicans' sectionalism or Know-Nothings' nativism and anti-Catholicism.[53] Old Whigs rose from the dead, or at least postponed departure, in order to aid the Democracy. A correspondent informed Democratic senator James A. Bayard that "Mr. Clayton is quite indisposed but says, if it becomes necessary he will take part in Delaware against Fillmore & Fremont." A short two months after the ailing John M. Clayton offered to assist the Democracy, Bayard received plaudits for his eulogy of the Delaware Whig.[54]

Many observers tried to divine the course of residual Whigs, such as the "fossiliferous Whiggery in New-England."[55] Conservative Whigs would have been "equally pleased with the election of Buchanan or Fillmore," provided Frémont and the "sectional" Republicans went down to defeat.[56] A New England bookseller related to a Democratic customer in Alabama that "Choate & Everett would be highly indignant if they were named in connection" with Know-Nothings. He forecast that "a large number of the prominent old Webster Whigs will be found voting for Buchanan this year."[57] Edward Everett, whose name would have lent gravitas to any party, ended up voting for Fillmore. Everett's course earned a gentle rebuke from Buchanan, who complained that he "witnessed with much regret & disappointment your march, under the lead of Mr. Fillmore, from the proud & patriotic old whig party into the ranks of the Know Nothings."[58] Robert Winthrop also enlisted in the Know-Nothing ranks, while Rufus Choate sanctioned fellow Whigs voting for Buchanan. New York's Hamilton Fish, upset that Fillmore could not win yet unable to stomach backing the Democrat, voted for Frémont "under a protest."[59] Many Old Whigs still preferred Buchanan to Republican radicalism. Everett explained to Buchanan that, although "I did not vote for you," he still wished the Democrat would "check the progress of sectional feeling" and revivify "the Conservative feeling of the North."[60]

Discomfort over Know-Nothingism made Buchanan the conservative choice for Whigs who thought nativism as serious an *ism* as abolitionism. Allen Hamilton, an influential Indiana Whig originally from Ireland, announced his support for Buchanan and revealed that he had been voting the Democratic ticket for two years. Hamilton explained his reasoning to William H. English: "The no nothing movement disgusted me." Buchanan, he reckoned, "will be conservative and pour oil on the troubled watters of our internal troubles." Bagging leading Whigs at the local level represented just as much a coup as securing an Everett or a Choate. Indiana Democrats fawned over Hamilton. Former congressman Thomas A. Hendricks was "greatly rejoiced when conservative & influential Whigs are found laboring with the democrats in this struggle."[61] A Maryland Whig parroted Democrats in his conclusion that the Democratic ticket would guarantee the "defence of Southern rights against the purposes of the Free Soilers, and defence of the rights of conscience in religious belief, and of the Constitutional rights of our naturalized citizens against the purposes of the American party."[62] For these Whigs, the Democracy was the only party that rejected *all* of the *isms*.

Yet Whiggery's influx did not cleave the Democracy from its Jacksonian roots, with Buchanan's aged body anchoring the 1850s party to that of Old Hickory. Democrats dredged up Buchanan's service during the party's heroic past and his personal ties to Jackson to energize partisans. The august Martin Van Buren, who could no longer attend rallies due to "advanced age," backed Buchanan in a public letter, lending his Jacksonian aura to a man whom Jackson had never liked. Amid their heated party battles, Jackson and Henry Clay had aligned in mistrust of the conniving Buchanan.[63] This fact did not prevent Democrats from associating Buchanan with the Old Hero, with one pamphlet noting, "Probably the most interesting part of Mr. Buchanan's history, was his early and effective support of General Jackson for the Presidency."[64]

Democrats often reminded Old Whigs that the issues of the second party system were dead. But when attempting to activate Jacksonian loyalties, they rehashed the great party struggles, with Buchanan in a starring role. In epic clashes such as those over the Bankruptcy Bill and internal improvements, Buchanan had demonstrated his devotion to "the cause of equal rights—for special privileges to none, and for justice to all."[65] The platform adopted by the

1856 Cincinnati national convention reiterated traditional Jacksonian maxims, such as acknowledging "the popular will" and ensuring that "the Federal Government is one of limited power" and "rigid economy." Democrats fitted these planks alongside those touting Kansas-Nebraska and disparaging the "political crusade" aimed at "Catholic and foreign-born" Americans. The continuity of Jacksonian thought was textually laid out in a platform that joined old and new issues and was embodied in a venerable old candidate whose career spanned both eras. Buchanan, Van Buren noted, was approaching "the evening of his life."[66] In the sectional politics of the 1850s, there was no clearer qualification for office in the minds of conservatives than being tied to dead men or being near death oneself. Buchanan was the last vestige of a nobler era, and it fell to his wisdom and conservatism to quell sectionalism and restore nationalism.

James Buchanan's National Body

According to Henry Wise, Buchanan's selection was "due to Pennsylvania," as well as to Virginia. Wise envisioned an intersectional coalition of the "great tier of Middle States," centered on the partnership of the "'sour krout' democracy" of the Keystone State and Virginia's "'red waistcoat' democracy of Thomas Jefferson." Although Wise's proposed alliance did not have the same ring to it as Van Buren's union "between the planters of the South and the plain Republicans of the North" a generation earlier, a Virginia-Pennsylvania backbone would reinvigorate the intersectional party that had earlier rested on Van Buren and Thomas Ritchie's New York–Virginia axis. The Democratic Party would continue to be *the* national party.[67]

The union of Wise and Buchanan personified Democrats' Unionism. The two men conflated their friendship with the political dalliance of their states. Wise vowed that "Virginia and Pennsylvania shall forever be united in democratic and patriotic triumphs." After his victory, the president-elect gushed to his "best friend" in the Old Dominion that "I respect, nay I venerate Virginia & my gratitude to her will end only with my life. She & Penn[a] united can preserve the Constitution & the Union, & may Heaven grant that they may never be separated." "As to our selves individually," he reassured Wise, "I entertain no apprehensions."[68] The childless bachelor and sagacious old statesman could effect this partnership between slave states and free states and was "the most congenial candidate to national men,"[69] because he could be father to the entire nation. Head of neither free labor nor plantation household, Buchanan embodied popular sovereignty by neutrally refereeing sectional passions, moral visions, and contrasting conceptions of the family.

Democrats presented bachelorhood as a boon to national statesmanship. After Buchanan's nomination, Pennsylvanian Samuel W. Black endeavored to "set Mr. Buchanan right on the matrimonial question." He told the raucous Cincinnati convention that, "though our beloved chieftain has not, in his own person, exactly (laughter) fulfilled (renewed laughter) the duties that every man owes to the sex, and to society, there is a reason. Ever since James Buchanan was a marrying man, he has been wedded to THE CONSTITUTION, *and in Pennsylvania we do not allow bigamy.*"[70] Democrats' claim that Buchanan "married his Country" prompted a "spunky Republican" to quip that Frémont had already "run off with Tom Benton's daughter, and next November he will run off with *Jem Buchanan's wife*, old as she is!" Democrats nonetheless contended that Buchanan should not be faulted for not fulfilling the "duties" of a man because he had "fulfilled" his "duties . . . to society" by abstaining from a worldly union of flesh to focus on preserving the Union of states.[71]

Childlessness would also enhance Buchanan's statesmanship. Another Pennsylvanian predicted that "Mr. Buchanan will make a good President. . . . He has no children [and] not many relations to provide for." Bereft of progeny, the nation was his charge. One pamphleteer glowed that "like Washington, Madison, and Jackson, Mr. Buchanan is childless. God has denied these benefactors children, 'that a nation might call them father.'"[72] Buchanan once referenced his childlessness to mollify a delegation of Democrats affiliated with the Young America movement, who were curious if he was just another of the "old fogies" retarding national progress. He assured them "that he was an old democrat and childless" and "had concluded long ago to maintain the best relations with the young men of the country to whom his attitude was almost paternal."[73] Childlessness made Buchanan a natural political harmonizer.

Democrats promised that, as the impartial father/statesman, Buchanan would pacify the territories, the site of contestation over slavery under popular sovereignty. Buchanan would ease sectional tension by "separat[ing] these angry foes, not by ideal lines and unequal privileges, but by giving the right to each to enter upon and occupy ample and abundant territory." Accepting his nomination, Buchanan postured as a wise patriarch managing quarrelsome children, advising, "Let the members of the family abstain from intermeddling with the exclusive domestic concerns of each other."⁷⁴ Free labor families and plantation households would rest secure under the paternal gaze of James Buchanan, whose lack of a family strengthened his ability to guarantee the manly autonomy and democratic self-determination of all white heads of household.

Buchanan's bachelorhood enabled his party to hoist him upon their platform. The Cincinnati platform embraced popular sovereignty as "the only sound and safe solution of the 'slavery question' upon which the great national idea of the people of this whole country can repose in its determined conservatism of the Union." Politicians used platforms to differentiate parties in a metaphorical sense; according to historian Jean H. Baker, platforms served as "a special place for Democrats to stand during the campaign." A Maine Democrat who attended the Cincinnati convention scorned "any of our Democrats that thinks the platform is to hard for their feet barefooted," continuing, "they better not step on and leave their room for others." And "ample room for all" there would be, for "the platform extends from one end of the nation" to the other.⁷⁵ All could stand on the platform, because popular sovereignty ostensibly treated all white men as equals. Platforms also facilitated the merger of men and principles, with a nominee bound by the planks upon which he stood. After his nomination, Buchanan mused, "Being the representative of the great Democratic party, and not simply James Buchanan, I must square my conduct according to the platform," which he judged to be "sufficiently broad and national for the whole Democratic party." The doctrine of popular sovereignty was mapped onto Buchanan's manly form, as the childless bachelor personified treating all white heads of household equally. Buchanan's conservative and national body became his party's platform. Like the platform, he was "a man upon whom all can unite."⁷⁶

James Buchanan's Southern Manhood

Preparing for his daughter's nuptials in the summer of 1856, Henry Wise schemed about the upcoming election. Relishing his national prominence, he invited his old friend not simply to attend the wedding but to escort his daughter. Buchanan sent his regrets, explaining that he could not "give away the bride" because he "could not, without giving great & perhaps just offences, leave home under existing circumstances." Convention barred Buchanan from appearing to campaign. Wise had ignored that stricture in 1855 by traversing Virginia to lambast Know-Nothings as beholden to untrustworthy Yankees.

Stumping for Buchanan in 1856, he needlessly reminded Virginians that "no one here or elsewhere will say I am an anti-slavery man."[77] Yet the steadfastly proslavery, occasionally secessionist, and thrice-married Wise was now entrusting white southern womanhood to a northern bachelor. By doing so, he vouched for Buchanan as a manly protector of white women from the imagined sexual ravages of enslaved insurrection. This pervasive fear reached acute levels in 1856, a distorted reflection of enslaved southerners' interest in the Republican campaign.[78] In this charged atmosphere, Democrats offered white southerners a candidate who would safeguard their households by rhetorically rendering Buchanan as a southern paternalist, an image that also resonated with northern audiences. That a northern man so enthusiastically upheld southern honor underscored the conservative nationalism of this Doughface and his Democracy.

Democrats drew on the elasticity of southern manhood and their party's own masculine culture to advance otherwise unorthodox men. In the slave states, manhood, and consequently political legitimacy, derived from two sources—household mastery and communally conferred honor. *Mastery* stemmed from control over household dependents, including white women and especially slaves. Despite mastery's domestic prerequisites, the public dimension of southern *honor,* performed before and mediated by the community, made manhood flexible. One could lay claim to manhood by performing mastery in public, and the public conferral of honor could compensate for an absence of mastery at home.[79]

Childless and unmarried southern men, along with those whose private lives transgressed norms of propriety, could demand public recognition of their honor and, correspondingly, their statesmanship. Vice President Richard Mentor Johnson, for instance, had long-term sexual relationships with women he owned.[80] Alexander H. Stephens, diminutive, sickly, and a lifelong bachelor, also achieved enviable political standing. One of Buchanan's intimate friends was fellow Democratic bachelor William Rufus King of Alabama. King successfully ran for vice president in 1852, although lamenting that his *"Friend Buchanan"* did not receive the presidential nomination, for which his "purity of character" and "long political experience" qualified him. Buchanan, in turn, expressed satisfaction to Wise over his friend, "one of the best & purest men I have ever known," receiving the second spot on the ticket.[81]

Both bachelors headed proxy families of nieces and nephews. They were similar to Andrew Jackson, with his legion of dependents but no biological children. Both men also took their favorite wards abroad on diplomatic errands, and Buchanan acted as surrogate father to his niece, Harriet Lane, who presided over his White House.[82] King was one of the dominant forces in Alabama politics dating back to that state's territorial phase. In their eulogies upon his death in 1853, several congressmen felt impelled to mention that King paled in comparison to the demigods who preceded him—Calhoun, Clay, and Webster. Yet his "brother Senator[s]" also recalled King's "manly firmness" and found that "his example in all the relations of life, public and private, may be safely commended to our children." According to R. M. T. Hunter, King's "public honors" resulted from his unimpeachable "personal honor."[83] King's status as a respected legislator and party leader hinted at the potential for shaping a bachelor's malleable manhood to the sectionally distinct norms of southern masculinity. Democrats went even further in 1856 to depict Buchanan, a northern bachelor, as a southern patriarch.

Master of neither wife nor children, King *was* a slaveholder. He thereby benefited from a tangible criterion of southern mastery and political legitimacy—he was master of, in the words of a campaign biography, "his people."[84] The best that Buchanan's supporters offered was that he had long broadcast his paternalism beyond his own home by protecting other men's dependents and their right to own slaves. Buchanan did head his own "family," with his campaign biography noting that "his family consists of himself and niece." But Buchanan's domestic responsibilities extended beyond Harriet Lane. To counter speculation that "he has no sympathy or regard for the [female] sex," campaign literature highlighted his role as the "perpetual benefactor of the poor widows" in his hometown of Lancaster. He acted as a surrogate husband and father by establishing a fund to provide "fuel for indigent females." As a result, "many a desolate hearth has been made glad by his noble charity" and mothers "teach their little ones to bless the name of James Buchanan." Democrats recycled these maudlin testimonials to prove that their unmarried candidate knew how to protect women and children and to show that his paternalism rippled outward to enfold numerous households.[85]

Buchanan's domestic life forecast the sectional fraternization he would oversee as president. He reposed at his pastoral Wheatland estate in southern Pennsylvania after the manner of a country squire. Hardly a "cold blooded, imperturbable and selfish old bachelor,"[86] Buchanan was noted for his "warm-hearted friendship," "hospitality," and "the hold he has upon the affections of the people among whom he resides." "The Sage of Wheatland" was comfortable among the southern gentry, who were frequent guests at his home.[87] Intersectional cohabitation was familiar to the Pennsylvanian. He related to a South Carolina friend how he had lived with William R. King "for many years as a brother" in a congressional boardinghouse. One visitor to Wheatland later recounted "finding in his library a likeness of the late Vice-President King, whom he loved (and who did not?)."[88] Wise trekked to Wheatland after the election to see "Old Buck," but refused a cabinet position. Although the Virginian declined to join the president-elect's official family, Buchanan told him that "I never enjoyed a visit from any man more in my life than I did your recent visit."[89] During the campaign, additionally, "many prominent whigs [were] at his house."[90] The patriarch of his party, Buchanan knew how to maintain a harmonious political household.

Old Buck's paternalism percolated beyond his home to encompass white southern women. Reaching back to congressional debates over the reception of abolitionist petitions in 1836, Democrats found that Buchanan had consistently defended plantation households. Arguing that Congress should not entertain such petitions lest they incite slaves, Senator Buchanan had proclaimed, "Touch this question of slavery seriously—let it once be made manifest to the people of the south that they cannot live with us, except in a state of continual apprehension and alarm for their wives and their children, for all that is near and dear to them upon the earth,—and the Union is from that moment dissolved." Such statements amounted to motifs in Buchanan's public speeches for the rest of his career. Twenty years later, the victorious Buchanan admonished the North: "With the South it is a question of self-preservation, of personal security around the family altar, of life or of death."[91]

In the conservative mind, fanaticism facilitated black political agency, culminating with interracial sex and the rape of white women. That Buchanan knew *"the consequences of abolition"* as well as any slaveholder solaced southern Democrats. Supporters publicized Buchanan's opposition to abolitionists' petitions and their mailings in the South. Wise, remembering his state's history, recollected, "When the issue of incendiary publications arose, he voted to violate the very mails rather than permit the agitators of a Nat Turner insurrection to light the fires of incendiarism."[92] While protecting southern women, Buchanan's own virility was never a threat. Foregrounding his bachelorhood, Wise and other Democrats had rhetorically neutered the aged northerner. Antislavery Americans cringed at the sexual depravity of "the slave driver's harem," referencing the access slaveholders forced upon enslaved women's bodies. If the slaveholding South was indeed a seraglio, then James Buchanan was its eunuch.[93]

Democrats cited Buchanan's protection of southern families from abolitionist meddling to prove that he was both more conservative than Millard Fillmore and more prosouthern. John W. A. Sanford Sr., a Know-Nothing candidate in Georgia, advised his Democratic son in Alabama that the issues of the second party system had "ceased to be subjects of discussion" and that, between Buchanan and Fillmore, "the question is how do they stand affected upon the subject of negro slavery." He doubted his son possessed "ingenuity enough to show a marked dissimilarity between" them. Democrats warmed to this challenge, prompting another Know-Nothing to report that "Buchanan's folks in the South are getting very much alarmed and are pitching into Mr. Fillmore . . . most relentlessly."[94] Southerners consulted both men's exhaustively reprinted record. Buchanan supported the gag rule against abolitionist petitions, while Fillmore voted with the likes of Joshua R. Giddings to consider them. Both Fillmore and Frémont, Democrats warned, were allied with Giddings, a fanatic who "look[ed] forward to the day when there shall be a *servile insurrection* in the South."[95]

Tennent Lomax, a Democrat in Georgia, compiled an authoritative scrapbook of the election. He recorded numerous bets he made on the race's outcome—wagering "one basket champagne," for instance, "that Buchanan would get more northern electoral votes than Fillmore." Most of his compendium featured annotated press clippings that exhaustively rehashed the two men's positions on issues such as "abolition petitions" and "incendiary publications." Fillmore, for example, seemingly supported citizenship for "free colored foreigners" in 1842, while, more recently, his congressional allies voted for the expulsion of Preston Brooks after his "deserved chastisement" of Charles Sumner. Southerners like Lomax pored over candidates' political histories before risking a vote for a Yankee.[96]

Democrats also deployed the politics of slavery against Know-Nothings by linking them to Republicans, a party more susceptible to charges of antislavery fanaticism. The American Party allegedly contained "Abolition Know Nothings [who] are out for Fremont." Know-Nothings and Republicans shared a common fanatical ideology, with John C. Frémont "the candidate for the Presidency of conjoined fanaticisms." The two parties were also connected on an organizational level through fusion movements.[97] Buchanan used racially and sexually suggestive language when he observed that in Pennsylvania, "the Black Republicans & Know nothings are coquetting with each other,—alternately abusing & coaxing."⁹⁸ "Every vote thrown for Mr. Fillmore is more or less an aid to John C. Fremont, to the extent that it may weaken James Buchanan," Democrats cautioned. The Know-Nothing ticket would split the conservative vote, ensuring Frémont's victory in the Republican-controlled House of Representatives. "This proves that the ticket," Henry Wise shrieked, "is a mongrel ticket—that the offspring of it is . . . a mulatto, or . . . a Mulungeon," with "Mulungeon" referring to free people of color of Native American, African, and European ancestry.⁹⁹ Democrats did not wage separate campaigns against Republicans and Know-Nothings but lumped them together in their nationwide defense of a racially pure white man's republic.

Buchanan circulated a letter among delegates at the Cincinnati convention pronouncing, "I have no patience at the distrust of any southern man in regard to my course on the subject of Slavery." Buchanan identified with white southerners politically and personally. During the election he bemoaned to a southern friend that the British were "gloating over the prospects of the emancipation of *our* slaves & the dissolution of the Union" (emphasis added).¹⁰⁰ Buchanan was also sound on white supremacy. His impartial paternalism applied to race relations. No past actions attested to "Mr. Buchanan's want of feeling to the colored men." Even so, his paternalism did not extend unduly to African Americans. "In his proverbial benevolence," he had never given "preference to the negro over the men of his own color and blood." Northern audiences read that Buchanan "regards this as a government of white men, and not a government of colored men."¹⁰¹

The politics of slavery played well before northern audiences in 1856. Although many northern Democrats counted themselves "the opponent[s] of the extension of slavery," they would still "guard the rights of the South under the Constitution." Free-state Democrats congratulated themselves on sticking up for the South and, echoing their candidate, often faulted their region for sectional tension. In a victory speech, Buchanan lectured, "All we of the North have to do is to permit our Southern neighbors to manage their own domestic affairs, as they permit us to manage ours. It is merely to adopt the golden rule."¹⁰² Northern Democrats understood Buchanan's stance not as Doughfacism but as manly Unionism—"an exhibition of firmness only too rare in those days among Northern men." Southerners likewise perceived Buchanan's advocacy of their unique rights not as preferential treatment but disinterested statesmanship. Encouraging the South Carolina Democracy to send a delegation to Cincinnati in 1856, which would be the state party's first delegation to the national convention in over a decade, James L. Orr anticipated that "the aid of the conservative men at the North" would "enable us to save a constitutional Union," as well as "ourselves and our institutions." The South could depend on these northerners, "who in their section have done good service against political abolitionism."[103] As northern fanaticism was the aggressor, to which southern fanaticism only responded, the South expected northern Democrats to tamp down zealotry at home for the good of the Union. Democratic nationalism found its embodiment in the southern-sympathizing Buchanan.

James Buchanan's Doughface Body

The Democracy's foes agreed that Buchanan was "the embodiment of the platform,"[104] so that belittling his gendered body was a means of disparaging Democratic principles, particularly popular sovereignty. Democrats contended that popular sovereignty was sectionally neutral. Their national platform meant that they did not have to opportunistically portray Buchanan as "a slave-holder at the South and an abolitionist at the North." Yet they had long tailored the doctrine to sectional audiences, telling northerners that settlers could vote against slavery in the territorial phase, while assuring southerners that it could only be banned upon statehood.[105] Rivals claimed that Kansas-Nebraska "was read one way at the South and another way at the North" in order to embarrass Buchanan as a sectional candidate.[106] A Frémont partisan attacked Buchanan because the proslavery "operation of squatter sovereignty" would "force slavery into Kansas." A southern Know-Nothing reached the opposite conclusion and reproached southerners for backing Buchanan, who, when "he gave the platform a voice," endorsed the northern version of popular sovereignty.[107] Democrats' supposedly national candidate easily succumbed to the stigma of sectionalism.

Along with sectionalism, opponents detected unmasculine dependence in Buchanan's symbiosis with his platform. Maryland's Charles B. Calvert juxtaposed Millard Fillmore's "manly independence, in qualifying his acceptance of the American platform" with "the subserviency of the acceptance of his competitor." Fellow Know-Nothing supporter Sam Houston observed that it was impossible to "separate the candidate and platform" because Buchanan "has merged himself in the platform."[108] Buchanan's personal shortcomings paralleled his political cravenness; Houston reportedly felt that his "great private fault was being a bachelor."[109] Know-Nothings had arisen as a reformist crusade against established parties. Their antipartisan culture primed them to interpret Buchanan's "entire dependence on the party that nominated him" as proof of political corruption in addition to unmanly degradation.[110]

That Buchanan "renounce[d] his Identity" when mounting a proslavery platform espousing popular sovereignty also convinced antislavery Americans that he was "the pliant instrument of the Slave power that nominated him."[111] In a speech in the Democratic candidate's hometown, Republican Thaddeus Stevens hissed that "there is no such person running as James Buchanan. He is dead of lockjaw. Nothing remains but a platform and a bloated mass of political putridity." One Republican pamphlet equated adhering to the platform with surrendering to the South, having Buchanan sing:

The South "demands more room"—the West and North must bow,
And the East must knuckle down—and the Niggers hold the plow,
    For "Platform" James am I.

Republicans agreed that Democrats could stand upon the body of "'Platform' James," although for them, his was an unmanly, proslavery body.[112] In one critical cartoon, a fire-eater and an enslaved southerner sit atop Buchanan's prone form, suggesting the degradation of allowing his body to serve as a prosouthern platform (fig. 2).

Antislavery Americans read Doughfaces' unsavory principles on such degraded bodies. Doughfaces constituted a distinct "race" or "species."[113] While for Democrats fanatics exhibited excess passion, their critics charged that Doughfaces suffered from a lack thereof after offering up their manhood to the Slave Power. They were "pale-blooded"—one of these northern men with southern principles had "not a drop of manly blood coursing through his veins."[114] Doughfaces failed to defend the North against southern aggression, and their doughy pallor indexed their deficient masculinity. Doughfaces were distinguished by "both *softness* and paleness, and these again a lack of *firmness*, or unmanliness."[115] Becoming slaves themselves, they also forfeited whiteness. A female correspondent to Frederick Douglass's newspaper questioned President Pierce's statesmanship by painting him as "a man of easy,

Figure 2. "The Democratic Platform," 1856. A fire-eater and enslaved southerner sit atop James Buchanan's body, the Democratic Party's platform. (Library of Congress, Prints and Photographs Division, LC-DIG-pga-04795)

gentlemanly manners; but he looks *far* more fit *to be ruled* than *to rule*." One northern Democrat confided that he "hate[d] a Dough-face" such as Pierce and hoped instead to "get a *white man* nominated at Cincinatti." While for him Buchanan passed this test, few Democrats proved acceptable to most antislavery northerners.[116]

Bachelorhood, Republicans alleged, only exacerbated Buchanan's unmanly Doughfacism. Both the lascivious rake, "who shall carry into the White House the crude and possibly gross tastes and experiences of a bachelor," and the effeminate man, who suffered from "a lack of some essential quality," populated campaign literature.[117] A newspaper correspondent writing under the pseudonym "An Ex-Old Maid" employed sexual innuendo: "Imagine the disgrace of having our National Palace converted into a bachelor's den; . . . our National fire poked by a single tong!" Bachelorhood jeopardized political legitimacy along with manhood. The same writer declared that "an Old Bachelor is at most but a half man." If this did not justify opposition to Buchanan, the writer then inquired, "How can such a person make more than a half-President?" Denunciations of Buchanan's bachelorhood, whether flippant or vicious, conveyed the message that statesmanship necessitated normative manhood and domesticity. The excitement surrounding Jessie Frémont showed that many Americans believed a married woman worthier of occupying the White House than the Democratic bachelor.[118]

Buchanan's abdication of domestic responsibilities precluded national statesmanship. That Buchanan never entered into marital union led many to ask whether he could administer the Union of North and South. As a Republican campaign song put it, Buchanan "is afraid of the girls and to union a foe."[119] John and Jessie, although native southerners, adhered to the norms of free labor society and bourgeois domesticity. As such, another song contrasted the Democratic bachelor with the Republican couple who represented the union of sections:

> The "White House" has no place
> That a bachelor can grace,
> So with "Jessie" we'll adorn it anew!
>
> "Fremont and Jessie" will be faithful;
> "Union"—"of hearts" be their sway,
> 'Tween the sunny, balmy South,
> And the steadfast, busy North,
> The dawn of FREEDOM'S GLORIOUS DAY![120]

The two senses of "union" were complementary. By conflating his marriage with the Union, Republicans refuted accusations that Frémont's election would amount to a sectional victory. Democrats employed the same analogy to bolster their nationalism. When Indiana governor Joseph A. Wright married a Kentuckian in 1854, papers in both states imbued the nuptials with political significance: "Indiana and Kentucky have always stood side by side, when danger threatened the unity of States, and now they have clasped hands across the altar of love." The governor of Kentucky helped Governor Wright celebrate this "union of hearts" and "union of States."[121] The metaphor foundered, however, with a bachelor candidate. As a Republican explained of Buchanan at a New York City mass meeting, "No wonder this man is a sectionalist. He was never for union in all his life."[122]

Bachelorhood amplified Buchanan's Doughfacism by blinding him to the plight of white northern families. He had "been rejected by the fair ladies of Pennsylvania" as a suitor, and northerners refused to vote for him "from the same reason which has kept him a bachelor—his utter want of human sympathy."[123] As president, he would not protect northern women in Bleeding Kansas, where Democratic territorial policy yielded "blighted maiden-wreaths and soiled matron-veils of Northern wives and daughters." Denying that the Democracy was friendlier to the foreign-born, a Republican speaker alerted German Americans that Buchanan could not empathize with their families in the territories. He cautioned, "The politicians who propose to the Germans, or to any other class of people, having families to provide for, to vote the Cincinnati platform, must think them insane." "It may be all very well for an old bachelor [applause and laughter] in easy circumstances, who has no posterity to take care of, to stand on that platform," he elaborated, but "we, for our part, have not the heart in us to take their future bread out of their mouths, to give it to a few great gentlemen, who live quite comfortably without it, on the labor of their slaves."[124] Selfish bachelors had more in common with idle slaveholders than they did with enterprising northern families.

Despite Republican attacks, James Buchanan and the National Democracy secured a plurality of the popular vote. Democrats throughout the Union, and around the world, sighed with relief. William T. King, nephew of the late vice president, relayed from Rome that Americans abroad received "the news of the election of Buchanan" with "profound satisfaction." From his diplomatic post in Paris, Henry Wise's son told his father that "until today, many of our good democrats here have looked very blue." But when word arrived, Buchanan's friend John Y. Mason, the American minister to France, hastened to wake the younger Wise and share the "gratifying news."[125] Historians have characterized the election as a "victorious defeat" for the young Republican Party, heralding sectional politics. Democrats swept the South, save Maryland, which went for Fillmore, while Republicans won eleven free states to Buchanan's five. Yet we would do well to read the results as testament to the resonance of Democrats' conservative nationalism and their gender appeals. "Fanaticism has been rebuked," rejoiced a Georgian, "in the election of that good and great man Mr. Buchanan as President."[126]

It required ingenuity to make Buchanan a "great man." Democrats first had to counteract bachelorhood's negative connotations. Buchanan, more than other Doughfaces, was politically conservative and immune to sectionalism *because* he was unmarried. Buchanan's manipulable domestic life and body gave Democrats a canvas upon which to project their gendered conservatism, which positioned all white men as equal masters, whether of free labor or plantation households. The party's gender ideology reinforced their conservative principles, especially popular sovereignty, which promised all white men, regardless of religion, slaveholding, or nativity, the democratic autonomy necessary to preserve their racial and gender prerogatives. The rhetorically amorphous Buchanan epitomized the interchangeability of white men in Democratic political culture. The election of 1856 revealed the gendered assumptions of Democrats' political thought, because their manly and conservative candidate was so painstakingly contrived.

Yet Buchanan and fellow Democrats soon learned that metaphors of masculinity, domesticity, and marriage were double-edged swords. The president's overt support for slavery offended some northern Democrats. In 1858 a Pennsylvanian complained that Buchanan "has thrown himself into the arms of the South and has disregarded the interests, and apeals of his Northern friends."[127] Buchanan's nickname was "Old Buck," and Doughface, although usually spelled "dough," was sometimes rendered as "doe." After Buchanan demanded the admission of Kansas into the Union as a slave state under the Lecompton constitution in 1857, another Democrat prophesized that he would "see a poor cold Buck leaving the White House without Horns having lost them on the Plains of Lecompton taking his Cause towards the Back Woods in Pennsylvania where party Packs of Blood Hounds will never be able to start him again." Old "Buck" metamorphosed into a "doe" face through the rhetorical emasculation of losing his antlers. This image contrasted with that of a virile buck outpacing competitors in an 1856 cartoon (fig. 3). "Buck" itself was a racially charged slur for black men. Now, fleeing from "Packs of Blood Hounds," Old Buck had also become a fugitive slave. Abasing himself before the Slave Power, Buchanan had relinquished both manhood and whiteness.[128]

Even Henry Wise broke with Buchanan over Kansas. In 1858 Buchanan chided Wise over the lapse in their correspondence during the Lecompton imbroglio. The embattled president, facing the defection of old allies and the sectional deterioration of his party, dusted off allusions to marriage and Union, pleading, "It is true I have regretted, most deeply regretted that we have differed upon a very important public question; but I have carefully

Figure 3. "The Buck Chase of 1856," 1856. James Buchanan as "Old Buck" surpasses his presidential opponents. (Library of Congress, Rare Book and Special Collections Division, Alfred Whital Stern Collection of Lincolniana)

guarded my 'heart, speech & behaviour' so as to prevent me from indulging a single feeling which could affect our friendly relations, which I trust may continue 'as long as we both shall live.'" Wise was unmoved. He countered, "I felt no necessity to 'guard' either my 'heart, speech or behavior,' to prevent our friendly relations from being affected." "'*As long as we both shall live*' are *marital* words," Wise retorted, "and I may well claim to appreciate their full force and meaning."[129]

The thrice-betrothed Wise, who had once brandished Old Buck's bachelorhood as conducive to statesmanship, now rebuffed his overtures of personal and political union as concepts incomprehensible to a bachelor. He publicly denounced Buchanan for supporting the Lecompton constitution, which territorial settlers had not approved. Wise explained that "the President is a bachelor, and he must, therefore, be excused for not comprehending a 'domestic institution' as well as we who have houses full of children." This childless bachelor had discredited popular sovereignty by not allowing Kansans to regulate their own "domestic institutions," including slavery.[130] The political divorce of James Buchanan and Henry Wise was but one manifestation of the intraparty feud over territorial slavery and popular sovereignty that would fracture the Democracy's nationalism and belie its conservatism after the party's success in 1856.

SIX

The Other Douglas Debates
DEMOCRATS DEBATE WHITE SUPREMACY AND POPULAR SOVEREIGNTY

> I should really like to hear from the author of the Nebraska bill,
> a philosophical theory, of the nature and origin of popular
> sovereignty. I wonder where he would begin,
> how he would proceed and where he would end.
> —Frederick Douglass, 1854

ABRAHAM LINCOLN began his 1858 campaign to unseat Senator Stephen A. Douglas with a charge of conspiracy. Four leading Democrats—Douglas, Pierce, Taney, and Buchanan—were colluding to spread slavery nationwide. The pieces fell into place with the repeal of the Missouri Compromise, the election of James Buchanan, and the *Dred Scott* decision. Lincoln employed one of his plebeian analogies for the Doughfaces' fait accompli: "When we see a lot of framed timbers, different portions of which we know have been gotten out at different times and places and by different workmen . . . and when we see these timbers joined together, and see they exactly make the frame of a house or a mill," then "we find it impossible not to believe that Stephen and Franklin and Roger and James all understood one another from the beginning."[1] Lincoln exaggerated the snugness of the Democratic edifice. While the collaborators he named regarded themselves as good Jacksonians and conservatives, and while critics considered them loyal tools of the Slave Power, they disagreed over much.

Serious divisions over popular sovereignty wracked the Democracy in the late 1850s and persisted until the party wrecked itself at Charleston in April 1860. Clarifying the doctrine was imperative, as its territorial implementation exposed its clumsiness as policy. Proslavery and antislavery settlers shedding blood for control of Kansas revealed the violent stakes of local democracy. Following Buchanan's 1856 election on a platform embracing popular sovereignty, the Supreme Court decreed Congress's impotence regarding territorial slavery in the 1857 *Dred Scott* decision. All Democrats already agreed on this point, but some read the decision as disempowering territorial legislatures as well. Douglas and many free-state Democrats had long held that territorial legislatures could outlaw or sanction slavery, while many southern Democrats contended that only constitutional conventions could do so when a territory became a state. *Dred Scott* made the dueling interpretations more than academic. The Lecompton constitution, Kansas's bid for slave-statehood, further strained popular sovereignty. In 1857 the Buchanan administration accepted the proslavery constitution as the product of Kansans' sovereignty, while Douglas condemned it. A majority of Kansans opposed Lecompton but had not been allowed to vote on its ratification. The Little Giant and his congressional allies rejected the constitution in early 1858, vindicating popular sovereignty but further alienating southern-rights Democrats and administration loyalists. Pedantic quibbling over popular sovereignty and the respective powers of legislatures and conventions evolved into a party-rending impasse on the eve of the 1860 presidential election.[2]

The party's introspection at the end of the decade dissatisfied many. Belonging to a party of ideas, Democrats fancied themselves political theorists. But they were also government officials and partisans. Beginning in 1847, Democrats had advertised popular sovereignty as a combination of pragmatism and principle, policy and theory. It was, most immediately, a balm for the sectional furor that flared up after the Mexican War. At the same time, it drew from Jacksonian ideology and the deeper reservoir of Revolutionary republicanism. Yet Democrats' public policy turned out to be riven with theoretical inconsistencies, unsurprising for men who philosophized from the stump. In 1859 Justice Robert C. Grier quipped that if Douglas "had been a trout fisher he would have known that an artificial fly may make an excellent bait, . . . but it will not bear a close examination or analysis of its materials."[3] The theory that the people rule themselves ran aground on the realities of governance and Democrats' own cultural assumptions, especially their racial qualifications for "the people" entitled to self-rule. Political theory faltered in practice, leaving the party's "wild vagaries and loose theorizing"[4] susceptible to conservative critique.

Because territorial popular sovereignty was a distillation of Democratic ideology, its practical difficulties roused slumbering contradictions within

Jacksonian thought. Democrats regarded the individual as the bearer of inviolable natural rights. Democratically self-governing, politically equal individuals advanced American progress. Yet Democrats were caught unaware by the possibility of democratic majorities infringing on individual rights. Douglas, for example, articulated a right of self-government that attached to territorial settlers collectively as a "political community." The interests of the community and of the individual need not align. A majority could abrogate one's rights.[5] Democrats were also chagrined when popular sovereignty subverted white male supremacy. Local democracy permitted political communities to set their own ethnic, religious, property-holding, gender, and racial prerequisites for belonging, potentially empowering women, nativists, religious bigots, and even African Americans. Democrats did not invent these conundrums. But they did foreground them by basing policy on an unstable mixture of individualism, majoritarian democracy, and white supremacy.

Douglas's squabbles over popular sovereignty, especially with Frederick Douglass and Attorney General Jeremiah Sullivan Black, forced Democrats to peer into their ideological oubliettes. These "other Douglas debates" rival the more famous ones between Douglas and Lincoln as examinations of the nature of sovereignty, the constitution of the body politic, and the racial limits of democracy. Democrats routinely boasted of their faith in the "great body of the American people [who] are eminently law-abiding and conservative." Devolving power to white male majorities, they had long promised, would engender stability in a turbulent era. Exaltations of "the great cardinal principle of freedom—the capacity of man for his own government,"[6] however, took on new meaning as diverse Americans appropriated popular sovereignty in unanticipated ways. Local majorities, Democrats learned, were neither necessarily silent nor conservative. Democrats came to disagree over who constituted "the people" as well as the scope of their power. In the Douglas debates of the late 1850s, Democrats attempted to reconcile conservatism and majoritarian democracy. Yet the self-proclaimed conservative party of white supremacy could not escape democracy's radical potential.

The "Black Douglass" and the "White Douglas": Democrats Debate the Racial Boundaries of "the People"

Popular sovereignty jeopardized Democrats' status as the white man's party. According to the political culture of Andrew Jackson's Democracy, white men interacted as political equals because of their mastery over women and Americans of color. Popular sovereignty was touted as a means to reinforce mastery by making the fate of African Americans the province of democratically equal white men. Yet Democrats pursued antagonistic goals: a racially pure republic *and* local self-determination. Local diversity and grassroots majoritarianism could disturb racial hierarchies. By arguing that each political community could define its own membership, Democrats imperiled white men's natural equality and broached black political agency. The "popular" dimension of popular sovereignty jarred with Jacksonian racial absolutism. No figure personified this unintended consequence more than the "Black Douglass." In Frederick Douglass's long-running personal feud with Stephen Douglas—the "White Douglas"—he staked a claim for African Americans in American democracy by leveling a moral and theoretical critique against popular sovereignty. Having articulated racial criteria for political participation that Frederick and others could attack as arbitrary, Stephen and his party realized that democracy endangered white supremacy.[7]

The "Black Douglass" confronted the "White Douglas" as a political equal to debate popular sovereignty. Commentators riffed on the two men's homonymous surnames, and Frederick frequently needled "his good namesake."[8] In 1854 he went to Illinois to challenge Stephen on Kansas-Nebraska. Frederick explained his rationale: "Ebony and ivory are thought to look better standing together than when separated. A white Douglas, canvassing the State for slavery, has suggested the idea of having black Douglass there to canvass the State for freedom."[9] Frederick censured the Little Giant in his hometown, offering a Chicago audience a pointed assessment of Stephen's doctrine. He defended genuine popular sovereignty against Democrats' racially restrictive formulation, telling Chicagoans, "The people in whose cause I come here to-night, are not among those whose right to regulate their own domestic concerns, is so feelingly and eloquently contended for." African Americans had "no Stephen Arnold Douglas—no Gen. Cass, to contend . . . for their Popular Sovereignty."[10]

Frederick Douglass found Democrats' policy a scrawny descendent of the theory inspiring the American Revolution. Territorial popular sovereignty positioned African Americans as objects, not agents, of democracy. It was a "miserable sophistry," he explained, to hold that whites should legislate for blacks—"they might as well say that wolves may be trusted to legislate for themselves, and why not for lambs . . . ?" Democrats were truckling to racism with the idea "that if the people of the territories can be trusted to make laws for white men, they may be safely left to make laws for black men." Rather than recognition of white men's superior claim to self-government, such pandering was "an appeal to all that is mean, cowardly, and vindictive in the breast of the white public." To purge American democracy of hypocrisy, Douglass demanded that African Americans not be regarded as "intruder[s]" at "the ballot box."[11] Drawing attention to African Americans' political absence, when the purpose of "this wicked measure"[12] was to determine their fate, constituted a powerful moral critique of Kansas-Nebraska.

Territorial popular sovereignty not only denied African Americans political rights but could result in the abnegation of all rights through enslavement. "The only seeming concession to the idea of popular sovereignty in this bill," Douglass observed, "is authority to enslave men, and to concede that right or authority is a hell black denial of popular sovereignty itself."[13] "Man," he explained in another speech, "is the owner of himself; the right to himself is inseparable from himself, and no power beneath the sky can take it from him."[14] Later in the decade Frederick explained that Stephen's construction of popular sovereignty "confounds *power* with *right*." It violated natural law, as "by his notion of human rights, everything depends upon the majority," even if the majority flouted moral or natural right.[15] Douglass highlighted a theoretical tension between majoritarianism and individual rights, one that would bedevil Democrats when those affected were white men.

Douglass mischievously sketched a plan to ensure genuine popular sovereignty in Kansas. "Colored men, Colored Citizens—for such they really are—native born Citizens to boot," he proposed, "*ought to go* into that Territory as *permanent* settlers." African Americans would possess a moral claim "when the day of election comes, and these people, with the other settlers of the territory, shall meet to determine what shall be the character of their institutions." One of the plan's supporters predicted that, although Congress had not anticipated African Americans taking part, a large number of free blacks in Kansas would force the issue: "'Popular Sovereignty,' as expressed by Gen. Cass and Stephen A. Douglas, would at once be invoked in this behalf. It would be pushing this 'popular rights' business to its extreme, but it would doubtless go." Douglass exploited Democrats' moral and theoretical inconsistency to push for the inclusion of black political actors.[16]

During Stephen's 1858 reelection campaign, a correspondent sent him a speech by "the '*Black Douglas*,'" in which Frederick endorsed Abraham Lincoln. "The white Douglas should occasionally meet his deserts at the hands of a black one," Frederick Douglass had joked, but "I now leave him in the hands of Mr. Lincoln."[17] Frederick's taunting of Stephen was not the only time the objects of popular sovereignty threatened to become its agents. Democrats themselves allowed for black and female political agency with the notion that the determinants of civic inclusion should vary across communities. Yet, when confronted by actual diversity, Democrats resorted to racial absolutism to shore up the white man's republic. Stephen regularly referenced "Lincoln's ally, in the person of FRED DOUGLASS, THE NEGRO," when campaigning in 1858.[18] The infamy of what Democrats called the "Black Republican party" was only compounded by "the addition of Fred. Douglass and his *black* republicans."[19] Alleging racial egalitarianism and interracial alliances, Democrats rhetorically transformed Republicans into black men. Racial demagoguery revealed Democrats' unwillingness to address popular sovereignty's challenge to racial uniformity.

In an example of theoretical consistency, some Democrats applied popular sovereignty to the color line. Stephen Douglas explained that "a negro, an Indian, or any other man of inferior race to a white man, should be permitted to enjoy, and humanity requires that he should have all the rights, privileges and immunities which he is capable of exercising consistent with the safety of society." This was Douglas's response to Lincoln's supposed penchant for "uniformity." During their 1858 campaign, when Lincoln declared that, regarding slavery, the Union must "become all one thing, or all the other," Douglas answered that it was untrue "that the States must all be free or must all be slave." Democrats had long cautioned that "uniformity is the parent of despotism," whereas "diversity, dissimilarity, variety in all our local and domestic institutions, is the great safeguard of our liberties."[20] For Douglas, it did not follow that "because the negro is our inferior that therefore he ought to be a slave." Douglas argued that Illinois had a right to ban slavery, without conferring political rights on African Americans. Virginia could enslave. Maine could enfranchise.[21] A broad spectrum of inferiority existed between slavery and equality, and the nationwide imposition of either extreme would prove dangerous. Uniform equality, for instance, would encourage that most harrowing homogenization: "repeal[ing] all laws making any distinction whatever on account of race and color, and authoriz[ing] negroes to marry white women on an equality with white men."[22]

Popular sovereignty's application to race relations complemented Democratic localism and states' rights. Each political community, whether a territory or a state, set criteria for membership. Senator Robert Toombs of Georgia defended territorial Kansans' right to "the highest but most delicate attribute of sovereignty to say who shall exercise the electoral franchise" when voting upon a state constitution.[23] Visiting Boston "to lecture the Yankees,"[24] he propounded that only "those upon whom each State, for itself, had adjudged it wise, safe, and prudent to confer it" had the power to elect constitutional "conventions [that] represented the sovereignty of each State." "Minors, women, slaves, Indians, Africans, bond and free" could be barred. The scope of disfranchisement Toombs granted a political community in the form of a sovereign state was expansive—even white men "were excluded because they had no land, others for the want of good characters."[25]

Ceding political communities such latitude allowed Democrats to fortify *Herrenvolk* democracy by including as many white men as possible. Local self-determination protected white men against nativism because, while the federal government standardized naturalization, states and territories could enfranchise anyone, including unnaturalized white immigrants. According to Philip Phillips, Alabama's fervent antinativist, permitting states to shape their own bodies politic stymied attempts to "consolidate the government by melting down into one common mould the rights of citizenship." A Tennessee Democrat likewise hailed the fact that "each State and Territory has the exclusive right to prescribe the rights of suffrage" as "our surest bulwark against consolidation and despotism." States and territories could even enfranchise women and Native Americans, although his goal was thwarting nativism by having polities bestow suffrage on all white men, "come from whatever part of the great Caucasian hive they may."[26]

But Democratic localism could cut both ways—the discretion given to political communities to combat nativist degradation could disempower white men and empower Americans of color. Rooting political rights in states and territories allowed each polity to proscribe those deemed unworthy, such as Indians, "paupers," and "persons enlisted in the army of the United States." Phillips admitted that "it is within the State power to require any length of probation, or to discriminate between native-born and foreigners, or even wholly to exclude foreigners." Federal or state citizenship, moreover, did not translate into rights when one emigrated to a new community.[27] In some states, for instance, "a man without a property qualification could not vote," even though "the man thus prescribed [*sic*] was a citizen of the United States."[28] Phillips even hinted that slave states and free states could implement "laws of exclusion" aimed at each other's "native-born citizens" to keep out opposing sectional viewpoints.²⁹

By letting local majorities dispense rights to racial minorities, Democrats raised the possibility that white men's rights were neither natural nor inalienable but manufactured within political communities. If the moral sense of the community defined the extent of African Americans' rights, why not those of white men? A New York Democrat opposed enfranchising African Americans in his state, even as he acknowledged that states *could* grant suffrage to noncitizens, whether white immigrants or African Americans, as a *"mere privilege,"* not an *"absolute right."*³⁰ Democratic localism opened the door to the organicism of European and Whiggish conservatism. In the first decades of the nineteenth century, Democrats had perfected their happy republic by substituting white men's natural equality for an organic conception of the polity, where social status determined rights and privileges. Empowering political communities as organic collectivities through popular sovereignty risked a democratically sanctioned return to a continuum of rights for white men, an outcome contravening the natural rights philosophy at the foundation of the white man's republic.³¹

Nativists co-opted Democratic reasoning to argue that if political rights could be denied to specific racial groups, so too could Know-Nothings prohibit their exercise by Catholics and the foreign-born. Political rights such as suffrage and officeholding, Know-Nothings agreed, were separable from basic legal rights. Just as Douglas argued that African Americans should exercise "all the rights they were capable of enjoying consistent with the good and safety of society," nativists were "willing to accord to all such privileges as they may have capacity to enjoy—but opposed to the policy that would thrust responsibilities upon raw foreigners, which they neither comprehend nor know how to discharge."³² If nativists could not bar Catholics and foreigners from the body politic, through legal restrictions or refusing to vote for them, then neither could Democrats omit racial others. A North Carolina Know-Nothing rejected *Herrenvolk* appeals and warned that if officeholding could not be closed to Catholics and white foreigners, then neither could it be withheld from "the motley half-breed of Indians, negroes, and Spaniards" in Mexico or the "inhabitants" of the "Sandwich Islands," should those areas be conquered.³³

Democrats' own enthusiasm for diversity weakened their racial barriers. Their zeal for religious toleration was expansive, with one pamphlet exclaiming in 1850 that "*every citizen of the requisite age, be he Jew, Mahometan; or Catholic, or whether he is poor or rich, is eligible to any office.* THIS IS RIGHT."[34] Philip Phillips proved his fealty to the "Separation of Church and State"[35] and religious toleration with his efforts on behalf of Jewish Americans. In 1857 a "national convention of Israelites" deputed him to present their grievances against a proposed treaty inimical to their rights. As their spokesman, Phillips secured President Buchanan's recognition of equality for "American citizen[s], of the Hebrew persuasion."[36] Democrats' willingness to include as many white men as possible in the polity led to demands by other groups. John R. Ridge, although professing his own "Douglasism," reproached the Little Giant. Noticing that Douglas "seem[ed] to put Indians and negroes upon an equality," Ridge volunteered that he was "of Indian descent." Surely, Ridge pleaded, Douglas did not mean that "Indians are no better, intellectually, than *negroes*." Douglas must recognize "Cherokees, and other civilized and intellectual tribes of the Western frontiers, as vastly superior, in every respect, to any portion of the Negro race." The Democracy claimed to stand fast against white men's degradation. Ridge hoped that "it may not be a degredation in me, as an Indian, to support you." This partisan had a personal stake in Douglas and other Democrats contending for the manhood of more than just white men.[37]

Massachusetts Democrat Caleb Cushing, meanwhile, championed multiple marginalized groups. In 1857 he charged an antislavery opponent with hypocrisy for calling for the "disfranchisement of the Chinese in California." A former diplomat in China, Cushing was incredulous that this "cultured and lettered race," which was "but a shade in color darker than ourselves," was not given the same regard as "the black savage of Africa."[38] Chinese immigrants were despised in nineteenth-century America—a Republican mocked Cushing for dining on "dog's meat" with a "Chinaman," while Douglas refused to "acknowledge that the Cooley imported into this country must necessarily be put upon an equality with the white race."[39] Still, Douglas would have each political community decide for itself, leaving an opening for sympathetic Democrats like Cushing, who also promoted Native American citizenship in Massachusetts in 1859. He explained that the "powers of sovereignty" allowed Massachusetts to enfranchise those without federal citizenship and "determine for itself the personal *status* of every person within the State." Echoing Douglas, Cushing wanted Native Americans to possess "all such civil and political rights as . . . they may be found competent to exercise."[40]

The Little Giant even reportedly extended popular sovereignty to white women. In 1859 Lucy Stone invited Douglas to attend a "Woman's Rights Convention" in Chicago. A published response had Douglas gush that, "after so many years of faithful labor in the cause of Popular Sovereignty," he supported women's "endeavors to obtain the liberty of governing yourselves in your own way." Douglas's letter, although possibly fabricated, captured Democrats' impetuousness over their doctrine. Frederick Douglass was unimpressed. He publicly rebuked Stone for fawning over a man who "notwithstanding his high sounding phrases about equal rights and popular sovereignty, has chiefly distinguished himself for his utter disregard of such rights." Only those "whose notions of human rights are not influenced or limited to any distinctions in the forms or colors of mankind" ought to receive such invitations. The Black Douglass understood the innate racial limits to popular sovereignty.[41]

Democrats compensated for their headiness, whether in support of women's rights or even black suffrage,[42] by always reaffirming white male supremacy. One commentator anticipated popular sovereignty leading to more than just black political actors in the territories: "In some they would establish freedom, and in others Slavery either black or white, or both."[43] For this anxious observer, territorial self-government promised white men's ultimate degradation. Douglas countered such fears by asserting that only popular sovereignty prevented racial and sexual disorder. Without sovereignty, territorial legislatures would have to recognize Muslim "polygamy" and racial "amalgamation." "A white man, with a negro wife and mulatto children, under a marriage lawful in Massachusetts," could claim legal rights in a territory "in defiance of the wishes of the people." While empowering territorial governments to close their borders to racial and gender disorder, Douglas ignored that "the wishes of the people" could just as easily legitimize fanaticism and erase the color line.[44]

Douglas and his party could always fall back on racial essentialism. The signers of the Declaration of Independence, Douglas argued, imagined equality solely for "white men, men of European birth and European descent, and had no reference either to the negro, the savage Indians, the Fejee, the Malay, or any other inferior and degraded race." A correspondent agreed that "the framers of the constitution and the signers of the Declaration of Independence never for one moment thought of conferring political equality upon savage or semi-civilized men."[45] Although Democrats interpreted parts of his *Dred Scott* decision differently, most welcomed Chief Justice Taney's *diktat* that

African Americans were not citizens.[46] The boundaries of their political culture circumscribed Democrats' toleration for diversity. Cushing, arraigned for favoring racial equality after defending Chinese immigrants, recanted, "I do *not* admit as my equals either the red men of America, or the yellow men of Asia, or the black men of Africa." Having momentarily forgotten the northern politics of slavery and race, Cushing acknowledged, "The Caucasian race are the masters of this country, its sovereigns."[47] Douglas, after his own doctrine opened theoretical space for black political agency, simply announced that natural inequality foreclosed that outcome. Assuming racial difference, whether justified as divinely ordained, as a "great natural law," as "strengthened by the force of habit," or as biologically indelible, was the Democracy's final redoubt against the logic of its own ideas.[48]

In their war against fanatical conformity, Democrats had enshrined their own uniformity—*all* white men had an equal place in an exclusive political sphere. Yet popular sovereignty, the point of which was to forestall centralization, proved a shaky foundation on which to erect a white man's republic. Democrats believed in inalienable rights for white men alongside democratically contingent rights for all others. This asymmetry left Democrats open to attacks by those who argued either that all rights were natural or that all rights were relative, with neither extreme serving as a solid basis for *Herrenvolk* democracy. Democrats had long bemoaned uniformity. But by relying on a policy that nurtured diversity, they inadvertently surrendered the one type of homogeneity they did countenance—uniformity in the racial and gender makeup of their political nation. The Douglas debates over who composed "the people" thereby made porous the racial delineations of Jacksonian Democracy and exposed the radicalism of a supposedly conservative doctrine.

"Dogmas as to Sovereignty": Democrats Debate the People's Power

When some Democrats proclaimed that they would "advocate Douglas' claims for the Presidency, and pure unadulterated Popular sovereignty,"[49] conservatives within and outside the Democracy winced. Conservatives were alarmed not only by the types of people practicing self-government but also by the magnitude of their unadulterated power. In addition to defining "popular," Democrats needed to clarify "sovereignty"—how much power did the people have, when could they exercise it, and how could it be limited? As policy, popular sovereignty failed to specify when territorial settlers could don the splendor of sovereignty. Douglas and like-minded Democrats, especially in the free states, held that territorial legislatures possessed that power, meaning that settlers could decide on slavery soon after territorial organization. Many southerners and northern Buchanan Democrats countered that only a constitutional convention antecedent to statehood could act upon the institution. They discredited Douglas's position as "Squatter Sovereignty." The derogatory epithet reflected slaveholders' anxiety over entrusting enslaved property to capricious majorities of what Alabama's fire-eating Democrat William F. Samford called the "free-soil rabble."[50]

This intraparty feud, nonetheless, transcended sectional disagreement over slavery. It also spoke to uncertainty over how much power the people could responsibly wield in a democratic republic. Democrats had relied on popular sovereignty to prove their commitment to white men's democracy since Doughfaces introduced it in 1847. Even as they backtracked on the extent of this power to reassure conservatives, the party of Jacksonian Democracy could not forswear self-government. Justice Grier was incredulous that Douglas persisted in preaching popular sovereignty: "I had supposed he had got up this phrase" to use "till the next election, but sense enough not to attempt to defend the absurdities represented by it."[51] More than mere pragmatism or campaign bombast, however, popular sovereignty was a principle that neither northern *nor* southern Democrats could disown, even as they were troubled by its application. Democrats betrayed their professed conservatism, because they dared not disown democracy.

Territorial democracy appalled southern *and* northern conservatives, because settlers endangered more than chattel slavery in the West. Popular sovereignty allowed them to shrug off convention and codify "institutions which might be against the will of Congress and the entire policy of a Christian civilization."[52] In 1859 a conservative critic concluded that Kansas-Nebraska authorized "Independent Sovereignties" that could validate "matrimony, slavery, polygamy, or socialism; or any religion they pleased, Christianity, Mahometism, Mormonism, or the worship of Juggernaut." In their "fanaticism" for catering to local tastes, Democrats would permit human sacrifice and "feast[ing] on human flesh," a Republican ranted.[53] Skeptics had long predicted this denouement. During the 1854 debates over Kansas-Nebraska, one observer asked John G. Davis, "How long will it be until our vast domain will have scatterd all over it some fifty or one hundred heterogenious petty sovrignties?" with some "protestant, some catholic, some mormon, some atheistic, and some hethanish."⁵⁴ The sovereign people could not be trusted to resist dabbling in fanaticism.

Turmoil in the territories convinced many that democratic excess eroded law and order. Surveying developments from California, home to extralegal vigilantism, Governor John B. Weller "deplore[d] the disposition, so frequently manifested by a portion of the people in different sections of the country, to take the law into their own hands." "The sovereignty of the people is manifested," he implored, through "a government of law." Governor Henry Wise pointed to the "committee of vigilance in the state of California," as well as to the uncouthness of backwoods settlers, the "state of Franklin," and the "Dorr revolution in Rhode Island," as popular disturbances adverse to the stability slavery required.⁵⁵ Thomas W. Dorr, boogeyman for antebellum conservatives, had approved of popular sovereignty as the Democracy's platform and associated it with his own democratic uprising, enthusing, "We have contended for the sovereignty of the People over all their political institutions."⁵⁶ Although some Democrats delighted in the resemblance between their "doctrine that '*The People govern*'" and "'*the people*' led by Gov Dorr," many were not eager to be classed as fellow travelers of Dorrites and other fanatical democrats.⁵⁷

"That portentous cloud which hangs upon our Western horizon,—the Territory of Utah," exemplified the perils of popular sovereignty on the nation's political littoral.⁵⁸ In 1859 a Virginia debating club solicited Attorney General Jeremiah Black's advice on their recent "hot dispute" over whether "if Utah, now a Territory, forms a constitution, tollerating poligamy, . . . 'That, when she applies to be admitted as a sister State, Congress is bound to admit her,' Bigotry to the contrary, notwithstanding."⁵⁹ Polygamy seemed to fall within popular sovereignty's grant of local control over "domestic institutions," a term usually referring to slavery.⁶⁰ While Kansas-Nebraska was under consideration, Brigham Young had teased Douglas that the bill's detractors were linking it to the Mormons' "domestic regulations." Some Democrats also made this connection and rejected federal oversight of both polygamy and slavery.⁶¹ There were, however, prevailing religious and gender conventions beyond which many Democrats would not venture. The transgression of sexual propriety represented by the "Mormon monstrosities"⁶² cooled their ardor for white men's religious diversity and domestic prerogative. In 1856 a visitor to Great Salt Lake City related to Lewis Cass the fruits of his doctrine. "Both Negro & Indian Slavery now exist," and "polygamy now exists to an extent that would make a man of your age blush, and almost disavow the female race." The Mormons hated the American government, he continued, "but endorse the 'Nebraska Bill.'"[63]

Rather than condone Utah's "infamous and disgusting practices," Democrats chose to "abolish the Territorial government" and snuff out Mormons' popular sovereignty. Decreeing them "unfit to exercise the right of self-government," Douglas sought to placate critics who blamed popular sovereignty for these "evils."[64] Opponents relished the hypocrisy. "He does not seem to have had the least idea," Attorney General Black chided, "that he was proposing to extinguish a sovereignty, or to trample upon the sacred rights of an independent people." Self-rule provoked its antithesis with the 1857–1858 Mormon War. *"If non-intervention . . . be the order of the error of the times,"* asked Henry Wise, then why did President Buchanan's use of federal forces against Brigham Young, *"the satyr of Utah,"* and *"the Mormon's harems of Salt Lake"* receive widespread support? Thus did polygamy reveal the difficulties of deploying abstract ideology as public policy in a complex cultural setting.[65]

Democrats had miscalculated in straitening the theoretical underpinnings of American institutions into governmental policy. The conservative, proslavery Philadelphian Sidney George Fisher explained that "all just and free government must be founded on the consent of the governed," adding, "on their consent, not necessarily on their votes." Like the English and American revolutionaries before him, and along with many contemporary American conservatives, Fisher heeded the people's sovereignty in the abstract but did not want that awesome power made tangible through direct democracy. Douglas "pilfer[ed] our birthright," according to one anonymous pamphleteer. He had taken "the doctrine of Popular Sovereignty [which] is the very germ of the Constitution, and the noble offspring of its founders" and had "emasculate[d] it."[66]

Recognizing the sovereignty of the people as an instrument of routine governance roused conservative ire because it consigned society to perpetual reenactments of the state of nature. States of nature are intrinsic to the social contract tradition as society's founding moments, when individuals, shorn of external constraints and abiding only by natural law, come together to inaugurate political order. Popular sovereignty in the western wilderness alluded to such scenes. Douglas supporter Reverdy Johnson contended that a territorial legislature's power over slavery was the only way to avoid primordial anarchy;

otherwise, "the territorial State would be almost without laws,—be one of nature." Should Know-Nothings triumph in "civil and religious persecution," Douglas held out hope that Americans could "flee to the wilderness, and find an asylum in Nebraska, where the principles of self-government have been firmly established."[67] Imagery of "an uncultivated waste" and "the primeval forest"[68] suggested that Americans would undergo repeated founding moments in the wild as they sprinted ever westward.

States of nature tessellating across space would foster cultural diversity but also political instability when "a rude people, in a wilderness"[69] regularly reforged society. Robert Winthrop, speaking for conservative Whigs, proclaimed that his party "seeks reforms by no riotous or revolutionary processes." Americans could no longer resort to "the great right of revolution," one means of leaving civil society and reentering the state of nature. Rather than "dissolve the whole social fabric, to fall into anarchy and trust to luck for a reorganization of society," preached a minister in Albany, good republicans should effect change through the "toilsome duties of peaceful reform."[70] Those who vouched for the people's right to defy the government, such as California's Vigilance Committee, cited the people's "inherent sovereign power"[71]—rhetoric identical to that of Democrats justifying their territorial policy. Democrats demystified the right of revolution by seemingly encouraging Americans to reclaim their undiluted sovereignty on a daily basis, giving conservatives pause before entering Democratic ranks.

Many American conservatives instead followed philosopher Edmund Burke in his theoretical skirting of the state of nature. Burke worked outside the social contract tradition by envisioning a polity that was not founded at the same moment, did not age as a unit, and thus never reached a point when "the whole fabric should be at once pulled down and the area cleared for the erection of a theoretic, experimental edifice in its place." Selective reinvigoration of the polity's components obviated the need to relapse wholesale into the state of nature "for the purpose of originating a new civil order out of the first elements of society." Sidney George Fisher, channeling Burke, observed that "happy is that country where political innovations are like those of time or the changes of the seasons, gradual and easy, not sudden and violent." Seismic departures could be avoided by recognizing that "the present of a Nation contains a portion of the past and of the future." American conservatives counseled evolutionary reform through existing institutions, not plunging society into elemental chaos whenever change was desired.[72]

Conservatives like former Whig Robert Toombs also took cues from Burke by defining rights "in a state of society" as opposed to locating them "in a state of nature."[73] According to the jurist George Ticknor Curtis, there was a difference between territorial settlers possessing the *"abstract right* of self-government" and demonstrating "a capacity of self-government."[74] The latter, hardly an a priori right, had to be inculcated by a "parent and patron power," added Henry Wise.[75] The territories—variously referred to as "republican nurselings," "fœtus of territory," and "inchoate, or minor states"[76]—required guidance *before* they could self-govern. For Sidney George Fisher, territorial settlers had a "right," not to self-government, but to be governed by the "General Government," as "a child has a right to the superior judgment of his father."[77] The people had to learn self-rule through tutelage and experience. "Train the people of every Territory, as fast as you practicably can, in the business of self-government," admonished Curtis.[78]

Amid the hand-wringing over unsupervised settlers in the wilderness, Douglas initiated a pamphlet war with the 1859 publication of his article "The Dividing Line between Federal and Local Authority: Popular Sovereignty in the Territories" in *Harper's New Monthly Magazine*. Having defeated the Buchanan administration on Lecompton and secured his reelection against Lincoln in 1858, Douglas positioned himself as the Democracy's leader and his doctrine as the party's platform for the 1860 presidential election. George Ticknor Curtis remarked on the novel "appearance, in a popular magazine, of an article on a constitutional question, written by a prominent candidate for the Presidency." He looked forward to Douglas's essay, quickly republished as a pamphlet, facilitating an intercourse "more deliberate" than usually allowed by "electioneering speeches."[79] Combatants in the ensuing pamphlet war did debate popular sovereignty in the parlance of political theory. Historians have not recognized the scale of this flurry of treatises, nor have they appreciated it as a theoretical dialogue. These ponderous pamphlets ransacked natural rights philosophy, common law, colonial history, and the law of nations. In couching disagreements in the language of sovereignty, constitutionalism, and the composition of the body politic, Democrats were not only wrangling over public policy or party factionalism but also seeking to make democracy amenable to conservatism.[80]

"The scribblers of the American Union are in a stew," Douglas was warned. His most formidable antagonist was Attorney General Jeremiah Sullivan

Black of Pennsylvania, speaking for the Buchanan administration. Douglas and Black riposted through eight texts.[81] "This agitating and important question" also "commanded the attention of some of the ablest minds in the country,"[82] with public intellectuals such as Henry Wise, Reverdy Johnson, George Ticknor Curtis, Horace Greeley, and Sidney George Fisher tossing off treatises. The pamphlet war encompassed all positions on slavery and sovereignty in the territories. Douglas defended sovereignty during the territorial phase. Black responded that only constitutional conventions had power over slavery. While Douglas and Black, like most Democrats, concurred on congressional non-intervention, other commentators preferred congressional regulation. Some congressional supremacists wanted Congress to legislate on slavery according to the will of the people, while Republicans sought outright proscription.[83] Radical states' rights southerners, meanwhile, demanded that the federal government, understood not as a supreme power but acting on behalf of the sovereign states, protect territorial slavery, most provocatively with a slave code.

Douglas intended his pamphlets to dampen opponents' glee over the 1857 *Dred Scott* decision, which President Buchanan and many southerners interpreted as guaranteeing slavery in the territories. Douglas pointed out that the Court had negated only Congress's power over territorial slavery, to which all Democrats had previously assented, leaving a territorial legislature's authority undefined. Yet many Democrats extended the ruling to legislatures, as they were created by Congress, which would undercut popular sovereignty in the territorial phase. Delaware senator James A. Bayard agreed with Douglas that the Court "made *no decision* as to the limits of territorial power," although he believed that "denying the powers of Congress to prohibit slavery in a territory" would logically apply to legislatures.[84] Upon Kansas-Nebraska's passage in 1854, northerners and southerners had left the authority of territorial legislatures to the arbitration of the courts.[85] Without a clear verdict on territorial legislative power in 1857, Douglas and his partisans insisted that the "compromise of '54" still held.[86] More importantly, Douglas simply sidestepped *Dred Scott* by arguing that territorial settlers' rights were natural, not derived from Congress. While Democrats had long labeled popular sovereignty an inherent right, the rhetoric took on added force when Douglas elevated the debate to the plane of political theory to circumvent *Dred Scott*'s constitutional morass.[87]

In his treatises, Douglas reaffirmed territorial settlers' right to "exercise exclusive legislation in respect to all matters pertaining to their internal polity," including marriage, property, and, of course, slavery. Douglas recognized sovereign power in "political communities," a slippery construction in terms of their membership and the mechanism through which they enacted their will. He was nevertheless emphatic that a political community's "right of local self-government" was "inalienable" and a "birth-right." He rooted territorial democracy in the natural rights tradition, with communities, as opposed to individuals, possessing inherent rights in territories that approximated states of nature.[88] At the same time, distancing himself from "squatter" sovereignty, Douglas clarified that political communities were more than the "few first settlers [who] were squatters on the public domain" able to "make laws binding the people who are to come after them."[89] Self-government, he specified, "pertains to the people collectively as a law-abiding and peaceful community."[90] The people acted through a government. "This right of self-government, being a political right," Douglas elaborated, "cannot be exercised by the people until they are formed and organized into a political community." Congress would verify "that they have people enough to constitute a political community" and "that they are capable of self-government."[91]

By designating popular sovereignty a "political right," as opposed to a natural one, Douglas erected barriers to its enjoyment. Yet he confused the issue by continuing to invoke the "inherent right of self-government." The notion of naturally inhering rights collided with an understanding of rights existing only within an ordered political community, sanctioned by Congress. Henry Wise noted that care had to be taken when defining "that word '*people*.'" One definition was that of "a mass of human beings, *organized*, by laws in municipalities and communities of government." But it could also mean "a mass of unorganized human beings, collected together by design or accident." Douglas claimed to hold the former view. Yet, after years of exalting the territorial people, and by continuing to present popular sovereignty as a political right which existed only in society *and* as a natural right, he left many unconvinced.[92]

One skeptic was the attorney general of the United States. Sovereignty, Jeremiah Black corrected, did not reside in a territory or its people prior to statehood. Yet, if left to Douglas, settlers would find lying on the plains "omnipotent sovereignty [that] is to be wielded by a few men suddenly drawn together from all parts of America and Europe, unacquainted with one another, and ignorant of their relative rights." Black regarded Douglas's political communities as governments with unchecked power. Territorial legislatures were "merely provisional and temporary," but "if Mr. Douglas is right, those governments have all the absolute power of the Russian Autocrat."[93] On the other hand, when Douglas denied that these legislatures were unlimited sovereigns, Black accused him of investing the unorganized people, acting through "voluntary mass meetings or at elections unauthorized by law," with sovereignty. Whether manifested institutionally through tyrannical territorial governments or chaotically through a *"mobocracy,"* Douglas had theorized unrepublican bastions of illimitable power in the territories.[94]

Black's alternative—that only constitutional conventions could rule on slavery when a territory morphed into a state—was conservative and precise. Black agreed that the territorial people, not Congress, were the ultimate shapers of their polity. But only a "competent local authority," not nebulous "political communities," could make the determination. John Forsyth, trying to suppress anti-Douglas sentiment in Alabama, explained that "the people of that territory, not as squatters, but as an organized political community" could regulate slavery. Like Douglas, however, he did not differentiate "an organized political community" from a despotic antislavery legislature. In contrast to such imprecision over the location and extent of sovereignty, Black's model boasted the merits of simplicity. The people, Black stipulated, had to "wait until they get a constitutional convention or the machinery of a State government into their hands," whereupon they earned the status of "competent local authority."[95]

Douglasites failed to buttress popular sovereignty's conservative facade because of their ultimate unwillingness to hamstring local government. Assaulted by Black's hectoring, Douglas responded, "I have never said or thought that our Territories were sovereign political communities." Still, unable to resist, he caveated that they did possess "attributes of sovereignty," a hedge that the attorney general dismissed.[96] Douglas tried to have it both ways, with obfuscations such as "but while the Territories are not sovereign, they have the inalienable right of self-government."[97] The difference between sovereignty and "the inalienable right of self-government" was lost on slaveholders and conservatives nationwide. Citing his "great reputation as a lawyer," Douglas welcomed the aid of Reverdy Johnson. A noted jurist involved in the *Dred Scott* case as well as a conservative Old Whig from a border slave state, his 1859 pro-Douglas pamphlet should have made popular sovereignty palatable. Instead, Johnson favored unfettered territorial sovereignty. He argued that it was best "to leave the question to the Territorial people, and to leave open for emigration the Territory to every citizen of the United States, without being subject, in regard to slavery, or any other domestic institution, to congressional mastery." That Johnson, like Douglas, categorized this as sovereignty in a "restricted sense" and not "in its more comprehensive meaning" did not practically diminish the power he accorded the people.[98]

Republicans helped Democrats incriminate their conservatism. In 1858 a supporter alerted Douglas that Illinois Republicans were challenging Democrats on "whether, under the Dred Scott decision . . . the territorial legislatures would have power to prohibit slavery." He shared his answer to the question when it "was poked up at me last night at a public meeting at Plainfield." "The people of the territories . . . were placed upon the same footing of the people of the states," and through their "territorial legislatures," he reasoned, "by virtue of their inherent sovereignty they might exercise all those powers of legislation." Douglas later replied to Lincoln's identical query during their Freeport debate by explaining that territorial legislatures, even if lacking legislative power to ban slavery, could withhold protective legislation from the institution.[99] Many Democrats, including southerners, had already conceded as much. The "Freeport Doctrine" was divisive, but not because it was new. In the polarized politics of the late 1850s, the doctrine rankled southerners who assumed *Dred Scott* had disempowered territorial settlers.[100] Douglasites, in turn, prioritized doctrinal purity over soothing slaveholders. By 1860, for instance, Reverdy Johnson had moved from grounding territorial sovereignty in law to basing it on the "inherent and paramount power" belonging to "the territorial people as a fundamental and inherent right."[101]

Johnson also belittled Black's "competent local authority." He asked if territorial settlers had to wait for "the necromancy of a State Constitution" to commence self-government. Douglas similarly elided the temporally slight yet theoretically vast gulf separating legislatures and conventions. While Johnson and Douglas meant to suggest that preventing citizens from governing themselves during the interim between territorial organization and statehood was unfair and socially disruptive, many Americans would have answered that a constitutional convention did exert a transformative effect. Henry Wise trembled before the mystical process by which a territory "ascend[ed] to the high priesthood of political rights." At this numinous moment, the people "are to put away childish things, and become more than men—an American, self-governed, sovereign people." Conventions *were* something special.[102]

In distinguishing between conventions and legislatures, Democrats perpetuated a centuries-old Anglo-American innovation acknowledging the people's abstract sovereignty while tempering its dislocating potential. In American constitutionalism, as developed during the Revolutionary era, legislatures are representative bodies; they do not possess sovereignty, which the people never abdicate. Conventions, on the contrary, are understood to be the people in their sovereign capacity. They constitute moments "when the people of the State were to meet with every attribute of original sovereignty."[103] Legislatures occupy an inferior status to conventions, which are antecedent to and constitutive of legislatures. Only conventions can draft constitutions, which constrain legislatures and transcend ordinary legislation. At the same time, these portals through which the people's sovereignty enters politics are exceptional and infrequent. The convention/legislature distinction allows for the recognition of the people's sovereignty, without relying on it for routine governance. "The very essence of republican government, is, that whilst the people possess all power, they exercise none," expounded fire-eater Louis T. Wigfall, taking the doctrine to its conservative extreme. In the United States, government lacks sovereignty. The people have it but lack the mechanism through which to regularly exercise it, making popular sovereignty conservative and safe.[104]

The difference between conventions and legislatures, foundational to American constitutional thought generally, also informed states' rights constitutionalism specifically. Belonging to what a New Yorker called "a strict States Rights party," northern and southern Democrats had long venerated state prerogative, especially over slavery. According to the 1856 Cincinnati national platform, slavery numbered among the "reserved rights of the States."[105] Some states' rights advocates went further. They agreed that the people were sovereign, but in their role as "the citizens of the several States" acting through state conventions.[106] John C. Calhoun had taught his disciples that "the General Government emanated from the people of the several States, forming distinct political communities, and acting in their separate and sovereign capacity, and not from all of the people forming one aggregate political community."[107] Many antislavery politicians responded that Congress could outlaw territorial slavery on behalf of a national conception of the sovereign American people.[108] While most Democrats would not have readily embraced nullification or secession, the culminations of Calhounite constitutionalism, they still respected states' rights and the pivotal function of sovereign state conventions.

Although hardly eschewing his party's states' rights tradition, Douglas deviated from this constitutional strain by arguing that territories were equally sovereign. Louis Wigfall held that, originally, "each State was a people, a political community, or nation, free, sovereign and independent."[109] Douglas and his adherents contended that territories were also political communities—they were simply "new States" or "territorial State[s]."[110] Sovereign political communities took multiple forms: "The people of every separate political community (dependent colonies, Provinces, and Territories as well as sovereign States) have an inalienable right to govern themselves."[111] This elastic definition of political communities was another example of how Douglas's theory chipped away at the buffers surrounding sovereign power. States, with constitutions born of conventions, held an esteemed place in American constitutionalism, yet Douglas "not only levels the Territories up to the States, but levels the States down to the Territories."[112] Douglas confused the nomenclature of power in America's federal system by according equality to other, inferior polities.

Douglas also rebuffed the extreme states' rights dictum that states projected their sovereignty into the territories. Radical states' rights theory mandated that "the federal government, as the general agent of the several States," guarantee citizens' ability to carry slavery into the "common territories." When emigrants removed to a territory, their state's sovereignty accompanied them—a protrusion of states' rights concocted to install slavery against the will of local majorities.[113] "The people of each State possess the inherent right of self-government," Douglas granted, and they lugged that right with them when "removing to a Territory of the United States." But in the territory, they ceased to bear that right as citizens of their former states. "The inherent right of self-government" that settlers carried "attaches to the people of the Territory" as a new political community. Attempting to obtrude their power into the territories, states would find sovereignty already present.[114] Douglas's disregard for the proslavery variant of states' rights constitutionalism again illustrated that he envisioned sources of political power prior to constitutional conventions and outside of accepted categories.

Collapsing the distinction between legislatures and conventions and between territories and states subverted the Revolutionary legacy of a people sovereign in the abstract by making them sovereign in practice. Douglas went further and swept away the republican partition between the sovereign people and government itself. He specified that only political communities institutionalized as a government, not the unorganized people out of doors, could wield power. Yet conservatives were unsure what restrained territorial governments prior to a constitutional convention. As a critical pamphleteer summarized Douglas and Reverdy Johnson's teachings, the people "possess the sovereign power inherently, and they can confer it upon a territorial legislature."[115] Popular sovereignty as public policy ignored the ancient enmity between "rulers" and "ruled," between the liberty-loving people and their power-hungry government. Jacksonians' heavily policed border between liberty and power became permeable. Maybe liberty and power were one and the same after all. Somewhere, John Quincy Adams smiled.

Douglas and his followers scrambled to refute the alarming notion that the people's sovereignty translated into tyrannical territorial legislatures. One pro-Douglas pamphleteer lamely trusted "the genius and character of our institutions" as implicit, unwritten checks. Americans somehow intuited that "with us power is everywhere limited and defined." Johnson postulated that Anglo-American political thought assumed limited sovereignty and such "implied conditions of all social power, . . . effectual to limit and restrict it as if in words repeated again and again."[116] To stifle power short of parchment barriers, however, was to forget that the American Revolution culminated with written constitutions. Black thus lauded the "Saxon race [who] have been laboring, planning, and fighting, during seven hundred years, for Great Charters, Bills of Rights, and Constitutions, to limit the sovereignty of all the governments they have lived under."[117] To invoke the people's sovereignty without abridging its exercise, "in words repeated again and again," betrayed white men's libertarian heritage.

Douglas, praising the people's democratic power, and Black, dreading the state's power, argued within a common ideology. Jefferson and Jackson had taught Democrats to rhapsodize over the people but to revile the state, a distinction Douglas muddled with his elision of the sovereign territorial people and their legislatures. Democrats instinctively wanted to limit state power, yet curbing state power means handicapping the people's democratic power. The contradiction between majoritarian democracy and antistatism had long hibernated at the core of Democratic thought. In turning their ideology into policy on territorial slavery, Democrats disentangled this paradox, with Douglas and Black each voicing one half of the Jacksonian mind. Douglas stubbornly persisted in praising the people, while Black stubbornly persisted in warning of their excess. Each agreed with his opponent's premises yet spoke past the other by emphasizing only one facet of an ideology that, once rent asunder, could not be sutured back together in time for a presidential election. Democrats also unraveled the other constitutive contradiction of Jacksonianism, that which existed between local diversity and the racial uniformity necessary to *Herrenvolk* democracy. In the Douglas debates, Democrats laid bare the clashing assumptions of their partisan ideology and alerted Americans to the radicalism of their democratic conservatism.

On to Charleston

The party teetered on schism as it lurched toward its 1860 national convention in Charleston. Winding down the pamphlet war, Black grandstanded, "I have regarded this dispute as on a question of constitutional law, far, very far, above party politics."[118] Questions of law and principle and those of factions and personality were, nonetheless, inseparable for this party of principles and of men. Douglas, in fact, could have single-handedly precipitated another round of the partisan realignment. With Douglas seemingly poised to engineer a new coalition, one Republican notified William Pitt Fessenden that he was "not *quite* prepared to give up the old leaders of the Republican party to enlist under a new man though he is a giant." Some Republicans feared an alliance with Douglas would seduce their party from its antislavery mission. Yet the Little Giant never contemplated defection and scorned those who did: "If there are any who choose to bolt, the fact only shows that they are not as good Democrats as I am."[119]

Douglas did not feel compelled to leave the Democracy because his feud with fellow Democrats took place over their shared ideology. "Your battle is the most noble one ever fought *not out* but *in* the *true* ranks of Democracy," beamed a sycophant.[120] A Republican also found that the Democracy's disagreement, "notwithstanding the laborious article and myriad speeches of Mr. Douglas, and the biting review of Judge Black, is the difference of tweedle-de and tweedle-dum." Douglas minimized discord yet conveyed truth when he thundered, "If there is one principle on earth which binds the Democracy together with more unanimity than any others throughout the entire land, it is this great principle of the right of every political community, loyal to the Constitution and the Union, to govern itself in respect to its internal concerns."[121] When fussing over enslaved property, Douglas's critics could sound undemocratic, like the Georgian who fumed about "allow[ing] 'the people of a territory' to lay their foul Squatter Sovereignty hands upon it." Yet, although differing on how and when, Democrats agreed that the people could create slave states or free states. Jefferson Davis, fast becoming Douglas's foe within the party, assured Lewis Cass in 1857, "We do not differ as to the principle of permitting a people to pass upon their constitution and to regulate their domestic affairs in their own way."[122]

The stalemate over popular sovereignty was not rigidly sectional. Although Douglas commanded the allegiance of many northern Democrats, others throughout the free states aligned with their southern counterparts in abjuring squatter sovereignty and hailing Black's "meritable discourse" as "the antidote to the poisonous influence which his [Douglas's] doctrine promulgated—a doctrine leading only to anarchy and revolution."[123] From Wilkes Barre, Pennsylvania, came affirmation that "Douglass, I regard, as simply a humbug, and his doctrine as bosh," while a Michigander hyperbolized that Black's argument "meets the views of three quarters of the Democrats" in his state. During the 1860 election, Caleb Cushing told Maine Democrats that they must adhere to Black's position that slavery could only be outlawed upon statehood—at which point the sovereign power could "do unjust things." He delivered the requisite paean: "We, in the United States, build up all government on the fundamental idea of the sovereignty of the people." Still, "the mystic name of popular sovereignty" required constitutional trammeling, especially given the sectionalism debilitating the Democracy and the Union.[124]

Southern Democrats were no more unanimous. Not all southerners condoned the automatic introduction of slavery into the territories, as supported by Black, or its positive protection there by a congressional slave code, as demanded by radical states' rights southerners. Slave code advocates joined Republicans in looking to Congress, one Alabamian surmised, because they distrusted the people and "the exercise of popular rights as agrarian and revolutionary—as one of the diseases of free Governments." For this pamphleteer, Cushing's call for congressional protection of slavery in the territories invalidated popular sovereignty. "Mr. Cushing," he charged, "has overlooked the fact that in this country the sovereign power is not in Constitutions and Governments, but in the people." Ceding Congress the power to enforce a slave code would give Republicans what they craved—the admission that the federal government possessed power over slavery.[125] According to a Georgia Douglasite, extreme southerners and Republicans "both are for *intervention*, though for different ends—the one, intervention against, and the other, intervention for slavery." A slave code would backfire if ever Congress decided to proscribe rather than safeguard.[126]

Many Democrats in the slave states continued to back the man who had permitted them to joust with free laborers as equals in the nation's hinterlands. In his attempt at a Senate seat in Arkansas in 1860, Albert Rust attacked the state's dominant Democratic clique, the "Little Rock junto and dynasty," in language similar to that of Douglasites maligning the dictatorial Buchanan administration. Rust transposed national issues onto a state election by supporting Douglas and popular sovereignty and opposing the federal administration, a congressional slave code, and disunion. Alabamian Daniel R. Hundley, in Chicago trying to publish his sociological study of the South, recorded Douglas's triumph over Lincoln in his diary. Douglas's essay in *Harper's*, "an abler article than I expected to find," he reflected, "won me over to its views." Although Hundley still anticipated that a "conservative Southerner, would make a better man & a better President," his hope was to "unite the Democratic party, and show an undivided front to the common enemy."[127]

Henry Wise's typically eccentric course regarding Kansas reveals the difficulties of painting his party's travails in stark sectional hues. Wise used his opposition to the proslavery Lecompton constitution to cultivate his intersectional iconoclasm. He addressed public letters to northern audiences supporting Douglas against the administration.[128] The Virginian flirted with a Wise-Douglas presidential ticket, provided the Illinoisan would "consent to be *Vice*." He even convinced himself that his celebrity gave him "more strength in the North than" Douglas.[129] In 1859, in addition to martyring John Brown, he authored the lengthiest, most idiosyncratic volume of the pamphlet war. He contended that states projected their sovereignty into the territories yet snubbed the nostrum of a federal slave code. Wise hewed a line between Douglas's *"squatter sovereignty"* and "such state rights as Jeff. Davis proclaims from Missi."[130] He had lost patience with how frequently "the South has poked its finger in its own eyes" through such brinksmanship.[131]

Wise disavowed territorial legislatures' power over slavery. But the people's sovereignty was inviolable at the statehood phase, and, for Wise, a sovereign convention was not sovereign enough. Only "the people, who alone are sovereign," could animate a constitution.[132] Vowing "to defend popular sovereignty,"[133] he broke with "his warm, personal friend" after President Buchanan endorsed the Lecompton constitution without popular ratification. The stakes were high. Forming a government "without submission to the sovereign people," Wise warned, was "a doctrine fit only for slaves." Sharing the Little Giant's reverence for the people's sovereignty, he publicly and privately cheered Douglas in his feud with the administration and interpreted his reelection as vindication of "the sovereignty of the organized people, supreme above all mere representative bodies, Conventions or Legislatures."[134]

All Democrats agreed that the sovereign people created constitutions. Those favoring Lecompton cited the supremacy of the popular will, focused through a sovereign constitutional convention. The governor of Alabama found Lecompton legitimate, drafted as it was by a "convention [that] was sovereign in its powers." That Lecompton was not ratified by plebiscite was not itself repudiation of democracy or of the constitutional theory of popular sovereignty. Both conventions and popular referenda were theoretically sound and established means of consecrating fundamental charters. Southerner Robert Toombs deemed popular ratification "prudent," although "not necessary to the validity" of a constitution. Concern over the mode of ratification, moreover, was distinct from damning complaints over the Lecompton convention's fraudulent and unrepresentative nature, for which many Democrats rejected its handiwork.[135] That some pro-Lecompton Democrats strayed from democratic purity to achieve short-term political goals, whether cauterizing Bleeding Kansas or acquiring a new slave state, hardly signified a renunciation of white men's democracy and certainly not a theoretical turn toward antimajoritarianism. Proud members of a party of ideas, Democrats were also pragmatic politicians at a perilous time. Despite the acrimony over *Dred Scott*, Lecompton, and Freeport, Democrats neither denied white men's sovereignty nor disowned democracy. Rather, their enthusiasm for democracy caused them trouble when principle collided with practice.[136]

A fraught political landscape magnified Democrats' internal tiff over popular sovereignty in the late 1850s. Fernando Wood entreated one of the dueling New York delegations to the Charleston convention to "go beyond and behind all hairsplitting discussion of territorial sovereignties," pleading, "the danger has become too imminent for us to stop and to discuss the abstract rights of a handful of men who seek homes in the wilderness." Reverdy Johnson also hoped that "inducements to harmony" outweighed "dogmas as to sovereignty." After explicating his own dogma, Johnson concluded his pamphlet by minimizing "all practical, immaterial differences of opinion on this question of popular sovereignty."[137] Concurring that at this juncture "the harmony & unity of the Democratic Party was so essential to the preservation of the Union," James Bayard bristled at Johnson's disingenuousness. Referencing what another reviewer dubbed Johnson's "bulky pamphlet," Bayard chastised, "Do you think that an elaborate argument on this Question of Popular Sovereignty, which has been raised, and needlessly raised by Mr Douglas, in support of his theoretical views, . . . is calculated to set aside immaterial differences of opinion?"[138]

Basing policy on "abstract rights" and "theoretical views," Democrats spurned practical conservatism to resemble the impassioned fanatics they had previously lampooned. The anti-*isms* party was now guilty of "DOUGLASISM."[139] Democrats had once lauded popular sovereignty as a demonstration of white men's masterly prerogative. In 1860 William Lowndes Yancey cast aside "the effete doctrine of squatter sovereignty," while a combatant in the pamphlet war dismissed Kansas-Nebraska as "hermaphrodite legislation."[140] Standing on a theory for a platform and then quarreling over it, Democrats parroted the impotent "wordy warfare" of "one-idea Abolitionists."[141] Douglas was "flourishing his lance in the empty air"; southern-rights Democrats were "fighting a shadow and for a shadow."[142] George Ticknor Curtis, a conservative finding fault with both Democrats and Republicans, lectured, "When a political party departs from established principles of the Constitution, seeking for new theories . . . , it must necessarily become divided against itself in the pursuit of such theories." Sidney George Fisher, another conservative critic, discredited Democrats' conservatism. Reflecting on the Democracy's self-immolation, he moralized, "Ideas, [and] principles, are sharp tools to play with."[143]

CONCLUSION

American Democracy, American Conservatism

All you are doing and saying is to America dangled mirages,
You have not learn'd of Nature—of the politics of Nature you have not
    learn'd the great amplitude, rectitude, impartiality,
You have not seen that only such as they are for these States,
And that what is less than they must sooner or later lift off from these
    States.
        —Walt Whitman, "To a President," 1860

IN LATE August 1864, former United States senator Benjamin Fitzpatrick fretted from his plantation outside Wetumpka, Alabama, about his son in Mobile, the coastal forts of which had recently fallen to the US military. He warned Elmore Fitzpatrick that "the fortunes of war may place you in the hands of the enemy." Fitzpatrick shared northern contacts who would provide "pecuniary or any other assistance" should Elmore find himself a prisoner of war. He recommended his son call upon George Pugh of Ohio; Indiana's Jesse Bright, expelled from the Senate in 1862 for aiding the Confederacy; John Kelly of New York, Irish Catholicism's lone representative in the House in the mid-1850s; and Fitzpatrick's intimate antebellum friend Franklin Pierce. All were Democrats, as Fitzpatrick had been before the war, and all, Fitzpatrick assured his son, would aid him, "whatever may be their opinion of this contest" that had severed their friendships, party, and nation.[1]

Residual connections between northern and southern Democrats augured well for postbellum reunification. The Democracy flourishes to this day. But what of the happy republic that the party had pledged to preserve? Having added armed treason to his already eclectic political accomplishments, Henry Wise resumed his prewar correspondence with Fernando Wood, Gotham's premier Doughface. In 1866 Wise beseeched Wood to "relieve my mind and heart of the painful doubt and anxiety which oppress them respecting the fate, not only of the Southern States and people, but of the Republic, and of the civil liberty which it was created to establish and defend." The New Yorker did not mince words, offering the Virginian advice quite unlike that which Martin Van Buren had given to Thomas Ritchie three decades earlier. Wood explained that they were living in "an interregnum, to be followed by such measures as will adapt the fundamental form of government to the new order of things; and incorporate into our system the principles thus established by force of arms." Rather than "State sovereignty," there would be "consolidation." Rather than "slavery," there would be black "freedom." Although he had opposed war and emancipation, Wood remained optimistic: "The new Americanism opens up before us, and common sense demands that we should conform to it." During the war, a Democrat had despaired over "abolition despotism" utilizing state power for "the elevation of the negro above the white man." In counseling acceptance of the "new Americanism," Wood was asking such Democrats to concede that fanaticism had overthrown the white man's republic.[2]

Fernando Wood offered Henry Wise and all Democrats a choice. Echoing what Democrats had told Old Whigs in their eulogies of the second party system, Wood announced that "the great questions which made issues between political parties have ceased." "My desire," he confided, "is that we shall realize this change and conform to it. It is folly to fight over the *dead past* when the *live present* and the GREAT FUTURE opens so brightly and beautifully before us." Striking a tone reminiscent of the antebellum party, he implored, "I want America to fill her mission. She is the fixed corner stone of universal liberty throughout the world."[3] Much is rightly made of a melancholy Republican's repurposing of the nation at Gettysburg in 1863. But before years of fratricidal bloodshed had wizened Abraham Lincoln into a gaunt prophet of American exceptionalism, Democrats had claimed stewardship of "the last great experiment of free government."[4] Wood informed his party that they could yet shepherd the republic on its world-historical errand or they could atrophy in recalcitrance. Wood gave Democrats a choice. They squandered it.

Thus did the party of Jefferson and Jackson enter its blighted decades. Democrats stood athwart history shrilly screaming stop. The Solid South's rotten boroughs enfeebled the national party. Neither Populists nor Progressives could shake the Democracy from its thralldom to pitchfork-toting, white-plumed demagogues. The party remained that of white male supremacy but neglected to pair it with a political economy that succored the people.

Industrialism's paupers ended up with Goldbugs instead of Loco-Focos. Dreary farmers endured grim prospects whether voting for staid Bourbons or New South modernizers, all the while yearning for Jackson to break up the monopolies spreading dependency in the wake of "progress." Boy Bryan's oratory could not sustain the yeomen when the party eviscerated Populism. Al Smith's urbanity could not console polyglot workingmen when the party sold its soul to a parochial bigotry that would have raised Henry Wise's hackles.

The Democracy nourished white men on race-baiting bile, an antebellum legacy the party honored. Democrats' white supremacy intensified after abolition and the granting of federal citizenship and suffrage to African Americans. In 1860 Mississippi's Albert Gallatin Brown, one of Stephen Douglas's antagonists over popular sovereignty, had reaffirmed for the Little Giant his "cordial personal friendship" and his "regard for you politically in all things; save *niggers*."[5] Brown mischaracterized the party's impasse. The Democracy came apart on a narrow, albeit theoretically profound, "conflict of opinion as to the source and extent of the power to legislate for the people of a Territory."[6] Democrats differed over white men's democratic power concerning slavery, not over the institution itself. The nation broke over the morality of slavery in 1861; the Democracy did not. Even Democrats hostile to slavery's expansion would have happily continued living in a slaveholding republic. After the war, southern and northern Democrats reunited on white supremacy, about which they had never disagreed.

Along with white male supremacy, the party still offered up local democracy, an increasingly stale shibboleth. Antebellum Democrats' effusions for democracy had not simply been electioneering humbug. Democratic self-governance constituted their identity. White men manifested their theoretical sovereignty and their racial and gender mastery when they gathered as equals to democratically determine others' rights. With emancipation, democracy no longer enabled a conservative defense of white men's exclusive power, but it did fuel a reactionary crusade. Democracy plumbed its nadir when local majorities harrowed minorities with patriotism, Protestantism, and prohibition and when racial terror received sanction as "home rule." Many Democrats ceased to value diversity, even among white men. They enforced uniformity within island communities and otherwise flailed against modernity. Self-rule descended into rancor between drys and wets, xenophobes and immigrants, urbanites and hayseeds.[7] The blunt deployment of democracy to defend privilege, initiated by Democrats in the interbellum era, was the party's contribution to American conservatism.

The 1850s Democracy rejuvenated conservatism by reimagining individualism and democracy as "conservative." Democrats lost their republic. But they did wrench American conservatism in a new direction. Traditional conservatism, taking solace in social organicism and antipathetic to liberal democracy, persists. Yet a thoroughly modern and distinctly American conservatism has also emerged. Individualism and democratic populism characterize contemporary conservatism in the United States, especially with the ascendance of the New Right after the Second World War. Americans trumpet their exceptionalism. They can at least cite their conservatism as unprecedented, untethered as it is from Europe's anti-Enlightenment reactionaries. The intellectual forerunners of this ideologically virile political coalition are antebellum Democrats, who squared liberal individualism and majoritarian democracy with social and racial order. Democrats discerned that those who opposed progress could not eschew democracy in a liberal democratic political culture, a culture they had themselves shaped in the early 1800s. No group could better articulate an American conservatism than the party that had already defined liberal democracy in the United States.

Classical liberals, devoted to individual rights, laissez-faire economics, and antistatism, usually find themselves relegated to today's Right. The Democracy's dependence on individualism as a conservative force in the 1850s helps account for how classical liberalism gradually became conservative libertarianism by the mid-twentieth century. Scholars of conservatism have not pushed the long history of libertarianism back far enough. Its roots reach to the antebellum period, before twentieth-century free-market zealots deified Austrian economists and even before Gilded Age classical liberals repurposed their dogmas to fortify private property and impede the state's amelioration of capitalist inequality. The Right's appropriation of classical liberalism, crassly bourgeois and selfishly individualistic to some traditionalists, was necessary in a liberal democratic landscape.[8]

The modern Right is also home to populist, democratic conservatives, who trust majorities within political communities not to spur change but to stymie it. Deference to local prescription is reconcilable with traditional conservatism except for a democratic edginess that would have made Federalists and Whigs shudder. Grassroots conservatives are comfortable with modernity, capitalism, and popular politics. They even exhibit Jackson's faith in the masses. Borrowing his populist idiom, they invoke "the people" to halt progress. After the executive, legislature, and judiciary countenance change, they can insist on ratification by the true sovereigns, making majoritarian democracy an insurmountable hurdle to reform. Jackson's nemesis, John Quincy Adams, once worried that state-led improvements could be "palsied by the will of our constituents," a seemingly undemocratic sentiment upon which Jacksonians pounced. Adams intuited the stultifying effects of kowtowing to the masses.[9]

Grassroots conservatism, unpredictably populist, and libertarian conservatism, wary when egalitarian impulses infringe on the individual, fraternize uneasily on the Right. The tension between local majoritarianism and individualism has prompted clever political and intellectual fusions. Many twentieth-century historians conclude that the crucible of racial and cultural backlash forged libertarian and communitarian conservatisms into an ecumenical New Right arrayed against liberal statism and progressive social movements.[10] Race and antifanaticism similarly synthesized interbellum Democrats' thought, when they theorized that local communities of self-governing individuals would preserve white supremacy through the democratic process. Previously, Democrats had sought to enlarge the body politic, a "progressive" endeavor conceived by Jefferson and consummated by Jackson. The white male individual whom they democratically empowered was the "liberal" individual of Enlightenment social contract theory, secure in his natural rights under a circumscribed state. Wearying of radicalism, Democrats turned him into an implement of social order, confident he would use majoritarian democracy to perpetuate inequality.

Democrats breathed new life into American conservatism by reducing democracy and individualism to brittle tools of exclusion. They pioneered the rhetorical and theoretical arguments employed by savvy conservatives ever since. Democrats' liberal individual, still a raced, gendered, and historically enmeshed entity, was enlisted by the New Right. The rhetoric of color-blind meritocracy and equal competition among abstract individuals occludes hierarchies, including those based on gender, race, and sexuality. The inviolability of individual rights prohibits an energetic state from addressing systemic injustice and dismantling agglomerations of power, something Jackson was willing to do for white men.[11] Modern conservatives have also been more successful than Douglas, Wise, and Buchanan in turning democracy toward conservative ends. Just as Douglas made the status of African Americans the purview of "political communities," individual and minority rights are often arbitrated by local majorities of the like-minded. America's little platoons dispense—or withhold—rights. In the United States, individualism *and* democracy can work together to consecrate an inegalitarian present.

Yet, as Democrats learned, while democracy is an asset in the hands of the privileged, it can be a means of advancement for everyone else. Majority rule applied to territorial slavery exposed the precariousness of relying on the people to forestall innovation. Democrats in the 1850s had somehow forgotten that the self-governing people do not always sanctify the status quo. By using democracy to conserve, Democrats injected a potentially subversive element into American conservatism. The party of Jackson teaches us that democracy, like conservatism, is a creature of context. Depending upon who can wield it, democracy can empower or marginalize. Democracy is power. Few have appreciated this truism so well as Andrew Jackson, and few have misunderstood it so brazenly as those who claimed his mantle in the 1850s. Jackson knew that the injustice that is most ineradicable, as well as the progress that is most far-reaching, is that which is consented to by "the people."

NOTES

Abbreviations

ADAH	Alabama Department of Archives and History
CG	*Congressional Globe*
DD	*Speeches; Correspondence, Etc., of the Late Daniel S. Dickinson*
DU	David M. Rubinstein Rare Book and Manuscript Library, Duke University
EFP	William Hayden English Family Papers, Manuscript and Visual Collections Department, William Henry Smith Memorial Library, Indiana Historical Society
FDP	*The Frederick Douglass Papers. Series One: Speeches, Debates, and Interviews*
HAW	*A Biographical Sketch of Henry A. Wise*, ed. James P. Hambleton
ISL	Manuscripts and Rare Books Division, Indiana State Library
JB	*The Works of James Buchanan*
JGD	John G. Davis Papers (microfilm), Manuscript and Visual Collections Department, William Henry Smith Memorial Library, Indiana Historical Society
LC	Manuscript Division, Library of Congress
LDD	*The Lincoln-Douglas Debates of 1858*, ed. Robert W. Johannsen
RMTH	"Correspondence of Robert M. T. Hunter, 1826–1876"
SAD	Stephen A. Douglas Papers, Special Collections Research Center, University of Chicago Library
SHC	Southern Historical Collection, Louis Round Wilson Special Collections Library, University of North Carolina at Chapel Hill
VHS	Virginia Historical Society
WCL	William L. Clements Library, University of Michigan
WFP	Wise Family Papers, 1777–1973, Virginia Historical Society
WHS	Wisconsin Historical Society

Introduction

1. Horton, *Life and Public Services*, 399–401 (quoted); Klein, *President James Buchanan*, 47–49, 53–56, 60–61, 252–53.

2. Buchanan to John E. Ward et al., Committee, June 16, 1856, in *JB*, 10:82.

3. National and Jackson Democratic Association, *Democratic Policy and Its Fruits*, 7.

4. Ward, *Speech . . . at a Democratic Meeting*, 4.

5. *(Indianapolis) Indiana Daily State Sentinel*, Mar. 4, 1854.

6. A. A. Coleman, "Antebellum Democratic Party Address, before 1861," manuscript speech, 6, 16, Coleman-Stuart Family Papers, WCL.

7. Ashworth, *"Agrarians" and "Aristocrats,"* 10–15, 21–34; Beeman, "Deference, Republicanism"; Ford, "Making the 'White Man's Country' White," 730–37; Fredrickson, *Black Image in the White Mind*, 58–64; Huston, *Stephen A. Douglas*, 1–24; Robertson, "Voting Rites and Voting Acts"; Roediger, *Wages of Whiteness;* Saxton, *Rise and Fall;* Stewart, "Emergence of Racial Modernity"; Sweet, *Bodies Politic;* Watson, *Liberty and Power*, 49–54; Wood, *Radicalism of the American Revolution*.

8. Horton, *Life and Public Services*, 427.

9. Hunter, *Democratic Demonstration at Poughkeepsie*, 16.

10. Paul S. Preston to Jackson Woodward, Oct. 28, 1847, Preston-Woodward Correspondence, WCL.

11. Robert McClelland to Alpheus Felch, Apr. 28, 1850, Alpheus Felch Papers, Bentley Historical Library, University of Michigan.

12. On cultural approaches, see Baker, *Affairs of Party;* Freeman, *Affairs of Honor;* Pasley, "Cheese and the Words"; Robertson, "Voting Rites and Voting Acts"; Ryan, *Civic Wars;* and Warner, *Letters of the Republic.* Scholars of republicanism earlier reminded us that political rhetoric conveyed substantive ideology, which some subsequent cultural approaches have obscured. Bailyn, *Ideological Origins of the American Revolution;* Watson, *Liberty and Power;* Wood, *Creation of the American Republic;* Wood, *Radicalism of the American Revolution*.

13. Quotations from J. C. Wales to Stephen A. Douglas, Mar. 28, 1856, SAD; I. R. Askew to Stephen A. Douglas, Jan. 8, 1848, SAD; and Cluskey, *Buchanan and Breckinridge*, 4.

14. Jeptha Dudley et al., Democratic Central Committee, to Holt, June 14, 1855 (quoted); Joseph Holt to Maggie Holt, Oct. 11, 14, 1856 (quoted); Thomas H. Holt to [Joseph Holt], Sept. 25, 1856; W. W. Trapp and J. Dudley to Holt, Oct. 10, 1856; W. W. Trapp to Holt, Oct. 16, 1856; Maggie Holt to Joseph Holt, Oct. 18, 1856, all Joseph Holt Papers, LC.

15. Nichols, *Disruption of American Democracy*, 25; Randall, "Blundering Generation." On ideology and sectionalism, see Baum, *Civil War Party System;* Earle, *Jacksonian Antislavery;* Foner, *Free Soil, Free Labor, Free Men*, 8–9; Foner, *Politics and Ideology*, 34–53; McCurry, *Masters of Small Worlds;* McManus, *Political Abolitionism in Wisconsin;* and Sinha, *Counterrevolution of Slavery.* Recent scholarship is examining often ignored compromisers, harmonizers, and nationalists. Conlin, "Dangerous *Isms* and the Fanatical *Ists*"; Mason, *Apostle of Union;* Shelden, *Washington Brotherhood*.

16. Earle, *Jacksonian Antislavery;* Feller, "Brother in Arms"; Foner, *Free Soil, Free Labor, Free Men*, 149–85; Hershock, "'Agitation Is as Necessary'"; Mueller, *Senator Benton and the People*, 226–59; Richards, *Slave Power*, 107–215; Schlesinger, *Age of Jackson*, 469–97; Wilentz, *Rise of American Democracy*, 663–64, 675–76, 703–6;

Wilentz, "Slavery, Antislavery, and Jacksonian Democracy." For 1850s Democrats as undemocratic and proslavery/prosouthern, see Baker, *James Buchanan;* Hettle, *Peculiar Democracy;* and Landis, *Northern Men with Southern Loyalties.*

17. Baker, *Affairs of Party,* 111–14.

18. Lynn, "From the Money Power"; Olson, *Abolition of White Democracy.*

19. Austin, *Buchananism Not Democracy,* 2. For Civil War–era northern Democrats' nationalism, racism, and antireformism, see Collins, "Ideology of the Antebellum Northern Democrats"; Etcheson, *Emerging Midwest,* 63–126; Rodgers, "Liberty, Will, and Violence"; and Silbey, *Respectable Minority,* 23–29, 66–88. Although blurring the antebellum, wartime, and postbellum periods, Jean H. Baker's rigorous cultural and intellectual analysis examines the northern Democracy's republicanism, conservatism, and racism and rebuts its superficial proslavery image. Largely ignoring southerners and minimizing slavery and race, Yonatan Eyal argues that the 1850s Democracy became more *progressive* due to the Young America movement. Michael Todd Landis's recent work on northern Democrats does not discuss ideology. In a rare work on southern Democratic ideology and culture, Wallace Hettle explores the tension between democratic ideas and white male supremacy. Baker, *Affairs of Party;* Eyal, *Young America Movement;* Landis, *Northern Men with Southern Loyalties;* Hettle, *Peculiar Democracy.*

20. For similar approaches to intellectual history, ideology, and political thought, see Ashworth, *"Agrarians" and "Aristocrats";* Baker, *Affairs of Party,* 143–47; Skinner, "Ideological Context of Hobbes's Political Thought"; and Skinner, "Meaning and Understanding." For political texts as simultaneously tracts on public policy and theoretical treatises, albeit divorced from historical context, see Strauss, "Machiavelli's Intention."

21. Edwards, *People and Their Peace;* Tomlins, *Law, Labor, and Ideology.*

22. Geertz, "Ideology as a Cultural System," 57–65. On political ideology, see Love, *Understanding Dogmas and Dreams,* 1–20; and Foner, *Free Soil, Free Labor, Free Men,* 4–10. On political culture, see Baker, *Affairs of Party,* 5–14; Baker, "Politics, Paradigms, and Public Culture"; Formisano, "Concept of Political Culture"; and Pasley, Robertson, and Waldstreicher, *Beyond the Founders.* On constructions of race, gender, and domesticity in partisan politics, see Edwards, "Domesticity versus Manhood Rights"; Pierson, *Free Hearts and Free Homes;* and Sinha, "Caning of Charles Sumner." For an opposite view of politics in daily life, see Altschuler and Blumin, *Rude Republic.*

23. Oakeshott, "On Being Conservative," quotations on 407, 408; Burke, *Reflections on the Revolution in France,* 7. On conservatism as an ideology, often derived from Burke, see Allen, "Modern Conservatism"; Huntington, "Conservatism as an Ideology," quotation on 468; Kirk, *Conservative Mind,* 3–70; and Rossiter, *Conservatism in America,* 3–66.

24. Bancroft to Cass, Oct. 22, 1848, Lewis Cass Papers, WCL.

25. Buchanan to William L. Marcy, Feb. 24, 1854, William L. Marcy Papers, LC; Higham, "From Boundlessness to Consolidation."

26. "Speech of Hon. D. S. Dickinson at the Democratic Convention at Syracuse," in *Proceedings of the Democratic State Convention*, 10.

27. *Last Appeal to Pennsylvania*, 7. Democrats called their party "the Democracy" to claim stewardship of American "democracy." The phrase "conservative Democracy" thus described the rebranding of their party and of democracy itself as conservative.

28. Michael F. Conlin and Adam I. P. Smith lump Democrats together with other late antebellum conservatives, inviting consideration of their unique conservatism. On early American conservatism, see Barkan, "Emergence of a Whig Persuasion"; Brown, *Politics and Statesmanship*, 49–92; Bruce, *Rhetoric of Conservatism;* Conlin, "Dangerous *Isms* and the Fanatical *Ists*"; Cotlar, *Tom Paine's America*, 82–114; Fischer, *Revolution of American Conservatism;* Fredrickson, *Inner Civil War*, 23–35; Genovese, *Southern Tradition;* Howe, *Political Culture of the American Whigs*, 210–37; Kirk, *Conservative Mind*, 71–113, 150–84, 225–59; Levine, "Conservatism, Nativism, and Slavery"; Risjord, *Old Republicans;* Roberts, "'Revolutions Have Become the Bloody Toy'"; Rossiter, *Conservatism in America*, 97–127; Sinha, *Counterrevolution of Slavery;* Smith, "Conservatism, Transformation"; and Wiecek, "'A Peculiar Conservatism.'"

29. Crick, "Strange Quest for an American Conservatism"; Hartz, *Liberal Tradition in America;* Maciag, *Edmund Burke in America*, 25–104; Rossiter, *Conservatism in America*, 67–96.

30. *James Buchanan, His Doctrines*, 2, 4.

31. Buchanan to William B. Reed, Feb. 29, 1856, in *JB*, 10:63.

32. Brinkley, "Problem of American Conservatism," 415–17; Huntington, "Conservatism as an Ideology," 472–73; Rossiter, *Conservatism in America*, 54–59.

1. The Northern Men and Their *National* Principle

1. Coleman, "Antebellum Democratic Party Address," 8–9; *1. Letter of Hon. James Shields*, 1; Jones, *Letter*, 15–16.

2. Bayard to Dr. Jno. Merritt, Oct. 24, 1854, copy, Thomas F. Bayard Papers, LC.

3. G. F. Corkeely[?] to John G. Davis, Jan. 12, 1854, JGD.

4. Buchanan, *Great Speech*, 13; [Wise] to [?], Dec. 2, 1846, Henry A. Wise Papers (microfilm), Eastern Shore of Virginia Historical Society.

5. Worth to Joseph Nill, Jan. 10, 1848, copy, EFP.

6. Kyle to Joseph A. Wright, May 10, 1852, Joseph A. Wright Correspondence and Papers, ISL; Etcheson, *Emerging Midwest*, 40–52.

7. English, draft speech in undated notebook, [1852?], EFP.

8. Franklin Pierce et al., Democratic State Central Committee, to Woodbury, Feb. 6, 1843, copy, Franklin Pierce Papers, LC; Woodbury to Franklin Pierce et al., Democratic State Central Committee, Feb. 11, 1843, Pierce Papers (quoted).

9. English, draft speech in undated notebook, [1852?], EFP.

10. Paul. S. Preston to Woodward, Aug. 21, 1845 (quoted), Oct. 28, 1847, Preston-Woodward Correspondence. For similar interpretations of Jacksonians as rational

actors ideologically contesting the Market Revolution's inegalitarian aspects, see Ashworth, *"Agrarians" and "Aristocrats"*; Schlesinger, *Age of Jackson;* Watson, *Liberty and Power;* and Wilentz, *Rise of American Democracy*. For differing interpretations of Jacksonianism, see Hofstadter, *American Political Tradition*, 44–66; Howe, *What Hath God Wrought*, 328–445, 498–501; Kohl, *Politics of Individualism;* Meyers, *Jacksonian Persuasion;* and Sellers, *Market Revolution*. For nuanced assessments of Jacksonian antistatism, see Richard, "The 'Great Depression'"; and Watson, "Andrew Jackson's Populism."

11. Dromgoole, *Address*, 1.

12. Elijah F. Purdy et al. to John Y. Mason, Dec. 1, 1847, printed invitation, John Y. Mason Papers, SHC; Ward, *Andrew Jackson*.

13. National and Jackson Democratic Association, *Democratic Policy and Its Fruits*, 1–4; Johannsen, *Stephen A. Douglas*, 183–85.

14. Dromgoole, *Address*, 1.

15. Dallas, Diary, Mar. 2, 1849, in "Mystery of the Dallas Papers. Part II," 515; Belohlavek, *George Mifflin Dallas*, 111–18.

16. Democratic Committee of Publication, *Life of George Mifflin Dallas*, 15.

17. Chapman, *Inaugural Address*, 3 (quoted); William Allen to Effie Allen, July 17 (quoted), 21, 24, 1846, William Allen Papers, LC.

18. Dallas, *Great Speech*, 16–17; Worth to Joseph Nill, Jan. 10, 1848, copy, EFP; Dorr to Edmund Burke, Oct. 3, 1849, Edmund Burke Papers, LC.

19. Hofstadter, *Idea of a Party System*, 236–38; Watson, *Liberty and Power*, 70–72, 87–88, 165–66.

20. George M. Dallas to Sophia Dallas, Dec. 11, 1848, Jan. 11, 1849, in "Mystery of the Dallas Papers. Part II," 484, 491; Daniel R. Hundley Diary, Dec. 7, 1859, WCL; Potter, *Impending Crisis*, 18–23.

21. Polk to Lewis Cass, Jan. 9, 1849, Cass Papers; [A. B. Conduitt] to W. A. Gorman, Feb. 11, 1850, EFP.

22. George R. Griswold to [Alpheus Felch], Jan. 16, Feb. 13 (quoted), 1848, Felch Papers; Henry Chipman to Alpheus Felch, Mar. 1, 1850, Felch Papers; Hershock, "'Agitation Is as Necessary,'" 143–50.

23. Tappan to Allen, Dec. 25, 1848, Allen Papers (quoted); H. C. Whitman to William Medill, Jan. 30, 1849, Allen Papers; Earle, *Jacksonian Antislavery*, 182–87; Feller, "Brother in Arms," especially 69–71.

24. *Indiana Daily State Sentinel*, Aug. 3, 1854.

25. Ashworth, *"Agrarians" and "Aristocrats,"* 177–223; Watson, *Liberty and Power*, 172–97. For the contrary argument that "ethnocultural" issues drove Jacksonian politics, see Benson, *Concept of Jacksonian Democracy;* Kleppner, *Cross of Culture;* Silbey, *Partisan Imperative*, 69–84; and Swierenga, "Ethnoreligious Political Behavior."

26. [Illegible] to Hall, June 28, 1853, Bolling Hall Family Papers, ADAH; L. W. Graves to John Perkins, July 30, 1855, John Perkins Papers, SHC; Robert McLane to Louis McLane, Jan. 31, 1854[?], Louis McLane Correspondence, LC.

27. [Illegible] to John G. Davis, Feb. 4, 1854, JGD.

28. "Mr. Hunter's Speech in Richmond," in *HAW*, 81; Bayard to Dr. Jno. Merritt, Oct. 24, 1854, copy, Bayard Papers; Leland R. [Illegible] to John G. Davis, Apr. 23, 1854, John Givan Davis Papers (microfilm), WHS.

29. Drake, *Address*, 3, 9–16.

30. King to Neil Blue, Apr. 11, 1850, Matthew P. Blue Family Papers, ADAH (quoted); King to Bolling Hall, Nov. 19, 1850, Hall Family Papers (quoted); King to Philip Phillips, Mar. 11, 1851, Philip Phillips Family Papers, LC; William R. King to William T. King, Mar. 27, 1851, photocopy, William R. King Family Papers, ADAH; "Resolutions from Sumter County, AL, Favoring the Resolutions of the Nashville Convention, 1850," draft manuscript, Coleman-Stuart Family Papers; Potter, *Impending Crisis*, 51–120.

31. Bayard to Henry Clay, July 1, 1850, draft, Bayard Papers.

32. N. T. Rosseter to Douglas, Jan. 2, 1848, SAD.

33. Gorman to A. B. Conduitt, Jan. 17, 1850, copy, EFP; [A. B. Conduitt] to Gorman, Feb. 11, 1850, EFP; Childers, *Failure of Popular Sovereignty*, 102–34.

34. J. F. Brown to Austin H. Brown, Aug. 2, 1850, Austin H. Brown Papers, ISL.

35. Dallas, *Great Speech*, 13–15.

36. "Speech on the Acquisition of Territory, and the Formation of Governments for the Territories.—The Doctrine of 'Popular Sovereignty' Proposed and Defended. Delivered in the Senate of the United States, January 12, 1848," in *DD*, 1:228 (quoted); Cass, *Letter*, 5 (quoted); *Territorial Slavery Question*, 7–11; Ambacher, "Pennsylvania Origins of Popular Sovereignty"; Belohlavek, *George Mifflin Dallas*, 126–28; Childers, *Failure of Popular Sovereignty*; Childers, "Interpreting Popular Sovereignty"; Johnson, "Genesis of Popular Sovereignty"; Klunder, "Lewis Cass, Stephen Douglas"; Klunder, "Seeds of Popular Sovereignty"; Potter, *Impending Crisis*, 72.

37. "Extract from Notes of P. Phillips Left for His Children," [ca. 1870–76], typescript, 2, Phillips Family Papers (quoted); Edmund Burke to Stephen A. Douglas, Jan. 9, 1854, SAD; Douglas, *Letter . . . in Reply to the Editor*, 6; Douglas, *Speech . . . on the "Measures of Adjustment*," 6–7; *Territorial Slavery Question*; Childers, *Failure of Popular Sovereignty*, 204–33; Etcheson, *Bleeding Kansas*, 9–27; Freehling, *Secessionists at Bay*, 536–65; Holt, *Fate of Their Country*, 92–111; Holt, "Politics, Patronage, and Public Policy"; Johannsen, *Stephen A. Douglas*, 395–434; Learned, "Relation of Philip Phillips"; Nichols, "Kansas-Nebraska Act"; Paulus, "America's Long Eulogy for Compromise," 28–39; Potter, *Impending Crisis*, 145–76; Rensink, "Nebraska and Kansas Territories."

38. Henry J. Wilde to Caleb Cushing, Mar. 4, 1853 [1854], Caleb Cushing Papers, LC; Clingman, *Address*, 8; Conlin, "Dangerous *Isms* and the Fanatical *Ists*," 207, 219–25.

39. [A. B. Conduitt] to W. A. Gorman, Feb. 11, 1850, EFP.

40. Loring, *Speech Delivered at Webster, Mass.*, 4–6; Polk to Lewis Cass, Dec. 15, 1848, Cass Papers.

41. Phillips, *Speech*, 14.

42. Cass, *Letter*, 6–7 (quoted); "Extract from Notes of P. Phillips," 5 (quoted); Douglas, *Letter . . . in Reply to the Editor*, 7; Ward, *Speech . . . at the Great Democratic Mass Meeting*, 8; Ramsdell, "Natural Limits of Slavery Expansion."

43. Cooley, *Review of the Administration*, 8–9 (quoted); Dix, *Speech*, 4, 11–14; Jarvis, *Facts and Arguments*, 60; Childers, *Failure of Popular Sovereignty*, 174–75, 234–35; Etcheson, *Bleeding Kansas*, 28–35, 42–43, 95–96; Finkelman, "Appeasement of 1850," 50–55; Freehling, *Secessionists at Bay*, 550–51; Freehling, *Secessionists Triumphant*, 123–28; Huston, *Stephen A. Douglas*, 72–80, 96; Potter, *Impending Crisis*, 173–74.

44. Cameron to Edmund Burke, June 15, 1849, Burke Papers.

45. Josiah H. Drummond to Hannibal Hamlin, Apr. 9, 1856, Hamlin Family Papers (microfilm), Special Collections Department, Raymond H. Fogler Library, University of Maine at Orono.

46. F. J. Betts to Alpheus Felch, July 30, 1856, Felch Papers; James A. Bayard to Thomas F. Bayard, July 9, 1854, Bayard Papers.

47. Thompson, *Squatter Sovereignty*, 8.

48. Randolph quoted in *Springfield (MA) Hampden Federalist and Public Journal*, Apr. 12, 1820; Lynn, "Half-Baked Men"; Richards, *Slave Power*, 83–215; Sperber and Tidwell, "Words and Phrases in American Politics," 95–100; Wood, "'A Sacrifice on the Altar of Slavery.'"

49. Quotations from *Vermont Intelligencer and Bellows' Falls Advertiser*, May 1, 1820; *Carlisle (PA) Republican*, Oct. 6, 1820; and *Providence (RI) Gazette*, Aug. 14, 1820.

50. "Dough-Face Song," in Whitman, *Complete Prose Works*, 334.

51. W. M. Prentiss, J. P. Christian, et al. to Robert McClelland and Alpheus Felch, July 17, 1848, Felch Papers.

52. Van Buren to [Jeremiah] Clemens, [1854?], Box 3, Folder 34, Cass Papers.

53. [Lyman], *Leaven for Doughfaces*, 17.

54. "Moral Responsibility of Statesmen. Speech of Hon. J. R. Giddings," *CG*, 33rd Cong., 1st Sess., 1853–54, 23, appendix: 989.

55. Polk to Cass, Nov. 14, 1848, Cass Papers; Daniel Hoit to [J. A. Bean], Jan. 31, 1851, Hoit Family Papers, WCL.

56. Wise, *Letter*, 6.

57. Walker, *Speech*, 14.

58. *Territorial Slavery Question*, 11.

59. Douglas to Lewis Cass, June 13, 1848, Cass Papers.

60. Johnson to Levi B. Smith et al. (Committee), June 8, 1855, copy, Herschel V. Johnson Papers, DU; Perkins, *Speech*, 31–32.

61. Seymour, *Speech*, 7.

62. John Law to Stephen A. Douglas, Dec. 6, 1851, SAD.

63. Robert McLane to Louis McLane, June 15, 1854, McLane Correspondence.

64. G. W. Hopkins to [Stephen A. Douglas], Jan. 18, 1848, SAD.

65. Lynn, "From the Money Power." For the contrary argument of Democrats and Whigs' convergence, see Holt, *Political Crisis of the 1850s*, 101–81.

66. *Territorial Slavery Question*, 6.

67. Cass, *Letter*, 7. On popular sovereignty as pragmatism, see Johannsen, *Stephen A. Douglas*, 233, 239–40; as principle and pragmatism, see Childers, *Failure of Popular Sovereignty*; Etcheson, *Bleeding Kansas*, 15, 20–22; and Huston, *Stephen A.*

Douglas; as political theory, see Huston, "Democracy by Scripture"; Jaffa, *Crisis of the House Divided;* and Johnson, "Genesis of Popular Sovereignty"; as proslavery and lacking substance, see Landis, *Northern Men with Southern Loyalties,* 101–19.

68. *Douglas' Doctrine of Popular Sovereignty,* 30–31 (quoted); Douglas, *Popular Sovereignty . . . Douglas in Reply,* 23; Johnson, *Speech,* 3.

69. McConnel to Douglas, Jan. 28, 1854, SAD.

70. James Buchanan to John E. Ward et al., Committee, June 16, 1856, in *JB,* 10:82–83.

71. Paine, *Common Sense,* 67 (quoted); Dillon, *Inquiry into the Nature;* Hobbes, *Leviathan,* chap. 18; Locke, *Second Treatise,* chaps. 2, 3, 9, 11, 19; Montesquieu, *Spirit of the Laws,* bk. 2, chaps. 2–3, bk. 3, chaps. 2–3; Dippel, "Changing Idea of Popular Sovereignty"; Kloppenberg, "Virtues of Liberalism," 23–25, 30–33; Morgan, *Inventing the People;* Wood, *Creation of the American Republic.*

72. Dickinson, "Speech on the Acquisition of Territory," 1:241; "Extracts of a Speech of Hon. A. H. Stephens, of Georgia," Feb. 17, 1854, in *Popular Sovereignty in the Territories,* 8.

73. Quotations from "Letter of Hon. Philip Phillips," *Pennsylvanian,* Oct. 24, 1855, clipping in bound volume, Box 13, Phillips Family Papers; and Phillips, *Speech,* 14.

74. Quotations from Jackson, "Farewell Address," Mar. 4, 1837, and "Fifth Annual Message," Dec. 3, 1833, in Richardson, *Compilation of the Messages,* 3:30, 306; Bailyn, *Ideological Origins of the American Revolution;* Holt, *Political Crisis of the 1850s;* Robbins, *Eighteenth-Century Commonwealthman;* Rodgers, "Republicanism"; Watson, *Liberty and Power;* Wood, *Creation of the American Republic;* Wood, *Radicalism of the American Revolution.*

75. "Speech of General Aaron Ward," in *Speeches Delivered at a Dinner,* 12; *Indiana Daily State Sentinel,* Mar. 9, 1854.

76. Paul S. Preston to Jackson Woodward, Aug. 3, 1848, Preston-Woodward Correspondence; Jackson, "Farewell Address," 3:295–99; Richards, *Slave Power,* 107–215; Shade, "'The Most Delicate and Exciting Topics'"; Watson, *Liberty and Power,* 70–72, 202–4, 240.

77. Jones, *Speech,* 3; English, *Letter,* 4.

78. Carlos W. Shane to William Allen, July 5, 1847, Allen Papers; Johannsen, *Stephen A. Douglas,* 221–25; Potter, *Impending Crisis,* 63–67.

79. Charles Richmond to Alpheus Felch, Dec. 21, 1848, Felch Papers (quoted); Robert McClelland to Alpheus Felch, Jan. 3, 1850, Felch Papers; Dallas, Diary, Dec. 13, 1848, 485.

80. Perkins, *Speech,* 29 (quoted); John W. Robinson to William P. Fessenden, Jan. 10, 1860, William P. Fessenden Papers, WCL; Etcheson, *Bleeding Kansas,* 9–10; Johannsen, *Stephen A. Douglas,* 395, 398–400.

81. Shields to Douglas, Mar. 6, 1856, SAD.

82. Childers, "Interpreting Popular Sovereignty," 54–57; Huston, "Democracy by Scripture," 197; Huston, *Stephen A. Douglas,* 91, 119, 156; Potter, *Impending Crisis,* 57–59.

83. Dickinson, "Speech on the Acquisition of Territory," 1:244.

84. Greeley, *Why I Am a Whig*, 16; Baker, *Affairs of Party*, 177–258; Ford, "Making the 'White Man's Country' White"; Fredrickson, *Black Image in the White Mind*, 58–70, 90–96; Howe, *What Hath God Wrought*, 342–57, 421–30, 524, 544–46, 584–86, 638–41; Ignatiev, *How the Irish Became White;* Mueller, *Senator Benton and the People;* Olson, *Abolition of White Democracy*, 31–63; Roediger, *Wages of Whiteness*, especially 55–60, 65–80, 140–44; Rothman, *Slave Country*, 119–62; Saxton, *Rise and Fall;* Stewart, "Emergence of Racial Modernity"; Watson, *Liberty and Power*, 13–14, 51–54, 104–13, 241–43; Wood, "'A Sacrifice on the Altar of Slavery.'"

85. Dix, *Speech*, 11–14; Foner, *Free Soil, Free Labor, Free Men*, 261–80; Foner, *Politics and Ideology*, 77–93. For interpretations minimizing racism's role in Jacksonianism, see Earle, *Jacksonian Antislavery;* Wilentz, *Rise of American Democracy*, 512–13, 598–99, 790–91; and Wilentz, "Slavery, Antislavery, and Jacksonian Democracy."

86. H. C. Whitman to William Medill, Jan. 30, 1849, Allen Papers; Fredrickson, *Black Image in the White Mind*, 133–35.

87. Childers, *Failure of Popular Sovereignty*, 4–5, 9–39; Etcheson, *Emerging Midwest*, 15–26; Hammond, *Slavery, Freedom, and Expansion;* Onuf, *Statehood and Union;* Wiebe, *Opening of American Society*, 131–42, 287–88; Wilson, *Space, Time, and Freedom*, 29–34.

88. Etcheson, *Bleeding Kansas*, 20–21; Greenberg, "Manifest Destiny's Hangover"; Mueller, *Senator Benton and the People*, 135–76; Rensink, "Nebraska and Kansas Territories"; Van Atta, "'A Lawless Rabble.'"

89. Charles F. Gowe to Hibbard, Apr. 7, 1850, Burke Papers; *Indiana Daily State Sentinel*, Mar. 2, 1854.

90. Holmes, *Harp and the Hickory Tree*, 6–8; Dickinson, "Speech on the Acquisition of Territory," 1:231, 233–35; Dallas, *Great Speech*, 13; Belohlavek, *George Mifflin Dallas*, 125; Watson, *Liberty and Power*, 53–54.

91. Douglas, *Speech . . . on the "Measures of Adjustment,"* 6–7.

92. Cass, *Letter*, 4 (quoted); Douglas, *Letter . . . in Reply to the Editor*, 3.

93. Charles F. Gowe to Harry Hibbard, Apr. 7, 1850, Burke Papers.

94. William S. Allen to Caleb Cushing, Feb. 20, 1854, Cushing Papers.

95. Joseph A. Wright to John G. Davis, Mar. 18, 1854, JGD (quoted); Dickinson, "Speech on the Acquisition of Territory," 1:243–44 (quoted); *Indiana Daily State Sentinel*, May 20, 1854; W. F. Stuart to William H. English, Mar. 13, 1854, EFP; Johannsen, *Stephen A. Douglas*, 428, 434; Nichols, "Kansas-Nebraska Act," 209–11. For a Democrat favoring the Clayton amendment, see David B. Smealey to Bolling Hall, June 21, 1854, Hall Family Papers.

96. Chadbourne to Charles G. Bellamy, Feb. 28, 1860, Charles G. Bellamy Papers, WCL; Clingman, *Address*, 10–11.

97. *Plain Facts and Considerations*, 27; *Indiana Daily State Sentinel*, Aug. 11, 1854.

98. Chase to Allen, Apr. 8, 1854, Allen Papers; Earle, *Jacksonian Antislavery*, 144–47, 154–62, 182–84.

99. Corry to Joseph Holt, Mar. 1, 1852, Holt Papers.

2. Conservatism and Fanaticism

1. Jonathan S. Wilcox Diaries, Mar. 6, Apr. 7, 1860, WCL.
2. Wilcox Diaries, July 31, 1859, Feb. 19, 1860.
3. Wilcox Diaries, Apr. 8, 1860.
4. *Sketches of the Lives,* 4; Orr, *Cincinnati Convention,* 3.
5. Quotations from *Infidelity and Abolitionism,* 5; "Speech of Hon. Isaac D. Jones," in Pearce, Pratt, Jones, and Crisfield, *Letter,* 13; Hallett et al., *Appeal to Democrats,* 4; and "Letter of Hon. W. R. Scurry, Austin, August 26th, 1856," in Oldham and Scurry, *Rights of the South,* 35.
6. Quotations from A. A. Coleman, "Address on Change in Boyhood Home, before 1861," manuscript speech, 13, Coleman-Stuart Family Papers; *Indiana Daily State Sentinel,* Nov. 27, 1854; *Document for All Thinking Men!,* 1; and "The Slavery Question. Speech of Hon. James A. Stewart," *CG,* 34th Cong., 1st Sess., 1855–56, 25, appendix: 991.
7. Quotations from Stewart, "The Slavery Question," 992; Wood, *Speech,* 4; "Speech of General Lewis Cass," in Cass et al., *Speeches Delivered at Tammany Hall,* 4; James Ferguson to Austin H. Brown, Oct. 14, 1848, Brown Papers; and "Speech on the Maine Law Question. Delivered at a Democratic Ratification Meeting, Held at the Broadway Tabernacle, New York, November 1, 1854," in *DD,* 1:506.
8. [Garnett], *Union, Past and Future,* 26.
9. Quotations from Brown, *Address . . . before the Democratic Association,* 6; "Speech 'On the Political Topics Now Prominent before the Country,' Delivered at Lowell, Mass., October 28, 1856," in Choate and Brown, *Works of Rufus Choate,* 2:393; and *Infidelity and Abolitionism,* 7.
10. *Plain Facts and Considerations,* 31.
11. "Insanity of the Times—Present Condition of Political Parties. Speech of Hon. S. S. Marshall," *CG,* 34th Cong., 1st Sess., 1855–56, 25, appendix: 1227.
12. Dallas, *Great Speech,* 7–8; Dromgoole, *Address,* 1–2.
13. English, *Letter,* 3.
14. *1. Letter of Hon. James Shields,* 1.
15. Quotations from Dallas, *Great Speech,* 28; and *Proceedings of the Celebration,* 11. Jean H. Baker helpfully explains how Democrats were simultaneously adherents of republicanism and of liberal individualism and pluralism. See *Affairs of Party,* 143–48. For a different account of Democratic progressivism, see Eyal, *Young America Movement.*
16. *1. Letter of Hon. James Shields,* 1–2.
17. Coleman, "Address on Change in Boyhood Home," 15.
18. Loring, *Speech Delivered at Webster, Mass.,* 4.
19. Hunter, *Address,* 4; Orr, *Address Delivered before the Philosophian,* 26–27.
20. Robert McClelland to Alpheus Felch, Jan. 17, 1852, Felch Papers.
21. Chandler, *Letter,* 4, 5.
22. Kemper, *Speech,* 14.
23. Quotations from Dallas, *Great Speech,* 21; and Dowdell, *Speech,* 1.

24. William A. Thurston to Douglas, Mar. 5, 1852, SAD; Ross, "Inaugural Address," 159.

25. M. Jordan to Mason, Oct. 29, 1849, Mason Papers; James B. Steedman to Douglas, Nov. 7, 1858, SAD.

26. *United States Magazine, and Democratic Review*, Oct. 1837, 2, 6, 11; "Speech of General E. Ward," in *Speeches Delivered at a Dinner*, 3; Ashworth, *"Agrarians" and "Aristocrats,"* 15–20; Kohl, *Politics of Individualism*, 24–26, 123–29; Rodgers, "Liberty, Will, and Violence," 148–50; Watson, *Liberty and Power*, 240–41.

27. Pugh, *Oration Delivered before the Triennial Convention*, 9–12; Marshall, "Insanity of the Times," 1226, 1227; Conlin, "Dangerous *Isms* and the Fanatical *Ists*," 205–6, 209–13.

28. Loring, *Speech Delivered at Webster, Mass.*, 22.

29. Brown, *Address . . . before the Democratic Association*, 6; Hunter, *Address*, 8.

30. Marshall, "Insanity of the Times," 1228; Wright, *Address*, 15.

31. Loring, *Speech Delivered at Webster, Mass.*, 6.

32. Seymour, *Speech*, 1–4.

33. "Resolutions," Aug. 13, 1853, in Drake, *Address*, 26–27.

34. "Speech of General Lewis Cass," 3.

35. Pugh, *Oration Delivered before the Triennial Convention*, 11–12 (quoted); *United States Democratic Review*, Oct. 1857, 311, 314 (quoted); *Indiana Daily State Sentinel*, Jan. 19, Aug. 26, 1854.

36. *Indiana Daily State Sentinel*, May 15, 1854 (quoted); Macon quoted in Watson, *Liberty and Power*, 62; Sampson W. Harris to Bolling Hall, Sept. 21, 1850, Hall Family Papers; Winston, *Inaugural Address*, 3–4; Dickinson and Lee, *Empire and Nation*, 14.

37. Quotations from Burton, "Inaugural Address," 88; and Wood, *Speech*, 4.

38. Quotations from *Last Appeal to Pennsylvania*, 6; and *Plain Facts and Considerations*, 29.

39. Charles Perkins to William Allen, Feb. 4, 1847, Allen Papers.

40. *Document for All Thinking Men!*, 2, 17.

41. Quotations from *Address of the National Democratic Volunteers*, 3–4; and Child, Wise, and Mason, *Correspondence*, 5.

42. *Address of the National Democratic Volunteers*, 3–4.

43. Wood, *Campaign in Connecticut*, 8.

44. "Speech Delivered in Faneuil Hall, October 31, 1855," in Choate and Brown, *Works of Rufus Choate*, 2:334.

45. Pugh, *Oration Delivered before the Triennial Convention*, 12.

46. Slicer, *Speech*, 5; "Speech Delivered at Barnwell C.H., S.C., October 29, 1858," in Hammond, *Selections from the Letters*, 344–45.

47. Hume, "Of Superstition and Enthusiasm," 77 (quoted); Voltaire, *Fanaticism*, 58 (quoted); Locke, *Letter Concerning Toleration*, especially 47–49; Montesquieu, *Persian Letters*, letters 55, 58, 59, 73, 83; Passmore, "Fanaticism, Toleration and Philosophy." For a sympathetic treatment of abolitionist "fanaticism," see Olson, "Freshness of Fanaticism."

48. Newman, *Fanatics and Hypocrites*.

49. Quotations from [Garnett], *Union, Past and Future*, 6; and *"Franklin Pierce and His Abolition Allies,"* 4.

50. Quotations from Dickinson, "Speech on the Maine Law Question," 499–500; and Seymour, *Speech*, 8.

51. Quotations from Clay, *Love of Truth*, 30; and *Plain Facts and Considerations*, 26.

52. Buchanan, *Mr. Buchanan's Administration*, 64.

53. Wilcox Diaries, Feb. 19 (quoted), Apr. 4, May 14, July 4, 1854, Oct. 7, 1860; Wise, *Lecompton Question*, 2.

54. *Sketches of the Lives*, 9.

55. Quotations from Horatio Seymour to James Campbell, Aug. 7, 1856, Horatio King Papers, LC; and Clay, *Love of Truth*, 12.

56. Quotations from *Document for All Thinking Men!*, 14; and *Proceedings of the Celebration*, 11.

57. "Civil and Religious Liberty Defended. Speech of Hon. John Kelly," *CG*, 34th Cong., 1st Sess., 1855–56, 25, appendix: 1264.

58. Hallett et al., *Appeal to Democrats*, 3.

59. Phillips, *Letter . . . on the Religious Proscription*, 7.

60. *Document for All Thinking Men!*, 14; Passmore, "Fanaticism, Toleration and Philosophy," 219–22.

61. *"Franklin Pierce and His Abolition Allies,"* 2.

62. "Mr. Cobb's Speech, in Depot Hall," in Cobb et al., *Speeches*, 23, 25.

63. "Mr. Cobb's Speech, in Depot Hall," 26.

64. Jones, *John G Davis*, 2.

65. Rufus W. Peckham [Sr.] to Wheeler H. Peckham, Jan. 4, Dec. 17 (quoted), 1860, Wheeler H. Peckham Family Papers, LC.

66. "Mr. Orr's Speech in Phœnix Hall," in Cobb et al., *Speeches*, 10.

67. Hundley Diary, Dec. 23, 1859.

68. Robertson, *South and the Democratic Party*, 9–11.

69. Quotations from "Mr. Cobb's Speech, in Depot Hall," 32; and *Plain Facts and Considerations*, 27.

70. Wilcox Diaries, Apr. 4, 1854.

71. Quotations from A *Maine Law* man, & a Republican to Hannibal Hamlin, Aug. 3, 1856, Hamlin Family Papers; and Drake, *Address*, 9.

72. Author unknown, "Ought a Man to Pledge Himself to Total Abstinence," manuscript speech, 1, Sydenham Moore Family Papers, ADAH; Moore to Mr. James, [1860?], Moore Family Papers.

73. [Illegible] to John G. Davis, Feb. 4, 1854, JGD; Wilcox Diaries, Oct. 7, 1860.

74. "National Politics. Speech of Hon. David Barclay," *CG*, 34th Cong., 1st Sess., 1855–56, 25, appendix: 1086, 1088 (quoted); *Agitation of Slavery*, 3–4; Brown, *Address . . . before the Democratic Association*, 13–15; Forney, *Address on Religious Intolerance*, 22–23.

75. Newman, *Fanatics and Hypocrites*, 21.

76. Sebastian, *Substance of the Speech*, 3.

77. *Address of the National Democratic Volunteers*, 4 (quoted); Ashworth, *"Agrarians" and "Aristocrats,"* 199–203; Schlesinger, *Age of Jackson*, 136–40 (quoted), 180–85, 350–60.

78. Wilcox Diaries, June 11, 1860; Woodbury quoted in *Whig Charge of Religious Intolerance*, 6.

79. Buchanan, *Great Speech*, 13 (quoted); Forney, *Address on Religious Intolerance*, 9–10, 38–44; Sebastian, *Substance of the Speech*, 1–2, 6–10.

80. Cass and Hughes, *Letter*, 10, 21, 23; newspaper clipping, June 16, 1854, enclosed in Lewis Cass to Horatio King, June 19, [1854], King Papers.

81. Kelly, "Civil and Religious Liberty Defended," 1264. For negative reaction to Campbell and Belmont, including from some Democrats, see Benjamin H. Brewster to Lewis Cass, Apr. 25, 1851, Cass Papers; Forney, *Address on Religious Intolerance*, 28; A. Dudley Mann to John Perkins, Dec. 21, 1855, Perkins Papers; "Speech of Lemuel Scroggins, Esq.," [1855], broadside, Box 1, Folder 3, Perkins Papers; [A. Dudley Mann], "The Present Administration," draft newspaper article, [1856], Box 1, Folder 5, Perkins Papers; Coleman, *Disruption of the Pennsylvania Democracy*, 65–67; and Holt, *Franklin Pierce*, 55.

82. Slicer, *Speech*, 4 (quoted); Douglas, *Speech . . . on the "Measures of Adjustment,"* 28–30 (quoted); Slicer to Alpheus Felch, Oct. 5, 1848, Felch Papers; Huston, "Democracy by Scripture."

83. Locke, *Letter Concerning Toleration*, 23–28, 31–36, 51–55; *Whig Charge of Religious Intolerance*, 7.

84. "Mr. Hunter's Speech in Richmond," 77–84.

85. [Anspach], *Sons of the Sires*, 219.

86. Quotations from *Infidelity and Abolitionism*, 6; Loring, *Speech Delivered at Webster, Mass.*, 9; and Horatio Seymour to Stephen A. Douglas, Apr. 10, 1856, SAD.

87. Quotations from Lovejoy, *True Democracy*, 12; Thomas A. Glover to R. M. T. Hunter, June 23, 1855, in RMTH, 165; and *Indiana Daily State Sentinel*, Aug. 10, 1854.

88. Leland R. [Illegible] to John G. Davis, Apr. 23, 1854, Davis Papers, WHS; Lovejoy, *True Democracy*, 10.

89. Douglas, *Letter . . . Vindicating His Character*, quotations on 9; George Miller to Douglas, Dec. 17, 1845; Brigham Young to [Douglas, Dec. 17, 1845]; Brigham Young, Heber C. Kimball, and Willard Richards to Douglas, July 20, 1849, all SAD; Cheathem, *Andrew Jackson, Southerner*, 122; Johannsen, *Stephen A. Douglas*, 104–10.

90. "Reply to a Memorial of Citizens of Connecticut on Kansas," Aug. 15, 1857, in *JB*, 10:122.

91. Garrigus to John G. Davis, Jan. 2, 1854, JGD; [Parmenas Taylor Turnley] to Stephen A. Douglas, Oct. 16, 1858, SAD.

92. D. P. Rhodes to Douglas, Mar. 27, 1854, SAD.

93. *Abolitionist Attack!*, 1.

94. *Letter of an Adopted Catholic*, 8.

95. "Mr. Brooks and Mr. Sumner. Speech of Hon. A. P. Butler," *CG*, 34th Cong., 1st Sess., 1855–56, 25, appendix: 626.

96. Wise, *Letter*, 6–7. On Democratic nationalism, see Baker, *Affairs of Party*, 317–27.

97. Madison, "The Federalist No. 10," in Publius, *Federalist Papers*, 50–58; Wiebe, *Opening of American Society*, 287–88; Wilson, *Space, Time, and Freedom*, 6–12.

98. Weller, *Inaugural Address*, 13; Ward, *Speech . . . at the Great Democratic Mass Meeting*, 8.

99. Pierce, "First Annual Message," Dec. 5, 1853, in Richardson, *Compilation of the Messages*, 5:222–24.

100. Eaton, *Union*, 19; "Speech of Stephen A. Douglas, Chicago, July 9, 1858," in *LDD*, 28–31.

101. Sebastian, *Substance of the Speech*, 13.

102. Cushing, *Speech Delivered in Faneuil Hall*, 13–14; Wiebe, *Opening of American Society*, 353–75; Wilson, *Space, Time, and Freedom*, 178–84.

103. Robertson, *South and the Democratic Party*, 9–11.

104. *Proceedings of the National Democratic Convention*, 36.

105. Quotations from "Extract. A Picture of Disunion. From a Speech Delivered at a Mass Meeting of the Democracy of Indiana. Held on the Battle Ground of Tippecanoe, September, 1856," in *DD*, 1:525; and Douglas, *Speech . . . at the Democratic Celebration*, 1.

106. Brown, *Address . . . before the Democratic Association*, 7.

107. *Frank. Pierce and His Abolition Allies*, 16.

108. "Mr. Orr's Speech in Phœnix Hall," 10; A. C. Scott to John G. Davis, Jan. 1, 1859, JGD.

109. Buchanan, *Great Speech*, 14.

110. Potter, "Historian's Use of Nationalism"; Herb and Kaplan, *Nested Identities*.

111. Wise to Austin H. Brown, Feb. 15, 1858, in *Popular Sovereignty. Proceedings of the Democratic State Convention*, 11; Wright, *Address*, 10–15; Wiebe, *Opening of American Society*, 281–90.

112. Buchanan to Wright, Dec. 8, 1854, Wright Correspondence and Papers.

113. Pugh, *Oration Delivered before the Triennial Convention*, 11; "Speech of General E. Ward," 4.

114. [Johnson], *Remarks on Popular Sovereignty*, 48; Hunter, *Democratic Demonstration at Poughkeepsie*, 14–15.

115. Robertson, *South and the Democratic Party*, 3 (quoted); "A Disquisition on Government," and "A Discourse on the Constitution and Government of the United States," in Calhoun, *Union and Liberty*, 3–284; Read, *Majority Rule versus Consensus*.

116. Pierce, "First Annual Message," 5:224. On American nationalism, see Kramer, *Nationalism in Europe and America;* Murrin, "Roof without Walls"; Parish, "Exception to Most of the Rules"; and Potter, *Impending Crisis*, 6–17.

117. Quotations from Joseph R. Chandler to John Perkins, Aug. 14, 1855, Perkins Papers; and Seymour, *Speech*, 4.

118. George M. Leeman to Charles G. Bellamy, Mar. 23, 1855, Bellamy Papers.

119. On mastery, see Bercaw, *Gendered Freedoms*, 75–93; Greenberg, *Masters and Statesmen;* Hettle, *Peculiar Democracy;* Heyrman, *Southern Cross*, 117–60; and McCurry, *Masters of Small Worlds*.

120. Benjamin, *Speech*, 11, 25–27.

121. Walker, *Speech*, 15.

122. Clay, *Love of Truth*, 20–26.

123. Dickinson, "Speech on the Acquisition of Territory," 1:234.

124. Lovejoy, *True Democracy*, 4.

125. "Speech upon the Issues and Candidates of the Presidential Campaign. Delivered in Tammany Hall, New York, August 19, 1848," in *DD*, 1:277, 280.

126. Clingman, *Address*, 10.

127. Chandler, *Letter*, 5; Seymour, *Speech*, 5.

128. Democratic Committee of Publication, *Life of George Mifflin Dallas*, 15 (quoted); George M. Dallas to Sophia Dallas, July 30, 1846, in "Mystery of the Dallas Papers. Part I," 386; Belohlavek, *George Mifflin Dallas*, 114.

129. Hallett et al., *Appeal to Democrats*, 4.

130. Loring, *Speech Delivered at Webster, Mass.*, 4, 9.

131. Forney, *Address on Religious Intolerance*, 16; "Coercive Temperance," 1855, in Tilden, *Writings and Speeches*, 1:283.

132. [Garnett], *Union, Past and Future*, 28.

133. Wise, *Lecompton Question*, 2; Edwards, *Angels in the Machinery*, 12–38; Edwards, "Domesticity versus Manhood Rights"; Hettle, *Peculiar Democracy;* McCurry, *Masters of Small Worlds;* Pierson, *Free Hearts and Free Homes*, especially 97–114 on the Democratic Party; Ryan, *Cradle of the Middle Class*, 18–59; Watson, *Liberty and Power*, 221–23. For a differing view of Democrats' conception of separate spheres, see Varon, *We Mean to Be Counted*, 82.

134. Thanks to Laura F. Edwards for helping me think through this. On the tension between mastery and egalitarian democracy, see Hettle, *Peculiar Democracy*, 18–38, 57–83.

135. [Garnett], *Union, Past and Future*, 22–29 (quoted); "Speech of General Lewis Cass," 4.

136. Benjamin Fitzpatrick to Aurelia Fitzpatrick, Mar. 9, 11, 1856, Fitzpatrick Family Papers, ADAH; Bolling Hall to Bolling Hall, Mary Louisa Hall to Bolling Hall, June 2, 1850, Hall Family Papers; William T. King to Thomas D. King, [Aug. 1844?], King Family Papers; McCurry, *Masters of Small Worlds*, 215–25; Rose, "Domestication of Domestic Slavery."

137. "Nebraska and Kansas. Speech of Hon. Lewis Cass," *CG*, 33rd Cong., 1st Sess., 1853–54, 23, appendix: 276.

138. E. B. Tyler to Stephen A. Douglas, Aug. 19, 1856, SAD.

139. Kemper, *Speech*, 20.

140. Rufus W. Peckham [Sr.] to Wheeler H. Peckham, Jan. 4, 1860, Peckham Family Papers; [Illegible] Peckham to Wheeler H. Peckham, May 22, 1861, Peckham Family Papers.

141. L. E. Mason to John Y. Mason, Apr. 9, 1849, Mason Papers; H. Stevenson to John Letcher, May 8, 1854, John Letcher Papers, 1770–1970, VHS; Forney, *Address on Religious Intolerance*, 15; McCurry, *Masters of Small Worlds*.

142. "Extract of a Speech of Hon. John B. Weller, of California," Feb. 13, 1854, in *Popular Sovereignty in the Territories*, 18.

143. Leonidas Howard to Bolling Hall, July 17, 1855, Hall Family Papers; Harry Hunter to Caleb Cushing, Mar. 25, 1854, Cushing Papers.

144. *Ritual of the Order of Know Nothings*, 3, 6; Douglas, *Speech . . . at the Democratic Celebration*, 7.

145. Coleman, "Address on Change in Boyhood Home," 15–18 (quoted); Sebastian, *Substance of the Speech*, 2 (quoted); Clay, *Love of Truth*, 20–26; "Mr. Hunter's Speech in Richmond," 77–78, 81.

146. Seymour, *Speech*, 2 (quoted); Burton, "Inaugural Address," 86 (quoted); Winston, *Inaugural Address*, 5–6, 8.

147. Seymour, *Speech*, 2; Jackson, "Farewell Address," 3:296.

148. Albert W. Blue to [Matthew P. Blue], Sept. 6, 1853, Blue Family Papers.

149. "Remarks at the Oxford Academy Jubilee. Held at Oxford, Chenango County, N.Y., August 1st and 2d, 1854," in *DD*, 1:475; Cushing, *Speech Delivered in Faneuil Hall*, 31.

150. James B. Hunt to Alpheus Felch, Jan. 24, 1848, Felch Papers; Nantz to English, June 21, 1854, EFP.

151. *Indiana Daily State Sentinel*, Feb. 18, 1854.

152. *Indiana Daily State Sentinel*, Jan. 7, 1854 (quoted); Millard Fillmore to Wilhelmine Smith, Oct. 17, 1860, Easby-Smith Family Papers, LC; William Russell Smith to Wilhelmine Smith, Jan. 12, [1861], Easby-Smith Family Papers; Baker, "Public Women and Partisan Politics"; Baker, "Domestication of Politics," 620–35; Edwards, *Angels in the Machinery*, 12–38; Graham, "'A Warm Politition'"; McGerr, "Political Style and Women's Power," 864–69; Pierson, *Free Hearts and Free Homes;* Sacher, "'Ladies Are Moving Everywhere'"; Varon, *We Mean to Be Counted*, especially 71–102; Welter, "Cult of True Womanhood."

153. Quotations from Yancey, *Speech*, 4–5; and Horton, *Life and Public Services*, 378; Varon, *We Mean to Be Counted*, 47–62; Zaeske, *Signatures of Citizenship*.

154. Mrs. M. E. Small to Davis, Feb. 21, 1860, Davis Papers, WHS; Portia L. Baldwin to Wise, Dec. 17, 1859, WFP.

155. Buchanan to Harriet Lane, Feb. 1, 1856, in *JB*, 10:29; Levi D. [Illegible] to Douglas, Nov. 1, 1848, SAD.

156. T. C. Wetmore to Stephen A. Douglas, Feb. 27, 1856, SAD.

157. Levi D. [Illegible] to Douglas, Nov. 1, 1848, SAD.

158. Douglas, Freeport Debate, Aug. 27, 1858, in *LDD*, 92–93.

159. *Proceedings of the Celebration*, 13; *Infidelity and Abolitionism*, 3.
160. *Infidelity and Abolitionism*, 5.
161. Sebastian, *Substance of the Speech*, 9.
162. Quotations from Brown, *Address . . . before the Democratic Association*, 7; [Illegible] Newkirk to William H. English, July 19, 1856, EFP; *Indiana Daily State Sentinel*, July 28, 1854; and Cushing, *Speech Delivered in Faneuil Hall*, 44.
163. Clingman, *Address*, 10.
164. *Letter of an Adopted Catholic*, 6.
165. Hunter, *Address*, 5–6; Jones, *Letter*, 2.
166. *Plain Facts and Considerations*, 26.
167. Bloch, "Gendered Meanings of Virtue"; Edwards, "Contradictions of Democracy"; Edwards, *People and Their Peace;* Horwitz, *Transformation of American Law;* Pateman, *Sexual Contract;* Smith-Rosenberg, "Dis-Covering the Subject"; Tomlins, *Law, Labor, and Ideology.*
168. Hobbes, *Leviathan*, 76 (quoted); Herzog, *Happy Slaves;* Smith, *Modernity and Its Discontents*, 67–87.

3. Resisting Realignment

1. Lewis Cass to Pierce, Aug. 30, 1853, Cass Papers; Holt, *Franklin Pierce*, 66–71.
2. Robert Toombs to Crawford, Apr. 26, 1854, Robert Toombs Correspondence, DU.
3. B. F. Hallett to Stephen A. Douglas, Mar. 10, 1854, SAD; Holt, *Fate of Their Country*, 97–104; Nichols, "Kansas-Nebraska Act," 197–212.
4. G. W. Newell to Marcy, Jan. 25, 1854, Marcy Papers (quoted); J. P. Jones to Marcy, Feb. 7, 1854, Marcy Papers; John Van Buren to Marcy, Feb. 12, 1854, Marcy Papers.
5. William S. Allen to Cushing, Feb. 3, 20, Mar. 25, 1854, Cushing Papers; Samuel Treat to Cushing, Mar. 25, 1854, Cushing Papers (quoted).
6. Robert McClelland to Alpheus Felch, July 5, 1854, Felch Papers.
7. William Barton Wade Dent to Herschel V. Johnson, June 13, 1854, Herschel V. Johnson Papers; Thomas C. Reynolds to Caleb Cushing, July 22, 1854, Cushing Papers.
8. Baum, *Civil War Party System*, 24–54; Foner, *Free Soil, Free Labor, Free Men*, especially 226–60; Huston, "Illinois Political Realignment of 1844–1860"; Levine, *Half Slave and Half Free*, especially 200–204; Levine, "'The Vital Element of the Republican Party'"; McManus, *Political Abolitionism in Wisconsin*, especially 99–114; McPherson, *Battle Cry of Freedom*, especially 130–44, 153–56.
9. Gienapp, *Origins of the Republican Party*, especially 99–102, 439–48; Holt, "Another Look at the Election of 1856," especially 155–81; Holt, *Political Crisis of the 1850s*, especially 155–81; Silbey, *Partisan Imperative*, 127–65.
10. Hunter, *Address*, 10.
11. Grant Thorburn to Horatio King, Mar. 6, 1855, King Papers.
12. "Gen. Cushing's Letter," *(Annapolis) State Capitol Gazette*, Nov. 19, 1853, clipping enclosed in O. H. Browne to Cushing, Feb. 2, 1854, Cushing Papers; Belohlavek, *Broken Glass*, 248–51.

13. Samuel S. Cox to [Stephen A. Douglas], Mar. 24, 1854, SAD.

14. Thomas C. Reynolds to Caleb Cushing, June 21, 1854, Cushing Papers.

15. Quotations from "Names of active Pierce democrats who joined the Know Nothing Order," [1854], Burke Papers; Lewis Cass to Samuel Beardsley, Dec. 13, 1853, Cass Papers; and S. T. Ensey to Joseph A. Wright, Feb. 24, 1854, Wright Correspondence and Papers.

16. Quotations from W. H. Collum to William H. English, July 24, 1854, EFP; Hallett et al., *Appeal to Democrats*, 3; and *Territorial Slavery Question*, 12.

17. John Y. Mason to Lewis Cass, Sept. 25, 1848, Cass Papers.

18. "Names of active Pierce democrats who joined the Know Nothing Order," [1854], Burke Papers.

19. Chandler, *Letter*, 3.

20. Lewis E. Harvie to R. M. T. Hunter, Mar. 17, 1855, in RMTH, 162–63.

21. J. O. Barnes to [Caleb Cushing], Nov. 4, 1854, Cushing Papers.

22. *Indiana Daily State Sentinel*, Jan. 11, 1854; A. L. Roache to John G. Davis, Feb. 13, 1854, JGD; Stampp, *Indiana Politics during the Civil War*, 1–30; Thornbrough, *Indiana in the Civil War Era*, 4–5, 27–28, 38–84. On the 1854 canvass, see Thornbrough, *Indiana in the Civil War Era*, 54–67; and Van Bolt, "Fusion Out of Confusion."

23. L. G. Matthews to William H. English, Dec. 26, 1853, EFP.

24. *Indiana Daily State Sentinel*, Jan. 16, 1854.

25. B. P. Douglass to William H. English, Apr. 4, 1854, EFP.

26. Scott Noel to John G. Davis, Mar. 8, 1854, JGD (quoted); [Illegible] to John G. Davis, Feb. 4, 1854, JGD (quoted); H. B. Pickett to John G. Davis, May 31, 1854, JGD; E. D. Logan to William H. English, Feb. 8, 1854, EFP; B. P. Douglass to William H. English, Apr. 4, 1854, EFP; *Indiana Daily State Sentinel*, Jan. 11, 14, 16, 25, Feb. 2, May 9, 1854.

27. David McClure to William H. English, May 1, 1854, EFP.

28. *Indiana Daily State Sentinel*, Jan. 16, June 30, July 1, 3, 6 (quoted), 29, Aug. 10, 1854.

29. B. H. Cornwell to John G. Davis, Apr. 26, 1854, JGD; William P. Bryant to John G. Davis, July 19, 1854, JGD (quoted); Douglas, *Letter . . . Vindicating His Character*.

30. Knownothing (Union Democrat) to Davis, Aug. 21, 1854, JGD; D. to Davis, Aug. 24, 1854, JGD (quoted); *Indiana Daily State Sentinel*, May 23, 24, June 29, July 19, 22, Aug. 16, 23, 29, 1854; Etcheson, *Emerging Midwest*, 84–90, 102–7.

31. E. C. Sugg to William H. English, Jan. 1, 1855, EFP.

32. Charles Wigely to Davis, Feb. 17, 1854; George W. Hanchett[?] to Davis, Mar. 21, 1854; W. Akers to Davis, Mar. 22, 1854; Samuel A. Fisher to [Davis], Apr. 4, 1854 (quoted), all JGD; John Hunt to Joseph A. Wright, July 22, 27, 1854, Wright Correspondence and Papers; *Indiana Daily State Sentinel*, July 26, 27, Aug. 4, 9, 1854; Stampp, *Indiana Politics during the Civil War*, 4, 9.

33. I. B. A. Archer to English, Feb. 23, 1854, EFP; A. L. Roache to [Davis], Feb. 18, 1854, JGD.

34. Daniel A. Farley to Davis, Jan. 21, 1854; Charles Wigely to Davis, Feb. 17, 1854; A. L. Roache to [Davis], Feb. 18, 1854; John S. Jennings to Davis, Feb. 23, 1854; A. L. Roache to Davis, Mar. 27, 1854; F. T. Brown to Davis, May 9, 1854; Wright to [Davis], May 29, 1854; William P. Bryant to Davis, July 19, 1854, all JGD; Bright to English, Sept. 2, 1850, Aug. 22, 1852, EFP; Bright to William L. Marcy, Jan. 23, 1854, Marcy Papers; Thornbrough, *Indiana in the Civil War Era*, 41–43; Van Bolt, "Fusion Out of Confusion," 361–66, 368–75.

35. B. H. Cornwell to Davis, Mar. 3, 1854; [Illegible] Noel to Davis, Mar. 21, 1854; Samuel A. Fisher to [Davis], Apr. 4, 1854; Nofsinger to [Davis], Apr. 14, 1854; Scott Noel to Davis, May 29, 1854 (quoted); Joseph A. Wright to Davis, June 1, 1854; Davis to Nofsinger, July 20, 1854, all JGD; *Indiana Daily State Sentinel*, July 8, 10, 25, 28, Aug. 4, 5, 1854.

36. Wright to Davis, Mar. 18, 1854, JGD (quoted); William P. Bryant to Davis, July 19, 1854, JGD; S. T. Ensey to Wright, Feb. 24, 1854, Wright Correspondence and Papers; John Hunt to Wright, July 22, 27, 1854, Wright Correspondence and Papers; *Indiana Daily State Sentinel*, Jan. 31, June 30, 1854; Van Bolt, "Fusion Out of Confusion," 370, 374.

37. Wright, *Address*, 13 (quoted); Wright to [Davis], Feb. 10 (quoted), Apr. 10 (quoted), May 8, 1854, JGD; *Indiana Daily State Sentinel*, Aug. 23, 1854.

38. *Indiana Daily State Sentinel*, Jan. 4, Feb. 11 (quoted), 25, Mar. 4, Aug. 22, 1854; Etcheson, *Emerging Midwest*, especially 108–26.

39. *Indiana Daily State Sentinel*, Aug. 21, 1854.

40. *Indiana Daily State Sentinel*, Aug. 23, 1854; Thornbrough, *Indiana in the Civil War Era*, 3–4.

41. *Indiana Daily State Sentinel*, Mar. 4, 1854.

42. Wright, *Letters*, 2.

43. E. D. Logan to William H. English, June 1, 1854, EFP.

44. A. Bassey to William H. English, July 13, 1854, EFP.

45. S. T. Ensey to Joseph A. Wright, Feb. 24, 1854, Wright Correspondence and Papers (quoted); W. R. Nofsinger to [John G. Davis], Apr. 14, 1854, JGD; Stoler, "Democratic Element," 185–86.

46. W. H. Collum to English, July 24, 1854, EFP; William P. Bryant to John G. Davis, July 19, 1854, JGD.

47. John Hunt to Joseph A. Wright, July 22, 27, 1854, Wright Correspondence and Papers.

48. Lewis Clark to Joseph A. Wright, Aug. 15, 1854, Wright Correspondence and Papers; Rodgers, "Liberty, Will, and Violence."

49. Jno. [Illegible]. Robinson to William H. English, Feb. 24, 1854, EFP; Van Bolt, "Fusion Out of Confusion," 381–82.

50. F. T. Brown to Davis, Dec. 21, 1854, JGD.

51. E. C. Sugg to William H. English, July, 20, 1854, EFP.

52. Stampp, *Indiana Politics during the Civil War*, 21–22; Stoler, "Democratic Element"; Thornbrough, "Race Issue in Indiana Politics," 166–67.

53. *Indiana Daily State Sentinel,* July 13, 1854.
54. *Indiana Daily State Sentinel,* July 20, 1854.
55. *Indiana Daily State Sentinel,* July 14, 28, 1854.
56. *Indiana Daily State Sentinel,* July 17, 1854.
57. *Indiana Daily State Sentinel,* July 31, 1854.
58. *Indiana Daily State Sentinel,* July 15, 1854.

59. Compare editorials in the *Indiana Daily State Sentinel* for Jan. 13, 14, Feb. 10, 14, 15 with those of May 13 and July 4 (quoted), 1854.

60. Garrigus to John G. Davis, Mar. 3, 1854, JGD; R. S. H. to Davis, Feb. 13, 1854, JGD.

61. *Indiana Daily State Sentinel,* May 12, 25, 1854.

62. Garrigus to E. M. Chamberlin, July 12, 1854, JGD; Garrigus to Davis, Mar. 3, 1854, JGD.

63. *Indiana Daily State Sentinel,* Jan. 11, 25, Feb. 9 (quoted), 24, 1854; Leland R. [Illegible] to John G. Davis, Apr. 23, 1854, Davis Papers, WHS; Drake, *Address,* 21–23.

64. *Indiana Daily State Sentinel,* May 23, 1854.
65. *Indiana Daily State Sentinel,* May 25, 1854.
66. *Indiana Daily State Sentinel,* Aug. 5, 1854.
67. *Indiana Daily State Sentinel,* July 18, 22, 1854.
68. *Indiana Daily State Sentinel,* May 24 (quoted), July 20, 1854.
69. *Indiana Daily State Sentinel,* July 20, 29 (quoted), 1854.
70. B. P. Douglass to English, Apr. 4, 1854, EFP.
71. David McClure to William H. English, May 1, 1854, EFP.

72. Cooper, *South and the Politics of Slavery;* Carter, *Politics of Rage;* Lassiter, *Silent Majority.* On Indianan and midwestern racism, see Etcheson, *Emerging Midwest,* 94–102; Fredrickson, *Black Image in the White Mind,* 133–35; Rodgers, "Liberty, Will, and Violence," 153–56; Thornbrough, *Indiana in the Civil War Era,* 12–28; and Thornbrough, "Race Issue in Indiana Politics."

73. *Indiana Daily State Sentinel,* July 19, 1854.
74. *Indiana Daily State Sentinel,* Aug. 3, 1854.
75. *Indiana Daily State Sentinel,* Aug. 2, 1854.
76. J. B. Norman to William H. English, Feb. 8, 1854, EFP.
77. *Indiana Daily State Sentinel,* May 9, 1854.

78. Scott Noel to John G. Davis, Apr. 27, 1854, JGD; R. S. Staunton to [John G. Davis], Oct. 21, 1854, JGD.

79. Jones, *John G Davis,* quotations on 2, 6; Jones to Davis, Dec. 23, 1855, JGD; Davis to [Jones], Dec. 28, 1855, JGD; Davis, "To the People of the 7th Congressional District of Indiana," *Daily Terre-Haute (IN) Journal,* extra, [1856].

80. Nofsinger to [Davis], Apr. 14, 1854, JGD.
81. Murray McConnel to Douglas, Jan. 28, 1854, SAD.
82. Barstow, *Speech,* 11.
83. Burke, *To the Democratic Members,* 2.
84. Garrigus to John G. Davis, Feb. 25, 1854, JGD.

85. *Ohio Politics*, 2, 3.
86. *Indiana Daily State Sentinel,* July 22, 1854.
87. Wick to English, June 5, 1854, EFP.
88. *Indiana Daily State Sentinel,* Aug. 24, 1854.
89. *Indiana Daily State Sentinel,* July 17, 1854.
90. *Indiana Daily State Sentinel,* July 1, 1854.
91. *Indiana Daily State Sentinel,* July 17, 1854.
92. *Indiana Daily State Sentinel,* July 1, 1854.
93. *Indiana Daily State Sentinel,* July 6, 1854.
94. *Indiana Daily State Sentinel,* Aug. 4, 1854.
95. *Indiana Daily State Sentinel,* Sept. 23, 1854.
96. English, *Letter,* 2.
97. E. C. Sugg to William H. English, Jan. 1, 1855, EFP.
98. Quotations from F. P. Stark to John G. Davis, July 27, 1854, JGD; and *Indiana Daily State Sentinel,* July 18, 1854.
99. *Indiana Daily State Sentinel,* Aug. 4, 1854.
100. Quotations from Bright to Hunter, Sept. 2, 1854, in RMTH, 159; and James Ferguson to Austin H. Brown, Sept. 27, 1848, Brown Papers.
101. E. C. Sugg to English, Jan. 1, 1855, EFP; Hendricks to Davis, Oct. 15, 1854, Davis Papers, WHS; Potter, *Impending Crisis,* 175.
102. Cass to Edmund Burke, Dec. 7, 1854, Burke Papers.
103. H. Martz to John Letcher, Nov. 10, 1854, Letcher Papers.
104. Van Buren quoted in Watson, *Liberty and Power,* 87; R. K. Meade to R. M. T. Hunter, Feb. 10, 1855, SAD (quoted); William F. Samford to Matthew P. Blue, Aug. 14, 1854, Blue Family Papers; Isaac Edward Holmes to R. M. T. Hunter, June 8, 1855, in RMTH, 164–65; Crofts, "Late Antebellum Virginia Reconsidered"; Link, *Roots of Secession;* Shade, *Democratizing the Old Dominion,* especially 92–113, 117–19, 283–85.
105. "Alliance in the North against the Democracy of Virginia," *Richmond Enquirer,* Dec. 13, 1854, Newspaper Clippings Scrapbook of Ellen Wright Wise, 1840–1896, Wise Papers, Eastern Shore of Virginia Historical Society.
106. Hunter to Wise, Jan. 12, 1853, Henry A. Wise Papers, DU (quoted); George Booker to Hunter, June 7, 1852, in RMTH, 144–45; James A. Seddon to Hunter, Dec. 3, 1855, in RMTH, 172–74; Roger A. Pryor to Hunter, Dec. 7, 9, 1856, Hunter Family Papers, 1766–1918, VHS; Wise to Hunter, Feb. 27, 1856, Hunter Family Papers; Wise, *Letter.* On Wise, see Eaton, "Henry A. Wise: A Study in Virginia Leadership"; Eaton, "Henry A. Wise, a Liberal of the Old South"; Eaton, "Henry A. Wise and the Virginia Fire Eaters"; and Simpson, *Good Southerner.* On Hunter, see Hitchcock, "Southern Moderates and Secession"; and Moore, "Robert M. T. Hunter."
107. Lewis E. Harvie to Hunter, Mar. 5, 17, 1855, in RMTH, 161–63. On Virginia "particularism," see Shade, *Democratizing the Old Dominion,* 225–61.
108. James A. Seddon to Hunter, Feb. 7, 1852, in RMTH, 136–39; Edmund W. Hubard to Hunter, May 8, 1852, in RMTH, 140–42 (quoted); Johannsen, *Stephen A. Douglas,* 347.

109. Wise to Franklin Pierce, June 22, 1852, copy, typescript, WFP; Buchanan to William L. Marcy, June 8, 1855, in *JB*, 9:357 (quoted).

110. "The Abolitionism of Know-Nothingism," *Richmond Enquirer*, June 3, 1855, Newspaper Clippings Scrapbook of Ellen Wright Wise. On the politics of slavery, see Cooper, *South and the Politics of Slavery*, 362–69; and Link, *Roots of Secession;* as central to the 1855 election, see Freehling, *Secessionists Triumphant*, 85–96. On Democrats' antinativism, see Bladek, "'Virginia Is Middle Ground'"; Eaton, "Henry A. Wise, a Liberal of the Old South," 490–91; and Simpson, *Good Southerner*, 106–22. For an argument minimizing nativism, see Rice, "Know-Nothing Party in Virginia."

111. "Speech of James B. Clay, Delivered at the Union Meeting in Mason County, Kentucky," in Pearce, Pratt, Crisfield, and Clay, *Old Line Whigs*, 13; Anbinder, *Nativism and Slavery*, xiv; Holt, "Politics of Impatience."

112. "Reasons Why I Am a Democrat and Not a Know Nothing," in *HAW*, 206, 213.

113. "Speech of Mr. Wise on Know Nothingism," Newspaper Clippings Scrapbook of Ellen Wright Wise; William F. Samford to Matthew P. Blue, Aug. 10, 1856, Blue Family Papers.

114. *Lynchburg Republican* and *Richmond Enquirer*, in *HAW*, 165–66.

115. *Richmond Enquirer*, in *HAW*, 428.

116. *Richmond Enquirer* and *Lynchburg Republican*, in *HAW*, 165–66.

117. *Richmond Enquirer*, in *HAW*, 166.

118. *Richmond Examiner*, in *HAW*, 251.

119. *Richmond Examiner*, in *HAW*, 352.

120. James Lawson Kemper, "For Buchanan vs. Fillmore," [1856], manuscript speech, 15, James Lawson Kemper Papers, 1837–1903, VHS.

121. Longstreet, *Know Nothingism Unveiled*, 8.

122. Quotations from Ezra Read to John G. Davis, Dec. 16, 1854, JGD; and R. S. Staunton to [John G. Davis], Oct. 21, 1854, JGD.

123. *Indiana Daily State Sentinel*, Aug. 16, 29, 1854.

124. James L. Kemper to Powell, Mar. 26, 1855, Paulus Powell Papers, 1848–1868, VHS (quoted); Jones, *Letter*, 14; "Mr. Hunter's Speech in Richmond," 75–77.

125. Camp, *Closer to Freedom*, especially 93–116; Crew, "'When the Victims of Oppression'"; Hahn, *Nation under Our Feet*, 13–61; Freehling, *South vs. the South*, 25–32; Link, *Roots of Secession;* Newman, "Protest in Black and White"; Waldstreicher, "Why Thomas Jefferson and African Americans."

126. Wise, *Religious Liberty*, 25; Brown, *Speech*, 6.

127. Quotations from "Mr. Hunter's Speech in Richmond," 89; Longstreet, *Know Nothingism Unveiled*, 4; and Wise, *Religious Liberty*, 2.

128. *Light for the People!*, 28–29.

129. "Letter from Henry A. Wise," July 1, 1855, *Richmond Enquirer*, in *HAW*, 431.

130. William L. Knox et al. to John Perkins Jr., June 5, 1855, Perkins Papers; Wise to George W. Jones, July 27, 1855, typescript, WFP; Freehling, *Secessionists Triumphant*, 92; Simpson, *Good Southerner*, 112.

131. R. P. Letcher to John Letcher, Mar. 29, 1855, Letcher Papers (quoted); Letcher to John Brooks, May 25, 1855, Letcher Papers; Wise to George Booker, Aug. 14, 1854, WFP (quoted); Wise to [Caleb Cushing], Sept. 6, 1854, Cushing Papers.

132. Quotations from Wise to George W. Jones, June 29, 1855, typescript, WFP; and Wise to George Booker, Aug. 14, 1854, WFP.

133. Wise to [?], Dec. 17, 1854, WFP.

134. Wise, *Religious Liberty*, 3–5; [Anspach], *Sons of the Sires*, 202 (quoted). For southern Know-Nothings' nativism, see their 1855 Virginia platform in *HAW*, 254–55; Rayner, *Reply;* Susan Piet to Charles James Faulkner, Feb. 12, 1855, Faulkner Family Papers, 1737–1954, VHS; and Bladek, "'Virginia Is Middle Ground,'" 37, 52–53. For a differing view, see Alexander, "'The Democracy Must Prepare for Battle.'"

135. The foreign-born population of Virginia did increase rapidly in the 1850s. Shade, *Democratizing the Old Dominion*, 22, 286; Stampp, *Indiana Politics during the Civil War*, 2, 9; Van Bolt, "Fusion Out of Confusion," 359–60.

136. *Three Letters on the Order*, 38.

137. Quotations from Wise, *Religious Liberty*, 11, 14; and "The Nominees of the Democratic Party," *Richmond Enquirer*, Dec. 5, 1854, Newspaper Clippings Scrapbook of Ellen Wright Wise.

138. Quotations from Wise, *Religious Liberty*, 24; and "Mr. Hunter's Speech in Richmond," 74.

139. Wise, *Religious Liberty*, 20, 30 (quoted); "An Appeal to the Clergy," in *HAW*, 270–72.

140. Phillips, *Letter . . . on the Religious Proscription*, 3, 8 (quoted); Bright, *Speech*, 13–14, 18 (quoted); Stephens and Tucker, *Letters*.

141. Wise to Curry, Dec. 11, 1854, manuscript letter inserted between pages 8 and 9 of Curry's personal copy of Wise, *Religious Liberty*, J. L. M. Curry Pamphlet Collection, ADAH; Longstreet, *Know Nothingism Unveiled*, 3, 4.

142. Heyrman, *Southern Cross*, 206–52; McCurry, *Masters of Small Worlds*, 130–207.

143. Phillips, *Letter . . . on the Religious Proscription*, 4 (quoted); Phillips, *Speech*.

144. Bright, *Speech*, 14–16.

145. "Letter of Hon. Philip Phillips," *Pennsylvanian*, Oct. 24, 1855, clipping in bound volume, Box 13, Phillips Family Papers.

146. Wise, *Religious Liberty*, 22.

147. S. Bassett French to Hunter, May 12, 1855, R. M. T. Hunter Papers, Library of Virginia.

148. Wise, *Religious Liberty*, 11.

149. *Richmond Enquirer*, in *HAW*, 28.

150. *Richmond Examiner*, Apr. 17, 1855, in *HAW*, 334–35.

151. "Correspondence," Thomas G. Pratt to John Walton et al., Sept. 13, 1855, broadside, Box 1, Folder 4, Perkins Papers (quoted); Thomas F. Carpenter to [Stephen A. Douglas], Apr. 15, 1854, SAD; *Letter of an Adopted Catholic;* Anbinder,

Nativism and Slavery, 45–46; Ignatiev, *How the Irish Became White*, 62–89; Osofsky, "Abolitionists, Irish Immigrants"; Roediger, *Wages of Whiteness*, 140–44.

152. *Official Proceedings*, 8.

153. "National Politics. Speech of Hon. J. H. Jewett," *CG*, 34th Cong., 1st Sess., 1855–56, 25, appendix: 1026.

154. Wise, *Religious Liberty*, 9; Peterson, *Jeffersonian Image in the American Mind*, 162–209.

155. "Nebraska and Kansas. Speech of Hon. John Pettit," *CG*, 33rd Cong., 1st Sess., 1853–54, 23, appendix: 214; Hunter, *Democratic Demonstration at Poughkeepsie*, 6–7.

156. Wise, *Religious Liberty*, 64.

157. *Richmond Examiner*, in *HAW*, 117.

158. "Mr. Hunter's Speech in Richmond," 83; Wise, *Religious Liberty*, 20.

159. Wise, *Religious Liberty*, 7 (quoted); "Know-Nothingism an Alias of Federalism," *Richmond Examiner*, Feb. 20, 1855, in *HAW*, 54–60.

160. "Mr. Hunter's Speech in Richmond," 87; Brown, *Speech*, 13.

161. Kemper, "For Buchanan vs. Fillmore," 18.

162. Hunter, *Democratic Demonstration at Poughkeepsie*, 6–10.

163. Hallett et al., *Appeal to Democrats*, 5.

164. Hunter, *Democratic Demonstration at Poughkeepsie*, 1, 6–10.

165. H. Martz to John Letcher, Nov. 10, 1854, Letcher Papers; Simpson, "Political Compromise."

166. Wise, *Address*, 9 (quoted); Wise, *Speech*; Freehling, *Secessionists Triumphant*, 89–93; Rice, "Know-Nothing Party in Virginia," 68.

167. Rayner, *Reply*, 3.

168. J.[?] H. Moore to R. M. T. Hunter, Mar. 7, 1856, Hunter Papers.

169. Wise, *Religious Liberty*, 50.

170. George W. Jones to Wise, July 8, 1855, WFP; Wise to George W. Jones, July 27, 1855, typescript, WFP.

171. Meade to Hunter, Feb. 10, 1855, SAD.

172. "Judge Douglas in Richmond," in *HAW*, 68.

173. *Indiana Daily State Sentinel*, Sept. 7, 1854.

174. Mann to [John Perkins], May 14, 1855, Perkins Papers (quoted); E. G. W. Butler to John Perkins, Sept. 5, 1855, Perkins Papers; Jeptha Dudley et al., Democratic Central Committee, to Joseph Holt, June 14, 1855, Holt Papers (quoted).

175. Joseph Allison et al., Committee, to Faulkner, Nov. 14, 1855, Faulkner Family Papers; Wright to Wise, Nov. 24, 1855, Joseph A. Wright Papers, Manuscript and Visual Collections Department, William Henry Smith Memorial Library, Indiana Historical Society.

176. "The Virginia Election—The Democratic Victory," reprinted from *Albany Atlas*, and "Democratic Rejoicings over the Virginia Election," Newspaper Clippings Scrapbook of Ellen Wright Wise.

177. George W. Jones to Wise, July 8, 1855, WFP; Pierce to Stephen A. Douglas, May 28, 1855, SAD.

178. Everett's sentiments conveyed in [H. A. Wise to Henry A. Wise], Sept. 27, 1855, Wise Family Papers, 1816–1898, VHS; Jones to Wise, Dec. 13, 1858, Schoff Civil War Collection, Letters and Documents, WCL.

4. Welcoming Realignment

1. *Robert C. Winthrop on Fusion*, 1–3 (quoted); Winthrop, *Memoir of Robert C. Winthrop*, 167–68, 170–95, 199–200, 202–9.

2. Everett to William Henry Trescot, June 6, 1855 [1856?] (quoted), Dec. 24, 1856, Edward Everett Papers (microfilm), Massachusetts Historical Society; Millard Fillmore to Everett, July 12, 1856, Everett Papers.

3. Alexander, "Persistent Whiggery in the Confederate South"; Baum, *Civil War Party System*, 26, 50–52; Crofts, "Southern Opposition"; Foner, *Free Soil, Free Labor, Free Men*, 186–225; Holt, "Another Look at the Election of 1856"; Holzer, *Lincoln at Cooper Union*, 42–44, 114–18, 119–23, 233–36; Levine, "Conservatism, Nativism, and Slavery"; Knupfer, "Crisis in Conservatism"; O'Connor, *Lords of the Loom*, 114–31; Smith, "Conservatism, Transformation."

4. *Whig Testimony against the Election*, quotation on 5; *Document for All Thinking Men!*, 4–5; Charles Fletcher to Webster, Aug. 17, 1852, in Webster, *Papers*, 7:344–48; Hilliard, *Letter*, 3–5; Henry W. Hilliard to Nathaniel Niles, Aug. 13, 1851, Nathaniel Niles Papers, DU; "Speech of Hon. Isaac D. Jones," 14–15; Holt, *Political Crisis of the 1850s*, 70–72, 97–98, 118–20, 148.

5. Webster to James Louis Petigru, Aug. 15, 1852, in Webster, *Papers*, 7:344; Baum, *Civil War Party System*, 26; O'Connor, *Lords of the Loom*, 114–31.

6. Alpheus Felch to [Lucretia Felch], Apr. 5, 1848, Felch Papers.

7. Address of R. M. T. Hunter, in *Obituary Addresses . . . of the Hon. William R. King*, 13. On death and mourning in the Civil War era, see Berry, *Weirding the War;* Faust, *This Republic of Suffering;* and Wills, *Lincoln at Gettysburg*, 63–89.

8. Quotations from "Letter of Hon. James A. Pearce, Washington, July 31, 1856," in Pearce, Pratt, Crisfield, and Clay, *Old Line Whigs*, 3; and Hilliard, *Letter*, 6.

9. E. C. Sugg to William H. English, Jan. 1, 1855, EFP; Burstein, "Immortalizing the Founding Fathers"; Dennis, "Patriotic Remains"; Henderson, *Grief and Genre in American Literature*, 47–68; Wills, *Lincoln at Gettysburg*. By "eulogy," I mean a variety of political print culture including funeral addresses.

10. Perkins, *Speech*, 31; Buchanan, *Great Speech*, 9.

11. *Boston Courier*, quoted in *Whig Testimony against the Election*, 12.

12. "Speech of Hon. Isaac D. Jones," 15; address of James A. Bayard, in *Obituary Addresses . . . of the Hon. John M. Clayton*, 8.

13. "Speech of Hon. Jno. W. Crisfield," in Pearce, Pratt, Crisfield, and Clay, *Old Line Whigs*, 10; "Letter to the Whig Convention at Worcester, Mass., Boston, October 1, 1855," in Choate and Brown, *Works of Rufus Choate*, 1:199.

14. "Speech of James B. Clay," 14.

15. W. H. Wilder to [Lucius Lyon], Aug. 21, 1848, Lucius Lyon Papers, WCL.

16. Quotations from addresses of Sampson Harris and John Taylor, in *Obituary Addresses . . . of the Hon. William R. King,* 36, 62–63.

17. Quotations from Hilliard, *Letter,* 5; and Yancey, *Speech,* 11.

18. *Sketches of the Lives,* 4.

19. Sheahan, *Life of Stephen A. Douglas,* 134; National Democratic Executive Committee, *Biographical Sketches,* 6.

20. *Short Answers to Reckless Fabrications,* 32 (quoted); *Hon. James B. Clay, to His Constituents,* quotation on 7; "Speech of James B. Clay," 15–16; Paulus, "America's Long Eulogy for Compromise."

21. Kemper, "For Buchanan vs. Fillmore," 13.

22. Douglas, Freeport Debate, 97–98; John Kierans to Douglas, Oct. 3, 1858, SAD; Guelzo, *Lincoln and Douglas,* 41–47, 70–4, 236–37, 288.

23. Kemper, "For Buchanan vs. Fillmore," 3; "Speech of James B. Clay," 16; Walker, *Speech,* 5.

24. *Sketches of the Lives,* 8.

25. Hofstadter, *Idea of a Party System;* Neely, *Union Divided.*

26. Abercrombie and White, *Letter,* 2.

27. W. H. Wilder to Lucius Lyon, June 17, 1848, Lyon Papers.

28. A. Logan to Stephen A. Douglas, Dec. 1, 1855, SAD; Ward, *Speech . . . at the Great Democratic Mass Meeting,* 4.

29. "Mr. Hunter's Speech in Richmond," 89–90.

30. Coleman, "Antebellum Democratic Party Address," 10.

31. *Plain Facts and Considerations,* 29–31.

32. Brown, *Speech,* 5–7.

33. Choate, "Speech Delivered in Faneuil Hall," 2:327–41.

34. Benjamin, *Speech,* 17.

35. Address of James A. Bayard, in *Obituary Addresses . . . of the Hon. John M. Clayton,* 8.

36. Choate, "Speech 'On the Political Topics,'" 2:392–93, 394.

37. "Speech of Hon. Isaac D. Jones," 13.

38. Toombs to Thomas, Feb. 9, 1856, Toombs Correspondence; "Speech of James B. Clay," 15.

39. Clingman, *Valedictory Address,* 3.

40. Choate, "Speech Delivered in Faneuil Hall," 2:330–33 (quoted); Choate, "Speech 'On the Political Topics,'" 2:412.

41. Faust, *This Republic of Suffering,* 3–31.

42. Quotations from Benedict, *"Wide Awake" Poem,* 6; and "Speech of the Hon. Wm. L. Yancey," June 23, 1860, *(Washington, DC) Constitution,* June 27, 1860.

43. Whitman, "Eighteenth Presidency!," 44; Kemper, "For Buchanan vs. Fillmore," 4.

44. *Appeal for the Union,* 11–12.

45. "Judge Douglas in Richmond," 68.

46. *Short Answers to Reckless Fabrications,* 7.

47. Douglas, Freeport Debate, 98.

48. Van Buren to Moses Tilden, Sept. 1, 1856, in Tilden, *Letters and Literary Memorials*, 1:119; Cooper, *South and the Politics of Slavery;* Shade, "'The Most Delicate and Exciting Topics.'"

49. Clingman, *Speech*, 9–14; "Speech to the Springfield Scott Club," Aug. 14, 26, 1852, in Lincoln, *Collected Works*, 2:157; H. A. Wise to Edward Everett, June 8, 1856, Everett Papers; Edward Everett to William Henry Trescot, June 9, July 27, 1856, Everett Papers.

50. For the Whig pamphlet, see *Frank. Pierce and His Abolition Allies*, 14, 15 (quoted); for the Democratic response, see *"Franklin Pierce and His Abolition Allies,"* 5, 7 (quoted). On whether Pierce was unduly proslavery, see *Abolitionist Attack!* On Whigs and racism, see Neely, *Boundaries of American Political Culture*, 97–127; and Saxton, *Rise and Fall*, 67–72.

51. "Letter of Hon. James A. Pearce," 3; *Robert C. Winthrop on Fusion*, 3.

52. Hallett et al., *Appeal to Democrats*, 5, 6.

53. Cox to [Douglas], Mar. 24, 1854, SAD.

54. Brown, *Speech*, 19.

55. *Plain Facts and Considerations*, 31.

56. *Whig Testimony against the Election*, 7–8 (quoted); *Abolitionist Attack!*, 2.

57. Coleman, "Antebellum Democratic Party Address," 11.

58. Brown, *Speech*, 20; "Speech of Hon. Jno. W. Crisfield," 11.

59. Wood, *Speech*, 3, 4.

60. "Letter of Hon. James A. Pearce," 4; Choate, "Speech 'On the Political Topics,'" 2:396, 402; Mason, *Apostle of Union*, 43–45.

61. "The Hybrid Ticket," *Richmond Enquirer*, in *HAW*, 165–66.

62. Wise, *Religious Liberty*, 58–59.

63. *Official Proceedings*, 10.

64. *Indiana Daily State Sentinel*, July 11 (quoted), 19, 28 (quoted), 1854; Jordan to English, Sept. 26, 1858, EFP.

65. "Freedom in the West Indies: An Address Delivered in Poughkeepsie, New York, on 2 August 1858," in *FDP*, 3:226–31.

66. "A Nation in the Midst of a Nation: An Address Delivered in New York, New York, on 11 May 1853," in *FDP*, 2:429–30.

67. Blair, *Voice from the Grave of Jackson!*, quotations on 8–9; Alexander, "Persistent Whiggery in the Confederate South"; Earle, *Jacksonian Antislavery*, 15–16; Hettle, *Peculiar Democracy*, 45–46, 85, 88; Schlesinger, *Age of Jackson*, 480–82, 488–90.

68. Benjamin, *Speech*, 20 (quoted); Benjamin to John Perkins Jr., July 2, 1856, Perkins Papers; John Irvine to Samuel [*sic*, Stephen] A. Doughlas, Apr. 28, 1856, SAD (quoted).

69. Blair, *Voice from the Grave of Jackson!*, 8; Whitman, "Eighteenth Presidency!," 24, 30.

70. Kelley, *Address*, 2, 7–8, 11–14.

71. *CG*, 34th Cong., 1st Sess., 1855–56, 25, pt. 2:1396–97.

72. Cole to Hamlin, June 6–7, 1856, Hamlin Family Papers.

73. F. H. Cushing to Hamlin, June 13, 1856, Hamlin Family Papers (quoted); John Bent to Hamlin, June 14, 1856, Hamlin Family Papers.

74. A *Maine law* man, & a Republican to Hamlin, Aug. 3, 1856, Hamlin Family Papers.

75. *CG,* 34th Cong., 1st Sess., 1855–56, 25, pt. 2:1396–97. For a critical assessment of defectors like Hamlin, see Baker, *Affairs of Party,* 52–63.

76. John Abbott to Cushing, Feb. 24, Nov. 15, 1854, Cushing Papers.

77. James[?] D. McIntire to Charles G. Bellamy, Mar. 28, 1857, Bellamy Papers.

78. Hallett et al., *Appeal to Democrats,* 4.

79. E. C. Sugg to William H. English, Jan. 1, 1855, EFP.

80. James N. Shine to Douglas, Feb. 16, 1856, SAD; Buchanan to David Lynch, Sept. 21, 1855, typescript, James Buchanan and Harriet Lane Johnston Papers, LC.

81. Welles became a Republican later in the 1850s and returned to the Democracy after the Civil War. "Correspondence," Thomas G. Pratt to John Walton et al., Sept. 13, 1855, broadside, Box 1, Folder 4, Perkins Papers (quoted); Welles to [Burke], Nov. 5[?], 1851, Burke Papers (quoted); "Letter of Hon. Thos. G. Pratt," in Pearce, Pratt, Crisfield, and Clay, *Old Line Whigs,* 7–10; Ashworth, *"Agrarians" and "Aristocrats,"* 205–18; Brown, *Politics and Statesmanship,* 6–12.

82. Day, *Democratic Party as It Was,* 1–2, 5–6.

83. Abraham Lincoln to Henry L. Pierce and Others, Apr. 6, 1859, in Lincoln, *Collected Works,* 3:374–76.

84. Harlan, *Democratic Party,* 2.

85. Abraham Lincoln to Anson G. Henry, Nov. 19, 1858, in Lincoln, *Collected Works,* 3:339 (quoted); Abraham Lincoln to Henry L. Pierce and Others, Apr. 6, 1859, in Lincoln, *Collected Works,* 3:374–76.

86. Buchanan to J. Glancy Jones, June 1, 1855, Buchanan and Johnston Papers.

87. Harlan, *Democratic Party,* 2. For Whigs converging with Democracy, see Clingman, *Address;* and Cushing, *Speech Delivered in Faneuil Hall.*

88. Day, *Democratic Party as It Was,* 2.

89. Lovejoy, *True Democracy,* 6, 10. On Whiggish conservatism, see Barkan, "Emergence of a Whig Persuasion"; Brown, *Politics and Statesmanship,* 49–92; Current, *Daniel Webster,* 103–8, 145–52, 193–202; Howe, *Political Culture of the American Whigs,* 210–37; Maciag, *Edmund Burke in America,* 73–104; and Mason, *Apostle of Union.*

90. "Reply to the Charge of Lunacy," Jan. 30, 1835, in Leggett, *Democratick Editorials,* 16, 18.

91. *Horrible Doctrines!!!,* 1, 2; Greeley, *Why I Am a Whig,* 1–4. On Jacksonian radicalism, see Fredrickson, *Inner Civil War,* 7–10, 19–22; Schlesinger, *Age of Jackson,* 159–89; and Wilentz, *Rise of American Democracy,* 352–58.

92. "Manifest Destiny, January 19, 1858," in Nicholas, *Conservative Essays,* 40–41; Van Atta, "'A Lawless Rabble.'"

93. *Appeal for the Union*, 4–10 (quoted); Benjamin, *Speech*, 18; Edward Everett to William Henry Trescot, June 6, 1855 [1856?], Sept. 12, 1856, Everett Papers; "Disunion. Extract from a Series of Numbers Published under This Title in the Summer and Fall of 1856," in Nicholas, *Conservative Essays*, 56; *Robert C. Winthrop on Fusion*, 2, 3.

94. Johnson, *Speech*, 4–5; Hilliard, *Letter*, 4.

95. George G. Dunn to A. B. Conduitt, Oct. 16, 1850, EFP.

96. Everett, *Stability and Progress*, 5–6; Cobban, *Edmund Burke;* Mason, *Apostle of Union*.

97. Greeley, *Why I Am a Whig*, 6–8, 12–13.

98. Lovejoy, *True Democracy*, 5.

99. Van Buren, *Inquiry into the Origin*, 352.

100. John Abbott to Caleb Cushing, Feb. 24, 1854, Cushing Papers; Isaac Chadbourne to Charles G. Bellamy, Feb. 28, 1860, Bellamy Papers.

101. Ford, *Origins of Southern Radicalism*, 308–37; Holt, *Political Crisis of the 1850s*, 101–81; Thornton, *Politics and Power*, 165–342. For Democrats' continued Jacksonianism in the 1850s, see Lynn, "From the Money Power."

102. Burke, *Reflections on the Revolution in France*, 40–44, 173; Everett, *Stability and Progress*, 8–10; Clark, *Coherent Variety;* Ryan, *Cradle of the Middle Class*, 145–85.

103. "Remarks Made during the Debate on His Resolutions, in Respect to the Rights of the States and the Abolition of Slavery,—December 27th, 1837, *et seq.*," in Calhoun, *Works*, 3:180; Toombs, *Lecture Delivered in the Tremont Temple*, 9, 12; Kirk, *Conservative Mind*, 150–84; Rossiter, *Conservatism in America*, 119–24.

104. Burke, *Reflections on the Revolution in France*, 41.

105. Coleman, "Address on Change in Boyhood Home," 13–16.

106. Mayo, *Capitol; or, the Higher Law*, 3.

107. Greeley, *Why I Am a Whig*, 6–8; Ashworth, *"Agrarians" and "Aristocrats,"* 52–84, 193–99; Howe, *What Hath God Wrought*, 582–85; Watson, *Liberty and Power*, 237–48; Wiebe, *Opening of American Society*, 131–42; Wilson, *Space, Time, and Freedom*, 49–119. For a differing view of Democrats as Burkeans, see Baker, *Affairs of Party*, 177–211.

108. Tocqueville, *Democracy in America*, 68–71; "Power of Majorities over Constitutions, March 3, 1858," in Nicholas, *Conservative Essays*, 19; Barkan, "Emergence of a Whig Persuasion"; Fischer, *Revolution of American Conservatism;* Hartz, *Liberal Tradition in America*, 89–142, 198–200; Schlesinger, *Age of Jackson*, 267–305; Wilentz, *Rise of American Democracy*, 482–507.

109. George G. Dunn to A. B. Conduitt, Oct. 16, 1850, EFP.

5. Doughface Triumphant

1. "Speech of Governor H. A. Wise, at Richmond, June 13, 1856," in *James Buchanan, His Doctrines*, 13, 14 (quoted); Jones to Wise, July 8, 1855, WFP (quoted);

Wise to Jones, June 29, 1855, typescript, WFP; O. Jennings Wise to Henry A. Wise, Dec. 28, 1855, WFP.

2. Wise to George Booker, Mar. 11, 1857, WFP.

3. Quotations from O. Jennings Wise to Henry A. Wise, Mar. 23, 1856, WFP; and Buchanan to J. Glancy Jones, Dec. 7, 1855, Buchanan and Johnston Papers.

4. Buchanan to Wise, Mar. 10, 18 (quoted), May 10, June 9, 1852, May 16, 1852 [1853], WFP; Simpson, *Good Southerner*, 89–91.

5. Wise to Pierce, June 22, 1852, copy, typescript, WFP (quoted); Wise to P. R. George, Dec. 11, 1852, copy, typescript, WFP.

6. "Speech of Governor H. A. Wise," 10 (quoted); O. Jennings Wise to Henry A. Wise, July 29, 1856, WFP; Eaton, "Henry A. Wise: A Study in Virginia Leadership," 190–94; Simpson, *Good Southerner*, 122–25.

7. Buchanan to John Y. Mason, Aug. 15, 1856, Mason Family Papers, 1805–1886, VHS.

8. For the election as separate campaigns, see Nichols and Klein, "Election of 1856," 1020, 1027–31; Nichols, *Disruption of American Democracy*, 32–34, 61–62; and Potter, *Impending Crisis*, 259–65. For northern Democrats' campaign as proslavery and prosouthern, see Landis, *Northern Men with Southern Loyalties*, 152–58. For the election as a national campaign from the Know-Nothing perspective, see Holt, "Another Look at the Election of 1856."

9. *Proceedings of the National Democratic Convention*, 33.

10. *Constitution and By-Laws*, 12.

11. Douglas, *Speech . . . Delivered in Richmond*, 1.

12. Buchanan to Henry A. Wise, Dec. 2, 1856, WFP. On Buchanan, see Auchampaugh, "James Buchanan, the Conservatives' Choice"; Klein, *President James Buchanan*; Baker, *James Buchanan*; Birkner, *James Buchanan*; and Quist and Birkner, *James Buchanan*.

13. *Stockton (CA) Weekly San Joaquin Republican*, Aug. 23, 1856.

14. *New York Herald*, July 1 (quoted), 11, 19, 20 (quoted), 23, Aug. 1, 7, Oct. 17, 1856; *(Columbus) Ohio State Journal*, Sept. 17, 1856; Editor's drawer, *Harper's New Monthly Magazine*, Aug. 1856, 421–22; *Weekly (Madison) Wisconsin Patriot*, Aug. 23, 1856; *Sacramento Daily Democratic State Journal*, Aug. 20, 1856.

15. Democratic State Central Committee of Pennsylvania, *Memoir of James Buchanan*, 11.

16. Bercaw, *Gendered Freedoms;* Glymph, *Out of the House of Bondage;* McCurry, *Masters of Small Worlds;* Pierson, *Free Hearts and Free Homes*, especially 115–63 for the 1856 election as a contest between gender and domestic ideologies from the Republican perspective; Silber, *Gender and the Sectional Conflict*, xi–36; Whites, *Gender Matters*, 11–24. Foregrounding sectional domestic differences can obscure the existence of northern patriarchal households, akin to those in the South, both of which Democrats represented.

17. *Boston Daily Atlas*, June 10, 1856.

18. Halstead, *Trimmers, Trucklers and Temporizers*, 24.

19. "Speech of Governor H. A. Wise," 10, 13; Mumford, "'Lost Manhood' Found," 37–41; Sellers, *Market Revolution*, 246–54; Smith-Rosenberg, "Sex as Symbol in Victorian Purity."

20. Horton, *Life and Public Services*, 369.

21. Quotations from Loring, *Speech Delivered at Webster, Mass.*, 6; "Mr. Cobb's Speech, in Depot Hall," 26; and Douglas, Ottawa Debate, Aug. 21, 1858, in *LDD*, 45.

22. *Infidelity and Abolitionism*, 5.

23. *Plain Facts and Considerations*, 26.

24. *United States Democratic Review*, July 1856, 574; H. A. Wise to Edward Everett, Feb. 20, 1856, Everett Papers.

25. *Salisbury (NC) Carolina Watchman*, May 31, 1859 (quoted); William M. Cooke to John Y. Mason Jr., Apr. 24, 1847, Mason Papers; John Letcher to [Paulus Powell], Sept. 25, 1854, Powell Papers; Bertolini, "Fireside Chastity"; Foster, "Reconsidering Libertines and Early Modern Heterosexuality"; Glover, *Southern Sons*, 132–34; Mandell, "What's Sex Got to Do with It?"; McCurdy, *Citizen Bachelors*, especially 84–119.

26. P. R. George to [Cushing], Sept. 26, [1854], Cushing Papers; Cushing to P. R. George, Sept. 30, 1854, draft, Cushing Papers (quoted); Belohlavek, *Broken Glass*, 49.

27. Cushing, *Speech Delivered in Faneuil Hall*, 31; Cott, *Public Vows*. For a differing view, see McCurdy, *Citizen Bachelors*, 198–200.

28. Wise, *Speech*, 11–12; Wise, *Religious Liberty*, 39; Simpson, *Good Southerner*, 76–77, 95.

29. *(Columbus) Ohio State Journal*, July 9, 1856.

30. Democratic State Central Committee of Pennsylvania, *Memoir of James Buchanan*, 16.

31. "Letter of Hon. James A. Pearce," 6.

32. Quotations from *Plain Facts and Considerations*, 3; and "Speech Delivered at Delhi, Delaware County, N.Y., at a Meeting of the 'Hardshell' or National Democracy of the County, September 29, 1854," in *DD*, 1:494.

33. *Infidelity and Abolitionism*, 5.

34. Quotations from Horton, *Life and Public Services*, 421; and "Letter of Hon. James A. Pearce," 5.

35. Quotations from Horton, *Life and Public Services*, 425; and Democratic State Central Committee of Pennsylvania, *Memoir of James Buchanan*, 3.

36. "Speech of Governor H. A. Wise," 10.

37. "Buchanan and Fremont," in *Songs for Freemen*, 15 (quoted); *Boston Daily Atlas*, June 27, Aug. 8, 1856; Pierson, *Free Hearts and Free Homes*, 115–63.

38. Frémont to Elizabeth Blair Lee, [Apr. 18, 1856], in Frémont, *Letters*, 98.

39. *Dallas Herald*, Sept. 6, 1856; Buchanan to Mason, Aug. 15, 1856, Mason Family Papers.

40. *Short Answers to Reckless Fabrications*, 28.

41. Lovejoy, *True Democracy*, 1.

42. Loring, *Speech Delivered at Webster, Mass.*, 17, 21; Pierson, *Free Hearts and Free Homes*, 117–29.

43. Quotations from Brown, *Address . . . before the Democratic Association,* 22; and Anthony Ten Eyck to Alpheus Felch, Jan. 27, 1856, Felch Papers.

44. Democratic State Central Committee of Pennsylvania, *Memoir of James Buchanan,* 3.

45. *Appeal for the Union,* 15.

46. Buchanan to William B. Reed, Feb. 29, 1856, in *JB,* 10:63.

47. *Last Appeal to Pennsylvania,* 7.

48. Quotations from *Agitation of Slavery,* 8; and letter from "Charles B. Calvert, of Maryland," in *Buchanan's Political Record,* 10.

49. Haven to James M. Smith, Mar. 12, 1856, Solomon G. Haven Family Papers, WCL; "Speech at a Mass Meeting Held to Ratify the Nominations of the Cincinnati Convention. Delivered at the Court-House in Binghamton, N.Y., June 21, 1856," in *DD,* 1:514; Holt, "Another Look at the Election of 1856," 47–54.

50. Brown, *Address on the Parties and Issues,* 35; Paulus, "America's Long Eulogy for Compromise," 43–46.

51. Reed, *Appeal to Pennsylvania,* 17, 20, 25.

52. Quotations from Democratic State Central Committee of Pennsylvania, *Memoir of James Buchanan,* 4; and Loring, *Speech Delivered at Webster, Mass.,* 21.

53. "Speech of James B. Clay," 15–16; Klein, *President James Buchanan,* 260; Schlesinger, *Age of Jackson,* 481.

54. O. K. Barrell to Bayard, Sept. 3, 1856, Bayard Papers (quoted); Thomas F. Bayard to James A. Bayard, Dec. 3, 1856, Bayard Papers; address of James A. Bayard, in *Obituary Addresses . . . of the Hon. John M. Clayton,* 5–10.

55. Millard Fillmore to Everett, July 12, 1856, Everett Papers; *New York Times,* clipping enclosed in Winthrop to Everett, July 28, 1856, Everett Papers (quoted); H. A. Wise to Everett, July 14, 16, 31, Aug. 12, 17, 23, 1856, Everett Papers; Henry A. Wise to Robert Tyler, Aug. 15, 1856, Wise Papers, DU.

56. Everett to William Henry Trescot, Sept. 12, Dec. 29, 1856, Everett Papers.

57. Levi L. Cushing Jr. to [John W. A. Sanford Jr.], Sept. 11, 1855, June 24, 1856, John W. A. Sanford Papers, ADAH.

58. Buchanan to Everett, Dec. 11, 1856, Everett Papers; Mason, *Apostle of Union,* 210–13.

59. Winthrop, *Memoir of Robert C. Winthrop,* 185–95; Choate, "Speech 'On the Political Topics,'" 2:412; Fish to Everett, Sept. 15, 1856, Everett Papers (quoted).

60. Joshua Bates to Everett, Dec. 5, 1856, Everett Papers; Everett to Buchanan, Dec. 8, 1856, copy, Everett Papers (quoted); Moore, *Letter,* 5.

61. Hamilton to English, June 12, 27, 1856, EFP (quoted); Jesse D. Bright to Hamilton, June 16, 1856, Hamilton Family Papers, ISL; Hendricks to Hamilton, Mar. 31, 1856, Hamilton Family Papers (quoted).

62. "Speech of Hon. Isaac D. Jones," 16.

63. Van Buren, *Letter,* 3 (quoted); William M. Corry to Joseph Holt, June 20, 1856, Holt Papers; *Buchanan's Political Record,* 4; "Speech of James B. Clay," 15–16; *Life*

of the Hon. James Buchanan, 6; Baker, *James Buchanan*, 28; Klein, *President James Buchanan*, 49–53, 56–59.

64. Democratic State Central Committee of Pennsylvania, *Memoir of James Buchanan*, 5 (quoted); Horton, *Life and Public Services*, 45–46, 68–70, 72–77, 356, 367.

65. Horton, *Life and Public Services*, 67, 137–38.

66. "Democratic Platform of 1856," in Porter and Johnson, *National Party Platforms*, 23–27; Van Buren, *Letter*, 8.

67. "Speech of Governor H. A. Wise," 10, 12, 14 (quoted); Wise to George Booker, Mar. 11, 1857, WFP; Van Buren quoted in Watson, *Liberty and Power*, 87; Eaton, "Henry A. Wise: A Study in Virginia Leadership," 190–94; Simpson, *Good Southerner*, 89.

68. "Speech of Governor H. A. Wise," 14 (quoted); Buchanan to Wise, Mar. 10, 1852, June 21, Nov. 26 (quoted), Dec. 2 (quoted), 1856, WFP.

69. Reed, *Appeal to Pennsylvania*, 5.

70. *Proceedings of the National Democratic Convention*, 36 (quoted); *Weekly Wisconsin Patriot*, July 5, 1856.

71. *(Columbus) Ohio State Journal*, Sept. 17, 1856; Terrill, "James Buchanan."

72. Quotations from A. Johnston to Allen Hamilton, Mar. 10, 1857, Hamilton Family Papers; and *Agitation of Slavery*, 35.

73. William M. Corry to Joseph Holt, June 20, 1856, Holt Papers.

74. *Agitation of Slavery*, 35; Buchanan to John E. Ward et al., Committee, June 16, 1856, in *JB*, 10:84.

75. "Democratic Platform of 1856," 25–26; Baker, *Affairs of Party*, 285; Isaac Chadbourne to Charles G. Bellamy, June 25, 1856, Bellamy Papers.

76. "Speech, June 9, 1856," in *JB*, 10:81; *Proceedings of the National Democratic Convention*, 35.

77. Buchanan to Wise, June 21, 1856, WFP; "Speech of Governor H. A. Wise," 10.

78. Egerton, "Slaves' Election"; Wish, "Slave Insurrection Panic of 1856."

79. On the "honor-mastery paradigm," see Friend and Glover, "Rethinking Southern Masculinity." On mastery, see Heyrman, *Southern Cross*, 117–60; and McCurry, *Masters of Small Worlds*. On honor, see Greenberg, *Masters and Statesmen;* Stowe, *Intimacy and Power;* and Wyatt-Brown, *Southern Honor*, especially 239–40 for southern bachelors. For southern manhood's performative dimension and the synthesis of mastery and honor, see Beilein, *Bushwhackers;* Bercaw, *Gendered Freedoms*, 75–93; Cheathem, *Andrew Jackson, Southerner;* Fennessy, "Master of an Interior World"; Glover, *Southern Sons;* Hettle, *Peculiar Democracy;* and Mayfield, *Counterfeit Gentlemen*.

80. Brown, "Miscegenation of Richard Mentor Johnson"; Mueller, *Senator Benton and the People*, 82–83.

81. King to Robert Tyler, June 28, 1852, photocopy, King Family Papers; Buchanan to Wise, June 9, 1852, WFP. On Buchanan and King's relationship, which some claim may have been romantic and sexual, see Baker, *James Buchanan*, 20–22, 25–26; and Balcerski, "Intimate Contests," 21–93. Despite this speculation, explicit charges of

same-sex sexuality were not prominent in the campaign. On historicizing nineteenth-century same-sex intimacy, see D'Emilio and Freedman, *Intimate Matters*, 121–30; Katz, *Love Stories*, especially 8–12, 331–43; and Yacovone, "Abolitionists and the 'Language of Fraternal Love.'"

82. William Thomas King to Thomas Devane King, Mar. 22, 1844[?], typescript, King Family Papers; Catherine Ellis to Thomas D. King, Aug. 20, 1845, King Family Papers; William R. King to William T. King, Mar. 27, 1851, photocopy, King Family Papers; Auchampaugh, "James Buchanan, the Bachelor"; Baker, *James Buchanan*, 47–51; Cheatham, *Andrew Jackson, Southerner*, 53–57, 79–89, 121; Cheatham, "'The High Minded Honourable Man'"; Klein, *President James Buchanan*, 206–10, 227.

83. *Obituary Addresses . . . of the Hon. William R. King*, 10, 16, 24, 25, 27, 67–68, 74.

84. *Sketches of the Lives*, 34 (quoted); Greenberg, *Masters and Statesmen*.

85. Horton, *Life and Public Services*, 18–19, 422–23, 424 (quoted); "Buchanan's Sympathy for Women," *Stockton Weekly San Joaquin Republican*, Sept. 27, 1856 (quoted); *Plain Facts and Considerations*, 6, 8–9.

86. *New York Herald*, July 19, 1856.

87. "Mr. Buchanan at Home," in Horton, *Life and Public Services*, 419–28 (quoted); "Mr. Buchanan's Character at Home," in *Short Answers to Reckless Fabrications*, 26–27; H. A. Wise to Edward Everett, Aug. 5, 1856, Everett Papers; Baker, *James Buchanan*, 25–26, 47, 137–38, 150, 151–52; Freehling, *Secessionists Triumphant*, 97–101; Klein, *President James Buchanan*, 206–7.

88. Buchanan to Francis W. Pickens, July 14, 1853, Buchanan and Johnston Papers; Horton, *Life and Public Services*, 424.

89. Wise to George Booker, Nov. 26, 1856, WFP (quoted); Buchanan to Wise, Dec. 2, 1856, WFP (quoted); Buchanan to J. Glancy Jones, Nov. 29, 1856, Buchanan and Johnston Papers.

90. Horton, *Life and Public Services*, 425.

91. *CG*, 24th Cong., 1st Sess., 1835–36, 3:222; "Speech at Wheatland," Nov. 6, 1856, in *JB*, 10:96; Freehling, *Secessionists at Bay*, 324–27.

92. *Agitation of Slavery*, 11–15; "Speech of Governor H. A. Wise," 10.

93. *Nebraska: A Poem*, 25; Walters, "Erotic South."

94. John W. A. Sanford [Sr.] to John W. A. Sanford [Jr.], July 29, 1856, Sanford Papers; Solomon G. Haven to James M. Smith, July 29, 1856, Haven Family Papers.

95. *Fearful Issue to Be Decided*, 9–10, 24 (quoted); *Agitation of Slavery*, especially 15–25, 29–30.

96. Tennent Lomax Scrapbook, "Bets," 48, 53¼, 58, 63, 82, 88, Tennent Lomax Papers, ADAH.

97. Quotations from *Fearful Issue to Be Decided*, 3 (see also 24); and *Infidelity and Abolitionism*, 1.

98. Buchanan to Henry A. Wise, Aug. 27, Sept. 13 (quoted), 1856, WFP.

99. *Fearful Issue to Be Decided*, 24 (quoted); "Speech of Governor H. A. Wise," 14 (quoted); Clingman, *Address*, 11–12; "Speech of Hon. Isaac D. Jones," 15–16.

100. Quotations from Buchanan to John Slidell, May 28, 1856, copy, Breckinridge Family Papers, LC; and Buchanan to John Y. Mason, Aug. 15, 1856, Mason Family Papers.
101. *Short Answers to Reckless Fabrications*, 25.
102. *Last Appeal to Pennsylvania*, 3; Buchanan, "Speech at Wheatland," 10:97.
103. Democratic State Central Committee of Pennsylvania, *Memoir of James Buchanan*, 10; Orr, *Cincinnati Convention*, 3; Ford, *Origins of Southern Radicalism*, 345–48.
104. *James Buchanan, His Doctrines*, 9.
105. Loring, *Speech Delivered at Webster, Mass.*, 21; Potter, *Impending Crisis*, 57–59.
106. Foster, *Speech*, 3.
107. "Letter from George Law on the Political Crisis," July 3, 1856, in Morgan, Law, and Shaffer, *Tract for Americans*, 10–11; Foster, *Speech*, 3–10.
108. Letter from "Charles B. Calvert, of Maryland," 11–12; "Gen. Sam Houston on the Presidency," in *Buchanan's Political Record*, 9.
109. *Austin (TX) State Gazette*, Oct. 4, 1856.
110. Letter from "Charles B. Calvert, of Maryland," 12; Holt, "Politics of Impatience," 313–20.
111. Quotations from *James Buchanan, His Doctrines*, 9; and "Letter from George Law," 10.
112. "Excerpt from Speech to Frémont and Dayton Rally, October 1, 1856, Lancaster," in Stevens, *Selected Papers*, 1:154; *Life of the Hon. James Buchanan*, 8.
113. Quotations from Lewis D. Campbell to William P. Fessenden, Oct. 16, 1855, Fessenden Papers; and [Marsh], *Bake-Pan*, 5.
114. Quotations from [Marsh], *Bake-Pan*, 3; and *Frederick Douglass' Paper* (Rochester, NY), Mar. 10, 1854.
115. [Marsh], *Bake-Pan*, 4.
116. *Frederick Douglass' Paper*, Mar. 3, 1854; Anthony Ten Eyck to Alpheus Felch, Jan. 27, 1856, Felch Papers.
117. *New York Herald*, July 23 (quoted), Aug. 1, 1856; Pierson, *Free Hearts and Free Homes*, 122–27.
118. *(Columbus) Ohio State Journal*, June 18, 1856 (quoted); "Jessie Fremont," in *Songs for Freemen*, 24; *Boston Daily Atlas*, June 27, 1856.
119. "The Bachelor Candidate," in *Songs for Freemen*, 41.
120. "Political Judgment Day," in *Songs for Freemen*, 28–29; Pierson, *Free Hearts and Free Homes*, 117–29.
121. *Indiana Daily State Sentinel*, Aug. 22, 1854.
122. *New York Herald*, Sept. 25, 1856.
123. *New York Herald*, Sept. 25, Oct. 17, 1856.
124. *Boston Daily Atlas*, Oct. 18, 1856.
125. King to Dr. Saltmarsh, Dec. 1, 1856, typescript, King Family Papers; O. Jennings Wise to Henry A. Wise, Oct. 29, 1856, WFP.

126. E. Randolph Harden to [Herschel V. Johnson], Nov. 23, 1856, Herschel V. Johnson Papers; Gienapp, *Origins of the Republican Party*, 413–48; Landis, *Northern Men with Southern Loyalties*, 157–58; Nichols and Klein, "Election of 1856," 1032–33; Nichols, *Disruption of American Democracy*, 60–65.

127. A. Johnston to Allen Hamilton, Nov. 1, 1858, Hamilton Family Papers.

128. William C. Davison to Stephen A. Douglas, Nov. 6, 1858, SAD; Roediger, *Wages of Whiteness*, 99.

129. Buchanan to Wise, Oct. 9, 1858, WFP (quoted); Wise to Buchanan, Oct. 12, 1858, copy, WFP (quoted); Buchanan to John B. Floyd, Aug. 14, 1859, photocopy, Buchanan and Johnston Papers.

130. Wise, *Lecompton Question*, 6.

6. The Other Douglas Debates

1. "Speech of Abraham Lincoln, Springfield, June 16, 1858," in *LDD*, 18–19.

2. Etcheson, *Bleeding Kansas;* Etcheson, "General Jackson Is Dead"; Etcheson, "Great Principle of Self-Government"; Potter, *Impending Crisis*, 199–224, 267–331; Stampp, *America in 1857*.

3. Grier to Jeremiah Sullivan Black, Sept. 15, 1859, Jeremiah S. Black Papers (microfilm), LC.

4. "Squatter Sovereignty: Response to the Essay on Popular Sovereignty Imputed to the Hon. R. J., December 3, 1858," in Nicholas, *Conservative Essays*, 55.

5. Jaffa, *New Birth of Freedom*, 474–82.

6. Quotations from Black, *Observations on Territorial Sovereignty*, 4–5; and Dickinson, "Speech on the Acquisition of Territory" 1:230.

7. Huston, "Putting African Americans in the Center"; Johnson, "Frederick Douglass and the Kansas-Nebraska Act"; Rucker, "Unpopular Sovereignty."

8. "Slavery the Live Issue: Addresses Delivered in Cincinnati, Ohio, on 11–13 April 1854," in *FDP*, 2:464 (quoted); "John Brown and the Slaveholders' Insurrection: An Address Delivered in Edinburgh, Scotland, on 30 January 1860," in *FDP*, 3:319.

9. *Frederick Douglass' Paper*, Sept. 29 (quoted), Oct. 27, Nov. 3, Dec. 1, 1854; Stauffer, *Giants*, 191–92.

10. "Slavery, Freedom, and the Kansas-Nebraska Act: An Address Delivered in Chicago, Illinois, on 30 October 1854," in *FDP*, 2:538–59, quotation on 542.

11. Douglass, "Slavery, Freedom, and the Kansas-Nebraska Act," 2:539, 554, 555.

12. Douglass to Charles Sumner, Feb. 27, 1854, in Douglass, *Life and Writings*, 2:280.

13. Douglass, "Slavery, Freedom, and the Kansas-Nebraska Act," 2:557.

14. Douglass, "Slavery the Live Issue," 2:462–63.

15. "Slavery and the Irrepressible Conflict: An Address Delivered in Geneva, New York, on 1 August 1860," in *FDP*, 3:383–84.

16. *Frederick Douglass' Paper*, Sept. 15 (quoted), Sept. 29 (quoted), Oct. 27, 1854. Concern that popular sovereignty could empower political actors of color dated to the

doctrine's inception. Childers, *Failure of Popular Sovereignty*, 127–28, 131–32, 151, 158–60, 183–85, 192–93.

17. J. R. Vaughan to Douglas, Aug. 3, 1858, SAD; Douglass, "Freedom in the West Indies," 3:233–37.
18. *LDD*, 39, 92, 189–90, 264.
19. Quotations from *LDD*, 39; and *Fearful Issue to Be Decided*, 20.
20. "Speech of Stephen A. Douglas, Chicago, July 9, 1858," 28–35; "Speech of Abraham Lincoln, Springfield, June 16, 1858," 14.
21. Douglas, Ottawa Debate, 44–48.
22. Douglas, *Remarks*, 7–11.
23. Toombs to Lewis Cass, July 28, 1857, Cass Papers.
24. Toombs to Thomas, Feb. 9, 1856, Toombs Correspondence.
25. Toombs, *Lecture Delivered in the Tremont Temple*, 2.
26. Phillips, *Letter on Naturalization and Citizenship*, quotation on 4; Jones, *Speech*, 10–16 (quoted); Brown, *Speech*, 9–10; Cushing, *Speech Delivered in Faneuil Hall*, 7–8; Wise, *Territorial Government*, 119–23; Quitt, *Stephen A. Douglas*, 89–95.
27. Phillips, *Letter on Naturalization and Citizenship*, quotations on 4, 5.
28. Cluskey, *Buchanan and Breckinridge*, 31.
29. Phillips, *Letter on Naturalization and Citizenship*, quotations on 4.
30. Callicot, *Speech*, 4–8.
31. Jean H. Baker argues for Douglas's Burkeanism, citing his notion that rights varied by community. Yet she confuses a theoretical impasse in Douglas's liberalism for philosophical conservatism. Baker, *Affairs of Party*, 177–96; Huston, "Democracy by Scripture," 195; Huston, *Stephen A. Douglas*, 84–91.
32. Douglas, *Remarks*, 10; [Anspach], *Sons of the Sires*, 203–12.
33. Rayner, *Reply*, 4–5, 8, 11–12, 22.
34. *Whig Charge of Religious Intolerance*, 8.
35. Phillips, *Letter . . . on the Religious Proscription*, 3.
36. "The Swiss Treaty and the Hebrew Convention," *Washington Union*, Nov. 5, 1857, clipping in bound volume, Box 13, Phillips Family Papers.
37. Ridge to Douglas, Sept. 19, 1858, SAD.
38. Cushing, *Speech Delivered in Faneuil Hall*, 23 (quoted); *Catalogue of the Private Library*.
39. Kelley, *Address*, 14; "Speech of Stephen A. Douglas, Chicago, July 9, 1858," 34.
40. "Remarks of Hon. Caleb Cushing, in Presenting the Bill Conferring Citizenship on the Indians of the Commonwealth of Massachusetts, in the Mass. House of Representatives, April 4th, 1859," manuscript speech, 7–11, 13, Box 207, Cushing Papers.
41. *Douglass' Monthly* (Rochester, NY), Oct. 1859; Douglas, *Letters*, 448.
42. Ward, *Speech . . . at the Great Democratic Mass Meeting*, 10.
43. [?] to [John G. Davis], Apr. 24, 1854, JGD.
44. Douglas, *Popular Sovereignty . . . Rejoinder of Judge Douglas*, 3–6.
45. Douglas, Jonesboro Debate, Sept. 15, 1858, in *LDD*, 127–28; David Christy to Douglas, July 23, 1858, SAD.

46. Wise, *Territorial Government*, 121–23; Stampp, *America in 1857*, 102.
47. Cushing, *Speeches on the Amendment*, 6–9.
48. Quotations from Douglas, *Remarks*, 7–11; and Wood, *Campaign in Connecticut*, 3–4; Baker, *Affairs of Party*, 177–211.
49. Austin H. Brown to John G. Davis, Jan. 16, 1859, JGD.
50. Samford to Bolling Hall, Nov. 9, 1855, Hall Family Papers (quoted); "Letter of Hon. W. R. Scurry," 24; Wise, *Territorial Government*, 86.
51. Grier to Jeremiah Sullivan Black, Sept. 15, 1859, Black Papers.
52. Curtis, *Just Supremacy of Congress*, 5, 19–23.
53. [Fisher], *Law of the Territories*, 80–81, 114–15; Lovejoy, *Fanaticism of the Democratic Party*, 6.
54. [? to Davis], Apr. 24, 1854, JGD (quoted); W. R. Nofsinger to [Davis], Apr. 14, 1854, JGD. For popular sovereignty in Nebraska, which was not characterized by Kansas's turbulence, see Etcheson, "Where Popular Sovereignty Worked."
55. Weller, *Inaugural Address*, 2–3 (quoted); Wise, *Territorial Government*, 38, 54–56 (quoted); Nicholas, "Manifest Destiny," 38–47; Etcheson, *Bleeding Kansas*, 69–79, 92–94, 210–11; Fritz, "Popular Sovereignty, Vigilantism."
56. Dorr to Edmund Burke, Apr. 9, 1851, Burke Papers.
57. A. E. to [Stephen A. Douglas, Sept. 1859], SAD; Wiecek, "'A Peculiar Conservatism.'"
58. Curtis, *Just Supremacy of Congress*, 5, 19–20, 33; Turner, "Unpopular Sovereignty."
59. C. S. Baron[?] Jr. to [Black], Apr. 18, 1859, Black Papers.
60. [Fisher], *Law of the Territories*, 75, 80, 114–15.
61. Young to Douglas, Apr. 29, 1854, SAD (quoted); William S. Allen to Caleb Cushing, Feb. 3, 1854, Cushing Papers.
62. Wise, *Territorial Government*, 38, 54–55.
63. W. W. Drummond to Cass, Apr. 1, 1856, Cass Papers.
64. Douglas, *Remarks*, 11–15.
65. Black, *Observations on Territorial Sovereignty*, 14 (quoted); Wise, *Territorial Government*, 38 (quoted); "First Annual Message, December 8, 1857," and "Proclamation on the Rebellion in Utah," [Apr. 6, 1858], in *JB*, 10:151–54, 202–6; MacKinnon, "Prelude to Armageddon"; Stampp, *America in 1857*, 196–208.
66. [Fisher], *Law of the Territories*, 29–30, 52–54, 80, 116–18; *Douglas' Doctrine of Popular Sovereignty*, 40–42.
67. [Johnson], *Remarks on Popular Sovereignty*, 16; Douglas, *Speech . . . at the Democratic Celebration*, 7.
68. Benjamin, *Speech*, 7.
69. [Fisher], *Law of the Territories*, 98.
70. *Robert C. Winthrop on Fusion*, 2; Mayo, *Capitol; or, the Higher Law*, 5–6.
71. John Perry Jr. to [Alpheus Felch], [1856], "Constitution and Address of the Vigilance Committee," printed circular, Felch Papers.

72. Burke, *Reflections on the Revolution in France*, 15–31, 111, 148–49, 190–91 (quoted); [Fisher], *Law of the Territories*, 45–48 (quoted); Calhoun, "A Disquisition on Government," 43–45; Howe, *Political Culture of the American Whigs*, 227–28, 233.

73. Burke, *Reflections on the Revolution in France*, 27–33, 50–55, 85–87, 161–63; Toombs, *Lecture Delivered in the Tremont Temple*, 9 (quoted); Cobban, *Edmund Burke*, 37–96; Maciag, *Edmund Burke in America*, 15–19.

74. Curtis, *Just Supremacy of Congress*, 19–23, 33.

75. Wise, *Territorial Government*, 89.

76. Quotations from *Douglas' Doctrine of Popular Sovereignty*, 13–14; Wise, *Territorial Government*, 54; and H. M., *Reflections on the Powers*, 4.

77. [Fisher], *Law of the Territories*, 55, 70, 80–81.

78. Curtis, *Just Supremacy of Congress*, 19–23.

79. Douglas, "Dividing Line"; Curtis, *Just Supremacy of Congress*, 3–4.

80. Robert Johannsen provides the only detailed treatment of the pamphlet war, but without much attention to its ideas. Harold Holzer mischaracterizes Douglas's article as "the final round of the Lincoln-Douglas debates." Nicole Etcheson examines disagreements over popular sovereignty as intellectually substantive but also places Douglas in dialogue with Lincoln, not Black and other Democrats. Don E. Fehrenbacher discusses some of the constitutional and legal questions involved and correctly identifies the debate as an intraparty one. Harry V. Jaffa captures the theoretical importance of Douglas's essay and treats him as a serious, albeit flawed, thinker. Johannsen, "Stephen A. Douglas, 'Harper's Magazine'"; Holzer, *Lincoln at Cooper Union*, 35–42; Etcheson, "'A Living, Creeping Lie,'" 19–25; Fehrenbacher, *Dred Scott Case*, 514–32; Jaffa, *New Birth of Freedom*, 473–87; Knupfer, "Crisis in Conservatism," 130–33.

81. William A. Seaver to Douglas, Oct. 3, 1859, SAD. The Douglas-Black exchange unfolded as follows: Douglas's *Harper's* article, republished as a pamphlet, *Dividing Line;* Black's response, "Observations," first published in the administration organ the *(Washington, DC) Constitution,* Sept. 10, 1859; Douglas, "Speech . . . at Wooster, Ohio"; Black, "Appendix" to his initial "Observations"; Douglas, *Popular Sovereignty . . . Douglas in Reply;* Black, "Rejoinder to Senator Douglas's Last"; and Douglas, *Popular Sovereignty . . . Rejoinder of Judge Douglas.* Black's three responses—"Observations," "Appendix," and "Rejoinder to Senator Douglas's Last"—were later compiled and reprinted in the pamphlet, *Observations on Territorial Sovereignty.* The pamphlet's preface constitutes the final text in the debate. All references to Black's separate responses are to their appearance in this compilation.

82. Quotations from [Rockwell], *States vs. Territories*, 1; and H. M., *Reflections on the Powers*, 3.

83. For arguments favoring congressional power, see Curtis, *Just Supremacy of Congress;* Horace Greeley, "History Vindicated: A Letter to the Hon. Stephen A. Douglas on His 'Harper' Essay," *New-York Daily Tribune*, Oct. 15, 1859; H. M., *Reflections on the Powers; Douglas' Doctrine of Popular Sovereignty*, 13–24, 41; Nicholas, "Squatter Sovereignty," 47–55; and Thompson, *Squatter Sovereignty*.

84. Douglas, *Dividing Line*, 25–27; Douglas, *Popular Sovereignty . . . Rejoinder of Judge Douglas*, 13–14; [Johnson], *Remarks on Popular Sovereignty*, 15; James A. Bayard to Thomas F. Bayard, Jan. 28, 1860, Bayard Papers (quoted); Fehrenbacher, *Dred Scott Case*, 379, 400, 494, 510, 517; Stampp, *America in 1857*, 86–104, 108.

85. Benjamin, *Speech*, 7–9; Phillips, *Speech*, 12–13; Fehrenbacher, *Dred Scott Case*, 197–201; Mendelson, "Dred Scott's Case—Reconsidered."

86. Johnson, *Speech*, 3–10 (quoted); [Johnson], *Remarks on Popular Sovereignty*, 44–45; Fehrenbacher, *Dred Scott Case*, 455–56, 476–77, 494, 517.

87. Jaffa, *New Birth of Freedom*, 473–87.

88. Douglas, *Dividing Line*, 11, 14, 20–22 (quoted); Douglas, "Speech . . . at Wooster, Ohio," 203–4, 208–10; Douglas, *Popular Sovereignty . . . Rejoinder of Judge Douglas*, 3–5.

89. Douglas, "Speech . . . at Wooster, Ohio," 214–15.

90. Douglas, *Dividing Line*, 40.

91. Douglas, *Popular Sovereignty . . . Douglas in Reply*, 11.

92. Douglas, *Popular Sovereignty . . . Douglas in Reply*, 11; Wise, *Territorial Government*, 132–35.

93. Black, "Observations," 11–13.

94. Black, "Appendix," 16–19.

95. Black, "Observations," 8–11, 15 (quoted); Black, preface to *Observations on Territorial Sovereignty*, 5–6; Forsyth, *Letters*, 2 (quoted).

96. Douglas, *Popular Sovereignty . . . Douglas in Reply*, 2–5, 7–11 (quoted); Black, "Appendix," 17–19; Black, "Rejoinder to Senator Douglas's Last," 23.

97. Douglas, "Speech . . . at Wooster, Ohio," 209–10, 220–21.

98. Douglas to Johnson, Oct. 21 (quoted), Nov. 4, 1859, Reverdy Johnson Papers (microfilm), LC; [Johnson], *Remarks on Popular Sovereignty*, 17–18, 25 (quoted).

99. S. W. Randall to [Douglas], Aug. 28, 1858, SAD; Douglas, *Freeport Debate*, 88–89.

100. "Mr. Orr's Speech in Phœnix Hall," 14–15; Fehrenbacher, *Dred Scott Case*, 455–58, 484–514; Stampp, *America in 1857*, 101, 103. Fehrenbacher explains how both *Dred Scott* and the idea behind Freeport were not initially controversial but became divisive in the polarized late 1850s.

101. Johnson, *Speech*, 8–9, 11–12.

102. [Johnson], *Remarks on Popular Sovereignty*, 28; Douglas, *Popular Sovereignty . . . Douglas in Reply*, 13–14; Douglas to John W. Forney et al., Feb. 6, 1858, in Douglas, *Letters*, 408–11; Wise, *Territorial Government*, 91–95.

103. Democratic Committee of Publication, *Life of George Mifflin Dallas*, 10.

104. Wigfall, *Speech*, 3; Morgan, *Inventing the People*, 78–93, 106–21, 254–62; Tate, "Social Contract in America"; Wood, *Creation of the American Republic*, 259–343.

105. "Remarks of Hon. Wm. H. Ludlow, on Taking the Chair as President of the Democratic State Conventton," in *Proceedings of the Democratic State Convention*, 9; "Democratic Platform of 1856," 25.

106. "Letter of Hon. W. R. Scurry," 30, 32–33.

107. "A Discourse on the Constitution and Government of the United States," and "The Fort Hill Address: On the Relations of the States and Federal Government," July 26, 1831 (quoted), in Calhoun, *Union and Liberty*, 81–102, 369–85, quotation on 370–71; Herschel V. Johnson to T. Lomax, June 21, 1855, Herschel V. Johnson Papers; Toombs, *Lecture Delivered in the Tremont Temple*, 2–3; Wigfall, *Speech*.

108. For a nationally sovereign people, see Curtis, *Just Supremacy of Congress*, 22–23; Dillon, *Inquiry into the Nature;* and *Douglas' Doctrine of Popular Sovereignty*, 21–24, 29–30, 36–37, 41.

109. Wigfall, *Speech*, 4.

110. Quotations from Douglas, *Dividing Line*, 32; and [Johnson], *Remarks on Popular Sovereignty*, 14–16, 23.

111. Douglas, *Dividing Line*, 17–21 (quoted); Douglas, "Speech . . . at Wooster, Ohio," 208–9.

112. Black, "Appendix," 18 (quoted); "Letter of Hon. W. R. Scurry," 32–33; W. S. Oldham, "Speech," in Oldham and Scurry, *Rights of the South*, 13–16, 19.

113. "Letter of Hon. W. R. Scurry," 28–32 (quoted); Toombs, *Lecture Delivered in the Tremont Temple*, 2–6 (quoted); W. S. Oldham, "Speech," 16–21; Bestor, "State Sovereignty and Slavery"; Sinha, *Counterrevolution of Slavery*, 19–26, 63–93. For a northern Democrat advocating the extreme states' rights argument, see Wood, *Campaign in Connecticut*, 6–8.

114. Douglas, *Popular Sovereignty . . . Douglas in Reply*, quotation on 11; Douglas, *Popular Sovereignty . . . Rejoinder of Judge Douglas*. For a differing view of Douglas, see Jaffa, *New Birth of Freedom*, 482–87.

115. *Popular Sovereignty Subjected to the Test*, 9.

116. "Popular Sovereignty," 18–20, 41–43; [Johnson], *Remarks on Popular Sovereignty*, 28–30.

117. Black, "Appendix," 16–19.

118. Black, "Rejoinder to Senator Douglas's Last," 24.

119. J. Lothrop [Lathrop?] to Fessenden, Dec. 25, 1857, Fessenden Papers (quoted); Douglas, Alton Debate, Oct. 15, 1858, in *LDD*, 295 (quoted); *Douglas' Disorganization;* Douglas, *Popular Sovereignty . . . Rejoinder of Judge Douglas*, 14; Winston S. Pierce to John G. Davis, Dec. 14, 1858, Davis Papers, WHS; W. P. Mulhallan to John G. Davis, Dec. 17, 1858, Davis Papers, WHS; Potter, *Impending Crisis*, 320–22, 328–31.

120. August Kruer to Douglas, Aug. 3, 1858, SAD.

121. Thompson, *Squatter Sovereignty*, 2; Douglas, "Speech . . . at Wooster, Ohio," 200, 222–23.

122. Gartrell, *Speech*, 5 (quoted); Davis to Cass, Aug. 3, 1857, Cass Papers (quoted); Robert Toombs to Cass, July 28, Aug. 11, 1857, Cass Papers; Black, "Observations," 15. On the tension between democracy and enslaved property rights, see Etcheson, *Bleeding Kansas*, 2–4, 46–48, 189; Huston, *Stephen A. Douglas*, 131, 136–37, 151–54; and Woods, "Davis-Douglas Debates."

123. William H. Bertling to Black, Sept. 15, 1859 (quoted); Samuel C. Reid Jr. to Black, Sept. 14, 1859 (quoted); H. S. Knapp to Black, Sept. 17, 1859; George W.

Woodward to Black, Sept. 19, 1859; John S. Bagg to James Buchanan, Sept. 22, 1859; Edward G. Loring to [Black], Sept. 26, 1859, all Black Papers.

124. Stanley Woodward to Black, Sept. 19, 1859, Black Papers; C. B. Benedict to Black, Sept. 20, 1859, Black Papers; Cushing, *Speech . . . in Norombega Hall*, quotations on 2, 6.

125. Macon, *Letters to Chas. O'Conor*, 12–15, 17, 26–38.

126. Herschel V. Johnson to Alexander H. Stephens, July 20, 1860, Herschel V. Johnson Papers.

127. Rust, *Address*, quotation on 6; Hundley Diary, Jan. 4, 5, 6, 26 (quoted), Sept. 12 (quoted), 1859.

128. Wise, *Lecompton Question*; Wise to Austin H. Brown, Feb. 15, 1858, in *Popular Sovereignty. Proceedings of the Democratic State Convention*, 11.

129. Wise to William F. Samford, Nov. 3, 1858, Samford-Wise Papers, Special Collections and Archives, Auburn University Libraries.

130. Wise, *Territorial Government*, 69–76, 144, 147–50; Wise to William F. Samford, Dec. 2, 1858 (quoted), Feb. 9, Mar. 24, Apr. 5, 1859, Samford-Wise Papers; Simpson, *Good Southerner*, 174–75, 180–82.

131. Wise to William F. Samford, Aug. 6, 1857, Jan. 27, 1859 (quoted), Samford-Wise Papers; Wise to Robert Tyler, Jan. 17, 1858, Henry A. Wise Papers, 1858–1874, VHS.

132. Wise, *Letter*, quotation on 9.

133. Wise, *Territorial Government*, 109.

134. Wise, *Lecompton Question*, quotations on 49, 65–67; Wise, *Territorial Government*, 91–110; Reverdy Johnson to Wise, Nov. 6, 1858, original and typescript, Reverdy Johnson Papers; Wise to William F. Samford, Jan. 27, 1859, Samford-Wise Papers; Wise to David Hubbard, Mar. 3, 1859, Wise Papers, DU; Wise to Douglas, Jan. 14, Nov. 12, 1858, SAD; Simpson, *Good Southerner*, 157–89.

135. Moore, *Inaugural Address*, 7–8 (quoted); Toombs to Lewis Cass, July 28, 1857, Cass Papers (quoted); Gartrell, *Speech*, 3; Baker, *Affairs of Party*, 274–76; Etcheson, *Bleeding Kansas*, 139–89; Klein, *President James Buchanan*, 305–6; Potter, *Impending Crisis*, 297–327; Siddali, *Frontier Democracy*, 97–8n90; Stampp, *America in 1857*, 266–81, 315.

136. For a differing view, see Childers, *Failure of Popular Sovereignty*, 257–68; and Landis, *Northern Men with Southern Loyalties*, 199–204.

137. Wood, *Speech*, 4–5; [Johnson], *Remarks on Popular Sovereignty*, 45–47.

138. Quotations from Bayard to [Johnson], Nov. 6, 1859, draft, Bayard Papers; and Nicholas, "Squatter Sovereignty," 47.

139. *Douglas' Disorganization*, 1.

140. "Speech of the Hon. Wm. L. Yancey"; *Douglas' Doctrine of Popular Sovereignty*, 31–32.

141. Dickinson, "Speech upon the Issues and Candidates," 1:274.

142. Quotations from Black, "Appendix," 16; and Forsyth, *Letters*, 2.

143. Curtis, *Just Supremacy of Congress*, 36; [Fisher], *Law of the Territories*, xxiv, 122.

Conclusion

1. Benjamin Fitzpatrick to Elmore Fitzpatrick, Aug. 30, 1864, typescript, Benjamin Fitzpatrick Papers, SHC (quoted); Pierce to Fitzpatrick, Dec. 10, 1857, Fitzpatrick Family Papers.

2. Wise and Wood, *Correspondence,* 2–3 (quoted); see the antebellum letters from Wise to Wood in Henry A. Wise Letters, 1841, 1858–1860, Library of Virginia; Jno. W. Kees to Samuel Sullivan Cox, Box 6, Folder 217, Samuel Sullivan Cox Papers, John Hay Library, Brown University (quoted).

3. Wise and Wood, *Correspondence,* 4.

4. Rust, *Address,* 16.

5. Brown to Douglas, Sept. 10, 1859, SAD.

6. "Letter of Hon. A. J. Hamilton, Representative from the Second Congressional District of Texas, in Reply to the Hon. P. B. Fouke, of Illinois," Mar. 10, 1860, in Taylor et al., *Presidential Controversy,* 6.

7. For island communities, see Wiebe, *Search for Order,* 44–110.

8. Hayek, "Why I Am Not a Conservative"; Phillips-Fein, *Invisible Hands.* On traditionalism and the critique of libertarianism as conservatism, see Genovese, *Southern Tradition;* Kirk, *Conservative Mind,* 337–74; Poole, *Never Surrender;* and Rossiter, *Conservatism in America,* 128–62. For a nuanced reassessment of Gilded Age liberals, see Cohen, *Reconstruction of American Liberalism.*

9. Adams, "First Annual Message," Dec. 6, 1825, in Richardson, *Compilation of the Messages,* 2:316; Critchlow, *Phyllis Schlafly and Grassroots Conservatism;* Kazin, *Populist Persuasion,* 165–93, 221–66; Lassiter, *Silent Majority.*

10. MacLean, *Democracy in Chains;* McGirr, *Suburban Warriors;* Nash, *Conservative Intellectual Movement in America,* 235–86; Phillips-Fein, *Invisible Hands,* 132–35, 142–48, 205–6, 213–35, 250–58; Sugrue and Skrentny, "White Ethnic Strategy."

11. MacLean, *Freedom Is Not Enough,* 185–261; Wall, *Inventing the "American Way."*

BIBLIOGRAPHY

Manuscript Collections

ALABAMA DEPARTMENT OF ARCHIVES AND HISTORY
Matthew P. Blue Family Papers
J. L. M. Curry Pamphlet Collection
Fitzpatrick Family Papers
Bolling Hall Family Papers (manuscript and digitized)
William R. King Family Papers
Tennent Lomax Papers
Sydenham Moore Family Papers
John W. A. Sanford Papers

AUBURN UNIVERSITY LIBRARIES, SPECIAL COLLECTIONS AND ARCHIVES
Samford-Wise Papers

BROWN UNIVERSITY, JOHN HAY LIBRARY
Samuel Sullivan Cox Papers

DUKE UNIVERSITY, DAVID M. RUBINSTEIN RARE BOOK
AND MANUSCRIPT LIBRARY
Herschel V. Johnson Papers
Nathaniel Niles Papers
Robert Toombs Correspondence
Henry A. Wise Papers

EASTERN SHORE OF VIRGINIA HISTORICAL SOCIETY
Henry A. Wise Papers (microfilm)

INDIANA HISTORICAL SOCIETY, WILLIAM HENRY SMITH MEMORIAL LIBRARY,
MANUSCRIPT AND VISUAL COLLECTIONS DEPARTMENT
John G. Davis Papers (microfilm)
William Hayden English Family Papers
Joseph A. Wright Papers

INDIANA STATE LIBRARY, MANUSCRIPTS AND RARE BOOKS DIVISION
Austin H. Brown Papers
Hamilton Family Papers
Joseph A. Wright Correspondence and Papers

LIBRARY OF CONGRESS, MANUSCRIPT DIVISION
William Allen Papers
Thomas F. Bayard Papers
Jeremiah S. Black Papers (microfilm)
Breckinridge Family Papers
James Buchanan and Harriet Lane Johnston Papers
Edmund Burke Papers
Caleb Cushing Papers
Easby-Smith Family Papers
Joseph Holt Papers
Reverdy Johnson Papers (microfilm)
Horatio King Papers
William L. Marcy Papers
Louis McLane Correspondence
Wheeler H. Peckham Family Papers
Philip Phillips Family Papers
Franklin Pierce Papers

LIBRARY OF VIRGINIA
R. M. T. Hunter Papers
Henry A. Wise Letters, 1841, 1858–1860

MASSACHUSETTS HISTORICAL SOCIETY
Edward Everett Papers (microfilm)

UNIVERSITY OF CHICAGO LIBRARY, SPECIAL COLLECTIONS RESEARCH CENTER
Stephen A. Douglas Papers

UNIVERSITY OF MAINE AT ORONO, RAYMOND H. FOGLER LIBRARY, SPECIAL COLLECTIONS DEPARTMENT
Hamlin Family Papers (microfilm)

UNIVERSITY OF MICHIGAN, BENTLEY HISTORICAL LIBRARY
Alpheus Felch Papers

UNIVERSITY OF MICHIGAN, WILLIAM L. CLEMENTS LIBRARY
Charles G. Bellamy Papers
Lewis Cass Papers
Coleman-Stuart Family Papers
William P. Fessenden Papers
Solomon G. Haven Family Papers
Hoit Family Papers
Daniel R. Hundley Diary
Lucius Lyon Papers
Preston-Woodward Correspondence

Schoff Civil War Collection, Letters and Documents
Jonathan S. Wilcox Diaries

UNIVERSITY OF NORTH CAROLINA AT CHAPEL HILL, LOUIS ROUND WILSON
SPECIAL COLLECTIONS LIBRARY, SOUTHERN HISTORICAL COLLECTION
Benjamin Fitzpatrick Papers
John Y. Mason Papers
John Perkins Papers

VIRGINIA HISTORICAL SOCIETY
Faulkner Family Papers, 1737–1954
Hunter Family Papers, 1766–1918
James Lawson Kemper Papers, 1837–1903
John Letcher Papers, 1770–1970
Mason Family Papers, 1805–1886
Paulus Powell Papers, 1848–1868
Henry A. Wise Papers, 1858–1874
Wise Family Papers, 1777–1973
Wise Family Papers, 1816–1898

WISCONSIN HISTORICAL SOCIETY
John Givan Davis Papers (microfilm)

Newspapers and Periodicals

Austin (TX) State Gazette
Boston Daily Atlas
Carlisle (PA) Republican
(Columbus) Ohio State Journal
Daily Terre-Haute (IN) Journal
Dallas Herald
Douglass' Monthly (Rochester, NY)
Frederick Douglass' Paper (Rochester, NY)
(Indianapolis) Indiana Daily State Sentinel
Weekly (Madison) Wisconsin Patriot
New-York Daily Tribune
New York Herald
Providence (RI) Gazette
Sacramento Daily Democratic State Journal
Salisbury (NC) Carolina Watchman
Springfield (MA) Hampden Federalist and Public Journal
Stockton (CA) Weekly San Joaquin Republican
United States Democratic Review

Vermont Intelligencer and Bellows' Falls Advertiser
(Washington, DC) Constitution

Published Primary Sources

Abercrombie, James, and Alexander White. *A Letter from Messrs. White and Abercrombie, of Alabama, to the Chairman of the Carrollton District Convention.* N.p.: Gideon, [1852].

The Abolitionist Attack! Abolitionists against General Pierce. N.p., [1852].

Address of the National Democratic Volunteers. March, 1860. New York: John W. Oliver, 1860.

The Agitation of Slavery. Who Commenced! And Who Can End It!! Buchanan and Fillmore Compared from the Record. Washington, DC: Union, 1856.

[Anspach, F. R.]. *The Sons of the Sires; A History of the Rise, Progress, and Destiny of the American Party, and Its Probable Influence on the Next Presidential Election. To Which Is Added a Review of the Letter of the Hon. Henry A. Wise, against the Know-Nothings. By an American.* Philadelphia: Lippincott, Grambo, 1855.

An Appeal for the Union. By a Philadelphia Whig. [Philadelphia, 1856].

Austin, Robert F. *Buchananism Not Democracy. Speech of the Hon. Robert F. Austin, of Jefferson, on the Governor's Message. In Assembly, February 9, 1858.* N.p., [1858].

Barstow, Benjamin. *Speech of Benjamin Barstow, of Salem, on the Abolition Propensities of Caleb Cushing. Delivered at the Massachusetts National Democratic Convention, Held at Boston, Sept. 22, 1853.* Boston: National Democrat, 1853.

Benedict, Almon H. *A "Wide Awake" Poem; In Which Are Recounted the Political Death and Burial of the Unlamented Buchanan; and the Wanderings of the Little Giant "In Search of His Mother": In It Are, Also, Briefly Set Forth the Merits of "Honest Old Abe," Our Next President.* Cortland Village, NY: Edward D. Van Slyck, 1860.

Benjamin, J. P. *Speech of Hon. J. P. Benjamin, of Louisiana, on the Kansas Question. Delivered in the Senate, May 3, 1856.* Washington, DC: Union, 1856.

Black, Jeremiah Sullivan. *Observations on Territorial Sovereignty, Consisting of Three Several Answers to the Magazine Article, Speeches, and Pamphlets of Senator Douglas, with an Introductory Preface.* Washington, DC: Thomas McGill, 1860.

Blair, Francis P. *A Voice from the Grave of Jackson! Letter from Francis P. Blair, Esq., to a Public Meeting in New York, Held April 29, 1856.* Washington, DC: Buell and Blanchard, [1856].

Bright, John M. *Speech of John M. Bright, Esq., against Know-Nothingism, at Flat Creek, Bedford County, September 11, 1855.* Nashville: G. C. Torbett, 1855.

Brown, Aaron V. *Address of Ex-Gov. Aaron V. Brown, before the Democratic Association of Nashville, June 24, 1856.* Nashville: G. C. Torbett, 1856.

———. *An Address on the Parties and Issues of the Presidential Election, by Ex-Gov. Aaron V. Brown, Delivered at Philadelphia, before the Key-Stone Club of That City, August 15, 1856.* Nashville: G. C. Torbett, 1856.

———. *Speech of Ex-Gov. Aaron V. Brown, on Know Nothingism, at Gallatin, July 4th, 1855.* Nashville: J. F. Morgan, 1855.
Buchanan, James. *Great Speech of the Honourable James Buchanan, Delivered at the Mass Meeting of the Democracy of Western Pennsylvania, at Greensburg, on Thursday, Oct. 7, 1852.* Philadelphia, 1852.
———. *Mr. Buchanan's Administration on the Eve of the Rebellion.* New York: D. Appleton, 1866.
———. *The Works of James Buchanan: Comprising His Speeches, State Papers, and Private Correspondence.* Edited by John Bassett Moore. 12 vols. Philadelphia: J. B. Lippincott, 1908–11.
Buchanan's Political Record. Let the South Beware! [Washington, DC: National Executive Committee of the American Party, 1856].
Burke, Edmund (1729–1797). *Reflections on the Revolution in France.* 1790. Reprint, edited by J. G. A. Pocock. Indianapolis: Hackett, 1987.
Burke, Edmund (1809–1882). *To the Democratic Members of the Legislature of the State of New-Hampshire.* Newport, NH: Carleton and Harvey, [1852?].
Burton, William. "Inaugural Address." January 18, 1859. In *Journal of the House of Representatives of the State of Delaware, at a Session of the General Assembly, Convened and Held at Dover, on Tuesday, the Fourth of January, in the Year of Our Lord One Thousand Eight Hundred and Fifty-Nine, and of the Independence of the United States the Eighty-Third,* 78–90. Dover, DE: James Kirk, 1859.
Calhoun, John C. *Union and Liberty: The Political Philosophy of John C. Calhoun.* Edited by Ross M. Lence. Indianapolis: Liberty Fund, 1992.
———. *The Works of John C. Calhoun.* Edited by Richard K. Crallé. 6 vols. New York: D. Appleton, 1853–55.
Callicot, Theophilus C. *Speech of Hon. Theophilus C. Callicot, of Kings County, against Granting Equal Suffrage to Men of Color. In Assembly—February 10, 1860.* Albany, NY: Atlas and Argus, 1860.
Cass, Lewis. *Letter from Hon. Lewis Cass, of Michigan, on the War and the Wilmot Proviso.* Washington, DC: Blair and Rives, 1847.
Cass, Lewis, Stephen A. Douglas, John L. Dawson, Robert McLane, Simon Cameron, and Willis A. Gorman. *Speeches Delivered at Tammany Hall, New York City, Sept. 2, 1852, by Hon. Lewis Cass, of Michigan. Hon. Stephen A. Douglas, of Illinois. Hon. John L. Dawson, of Pennsylvania. Hon. Robert McLane, of Maryland. Hon. Simon Cameron, of Pennsylvania. Hon. Willis A. Gorman, of Indiana. Also Kentucky and Virginia Resolutions of 1798 and 1799.* [New York]: Evening Post, [1852].
Cass, Lewis, and John Hughes. *Letter of the Most Rev. Archbishop Hughes, on the Madiai. Speech of Hon. Lewis Cass, on Religious Freedom Abroad. Letter of the Most Rev. Archbishop Hughes, in Reply to Hon. Lewis Cass, on Religious Toleration.* Baltimore: Murphy, [1854].
Catalogue of the Private Library of the Late Hon. Caleb Cushing, of Newburyport, Mass. Boston: W. F. Brown, 1879.

Chandler, Daniel. *Letter from Daniel Chandler, Esq. on the Principles of the Know Nothing Party*. N.p., [1855].

Chapman, Reuben. *The Inaugural Address of Governor Chapman, Delivered December 16, 1847*. Montgomery, AL: McCormick and Walsh, 1847.

Child, Lydia Maria, Henry A. Wise, and M. J. C. Mason. *Correspondence between Lydia Maria Child and Gov. Wise and Mrs. Mason, of Virginia*. Boston: American Anti-Slavery Society, 1860.

Choate, Rufus, and Samuel Gilman Brown. *The Works of Rufus Choate with a Memoir of His Life*. 2 vols. Boston: Little, Brown, 1862.

Clay, Clement C., Jr. *The Love of Truth for Its Own Sake: An Address before the Erosophic and Philomathic Societies of the University of Alabama, at Its Commencement, in July, 1855*. Tuscaloosa, AL: M. D. J. Slade, 1855.

Clay, James B. *Hon. James B. Clay, to His Constituents of the Ashland District*. N.p., [1858].

Clingman, Thomas L. *Address of Hon. Thomas L. Clingman, on the Political Condition and Prospects of the Country, to the Freemen of the Eighth Congressional District of North Carolina*. N.p., [1856].

———. *Speech of T. L. Clingman, of North Carolina, on the Principles of the Whig and Democratic Parties. Delivered in the House of Representatives, March 7, 1844*. Washington, DC: Gales and Seaton, 1844.

———. *Valedictory Address of Thomas L. Clingman. To the Freemen of the Eighth Congressional District of North Carolina*. Washington, DC: Gideon, [1858].

Cluskey, Michael W., ed. *Buchanan and Breckinridge. The Democratic Hand-Book, Compiled by Mich. W. Cluskey, of Washington City, D.C. Recommended by the Democratic National Committee*. Washington, DC: R. A. Waters, 1856.

Cobb, Howell, James H. Lane, James L. Orr, and John B. Weller. *Speeches of Messrs. Weller, Orr, Lane, and Cobb, Delivered in Phœnix and Depot Halls, Concord, N.H., at a Mass Meeting of the Democratic Party of Merrimac County*. N.p., [1856?].

Constitution and By-Laws of the Young Men's Democratic Club of Boston. Boston: Franklin, 1857.

Cooley, James E. *Review of the Administration of General Pierce. Anti-Nebraska, Anti-Administration and Anti-Rum Platform: Speech of Hon. James E. Cooley, at a Meeting of the Democracy, Assembled on Saturday, Nov. 4th, 1854, at the Village of Patchogue, in Suffolk CO, L.I.* New York: John F. Trow, 1854.

Curtis, George Ticknor. *The Just Supremacy of Congress over the Territories*. Boston: A. Williams, 1859.

Cushing, Caleb. *Speech Delivered in Faneuil Hall, Boston, October 27, 1857. Also, Speech Delivered in City Hall, Newburyport, October 31, 1857*. [Boston]: Boston Post, 1857.

———. *Speech of Hon. Caleb Cushing, in Norombega Hall, Bangor, October 2, 1860, before the Democracy of Maine*. N.p., [1860].

———. *Speeches on the Amendment of the Constitution of Massachusetts, Imposing Disabilities on Naturalized Citizens of the United States*. [Boston]: Boston Post, 1859.

Dallas, George M. *Great Speech of the Hon. George Mifflin Dallas, upon the Leading Topics of the Day, Delivered at Pittsburgh, PA., with a Brief Biographical Sketch, &c., &c.* Philadelphia: Times and Keystone, 1847.

———. "The Mystery of the Dallas Papers. Part I." Edited by Roy F. Nichols. *Pennsylvania Magazine of History and Biography* 73, no. 3 (July 1949): 349–92.

———. "The Mystery of the Dallas Papers. Part II: Diary and Letters of George M. Dallas, December 4, 1848–March 6, 1849." [Edited by Roy F. Nichols.] *Pennsylvania Magazine of History and Biography* 73, no. 4 (Oct. 1949): 475–517.

Day, Timothy C. *The Democratic Party as It Was and as It Is! Speech of Hon. Timothy C. Day, of Ohio, in the House of Representatives, April 23, 1856.* N.p., [1856].

Democratic Committee of Publication. *Life of George Mifflin Dallas, Vice President of the United States.* Rev. ed. Philadelphia: Times and Keystone, 1847.

Democratic State Central Committee of Pennsylvania. *Memoir of James Buchanan, of Pennsylvania.* Philadelphia: C. Sherman and Son, 1856.

Dickinson, Daniel S. *Speeches; Correspondence, Etc., of the Late Daniel S. Dickinson, of New York. Including: Addresses on Important Public Topics; Speeches in the State and United States Senate, and in Support of the Government during the Rebellion; Correspondence, Private and Political (Collected and Arranged by Mrs. Dickinson), Poems (Collected and Arranged by Mrs. Mygatt), Etc.* Edited by John R. Dickinson. 2 vols. New York: G. P. Putnam and Son, 1867.

Dickinson, John, and Richard Henry Lee. *Empire and Nation: Letters from a Farmer in Pennsylvania and Letters from the Federal Farmer.* 2nd ed. Edited by Forrest McDonald. Indianapolis: Liberty Fund, 1999.

Dillon, John B. *An Inquiry into the Nature and Uses of Political Sovereignty.* Indianapolis: Journal Company, 1860.

Dix, John A. *Speech of Hon. John A. Dix, of New York, on the Bill to Establish Governments in the Territories. Delivered in the Senate of the United States, July 26, 1848.* Washington, DC: Congressional Globe, 1848.

A Document for All Thinking Men! The Political Letters and Writings of General Scott, Reviewed, Discussed, and Compared. N.p., [1852].

Douglas, Stephen A. "The Dividing Line between Federal and Local Authority: Popular Sovereignty in the Territories." *Harper's New Monthly Magazine*, September 1859, 519–37.

———. *The Dividing Line between Federal and Local Authority: Popular Sovereignty in the Territories.* New York: Harper and Brothers, 1859.

———. *Letter of Senator Douglas, in Reply to the Editor of the State Capitol Reporter, Concord, N.H.* Washington, DC: Sentinel, 1854.

———. *Letter of Senator Douglas, Vindicating His Character and His Position on the Nebraska Bill against the Assaults Contained in the Proceedings of a Public Meeting Composed of Twenty-Five Clergymen of Chicago.* Washington, DC: Sentinel, 1854.

———. *The Letters of Stephen A. Douglas.* Edited by Robert W. Johannsen. Urbana: University of Illinois Press, 1961.

———. *Popular Sovereignty in the Territories: Judge Douglas in Reply to Judge Black.* N.p., [1859].

———. *Popular Sovereignty in the Territories: Rejoinder of Judge Douglas to Judge Black*. N.p., [1859].

———. *Remarks of the Hon. Stephen A. Douglas, on Kansas, Utah, and the Dred Scott Decision. Delivered at Springfield, Illinois, June 12th, 1857*. Chicago: Daily Times, 1857.

———. *Speech of Hon. Stephen A. Douglas, of Illinois, Delivered in Richmond, Virginia, July 9, 1852*. N.p., [1852].

———. *Speech of Hon. Stephen A. Douglas, on the "Measures of Adjustment," Delivered in the City Hall, Chicago, October 23, 1850*. Washington, DC: Gideon, 1851.

———. *Speech of Senator Douglas, at the Democratic Celebration of the Anniversary of American Freedom, in Independence Square, Philadelphia, July 4, 1854*. N.p., [1854].

———. "Speech of Stephen A. Douglas, at Wooster, Ohio, September 16, 1859." In *In the Name of the People: Speeches and Writings of Lincoln and Douglas in the Ohio Campaign of 1859*, edited by Harry V. Jaffa and Robert W. Johannsen, 200–230. Columbus: Ohio State University Press, 1959.

Douglas, Stephen A., and Abraham Lincoln. *The Lincoln-Douglas Debates of 1858*. Edited by Robert W. Johannsen. 1965. Reprint, New York: Oxford University Press, 2008.

The Douglas' Disorganization. N.p., [1859].

Douglas' Doctrine of Popular Sovereignty in the Territories; Its Counterpart. By a Missourian. St. Louis: R. V. Kennedy, 1860.

Douglass, Frederick. *The Frederick Douglass Papers. Series One: Speeches, Debates, and Interviews*. Edited by John W. Blassingame. 5 vols. New Haven, CT: Yale University Press, 1979–92.

———. *The Life and Writings of Frederick Douglass*. Edited by Philip S. Foner. 5 vols. New York: International Publishers, 1950–75.

Dowdell, J. F. *Speech of Hon. J. F. Dowdell, Delivered in the Court House at La Fayette, on Monday, December 12th, 1859*. N.p., [1859?].

Drake, Thomas M. *An Address, on the Doctrine and Discipline of the Democratic Party; and the Heresy of the Maine Liquor Law and Free Soilism, or Other Side Issues Being Incorporated into Its Creed. Delivered in Zanesville, Ohio, prior to the Late Election*. Zanesville, OH: E. C. Church, 1853.

Dromgoole, George C. *Address of Mr. George C. Dromgoole to His Constituents*. N.p.: J. and G. S. Gideon, [1847].

Eaton, W. W. *The Union; Past, Present, and Future. A Speech Delivered by Hon. W. W. Eaton, at City Hall, Hartford, on Saturday Evening, March 3d, 1860*. N.p., 1860.

English, William H. *Letter from William H. English, of Indiana, in Response to a Nomination for Reëlection to Congress, Tendered to Him by the Democracy of the Second Congressional District*. [Washington, DC]: Congressional Globe, [1856].

Everett, Edward. *Stability and Progress. Remarks Made on the 4th of July, 1853, in Faneuil Hall*. Boston: Eastburn's, 1853.

The Fearful Issue to Be Decided in November Next! Shall the Constitution and the Union Stand or Fall? Fremont, the Sectional Candidate of the Advocates of Dissolution! Buchanan, the Candidate of Those Who Advocate One Country! One Union! One Constitution! And One Destiny! N.p., [1856].

[Fisher, Sidney George]. *The Law of the Territories.* Philadelphia: C. Sherman and Son, 1859.

Forney, John W. *Address on Religious Intolerance and Political Proscription, Delivered at Lancaster, PA., on the Evening of the 24th of September.* Washington, DC, 1855.

Forsyth, John. *Letters of Hon. John Forsyth, of Alabama, Late Minister to Mexico, to Wm. F. Samford, Esq., in Defence of Stephen A. Douglas.* [Washington, DC]: Lemuel Towers, [1859].

Foster, N. G. *Speech of Hon. N. G. Foster, of Georgia, on the Presidential Issues. Delivered in the House of Representatives of the United States on the 9th of August, 1856.* Washington, DC: American Organ, 1856.

Frank. *Pierce and His Abolition Allies.* N.p., Daily American Telegraph, [1852].

"Franklin Pierce and His Abolition Allies." N.p., [1852].

Frémont, Jessie Benton. *The Letters of Jessie Benton Frémont.* Edited by Pamela Herr and Mary Lee Spence. Urbana: University of Illinois Press, 1993.

[Garnett, Muscoe R. H.]. *The Union, Past and Future: How It Works, and How to Save It. By a Citizen of Virginia.* 3rd ed. Washington, DC: John T. Towers, 1850.

Gartrell, Lucius J. *Speech of Hon. Lucius J. Gartrell, at the Breckinridge and Lane Ratification Meeting of Fulton County, Georgia. Delivered at the City Hall, Atlanta, July 14th, 1860.* Atlanta: Atlanta Intelligencer, [1860].

Greeley, Horace. *Why I Am a Whig: Reply to an Inquiring Friend.* New York: Tribune, [1852?].

Hallett, B. F., James Cheever, Silas Peirce, Stephen D. Massey, and Benjamin J. Gerrish (Committee). *Appeal to Democrats and Union Men against Northern Fusion and Sectionalism. From the Democracy of Boston and Suffolk. Adopted by the Ward and County Committees, in Convention, October, 1855.* [Boston]: Boston Post, [1855].

Halstead, Murat. *Trimmers, Trucklers and Temporizers: Notes of Murat Halstead from the Political Conventions of 1856.* Edited by William B. Hesseltine and Rex G. Fisher. Madison: State Historical Society of Wisconsin, 1961.

Hambleton, James P., ed. *A Biographical Sketch of Henry A. Wise, with a History of the Political Campaign in Virginia in 1855. To Which Is Added a Review of the Position of Parties in the Union, and a Statement of the Political Issues: Distinguishing Them on the Eve of the Presidential Campaign of 1856.* Richmond, VA: J. W. Randolph, 1856.

Hammond, James Henry. *Selections from the Letters and Speeches of the Hon. James H. Hammond, of South Carolina.* New York: John F. Trow, 1866.

Harlan, James. *The Democratic Party: Its Responsibility, Its Practice and Policy, since the Inauguration of Franklin Pierce, March 4th, 1853. Speech of Hon. James*

Harlan, *of Iowa. Delivered June 22nd, at Des Moines City, before the Republican State Convention*. Mt. Pleasant, IA: Republican News, 1859.

Harper's New Monthly Magazine. Editor's Drawer. Aug. 1856.

Hayek, F. A. "Why I Am Not a Conservative." In *The Constitution of Liberty: The Definitive Edition*, edited by Ronald Hamowy, 518–33. Vol. 17 of *The Collected Works of F. A. Hayek*, edited by Bruce Caldwell. Chicago: University of Chicago Press, 2011.

Hilliard, Henry W. *Letter of Hon. Henry W. Hilliard, on the Political Issues of the Day*. Montgomery, AL: Confederation, 1858.

Hobbes, Thomas. *Leviathan*. 1651. Reprint, edited by Edwin Curley. Indianapolis: Hackett, 1994.

Holmes, Oliver. *The Harp and the Hickory Tree: An Address Delivered before the Baltimore Democratic Association*. Baltimore: Sherwood, 1853.

Horrible Doctrines!!! Loco Focoism Unmasked!! Read and Ponder Well! The Sub Treasury Has Passed and Here Is What Is to Come Next!!!! N.p., [1840].

Horton, R. G. *The Life and Public Services of James Buchanan. Late Minister to England and Formerly Minister to Russia, Senator and Representative in Congress, and Secretary of State: Including the Most Important of His State Papers*. New York: Derby and Jackson, 1856.

Hume, David. "Of Superstition and Enthusiasm." In *Essays: Moral, Political, and Literary*. 1777. Reprint, edited by Eugene F. Miller, 73–79. Indianapolis: Liberty Classics, 1985.

Hunter, R. M. T. *Address of R. M. T. Hunter, of Virginia, before the Democratic Association of Richmond, October 1, 1852*. Washington, DC: Congressional Globe, 1853.

———. "Correspondence of Robert M. T. Hunter, 1826–1876." Edited by Charles Henry Ambler. In *Annual Report of the American Historical Association for the Year 1916*. Vol. 2. Washington, DC, 1918.

———. *The Democratic Demonstration at Poughkeepsie. Speech of Hon. R. M. T. Hunter, of Virginia*. N.p., [1856].

Infidelity and Abolitionism: An Open Letter to the Friends of Religion, Morality, and the American Union. N.p., [1856].

James Buchanan, His Doctrines and Policy as Exhibited by Himself and Friends. New York: Greeley and McElrath, Tribune, [1856].

Jarvis, Russell. *Facts and Arguments against the Election of General Cass, Respectfully Addressed to the Whigs and Democrats of All the Free States. By an Anti-Abolitionist*. New York: R. Craighead, 1848.

[Johnson, Reverdy]. *Remarks on Popular Sovereignty, as Maintained and Denied Respectively by Judge Douglas, and Attorney-General Black. By a Southern Citizen*. Baltimore: Murphy, 1859.

———. *Speech of the Hon. Reverdy Johnson, of Maryland, Delivered before the Political Friends of Hon. Stephen A. Douglas, at a Meeting in Faneuil Hall, Boston, on Thursday, June 7, 1860. To Which Is Added the Letter of the Hon. Reverdy*

Johnson, to the Chairman of the Douglas Meeting in New York on the 22d of May, *1860*. Baltimore: John Murphy, 1860.
Jones, G. W. *Letter of Hon. G. W. Jones, of Tennessee, to His Constituents*. N.p., [1856].
Jones, J. O. *John G Davis. His Opinions upon the Repeal of the Missouri Compromise; His Opinions upon the Fugitive Slave Law. Choice Extracts from His Correspondence. Remarks by J. O. Jones*. Terre Haute, IN: Western Star, [1856?].
Jones, Joel J. *Speech of Joel J. Jones, of Lincoln, in the Senate of Tennessee, January 13th and 14th, 1858*. N.p., [1858].
Kelley, William D. *An Address Delivered by Hon. William D. Kelley, at Spring Garden Hall, Philadelphia, on September 9th, 1856*. Philadelphia: Philadelphia Morning Times, [1856].
Kemper, James Lawson. *Speech of James L. Kemper, Delegate from Madison, on the Public Defences of the Commonwealth—The Relations of Slavery—Southern Resistance and Retaliation. Delivered in the House of Delegates of Virginia, Monday, February 25th, 1856*. Richmond, VA: Charles H. Wynne, 1856.
The Last Appeal to Pennsylvania. N.p., [1856].
Leggett, William. *Democratick Editorials: Essays in Jacksonian Political Economy*. Edited by Lawrence H. White. Indianapolis: Liberty Press, 1984.
Letter of an Adopted Catholic, Addressed to the President of the Kentucky Democratic Association of Washington City, on Temporal Allegiance to the Pope, and the Relations of the Catholic Church and Catholics, Both Native and Adopted, to the System of Domestic Slavery and Its Agitation in the United States. N.p., [1856].
1. Letter of Hon. James Shields. 2. An Article from the Boston Pilot, Exposing the Falsehoods of the Scott Whigs Respecting General Pierce. 3. Extracts from Speeches of General Franklin Pierce before the Constitutional Convention, and before the People, upon the Religious Test. 4. Voice of the Catholics of New Hampshire. 5. General Scott's Letter to G. W. Reed and Others, of Philadelphia, in 1844. N.p., [1852].
The Life of the Hon. James Buchanan, as Written by Himself, and Set to Music by an Old Democrat, to the Tune of "Poor Old Horse Let Him Die!" Price—"Half a Jimmy!" N.p., 1856.
Light for the People! Read! The Know-Nothing Delusion Exposed! The Warning Voice of the Great Men of the Nation! Opinions of Distinguished Democrats. Montgomery, AL: Advertiser, n.d.
Lincoln, Abraham. *The Collected Works of Abraham Lincoln*. Edited by Roy P. Basler. 9 vols. New Brunswick, NJ: Rutgers University Press, 1953, 1955.
Locke, John. *A Letter Concerning Toleration*. 1689. Reprint, edited by James H. Tully. Indianapolis: Hackett, 1983.
———. *Second Treatise of Government*. 1690. Reprint, edited by C. B. Macpherson. Indianapolis: Hackett, 1980.
Longstreet, Augustus Baldwin. *Know Nothingism Unveiled. Letter of Judge A. B. Longstreet, of Mississippi*. [Washington, DC]: Congressional Globe, [1855].

Loring, George B. *A Speech Delivered at Webster, Mass., Providence, R.I., Nashua, N.H., and Other Places, during the Presidential Campaign of 1856, in Support of James Buchanan, by George B. Loring, of Salem.* [Boston]: Boston Post, 1856.

Lovejoy, J. C. *The True Democracy. A Speech Delivered at East Cambridge, Sept. 29, 1854. By J. C. Lovejoy, of Cambridgeport.* Boston: C. C. F. Moody, [1856?].

Lovejoy, Owen. *The Fanaticism of the Democratic Party. Speech of Hon. Owen Lovejoy, of Illinois. Delivered in the House of Representatives, February 21, 1859.* Washington, DC: Buell and Blanchard, 1859.

[Lyman, Darius]. *Leaven for Doughfaces; or Threescore and Ten Parables Touching Slavery. By a Former Resident of the South.* Cincinnati: Bangs, 1856.

M., H. *Reflections on the Powers of the General Government and the Inherent Rights of American Citizens: Suggested by a Perusal of the Constitution and the Congressional Debates in Relation to Territorial Governments.* Kalamazoo, MI: Gazette, 1857.

Macon, Nathaniel [pseud.]. *Letters to Chas. O'Conor. The Destruction of the Union Is Emancipation. The Status of Slavery. The Rights of the States and Territories.* N.p., [1860].

[Marsh, Leonard]. *A Bake-Pan. For the Dough-Faces. By One of Them.* Burlington, VT: C. Goodrich, 1854.

Mayo, A. D. *The Capitol; or, the Higher Law. A Lecture Delivered in the Division-St. Church, Albany, Sunday, February 21st, 1858.* N.p., [1858?].

Montesquieu. *Persian Letters.* 1721. Reprint, edited by Andrew Kahn. Translated by Margaret Mauldon. Oxford: Oxford University Press, 2008.

———. *The Spirit of the Laws.* 1748. Reprint, edited and translated by Anne M. Cohler, Basia Carolyn Miller, and Harold Samuel Stone. Cambridge: Cambridge University Press, 2009.

Moore, Andrew B. *Inaugural Address of Gov. Andrew B. Moore, to the General Assembly of Alabama. Delivered on Tuesday, December 1, 1857, at 12 O'clock, M.* Montgomery, AL: N. B. Cloud, 1857.

Moore, O. F. *Letter of Hon. O. F. Moore, of Ohio, to His Constituents.* Washington, DC: American Organ, 1856.

Morgan, E. B., George Law, and Chauncey Shaffer. *Tract for Americans. Fillmore's Political History and Position. George Law and Chauncey Shaffer's Reasons for Repudiating Fillmore and Donelson, and the Action of the Know-Nothing State Convention at Syracuse on the Resolutions Censuring Brooks's Assault on Senator Sumner, &c.* New York: Greeley and McElrath, Tribune, [1856].

The National and Jackson Democratic Association. *The Democratic Policy and Its Fruits.* N.p., [1848].

National Democratic Executive Committee. *Biographical Sketches of Hon. John C. Breckinridge, Democratic Nominee for President, and General Joseph Lane, Democratic Nominee for Vice-President.* Washington, DC, 1860.

Nebraska: A Poem, Personal and Political. Boston: John P. Jewett, 1854.

Nicholas, S. S. *Conservative Essays, Legal and Political.* Philadelphia: J. B. Lippincott, 1863.

Obituary Addresses on the Occasion of the Death of the Hon. John M. Clayton, of Delaware, in the Senate and House of Representatives of the United States, December 3, 1856. Washington, DC: A. O. P. Nicholson, 1857.
Obituary Addresses on the Occasion of the Death of the Hon. William R. King, of Alabama, Vice President of the United States Delivered in the Senate and in the House of Representatives of the United States, Eighth of December, 1853. Washington, DC: Beverley Tucker, 1854.
Official Proceedings of the Democratic and Anti-Know-Nothing State Convention of Alabama, Held in the City of Montgomery, January 8th and 9th, 1856. Montgomery, AL: Advertiser and Gazette, 1856.
Ohio Politics. Cox after Giddings. [Washington, DC]: Lemuel Towers, [1859?].
Oldham, W. S., and William R. Scurry. *Rights of the South in Opposition to "Squatter Sovereignty." Speech of Hon. W. S. Oldham, at the Capitol, Delivered on the 27th Day of August, 1856, and Letter of Hon. William R. Scurry.* Austin, TX: Marshall and Oldham, 1856.
Orr, James L. *An Address Delivered before the Philosophian and Adelphian Societies of the Furman University, at Their Annual Meeting, Greenville, S.C., July 18, 1855.* Greenville, SC: G. E. Elford, 1855.
———. *The Cincinnati Convention. Letter from James L. Orr, of South Carolina, to Hon. C. W. Dudley, on the Propriety of Having the State of South Carolina Represented in the Democratic National Convention, to Be Held in Cincinnati.* Washington, DC: H. Polkinhorn, [1855].
Paine, Thomas. *Common Sense.* 1776. Reprint, edited by Isaac Kramnick. London: Penguin Books, 1986.
Pearce, James Alfred, Thomas G. Pratt, J. W. Crisfield, and James B. Clay. *Old Line Whigs for Buchanan and Breckinridge: Letters from Hon. James Alfred Pearce, and Hon. Thomas G. Pratt, to the Whigs of Maryland. Speeches of Hon. J. W. Crisfield, of Maryland, and Hon. James B. Clay, of Kentucky.* N.p., [1856].
Pearce, James Alfred, Thomas G. Pratt, Isaac D. Jones, and John W. Crisfield. *Letter from the Hon. James Alfred Pearce, United States Senator from Maryland, on the Politics of the Day. Letter from the Hon. Thomas G. Pratt, United States Senator from Maryland, to the Whigs of That State. Speech of the Hon. Isaac D. Jones, Delivered in Response to the Call of a Democratic Procession at Princess Anne, Somerset County, Md., on the Evening of Tuesday, July 15, 1856. Speech of the Hon. John W. Crisfield, Delivered at Princess Anne, Somerset County, Md., on Tuesday Evening, July 15, 1856, Responding to the Call of a Democratic Procession.* Washington, DC: Standard, 1856.
Perkins, John, Jr. *Speech of Hon. John Perkins, Jr., of Louisiana, on the Results of Two Years' Democratic Rule in the Country.* N.p., [1855].
Phillips, Philip. *Letter of Hon. P. Phillips, of Mobile, Ala., on the Religious Proscription of Catholics.* N.p., [1855].
———. *Letter on Naturalization and Citizenship, from Hon. Philip Phillips, of Alabama. December 18, 1854.* Washington, DC: A. O. P. Nicholson, 1854.

———. *Speech of Hon. P. Phillips, of Alabama, on the Territorial Bill. Delivered in the House of Representatives, April 24, 1854*. N.p.: Towers, [1854].

Plain Facts and Considerations: Addressed to the People of the United States, without Distinction of Party, in Favor of James Buchanan, of Pennsylvania, for President, and John C. Breckinridge, of Kentucky, for Vice President. By an American Citizen. Boston: Brown, Bazin, 1856.

Popular Sovereignty in the Territories. The Democratic Record. Baltimore: Murphy, [1860].

Popular Sovereignty. Proceedings of the Democratic State Convention, Held at Indianapolis, Indiana, February 23d, 1858, with the Letters of Gov. Henry A. Wise, of Va.; Gov. Robert J. Walker; Hon. John W. Forney, and Others; and the Speeches of Hon. S. D. Johnston, of Kansas; Hon. H. B. Payne of Ohio, and Others. Indianapolis: Cameron and M'Neely, 1858.

Popular Sovereignty Subjected to the Test of Fundamental Principles, by a Constitutional Democrat. Washington, DC: O. E. Duffy, n.d.

"*Popular Sovereignty.*" *The Reviewer Reviewed. By a Southern Inquirer.* N.p., [1859].

Porter, Kirk H., and Donald Bruce Johnson, eds. *National Party Platforms, 1840–1964.* Urbana: University of Illinois Press, 1966.

Proceedings of the Celebration of the Fourth of July, 1856, by the Jackson Democratic Association of Washington, at the Bladensburg Spa Spring Grove. Containing the Oration of Hon. A. E. Maxwell, of Florida, and Sketches of the Remarks of the Other Speakers. N.p.: Office of "The National," 1856.

Proceedings of the Democratic State Convention, Held at Syracuse, N.Y., September 14 and 15, 1859. Albany, NY: Comstock and Cassidy, 1859.

Proceedings of the National Democratic Convention, Held in Cincinnati, June 2–6, 1856. Cincinnati: Enquirer, 1856.

Publius [Alexander Hamilton, James Madison, and John Jay]. *The Federalist Papers.* 1787–88. Reprint, New York: Bantam Classic, 2003.

Pugh, George E. *Oration Delivered before the Triennial Convention of the Alpha Delta Phi, at Miami University, Oxford, Ohio, July 5, 1859.* Washington, DC: Lemuel Towers, 1860.

Rayner, Kenneth. *Reply of Hon. Kenneth Rayner to the Manifesto of Hon. Henry A. Wise.* Washington, DC: American Organ, 1855.

Reed, William B. *The Appeal to Pennsylvania and the Middle States. A Speech by William B. Reed: Delivered at a Meeting of the Friends of Buchanan and Breckenridge, at Somerset, Pa., September 24, 1856.* [Philadelphia?, 1856].

Richardson, James D., ed. *A Compilation of the Messages and Papers of the Presidents, 1789–1897.* 10 vols. Washington, DC: Government Printing Office, 1896–99.

The Ritual of the Order of Know Nothings, with the Initiation Oaths Taken by James Pollock, Now Governor of Pennsylvania. N.p., n.d.

Robertson, D. A. *The South and the Democratic Party. A Speech by D. A. Robertson, Delivered in St. Paul, Wednesday, Sept. 30.* Saint Paul, MN: Goodrich, Somers, 1857.

[Rockwell, John A.]. *States vs. Territories: A True Solution of the Territorial Question. By an Old Line Whig.* N.p., 1860.
Ross, William H. "Inaugural Address." January 21, 1851. In *Journal of the House of Representatives of the State of Delaware, at a Session of the General Assembly, Commenced and Held at Dover, on Tuesday, the Seventh Day of January, in the Year of Our Lord, One Thousand Eight Hundred and Fifty-One, and of the Independence of the United States, the Seventy-Fifth,* 150–60. Dover, DE: S. Kimmey, 1851.
Rust, Albert. *Address of Hon. Albert Rust, to the People of Arkansas.* Washington, DC: Lemuel Towers, [1860].
Sebastian, William K. *Substance of the Speech of Hon. W. K. Sebastian, Made before the Democratic Mass Meeting, at Helena, November 23, 1855.* Washington, DC: Congressional Globe, [1855].
Seymour, Horatio. *Speech of the Hon. Horatio Seymour at Springfield, Mass., July 4, 1856.* Buffalo, NY: Campaign Courier, 1856.
Sheahan, James W. *The Life of Stephen A. Douglas.* New York: Harper and Brothers, 1860.
Short Answers to Reckless Fabrications, against the Democratic Candidate for President, James Buchanan. Philadelphia: William Rice, 1856.
Sketches of the Lives of Franklin Pierce and Wm. R. King, Candidates of the Democratic Republican Party for the Presidency and Vice Presidency of the United States. N.p., [1852].
Slicer, Henry. *Speech of Rev. Henry Slicer, Delivered in the General Conference at Indianapolis, 28th May, 1856, on the Subject of the Proposed Change in the Methodist Discipline, Making Non-Slave-Holding a Test or Condition of Membership in Said Church.* Washington, DC: H. Polkinhorn, [1856?].
Songs for Freemen: A Collection of Campaign and Patriotic Songs for the People. Adapted to Familiar and Popular Melodies, and Designed to Promote the Cause of "Free Speech, Free Press, Free Soil, Free Men, and Fremont." Utica, NY: H. H. Hawley, 1856.
Speeches Delivered at a Dinner, Given to Hon. Stephen A. Douglas, by Gen. Elijah Ward, in New York City, June 9th, 1854. N.p.: National Democrat, [1854].
Stephens, Alexander H., and H. H. Tucker. *Letters of Hon. A. H. Stephens and Rev. H. H. Tucker, on Religious Liberty.* Atlanta: C. R. Hanleiter, 1855.
Stevens, Thaddeus. *The Selected Papers of Thaddeus Stevens.* Edited by Beverly Wilson Palmer. 2 vols. Pittsburgh: University of Pittsburgh Press, 1997–98.
Taylor, Miles, John E. Bouligny, P. B. Fouke, and A. J. Hamilton. *The Presidential Controversy. The True Policy for the South. Letters of Messrs. Taylor, Bouligny, Fouke, and Hamilton, on the Political Questions of the Day.* [Washington, DC]: Lemuel Towers, [1860].
The Territorial Slavery Question. Non-Intervention Principle. Position of the National Democracy. N.p., [1854?].
Thompson, John. *Squatter Sovereignty. Review of the Article of Stephen A. Douglas in Harper's Magazine, September, 1859.* N.p., [1859?].

Three Letters on the Order of the Know Nothings, Addressed to the Hon. A. P. Butler. By a Citizen. Charleston, SC: A. J. Burke, 1855.

Tilden, Samuel J. *Letters and Literary Memorials of Samuel J. Tilden.* Edited by John Bigelow. 2 vols. New York: Harper and Brothers, 1908.

———. *The Writings and Speeches of Samuel J. Tilden.* Edited by John Bigelow. 2 vols. New York: Harper and Brothers, 1885.

Tocqueville, Alexis de. *Democracy in America and Two Essays on America.* 1835–40. Reprint, edited by Isaac Kramnick. Translated by Gerald E. Bevan. London: Penguin Books, 2003.

Toombs, Robert. *A Lecture Delivered in the Tremont Temple, Boston, Massachusetts, on the 24th January, 1856, by R. Toombs. Slavery—Its Constitutional Status—Its Influence on the African Race and Society.* N.p., [1856].

US Congress. *Congressional Globe.* 46 vols. Washington, DC, 1834–73.

Van Buren, Martin. *Inquiry into the Origin and Course of Political Parties in the United States.* New York: Hurd and Houghton, 1867.

———. *Letter of Ex-President Van Buren. June 28, 1856.* Philadelphia: William Rice, [1856].

Voltaire. *Fanaticism, or Mahomet the Prophet.* 1741. Reprint, translated by Hanna Burton. Sacramento, CA: Litwin Books, 2013.

Walker, Richard W. *Speech of Richard W. Walker, Esq., on the Presidential Election, Delivered at Huntsville, ALA. On Thursday, the 28th of August, 1856.* Florence, AL: Gazette, 1856.

Ward, Aaron. *Speech of General Aaron Ward, at the Great Democratic Mass Meeting, at White Plains, N.Y., on September 16, 1856.* New York: J. W. Bell, Daily News, [1856].

———. *Speech of General Aaron Ward, of Westchester County, New York, at a Democratic Meeting Held at New Rochelle, March 27, 1858, at Which Richard Lathers, Esq., Presided.* New York: J. W. Bell, Daily News, 1858.

Webster, Daniel. *The Papers of Daniel Webster. Series One: Correspondence.* Edited by Charles M. Wiltse and Michael J. Birkner. 7 vols. Hanover, NH: University Press of New England, 1974–86.

Weller, John B. *Inaugural Address.* N.p., [1858].

The Whig Charge of Religious Intolerance against the New Hampshire Democracy and General Franklin Pierce. N.p., [1852].

Whig Testimony against the Election of General Scott to the Presidency of the U. S.: Opinions of Henry Clay—Thos. G. Pratt—Geo. E. Badger, and Other Distinguished Whigs, and the Whig Press. N.p.: C. Alexander, [1852].

Whitman, Walt. *The Complete Poems.* Edited by Francis Murphy. London: Penguin Books, 2004.

———. *Complete Prose Works: Specimen Days and Collect, November Boughs and Good Bye My Fancy.* 1881. Reprint, Boston: Small, Maynard, 1901.

———. "The Eighteenth Presidency! Voice of Walt Whitman to Each Young Man in the Nation, North, South, East, and West." 1856. In *The Eighteenth Presidency:*

A Critical Text, edited by Edward F. Grier, 19–44. Lawrence: University of Kansas Press, 1956.

Wigfall, Louis T. *Speech of Louis T. Wigfall, on the Pending Political Issues; Delivered at Tyler, Smith County, Texas, September 3, 1860. Published by Request of the Breckinridge and Lane Club of Smith County.* Washington, DC: Lemuel Towers, [1860].

Winston, John A. *Inaugural Address of Governor John A. Winston, Delivered in the Representative Hall, December 20, 1853.* Montgomery, AL: Brittan and Blue, 1853.

Winthrop, Robert C. *Robert C. Winthrop on Fusion.* N.p., [1855].

Winthrop, Robert C., Jr. *A Memoir of Robert C. Winthrop. Prepared for the Massachusetts Historical Society.* Boston: Little, Brown, 1897.

Wise, Henry A. *Address Delivered by Gov. Henry A. Wise, in October 1856, before the Virginia Mechanics Institute of the City of Richmond.* Richmond, VA: Ritchie and Dunnavant, 1857.

———. *The Lecompton Question. Governor Wise's Tammany, Philadelphia and Illinois Letters, Together with Letters to Charles W. Russell, Esq. by a Virginia Democrat.* [Richmond, VA?, 1858?].

———. *Letter of Governor Wise, of Virginia, on the Senatorial Election and the Kansas Policy of the Administration.* Washington, DC, 1857.

———. *Religious Liberty. Equality of Civil Rights among Native and Naturalized Citizens. The Virginia Campaign of 1855. Governor Wise's Letter on Know-Nothingism, and His Speech at Alexandria.* N.p., [1855].

———. *Speech Delivered by Henry A. Wise, at the Free School Celebration, in the County of Northampton, on the Fourth of July, 1850; Dedicated to the People of Accomack and Northampton, and Now Addressed through Them to the People of the State of Virginia.* Baltimore: Bull and Tuttle, 1850.

———. *Territorial Government, and the Admission of New States into the Union: A Historical and Constitutional Treatise.* N.p., [1859].

Wise, Henry A., and Fernando Wood. *Correspondence between Hon. Henry A. Wise and Hon. Fernando Wood.* N.p., [1866?].

Wood, Fernando. *The Campaign in Connecticut. Speech of the Hon. Fernando Wood, at the Great Democratic Meeting, Held in Norwalk, on the 20th of March, 1860.* [New York]: Daily News, [1860].

———. *Speech of Fernando Wood, Delivered before the Meeting of the National Democratic Delegation to the Charleston Convention, at Syracuse, February 7, 1860.* New York: Daily News, [1860].

Wright, Joseph A. *An Address Delivered by Gov. Joseph A. Wright, on the 6th Day of October, 1853, at Livonia, Washington County, Indiana, to the District Agricultural Society, Composed of the Counties of Washington and Orange.* Indianapolis: Austin H. Brown, 1854.

———. *Letters from Governor Joseph A. Wright, to James H. Lane and Others, of Kansas, and the State Officers of Michigan, on the Kansas Difficulties.* Indianapolis: Elder and Harkness, [1856].

Yancey, William Lowndes. *Speech of the Hon. William L. Yancey, of Alabama, Delivered in the National Democratic Convention, Charleston, April 28th, 1860. With the Protest of the Alabama Delegation.* Charleston, SC: Walker, Evans, [1860].

Secondary Sources

Alexander, Erik B. "'The Democracy Must Prepare for Battle': Know-Nothingism in Alabama and Southern Politics, 1851–1859." *Southern Historian: A Journal of Southern History* 27 (Spring 2006): 23–37.

Alexander, Thomas B. "Persistent Whiggery in the Confederate South, 1860–1877." *Journal of Southern History* 27, no. 3 (Aug. 1961): 305–29.

Allen, David Y. "Modern Conservatism: The Problem of Definition." *Review of Politics* 43, no. 4 (Oct. 1981): 582–603.

Altschuler, Glenn C., and Stuart M. Blumin. *Rude Republic: Americans and Their Politics in the Nineteenth Century.* Princeton, NJ: Princeton University Press, 2000.

Ambacher, Bruce I. "The Pennsylvania Origins of Popular Sovereignty." *Pennsylvania Magazine of History and Biography* 98, no. 3 (July 1974): 339–52.

Anbinder, Tyler. *Nativism and Slavery: The Northern Know Nothings and the Politics of the 1850s.* New York: Oxford University Press, 1992.

Ashworth, John. *"Agrarians" and "Aristocrats": Party Political Ideology in the United States, 1837–1846.* London: Royal Historical Society, 1983.

Auchampaugh, Philip G. "James Buchanan, the Bachelor of the White House: An Inquiry on the Subject of Feminine Influence in the Life of Our Fifteenth President." *Tyler's Quarterly Historical and Genealogical Magazine* 20, no. 1 (July 1938): 154–66, 218–34.

———. "James Buchanan, the Conservatives' Choice, 1856: A Political Portrait." *Historian* 7, no. 2 (Spring 1945): 77–90.

Bailyn, Bernard. *The Ideological Origins of the American Revolution.* Rev. ed. Cambridge, MA: Harvard University Press, 1992.

Baker, Jean H. *Affairs of Party: The Political Culture of Northern Democrats in the Mid-Nineteenth Century.* 1983. Reprint, New York: Fordham University Press, 1998.

———. *James Buchanan.* New York: Times Books, 2004.

———. "Politics, Paradigms, and Public Culture." *Journal of American History* 84, no. 3 (Dec. 1997): 894–99.

———. "Public Women and Partisan Politics, 1840–1860." In Gallagher and Shelden, 64–81.

Baker, Paula. "The Domestication of Politics: Women and American Political Society, 1780–1920." *American Historical Review* 89, no. 3 (June 1984): 620–47.

Balcerski, Thomas John. "Intimate Contests: Manhood, Friendship, and the Coming of the Civil War." PhD diss., Cornell University, 2014.

Barkan, Elliott R. "The Emergence of a Whig Persuasion: Conservatism, Democratism, and the New York State Whigs." *New York History* 52, no. 4 (Oct. 1971): 367–95.

Baum, Dale. *The Civil War Party System: The Case of Massachusetts, 1848–1876.* Chapel Hill: University of North Carolina Press, 1984.

Beeman, Richard R. "Deference, Republicanism, and the Emergence of Popular Politics in Eighteenth-Century America." *William and Mary Quarterly,* 3rd ser., 49, no. 3 (July 1992): 401–30.

Beilein, Joseph M., Jr. *Bushwhackers: Guerilla Warfare, Manhood, and the Household in Civil War Missouri.* Kent, OH: Kent State University Press, 2016.

Belohlavek, John M. *Broken Glass: Caleb Cushing and the Shattering of the Union.* Kent, OH: Kent State University Press, 2005.

———. *George Mifflin Dallas: Jacksonian Patrician.* University Park: Pennsylvania State University Press, 1977.

Benson, Lee. *The Concept of Jacksonian Democracy: New York as a Test Case.* Princeton, NJ: Princeton University Press, 1961.

Bercaw, Nancy. *Gendered Freedoms: Race, Rights, and the Politics of Household in the Delta, 1861–1875.* Gainesville: University Press of Florida, 2003.

Berry, Stephen, ed. *Weirding the War: Stories from the Civil War's Ragged Edges.* Athens: University of Georgia Press, 2011.

Bertolini, Vincent J. "Fireside Chastity: The Erotics of Sentimental Bachelorhood in the 1850s." *American Literature* 68, no. 4 (Dec. 1996): 707–37.

Bestor, Arthur. "State Sovereignty and Slavery: A Reinterpretation of Proslavery Constitutional Doctrine, 1846–1860." *Journal of the Illinois State Historical Society* 54, no. 2 (Summer 1961): 117–80.

Birkner, Michael J., ed. *James Buchanan and the Political Crisis of the 1850s.* Selinsgrove, PA: Susquehanna University Press, 1996.

Bladek, John David. "'Virginia Is Middle Ground': The Know Nothing Party and the Virginia Gubernatorial Election of 1855." *Virginia Magazine of History and Biography* 106, no. 1 (Winter 1998): 35–70.

Bloch, Ruth H. "The Gendered Meanings of Virtue in Revolutionary America." *Signs* 13, no. 1 (Autumn 1987): 37–58.

Brinkley, Alan. "The Problem of American Conservatism." *American Historical Review* 99, no. 2 (Apr. 1994): 409–29.

Brown, Thomas. "The Miscegenation of Richard Mentor Johnson as an Issue in the National Election Campaign of 1835–1836." *Civil War History* 39, no. 1 (Mar. 1993): 5–30.

———. *Politics and Statesmanship: Essays on the American Whig Party.* New York: Columbia University Press, 1985.

Bruce, Dickson D., Jr. *The Rhetoric of Conservatism: The Virginia Convention of 1829–30 and the Conservative Tradition in the South.* San Marino, CA: Huntington Library, 1982.

Burstein, Andrew. "Immortalizing the Founding Fathers: The Excesses of Public Eulogy." In Isenberg and Burstein, 91–107.

Camp, Stephanie M. H. *Closer to Freedom: Enslaved Women and Everyday Resistance in the Plantation South.* Chapel Hill: University of North Carolina Press, 2004.

Carter, Dan T. *The Politics of Rage: George Wallace, the Origins of the New Conservatism, and the Transformation of American Politics.* 2nd ed. Baton Rouge: Louisiana State University Press, 2000.

Cheathem, Mark R. *Andrew Jackson, Southerner.* Baton Rouge: Louisiana State University Press, 2013.

———. "'The High Minded Honourable Man': Honor, Kinship, and Conflict in the Life of Andrew Jackson Donelson." *Journal of the Early Republic* 27, no. 2 (Summer 2007): 265–92.

Childers, Christopher. *The Failure of Popular Sovereignty: Slavery, Manifest Destiny, and the Radicalization of Southern Politics.* Lawrence: University Press of Kansas, 2012.

———. "Interpreting Popular Sovereignty: A Historiographical Essay." *Civil War History* 57, no. 1 (Mar. 2011): 48–70.

Clark, Michael D. *Coherent Variety: The Idea of Diversity in British and American Conservative Thought.* Westport, CT: Greenwood, 1983.

Cobban, Alfred. *Edmund Burke and the Revolt against the Eighteenth Century: A Study of the Political and Social Thinking of Burke, Wordsworth, Coleridge and Southey.* 2nd ed. London: George Allen and Unwin, 1960.

Cohen, Nancy. *The Reconstruction of American Liberalism, 1865–1914.* Chapel Hill: University of North Carolina Press, 2002.

Coleman, John F. *The Disruption of the Pennsylvania Democracy, 1848–1860.* Harrisburg: Pennsylvania Historical and Museum Commission, 1975.

Collins, Bruce. "The Ideology of the Ante-bellum Northern Democrats." *Journal of American Studies* 11, no. 1 (Apr. 1977): 103–21.

Conlin, Michael F. "The Dangerous *Isms* and the Fanatical *Ists:* Antebellum Conservatives in the South and the North Confront the Modernity Conspiracy." *Journal of the Civil War Era* 4, no. 2 (June 2014): 205–33.

Cooper, William J., Jr. *The South and the Politics of Slavery, 1828–1856.* Baton Rouge: Louisiana State University Press, 1978.

Cotlar, Seth. *Tom Paine's America: The Rise and Fall of Transatlantic Radicalism in the Early Republic.* Charlottesville: University of Virginia Press, 2011.

Cott, Nancy F. *Public Vows: A History of Marriage and the Nation.* Cambridge, MA: Harvard University Press, 2000.

Crew, Spencer R. "'When the Victims of Oppression Stand Up Manfully for Themselves': The Fugitive Slave Law of 1850 and the Role of African Americans in Obstructing Its Enforcement." In Finkelman and Kennon, 120–42.

Crick, Bernard. "The Strange Quest for an American Conservatism." *Review of Politics* 17, no. 3 (July 1955): 359–76.

Critchlow, Donald T. *Phyllis Schlafly and Grassroots Conservatism: A Woman's Crusade.* Princeton, NJ: Princeton University Press, 2005.

Crofts, Daniel W. "Late Antebellum Virginia Reconsidered." *Virginia Magazine of History and Biography* 107, no. 3 (Summer 1999): 253–86.

———. "The Southern Opposition and the Crisis of the Union." In Gallagher and Shelden, 85–111.

Current, Richard N. *Daniel Webster and the Rise of National Conservatism.* Boston: Little, Brown, 1955.
D'Emilio, John, and Estelle B. Freedman. *Intimate Matters: A History of Sexuality in America.* New York: Harper and Row, 1988.
Dennis, Matthew. "Patriotic Remains: Bones of Contention in the Early Republic." In Isenberg and Burstein, 136–48.
Dippel, Horst. "The Changing Idea of Popular Sovereignty in Early American Constitutionalism: Breaking Away from European Patterns." *Journal of the Early Republic* 16, no. 1 (Spring 1996): 21–45.
Earle, Jonathan H. *Jacksonian Antislavery and the Politics of Free Soil, 1824–1854.* Chapel Hill: University of North Carolina Press, 2004.
Eaton, Clement. "Henry A. Wise, a Liberal of the Old South." *Journal of Southern History* 7, no. 4 (Nov. 1941): 482–94.
———. "Henry A. Wise: A Study in Virginia Leadership, 1850–1861." *West Virginia History* 3 (1942): 187–204.
———. "Henry A. Wise and the Virginia Fire Eaters of 1856." *Mississippi Valley Historical Review* 21, no. 4 (Mar. 1935): 495–512.
Edwards, Laura F. "The Contradictions of Democracy in American Institutions and Practices." In *Re-imagining Democracy in the Age of Revolutions: America, France, Britain, Ireland, 1750–1850,* edited by Joanna Innes and Mark Philp, 40–56. Oxford: Oxford University Press, 2013.
———. *The People and Their Peace: Legal Culture and the Transformation of Inequality in the Post-Revolutionary South.* Chapel Hill: University of North Carolina Press, 2009.
Edwards, Rebecca. *Angels in the Machinery: Gender in American Party Politics from the Civil War to the Progressive Era.* New York: Oxford University Press, 1997.
———. "Domesticity versus Manhood Rights: Republicans, Democrats, and 'Family Values.'" In *The Democratic Experiment: New Directions in American Political History,* edited by Meg Jacobs, William J. Novak, and Julian E. Zelizer, 175–97. Princeton, NJ: Princeton University Press, 2009.
Egerton, Douglas R. "The Slaves' Election: Frémont, Freedom, and the Slave Conspiracies of 1856." *Civil War History* 61, no. 1 (Mar. 2015): 35–63.
Etcheson, Nicole. *Bleeding Kansas: Contested Liberty in the Civil War Era.* Lawrence: University Press of Kansas, 2004.
———. *The Emerging Midwest: Upland Southerners and the Political Culture of the Old Northwest, 1787–1861.* Bloomington: Indiana University Press, 1996.
———. "General Jackson Is Dead: James Buchanan, Stephen A. Douglas, and Kansas Policy." In Quist and Birkner, 86–110.
———. "The Great Principle of Self-Government: Popular Sovereignty and Bleeding Kansas." *Kansas History: A Journal of the Central Plains* 27 (Spring–Summer 2004): 14–29.
———. "'A Living, Creeping Lie': Abraham Lincoln on Popular Sovereignty." *Journal of the Abraham Lincoln Association* 29, no. 2 (Summer 2008): 1–25.

———. "Where Popular Sovereignty Worked: Nebraska Territory and the Kansas-Nebraska Act." In Wunder and Ross, 159–81.

Eyal, Yonatan. *The Young America Movement and the Transformation of the Democratic Party, 1828–1861.* Cambridge: Cambridge University Press, 2007.

Faust, Drew Gilpin. *This Republic of Suffering: Death and the American Civil War.* New York: Vintage Books, 2008.

Fehrenbacher, Don E. *The Dred Scott Case: Its Significance in American Law and Politics.* New York: Oxford University Press, 1978.

Feller, Daniel. "A Brother in Arms: Benjamin Tappan and the Antislavery Democracy." *Journal of American History* 88, no. 1 (June 2001): 48–74.

Fennessy, Brian. "Master of an Interior World: Masculinity, Sensibility, and William Gilmore Simms." *Simms Review* 19, nos. 1–2 (Summer–Winter 2011): 63–82.

Finkelman, Paul. "The Appeasement of 1850." In Finkelman and Kennon, 36–79.

Finkelman, Paul, and Donald R. Kennon, eds. *Congress and the Crisis of the 1850s.* Athens: Ohio University Press, 2012.

Fischer, David Hackett. *The Revolution of American Conservatism: The Federalist Party in the Era of Jeffersonian Democracy.* New York: Harper and Row, 1965.

Foner, Eric. *Free Soil, Free Labor, Free Men: The Ideology of the Republican Party before the Civil War.* London: Oxford University Press, 1970.

———. *Politics and Ideology in the Age of the Civil War.* Oxford: Oxford University Press, 1980.

Ford, Lacy K., Jr. "Making the 'White Man's Country' White: Race, Slavery, and State-Building in the Jacksonian South." *Journal of the Early Republic* 19, no. 4 (Winter 1999): 713–37.

———. *Origins of Southern Radicalism: The South Carolina Upcountry, 1800–1860.* New York: Oxford University Press, 1988.

Formisano, Ronald P. "The Concept of Political Culture." *Journal of Interdisciplinary History* 31, no. 3 (Winter 2001): 393–426.

Foster, Thomas. "Reconsidering Libertines and Early Modern Heterosexuality: Sex and American Founder Gouverneur Morris." *Journal of the History of Sexuality* 22, no. 1 (Jan. 2013): 65–84.

Fredrickson, George M. *The Black Image in the White Mind: The Debate on Afro-American Character and Destiny, 1817–1914.* New York: Harper and Row, 1971.

———. *The Inner Civil War: Northern Intellectuals and the Crisis of the Union.* New York: Harper and Row, 1965.

Freehling, William W. *Secessionists at Bay, 1776–1854.* Vol. 1 of *The Road to Disunion.* New York: Oxford University Press, 1990.

———. *Secessionists Triumphant, 1854–1861.* Vol. 2 of *The Road to Disunion.* Oxford: Oxford University Press, 2007.

———. *The South vs. the South: How Anti-Confederate Southerners Shaped the Course of the Civil War.* Oxford: Oxford University Press, 2001.

Freeman, Joanne B. *Affairs of Honor: National Politics in the New Republic.* New Haven, CT: Yale University Press, 2001.

Friend, Craig Thompson, and Lorri Glover. "Rethinking Southern Masculinity: An Introduction." In *Southern Manhood: Perspectives on Masculinity in the Old South*, edited by Craig Thompson Friend and Lorri Glover, vii–xvii. Athens: University of Georgia Press, 2004.

Fritz, Christian G. "Popular Sovereignty, Vigilantism, and the Constitutional Right of Revolution." *Pacific Historical Review* 63, no. 1 (Feb. 1994): 39–66.

Gallagher, Gary W., and Rachel A. Shelden, eds. *A Political Nation: New Directions in Mid-Nineteenth-Century American Political History*. Charlottesville: University of Virginia Press, 2012.

Geertz, Clifford. "Ideology as a Cultural System." In *Ideology and Discontent*, edited by David E. Apter, 47–76. New York: Free Press, 1964.

Genovese, Eugene D. *The Southern Tradition: The Achievement and Limitations of an American Conservatism*. Cambridge, MA: Harvard University Press, 1994.

Gienapp, William E. *The Origins of the Republican Party, 1852–1856*. New York: Oxford University Press, 1987.

Glover, Lorri. *Southern Sons: Becoming Men in the New Nation*. Baltimore: Johns Hopkins University Press, 2007.

Glymph, Thavolia. *Out of the House of Bondage: The Transformation of the Plantation Household*. Cambridge: Cambridge University Press, 2008.

Graham, Susan. "'A Warm Politition and Devotedly Attached to the Democratic Party': Catharine Read Williams, Politics, and Literature in Antebellum America." *Journal of the Early Republic* 30, no. 2 (Summer 2010): 253–78.

Greenberg, Amy S. "Manifest Destiny's Hangover: Congress Confronts Territorial Expansion and Martial Masculinity in the 1850s." In Finkelman and Kennon, 97–119.

Greenberg, Kenneth S. *Masters and Statesmen: The Political Culture of American Slavery*. Baltimore: Johns Hopkins University Press, 1985.

Guelzo, Allen C. *Lincoln and Douglas: The Debates That Defined America*. New York: Simon and Schuster, 2008.

Hahn, Steven. *A Nation under Our Feet: Black Political Struggles in the Rural South from Slavery to the Great Migration*. Cambridge, MA: Harvard University Press, 2003.

Hammond, John Craig. *Slavery, Freedom, and Expansion in the Early American West*. Charlottesville: University of Virginia Press, 2007.

Hartz, Louis. *The Liberal Tradition in America: An Interpretation of American Political Thought since the Revolution*. New York: Harcourt, Brace and World, 1955.

Henderson, Desirée. *Grief and Genre in American Literature, 1790–1870*. Surrey, UK: Ashgate, 2011.

Herb, Guntram H., and David H. Kaplan, eds. *Nested Identities: Nationalism, Territory, and Scale*. Lanham, MD: Rowman and Littlefield, 1999.

Hershock, Martin J. "'Agitation Is as Necessary as Tranquility Is Dangerous': Kinsley S. Bingham Becomes a Republican." In Finkelman and Kennon, 143–58.

Herzog, Don. *Happy Slaves: A Critique of Consent Theory*. Chicago: University of Chicago Press, 1989.

Hettle, Wallace. *The Peculiar Democracy: Southern Democrats in Peace and Civil War.* Athens: University of Georgia Press, 2001.
Heyrman, Christine Leigh. *Southern Cross: The Beginnings of the Bible Belt.* Chapel Hill: University of North Carolina Press, 1997.
Higham, John. "From Boundlessness to Consolidation: The Transformation of American Culture, 1848–1860." In *Hanging Together: Unity and Diversity in American Culture,* edited by Carl J. Guarneri, 149–65. New Haven, CT: Yale University Press, 2001.
Hitchcock, William S. "Southern Moderates and Secession: Senator Robert M. T. Hunter's Call for Union." *Journal of American History* 59, no. 4 (Mar. 1973): 871–84.
Hofstadter, Richard. *The American Political Tradition, and the Men Who Made It.* New York: Alfred A. Knopf, 1948.
——— . *The Idea of a Party System: The Rise of Legitimate Opposition in the United States, 1780–1840.* Berkeley: University of California Press, 1969.
Holt, Michael F. "Another Look at the Election of 1856." In Birkner, 37–67.
——— . *The Fate of Their Country: Politicians, Slavery Extension, and the Coming of the Civil War.* New York: Hill and Wang, 2004.
——— . *Franklin Pierce.* New York: Times Books, 2010.
——— . *The Political Crisis of the 1850s.* New York: John Wiley and Sons, 1978.
——— . "The Politics of Impatience: The Origins of Know Nothingism." *Journal of American History* 60, no. 2 (Sept. 1973): 309–31.
——— . "Politics, Patronage, and Public Policy: The Compromise of 1850." In Finkelman and Kennon, 18–35.
Holzer, Harold. *Lincoln at Cooper Union: The Speech That Made Abraham Lincoln President.* New York: Simon and Schuster Paperbacks, 2004.
Horwitz, Morton J. *The Transformation of American Law, 1780–1860.* Cambridge, MA: Harvard University Press, 1977.
Howe, Daniel Walker. *The Political Culture of the American Whigs.* Chicago: University of Chicago Press, 1979.
——— . *What Hath God Wrought: The Transformation of America, 1815–1848.* Oxford: Oxford University Press, 2007.
Huntington, Samuel P. "Conservatism as an Ideology." *American Political Science Review* 51, no. 2 (June 1957): 454–73.
Huston, James L. "Democracy by Scripture versus Democracy by Process: A Reflection on Stephen A. Douglas and Popular Sovereignty." *Civil War History* 43, no. 3 (Sept. 1997): 189–200.
——— . "The Illinois Political Realignment of 1844–1860: Revisiting the Analysis." *Journal of the Civil War Era* 1, no. 4 (Dec. 2011): 506–35.
——— . "Putting African Americans in the Center of National Political Discourse: The Strange Fate of Popular Sovereignty." In McDonough and Noe, 96–128.
——— . *Stephen A. Douglas and the Dilemmas of Democratic Equality.* Lanham, MD: Rowman and Littlefield, 2007.

Ignatiev, Noel. *How the Irish Became White.* New York: Routledge, 1995.
Isenberg, Nancy, and Andrew Burstein, eds. *Mortal Remains: Death in Early America.* Philadelphia: University of Pennsylvania Press, 2003.
Jaffa, Harry V. *Crisis of the House Divided: An Interpretation of the Issues in the Lincoln-Douglas Debates.* Garden City, NY: Doubleday, 1959.
———. *A New Birth of Freedom: Abraham Lincoln and the Coming of the Civil War.* Lanham, MD: Rowman and Littlefield, 2000.
Johannsen, Robert W. *Stephen A. Douglas.* New York: Oxford University Press, 1973.
———. "Stephen A. Douglas, 'Harper's Magazine,' and Popular Sovereignty." *Mississippi Valley Historical Review* 45, no. 4 (Mar. 1959): 606–31.
Johnson, Allen. "The Genesis of Popular Sovereignty." *Iowa Journal of History and Politics* 3, no. 1 (Jan. 1905): 3–19.
Johnson, Tekla Ali. "Frederick Douglass and the Kansas-Nebraska Act: From Reformer to Revolutionary." In Wunder and Ross, 113–28.
Katz, Jonathan Ned. *Love Stories: Sex between Men before Homosexuality.* Chicago: University of Chicago Press, 2001.
Kazin, Michael. *The Populist Persuasion: An American History.* New York: Basic Books, 1995.
Kirk, Russell. *The Conservative Mind: From Burke to Eliot.* 7th rev. ed. 1986. Reprint, Washington, DC: Gateway Editions, 2014.
Klein, Philip S. *President James Buchanan: A Biography.* University Park: Pennsylvania State University Press, 1962.
Kleppner, Paul. *The Cross of Culture: A Social Analysis of Midwestern Politics, 1850–1900.* New York: Free Press, 1970.
Kloppenberg, James T. "The Virtues of Liberalism: Christianity, Republicanism, and Ethics in Early American Political Discourse." *Journal of American History* 74, no. 1 (June 1987): 9–33.
Klunder, Willard Carl. "Lewis Cass, Stephen Douglas, and Popular Sovereignty: The Demise of Democratic Party Unity." In McDonough and Noe, 129–53.
———. "The Seeds of Popular Sovereignty: Governor Lewis Cass and Michigan Territory." *Michigan Historical Review* 17, no. 1 (Spring 1991): 64–81.
Knupfer, Peter. "A Crisis in Conservatism: Northern Unionism and the Harpers Ferry Raid." In *His Soul Goes Marching On: Responses to John Brown and the Harpers Ferry Raid*, edited by Paul Finkelman, 119–48. Charlottesville: University Press of Virginia, 1995.
Kohl, Lawrence Frederick. *The Politics of Individualism: Parties and the American Character in the Jacksonian Era.* New York: Oxford University Press, 1989.
Kramer, Lloyd. *Nationalism in Europe and America: Politics, Cultures, and Identities since 1775.* Chapel Hill: University of North Carolina Press, 2011.
Landis, Michael Todd. *Northern Men with Southern Loyalties: The Democratic Party and the Sectional Crisis.* Ithaca, NY: Cornell University Press, 2014.
Lassiter, Matthew D. *The Silent Majority: Suburban Politics in the Sunbelt South.* Princeton, NJ: Princeton University Press, 2006.

Learned, Henry Barrett. "The Relation of Philip Phillips to the Repeal of the Missouri Compromise in 1854." *Mississippi Valley Historical Review* 8, no. 4 (Mar. 1922): 303–17.
Levine, Bruce. "Conservatism, Nativism, and Slavery: Thomas R. Whitney and the Origins of the Know-Nothing Party." *Journal of American History* 88, no. 2 (Sept. 2001): 455–88.
———. *Half Slave and Half Free: The Roots of Civil War.* Rev. ed. New York: Hill and Wang, 2005.
———. "'The Vital Element of the Republican Party': Antislavery, Nativism, and Abraham Lincoln." *Journal of the Civil War Era* 1, no. 4 (Dec. 2011): 481–505.
Link, William A. *Roots of Secession: Slavery and Politics in Antebellum Virginia.* Chapel Hill: University of North Carolina Press, 2003.
Love, Nancy S. *Understanding Dogmas and Dreams: A Text.* 2nd ed. Washington, DC: CQ Press, 2006.
Lynn, Joshua A. "From the Money Power to the *Antislavery* Power: Jacksonian Democracy and White Supremacy after Jackson." *Tennessee Historical Quarterly* 76, no. 3 (Fall 2017): 276–91.
———. "Half-Baked Men: Doughface Masculinity and the Antebellum Politics of Household." Master's thesis, University of North Carolina at Chapel Hill, 2010.
Maciag, Drew. *Edmund Burke in America: The Contested Career of the Father of Modern Conservatism.* Ithaca, NY: Cornell University Press, 2013.
MacKinnon, William P. "Prelude to Armageddon: James Buchanan, Brigham Young, and a President's Initiation to Bloodshed." In Quist and Birkner, 46–85.
MacLean, Nancy. *Democracy in Chains: The Deep History of the Radical Right's Stealth Plan for America.* New York: Viking, 2017.
———. *Freedom Is Not Enough: The Opening of the American Workplace.* Cambridge, MA: Harvard University Press, 2006.
Mandell, Laura. "What's Sex Got to Do with It? Marriage versus Circulation in *The Pennsylvania Magazine*, 1775–1776." In *Long before Stonewall: Histories of Same-Sex Sexuality in Early America*, edited by Thomas A. Foster, 331–56. New York: New York University Press, 2007.
Mason, Matthew. *Apostle of Union: A Political Biography of Edward Everett.* Chapel Hill: University of North Carolina Press, 2016.
Mayfield, John. *Counterfeit Gentlemen: Manhood and Humor in the Old South.* Gainesville: University Press of Florida, 2009.
Mendelson, Wallace. "Dred Scott's Case—Reconsidered." *Minnesota Law Review* 38, no. 1 (Dec. 1953): 16–28.
McCurdy, John Gilbert. *Citizen Bachelors: Manhood and the Creation of the United States.* Ithaca, NY: Cornell University Press, 2009.
McCurry, Stephanie. *Masters of Small Worlds: Yeoman Households, Gender Relations, and the Political Culture of the Antebellum South Carolina Low Country.* New York: Oxford University Press, 1995.

McDonough, Daniel, and Kenneth W. Noe, eds. *Politics and Culture of the Civil War Era: Essays in Honor of Robert W. Johannsen*. Selinsgrove, PA: Susquehanna University Press, 2006.
McGerr, Michael. "Political Style and Women's Power, 1830–1930." *Journal of American History* 77, no. 3 (Dec. 1990): 864–85.
McGirr, Lisa. *Suburban Warriors: The Origins of the New American Right*. Princeton, NJ: Princeton University Press, 2001.
McManus, Michael J. *Political Abolitionism in Wisconsin, 1840–1861*. Kent, OH: Kent State University Press, 1998.
McPherson, James M. *Battle Cry of Freedom: The Civil War Era*. Oxford: Oxford University Press, 1988.
Meyers, Marvin. *The Jacksonian Persuasion: Politics and Belief*. Stanford, CA: Stanford University Press, 1957.
Moore, R. Randall. "Robert M. T. Hunter and the Crisis of the Union, 1860–1861." *Southern Historian* 13 (Spring 1992): 25–35.
Morgan, Edmund S. *Inventing the People: The Rise of Popular Sovereignty in England and America*. New York: W. W. Norton, 1988.
Mueller, Ken S. *Senator Benton and the People: Master Race Democracy on the Early American Frontiers*. DeKalb: Northern Illinois University Press, 2014.
Mumford, Kevin J. "'Lost Manhood' Found: Male Sexual Impotence and Victorian Culture in the United States." *Journal of the History of Sexuality* 3, no. 1 (July 1992): 33–57.
Murrin, John M. "A Roof without Walls: The Dilemma of American National Identity." In *Beyond Confederation: Origins of the Constitution and American National Identity*, edited by Richard Beeman, Stephen Botein, and Edward C. Carter II, 333–48. Chapel Hill: University of North Carolina Press, 1987.
Nash, George H. *The Conservative Intellectual Movement in America since 1945*. Rev. ed. Wilmington, DE: ISI Books, 2006.
Neely, Mark E., Jr. *The Boundaries of American Political Culture in the Civil War Era*. Chapel Hill: University of North Carolina Press, 2005.
———. *The Union Divided: Party Conflict in the Civil War North*. Cambridge, MA: Harvard University Press, 2002.
Newman, Jay. *Fanatics and Hypocrites*. Buffalo: Prometheus Books, 1986.
Newman, Richard. "Protest in Black and White: The Formation and Transformation of an African American Political Community during the Early Republic." In Pasley, Robertson, and Waldstreicher, 180–204.
Nichols, Roy Franklin. *The Disruption of American Democracy*. 1948. Reprint, New York: Free Press, 1968.
———. "The Kansas-Nebraska Act: A Century of Historiography." *Mississippi Valley Historical Review* 43, no. 2 (Sept. 1956): 187–212.
Nichols, Roy F., and Philip S. Klein. "Election of 1856." In *History of American Presidential Elections, 1789–1968*, edited by Arthur M. Schlesinger Jr., 2:1005–33. New York: Chelsea House, 1971.

Oakeshott, Michael. "On Being Conservative." In *Rationalism in Politics and Other Essays*. Rev. ed., 407–37. Indianapolis: Liberty Fund, 1991.

O'Connor, Thomas H. *Lords of the Loom: The Cotton Whigs and the Coming of the Civil War*. New York: Charles Scribner's Sons, 1968.

Olson, Joel. *The Abolition of White Democracy*. Minneapolis: University of Minnesota Press, 2004.

———. "The Freshness of Fanaticism: The Abolitionist Defense of Zealotry." *Perspectives on Politics* 5, no. 4 (Dec. 2007): 685–701.

Onuf, Peter S. *Statehood and Union: A History of the Northwest Ordinance*. Bloomington: Indiana University Press, 1987.

Osofsky, Gilbert. "Abolitionists, Irish Immigrants, and the Dilemmas of Romantic Nationalism." *American Historical Review* 80, no. 4 (Oct. 1975): 889–912.

Parish, Peter J. "An Exception to Most of the Rules: What Made American Nationalism Different in the Mid-Nineteenth Century?" *Prologue: Quarterly of the National Archives* 27, no. 3 (Fall 1995): 219–29.

Pasley, Jeffrey L. "The Cheese and the Words: Popular Political Culture and Participatory Democracy in the Early American Republic." In Pasley, Robertson, and Waldstreicher, 31–56.

Pasley, Jeffrey L., Andrew W. Robertson, and David Waldstreicher, eds. *Beyond the Founders: New Approaches to the Political History of the Early American Republic*. Chapel Hill: University of North Carolina Press, 2004.

Passmore, John. "Fanaticism, Toleration and Philosophy." *Journal of Political Philosophy* 11, no. 2 (June 2003): 211–22.

Pateman, Carol. *The Sexual Contract*. Stanford, CA: Stanford University Press, 1988.

Paulus, Sarah Bischoff. "America's Long Eulogy for Compromise: Henry Clay and American Politics, 1854–58." *Journal of the Civil War Era* 4, no. 11 (Mar. 2014): 28–52.

Peterson, Merrill D. *The Jeffersonian Image in the American Mind*. New York: Oxford University Press, 1960.

Phillips-Fein, Kim. *Invisible Hands: The Making of the Conservative Movement from the New Deal to Reagan*. New York: W. W. Norton, 2009.

Pierson, Michael D. *Free Hearts and Free Homes: Gender and American Antislavery Politics*. Chapel Hill: University of North Carolina Press, 2003.

Poole, W. Scott. *Never Surrender: Confederate Memory and Conservatism in the South Carolina Upcountry*. Athens: University of Georgia Press, 2004.

Potter, David M. "The Historian's Use of Nationalism and Vice Versa." In *The South and the Sectional Conflict*, 34–83. Baton Rouge: Louisiana State University Press, 1968.

———. *The Impending Crisis, 1848–1861*. Completed and edited by Don E. Fehrenbacher. New York: Harper and Row, 1976.

Quist, John W., and Michael J. Birkner, eds. *James Buchanan and the Coming of the Civil War*. Gainesville: University Press of Florida, 2013.

Quitt, Martin H. *Stephen A. Douglas and Antebellum Democracy.* Cambridge: Cambridge University Press, 2012.

Ramsdell, Charles W. "The Natural Limits of Slavery Expansion." *Mississippi Valley Historical Review* 16, no. 2 (Sept. 1929): 151–71.

Randall, J. G. "The Blundering Generation." *Mississippi Valley Historical Review* 27, no. 1 (June 1940): 3–28.

Read, James H. *Majority Rule versus Consensus: The Political Thought of John C. Calhoun.* Lawrence: University Press of Kansas, 2009.

Rensink, Brenden. "Nebraska and Kansas Territories in American Legal Culture: Territorial Statutory Context." In Wunder and Ross, 47–66.

Rice, Philip Morrison. "The Know-Nothing Party in Virginia, 1854–1856." Pts. 1 and 2. *Virginia Magazine of History and Biography* 55, no. 1 (Jan. 1947): 61–75; 55, no. 2 (Apr. 1947): 159–67.

Richard, Robert. "The 'Great Depression,' the People's Bank, and Jacksonian Fiscal Populism in North Carolina, 1819–1833." *Tennessee Historical Quarterly* 76, no. 3 (Fall 2017): 240–57.

Richards, Leonard L. *The Slave Power: The Free North and Southern Domination, 1780–1860.* Baton Rouge: Louisiana State University Press, 2000.

Risjord, Norman K. *The Old Republicans: Southern Conservatism in the Age of Jefferson.* New York: Columbia University Press, 1965.

Robbins, Caroline. *The Eighteenth-Century Commonwealthman: Studies in the Transmission, Development and Circumstance of English Liberal Thought from the Restoration of Charles II until the War with the Thirteen Colonies.* Cambridge, MA: Harvard University Press, 1959.

Roberts, Timothy M. "'Revolutions Have Become the Bloody Toy of the Multitude': European Revolutions, the South, and the Crisis of 1850." *Journal of the Early Republic* 25, no. 2 (Summer 2005): 259–83.

Robertson, Andrew W. "Voting Rites and Voting Acts: Electioneering Ritual, 1790–1820." In Pasley, Robertson, and Waldstreicher, 57–78.

Rodgers, Daniel T. "Republicanism: The Career of a Concept." *Journal of American History* 79, no. 1 (June 1992): 11–38.

Rodgers, Thomas E. "Liberty, Will, and Violence: The Political Ideology of the Democrats of West-Central Indiana during the Civil War." *Indiana Magazine of History* 92 (June 1996): 133–59.

Roediger, David R. *The Wages of Whiteness: Race and the Making of the American Working Class.* Rev. ed. London: Verso, 1999.

Rose, Willie Lee. "The Domestication of Domestic Slavery." In *Slavery and Freedom,* edited by William W. Freehling, 18–36. New York: Oxford University Press, 1982.

Rossiter, Clinton. *Conservatism in America: The Thankless Persuasion.* 2nd ed. New York: Vintage Books, 1962.

Rothman, Adam. *Slave Country: American Expansion and the Origins of the Deep South.* Cambridge, MA: Harvard University Press, 2005.

Rucker, Walter C. "Unpopular Sovereignty: African American Resistance and Reactions to the Kansas-Nebraska Act." In Wunder and Ross, 129–58.

Ryan, Mary P. *Civic Wars: Democracy and Public Life in the American City during the Nineteenth Century*. Berkeley: University of California Press, 1997.

———. *Cradle of the Middle Class: The Family in Oneida County, New York, 1790–1865*. Cambridge: Cambridge University Press, 1981.

Sacher, John M. "'The Ladies Are Moving Everywhere': Louisiana Women and Antebellum Politics." *Louisiana History: The Journal of the Louisiana Historical Association* 42, no. 4 (Autumn 2001): 439–57.

Saxton, Alexander. *The Rise and Fall of the White Republic: Class Politics and Mass Culture in Nineteenth-Century America*. London: Verso, 1990.

Schlesinger, Arthur M., Jr. *The Age of Jackson*. Boston: Little, Brown, 1945.

Sellers, Charles. *The Market Revolution: Jacksonian America, 1815–1846*. New York: Oxford University Press, 1991.

Shade, William G. *Democratizing the Old Dominion: Virginia and the Second Party System, 1824–1861*. Charlottesville: University Press of Virginia, 1996.

———. "'The Most Delicate and Exciting Topics': Martin Van Buren, Slavery, and the Election of 1836." *Journal of the Early Republic* 18, no. 3 (Autumn 1998): 459–84.

Shelden, Rachel A. *Washington Brotherhood: Politics, Social Life, and the Coming of the Civil War*. Chapel Hill: University of North Carolina Press, 2013.

Siddali, Silvana R. *Frontier Democracy: Constitutional Conventions in the Old Northwest*. New York: Cambridge University Press, 2016.

Silber, Nina. *Gender and the Sectional Conflict*. Chapel Hill: University of North Carolina Press, 2008.

Silbey, Joel H. *The Partisan Imperative: The Dynamics of American Politics before the Civil War*. New York: Oxford University Press, 1985.

———. *A Respectable Minority: The Democratic Party in the Civil War Era, 1860–1868*. New York: W. W. Norton, 1977.

Simpson, Craig M. *A Good Southerner: The Life of Henry A. Wise of Virginia*. Chapel Hill: University of North Carolina Press, 1985.

———. "Political Compromise and the Protection of Slavery: Henry A. Wise and the Virginia Constitutional Convention of 1850–1851." *Virginia Magazine of History and Biography* 83, no. 4 (Oct. 1975): 387–405.

Sinha, Manisha. "The Caning of Charles Sumner: Slavery, Race, and Ideology in the Age of the Civil War." *Journal of the Early Republic* 23, no. 2 (Summer 2003): 233–62.

———. *The Counterrevolution of Slavery: Politics and Ideology in Antebellum South Carolina*. Chapel Hill: University of North Carolina Press, 2000.

Skinner, Quentin. "The Ideological Context of Hobbes's Political Thought." *Historical Journal* 9, no. 3 (1966): 286–317.

———. "Meaning and Understanding in the History of Ideas." *History and Theory* 8, no. 1 (1969): 3–53.

Smith, Adam I. P. "Conservatism, Transformation, and the War for the Union." In *Reconfiguring the Union: Civil War Transformations*, edited by Iwan W. Morgan and Philip John Davies, 41–57. New York: Palgrave Macmillan, 2013.

Smith, Steven B. *Modernity and Its Discontents: Making and Unmaking the Bourgeois from Machiavelli to Bellow*. New Haven, CT: Yale University Press, 2016.

Smith-Rosenberg, Carroll. "Dis-covering the Subject of the 'Great Constitutional Discussion,' 1786–1789." *Journal of American History* 79, no. 3 (Dec. 1992): 841–73.

———. "Sex as Symbol in Victorian Purity: An Ethnohistorical Analysis of Jacksonian America." *American Journal of Sociology* 84, supplement (1978): S212–47.

Sperber, Hans, and James N. Tidwell. "Words and Phrases in American Politics." *American Speech* 25, no. 2 (May 1950): 91–100.

Stampp, Kenneth M. *America in 1857: A Nation on the Brink*. New York: Oxford University Press, 1990.

———. *Indiana Politics during the Civil War*. Indianapolis: Indiana Historical Bureau, 1949.

Stauffer, John. *Giants: The Parallel Lives of Frederick Douglass and Abraham Lincoln*. New York: Twelve, 2008.

Stewart, James Brewer. "The Emergence of Racial Modernity and the Rise of the White North, 1790–1840." *Journal of the Early Republic* 18, no. 2 (Summer 1998): 181–217.

Stoler, Mildred C. "The Democratic Element in the New Republican Party in Indiana." *Indiana Magazine of History* 36, no. 3 (Sept. 1940): 185–207.

Stowe, Steven M. *Intimacy and Power in the Old South: Ritual in the Lives of the Planters*. Baltimore: Johns Hopkins University Press, 1987.

Strauss, Leo. "Machiavelli's Intention: The Prince." *American Political Science Review* 51, no. 1 (Mar. 1957): 13–40.

Sugrue, Thomas J., and John D. Skrentny. "The White Ethnic Strategy." In *Rightward Bound: Making America Conservative in the 1970s*, edited by Bruce J. Schulman and Julian E. Zelizer, 171–92. Cambridge, MA: Harvard University Press, 2008.

Sweet, John Wood. *Bodies Politic: Negotiating Race in the American North, 1730–1830*. Baltimore: Johns Hopkins University Press, 2003.

Swierenga, Robert P. "Ethnoreligious Political Behavior in the Mid-Nineteenth Century: Voting, Values, Cultures." In *Religion and American Politics: From the Colonial Period to the 1980s*, edited by Mark A. Noll, 146–71. New York: Oxford University Press, 1990.

Tate, Thad W. "The Social Contract in America, 1774–1787: Revolutionary Theory as a Conservative Instrument." *William and Mary Quarterly*, 3rd ser., 22, no. 3 (July 1965): 375–91.

Terrill, Robert E. "James Buchanan: Romancing the Union." In *Before the Rhetorical Presidency*, edited by Martin J. Medhurst, 166–93. College Station: Texas A&M University Press, 2008.

Thornbrough, Emma Lou. *Indiana in the Civil War Era, 1850–1880*. Vol. 3 of *The History of Indiana*. Indianapolis: Indiana Historical Bureau and Indiana Historical Society, 1965.

———. "The Race Issue in Indiana Politics during the Civil War." *Indiana Magazine of History* 47, no. 2 (June 1951): 165–88.

Thornton, J. Mills, III. *Politics and Power in a Slave Society: Alabama, 1800–1860*. Baton Rouge: Louisiana State University Press, 1978.

Tomlins, Christopher L. *Law, Labor, and Ideology in the Early American Republic*. Cambridge: Cambridge University Press, 1993.

Turner, John G. "Unpopular Sovereignty: Brigham Young and the U.S. Government, 1847–1877." In *Mormonism and American Politics*, edited by Randall Balmer and Jana Riess, 14–31. New York: Columbia University Press, 2016.

Van Atta, John R. "'A Lawless Rabble': Henry Clay and the Cultural Politics of Squatters' Rights, 1832–1841." *Journal of the Early Republic* 28, no. 3 (Fall 2008): 337–78.

Van Bolt, Roger H. "Fusion Out of Confusion, 1854." *Indiana Magazine of History* 49, no. 4 (Dec. 1953): 353–90.

Varon, Elizabeth R. *We Mean to Be Counted: White Women and Politics in Antebellum Virginia*. Chapel Hill: University of North Carolina Press, 1998.

Waldstreicher, David. "Why Thomas Jefferson and African Americans Wore Their Politics on Their Sleeves: Dress and Mobilization between American Revolutions." In Pasley, Robertson, and Waldstreicher, 79–103.

Wall, Wendy L. *Inventing the "American Way": The Politics of Consensus from the New Deal to the Civil Rights Movement*. Oxford: Oxford University Press, 2008.

Walters, Ronald G. "The Erotic South: Civilization and Sexuality in American Abolitionism." *American Quarterly* 25, no. 2 (May 1973): 177–201.

Ward, John William. *Andrew Jackson: Symbol for an Age*. New York: Oxford University Press, 1955.

Warner, Michael. *The Letters of the Republic: Publication and the Public Sphere in Eighteenth-Century America*. Cambridge, MA: Harvard University Press, 1990.

Watson, Harry L. "Andrew Jackson's Populism." *Tennessee Historical Quarterly* 76, no. 3 (Fall 2017): 218–39.

———. *Liberty and Power: The Politics of Jacksonian America*. Rev. ed. New York: Hill and Wang, 2006.

Welter, Barbara. "The Cult of True Womanhood: 1820–1860." *American Quarterly* 18, no. 2 (Summer 1966): 151–74.

Whites, LeeAnn. *Gender Matters: Civil War, Reconstruction, and the Making of the New South*. New York: Palgrave Macmillan, 2005.

Wiebe, Robert H. *The Opening of American Society: From the Adoption of the Constitution to the Eve of Disunion*. New York: Alfred A. Knopf, 1984.

———. *The Search for Order, 1877–1920*. New York: Hill and Wang, 1967.

Wiecek, William M. "'A Peculiar Conservatism' and the Dorr Rebellion: Constitutional Clash in Jacksonian America." *American Journal of Legal History* 22, no. 3 (July 1978): 237–53.

Wilentz, Sean. *The Rise of American Democracy: Jefferson to Lincoln*. New York: W. W. Norton, 2005.
———. "Slavery, Antislavery, and Jacksonian Democracy." In *The Market Revolution in America: Social, Political, and Religious Expressions, 1800–1880*, edited by Melvyn Stokes and Stephen Conway, 202–23. Charlottesville: University Press of Virginia, 1996.
Wills, Garry. *Lincoln at Gettysburg: The Words that Remade America*. New York: Simon and Schuster Paperbacks, 1992.
Wilson, Major L. *Space, Time, and Freedom: The Quest for Nationality and the Irrepressible Conflict, 1815–1861*. Westport, CT: Greenwood, 1974.
Wish, Harvey. "The Slave Insurrection Panic of 1856." *Journal of Southern History* 5, no. 2 (May 1939): 206–22.
Wood, Gordon S. *The Creation of the American Republic, 1776–1787*. Chapel Hill: University of North Carolina Press, 1969.
———. *The Radicalism of the American Revolution*. New York: Alfred A. Knopf, 1992.
Wood, Nicholas. "'A Sacrifice on the Altar of Slavery': Doughface Politics and Black Disenfranchisement in Pennsylvania, 1837–1838." *Journal of the Early Republic* 31, no. 1 (Spring 2011): 75–106.
Woods, Michael E. "The Davis-Douglas Debates: Race, Property, and the Fate of Democracy in 1860." Paper presented at the Annual Meeting of the Organization of American Historians, New Orleans, LA, Apr. 2017.
Wunder, John R., and Joann M. Ross, eds. *The Nebraska-Kansas Act of 1854*. Lincoln: University of Nebraska Press, 2008.
Wyatt-Brown, Bertram. *Southern Honor: Ethics and Behavior in the Old South*. New York: Oxford University Press, 1982.
Yacovone, Donald. "Abolitionists and the 'Language of Fraternal Love.'" In *Meanings for Manhood: Constructions of Masculinity in Victorian America*, edited by Mark C. Carnes and Clyde Griffen, 85–95. Chicago: University of Chicago Press, 1990.
Zaeske, Susan. *Signatures of Citizenship: Petitioning, Antislavery, and Women's Political Identity*. Chapel Hill: University of North Carolina Press, 2003.

INDEX

abolitionists and antislavery movement: Bleeding Kansas and, 146–47; Buchanan and, 135–36, 139; Democrats' response to, 6, 12, 26–29, 35–36, 46, 50, 71; fanaticism and, 18–20, 40, 42, 59–60, 63–64, 69; in Indiana, 71, 78; Jacksonian sensibilities in, 32–33; Jackson on, 12, 14; Know-Nothings and, 84–87, 89–90; masculinity vs., 123, 125; partisan realignment and, 75, 78–79, 101, 103, 106–8, 110–11; popular sovereignty and, 21, 30–31, 166; Republican Party and, 103, 109; Whigs and, 97; Wilmot Proviso and, 16. *See also* fanaticism; Free Soilers

Adams, John Quincy, 168, 179

African Americans: black codes and, 29; Democrats on, 46, 53; *Dred Scott* and, 156; expanding rights for, 3; in household hierarchies, 62; local democracy marginalizing, 179–80; political agency of, 28, 29, 31, 64–66, 77, 80, 84, 86–87, 106–8, 135, 148, 151; popular sovereignty and, 12, 31, 149–56; suffrage for, 177; zero-sum racial absolutism and, 92

agency of disfranchised: Democrats on, 62–66; fanaticism and, 106–8, 123, 135; Frémont and, 125; Know-Nothings and, 86–87; local democracy enabling, 148, 149, 151; popular sovereignty forestalling, 31; racial amalgamation and, 84, 135; white men's sovereignty vs., 28, 80. *See also* African Americans; women

alcohol. *See* temperance

Allen, William, 15, 16

amalgamation: black political agency and, 64–66; Know-Nothings and, 84–86, 107; partisan realignment and, 70, 80–81, 105–8; politics of slavery and, 77; popular sovereignty and, 155

American Party. *See* Know-Nothing Party

American Revolution: Jacksonian principles from, 25–26, 38, 149–50; sovereignty of conventions vs. legislatures from, 166, 168

anticlericalism, 48–51, 71–72, 74, 77, 88–89

antinativism. *See* nativism

antistatism: conservatism and, 109; Democratic views of human nature and, 39; individualism and, 2; majoritarianism vs., 168; nationalism and, 56; people's power vs., 168; racial boundaries of, 14; from white egalitarianism, 40, 61

bachelorhood of Buchanan, 121–26, 131–35, 139–44

Baker, Jean H., 132, 183n19, 190n15, 217n31

Bancroft, George, 8, 9

Bank War. *See* national bank

Barbour, Lucian, 78
Bayard, James A., 12–13, 17, 18, 99, 128, 162, 172–73
Beecher, Henry Ward, 43–44
Belmont, August, 49
Benjamin, Judah P., 109
Benton, Thomas Hart, 68
Black, Jeremiah Sullivan, 158–59, 162–65, 168–70, 219n81
Black, Samuel W., 131
black codes, 29
Black Republicanism. *See* Republican Party
Blair, Francis P., 109
Bleeding Kansas, 73–74, 142, 146–47
Blue, Albert, 62
Blue, Matthew Powers, 62
Breckinridge, John C., 51, 100
Bright, Jesse D., 72, 81, 175
Brooks, Preston, 136
Brown, Aaron V., 102
Brown, Albert Gallatin, 177
Brown, John, 42
Bryan, William Jennings, 177
Buchanan, James: on 1855 Virginia gubernatorial election, 83; on African Americans, 64; anticlericalism and, 50; bachelorhood and, 121–26, 131–35, 139–44; Clay's legacy and, 100–101; conservatism of, 10, 96, 123–27, 133, 143; on democracy and arbitrary power, 1, 3; Doughface body of, 138–43; on European revolutionaries, 8–9; on fanaticism, 43; on individualism and nationality, 55; on Irish Americans, 13; Jackson and, 129, 133–34; King and, 213–14n81; Lecompton constitution and, 143, 147, 161; Lincoln on, 146; masculinity of, 121–26, 132–43; Mormon War (1857–1858) and, 159; national body of, 130–32; nonpartisan body of, 126–30; on partisan realignment, 111; sectionalism and, 130–32, 134–35, 138, 141–43; southern sympathy of, 132–38, 143; on Whigs, 99, 111, 112; Wise and, 119–20, 123, 125, 126, 130–33, 135–36, 143–45, 171
Burke, Edmund (New Hampshire politician), 79
Burke, Edmund (political theorist), 1, 8, 115–17, 160–61, 217n31
Burns, Anthony, 90
Butler, Andrew Pickens, 51
Butler, Benjamin F., 124

Calhoun, John C., 18, 100, 116, 166
California, 20, 21
Calvert, Charles B., 138
Cameron, Simon, 21
Campbell, James, 49
capitalism, 178
Cass, Lewis: Douglas on, 23; on fanaticism, 82; on Federalists and Whigs, 41; loss in presidential election (1848), 16; on Mexican Cession, 21; on moderation, 11; on religious toleration, 48–49; on slavery in the territories, 19, 20, 22, 25; on white men in the household, 31, 59; Wilmot Proviso rejected by, 16
Catholics and Catholicism: Frémont and, 121–22; nativism and, 44, 58, 84, 88–92, 153; religious toleration and, 48–50, 153–54; slavery and, 90–91
centralization, 39–43
Chadbourne, Isaac, 32
Chapman, Jacob P., 78
Charleston national convention (1860), 169–72
Chase, Salmon P., 32–33
Chinese immigrants, 154, 156
Choate, Rufus, 99, 103–4, 107, 108, 128
church and state, 48–51, 61, 77, 88–91, 154
Church of Jesus Christ of Latter-day Saints. *See* Mormons

Cincinnati national convention (1856), 120–21, 130–32, 137, 166
Civil War, Democratic Party and, 175
classical liberalism: conservatism and, 10, 67, 178; in contemporary politics, 178; Democratic Party and, 14; of Jacksonian Democrats, 2; racial boundaries for, 3
Clay, Clement Claiborne, 44, 57
Clay, Henry, 100–102, 106, 129
Clay, James B., 100–101, 103–4, 128
Clayton, John M., 31, 99, 100, 103, 128
Clingman, Thomas L., 58
Cobb, Howell, 45
coercion by the state, 44–47, 76–77, 124
Cole, Ichabod, 110
Coleman, A. A., 61
color-blind meritocracy, 179
communalism, 40
Compromise of 1850, 18–20, 25, 31, 68, 71, 97, 100–102
conservatism: Buchanan and, 10, 96, 123–27, 133, 143; contemporary grassroots, 178–79; cultural values and, 7, 59; as defense of privilege, 177; definitions of, 8; Democratic radicalism from, 169; Democratic reinvention of, 3–4, 7, 9–10, 36–37, 67, 98, 117–18, 177–78; fanaticism vs., 56–62, 69, 95, 98, 107, 119; from individualism, 36–37; masculinity and, 121–22; partisan realignment around, 96–97, 103, 104–5; people's, 10; popular sovereignty and, 20–22, 143, 148; second party system and, 98–99; Whig vs. Democratic, 109–18, 178; from white mastery, 61–62
conventions, sovereignty of, 165–68, 172
corporations as concentrations of power, 13–14
Corry, William M., 33
Cox, Samuel S., 79, 106
Curtis, George Ticknor, 161, 162, 173

Cushing, Caleb: on bachelorhood, 124; diversity and, 154, 156; Douglass on, 108; partisan realignment and, 68, 69, 79, 96; on popular sovereignty, 170; on women in politics, 63

Dallas, George Mifflin, 15, 16, 19, 30, 37, 58
Davis, Jefferson, 169–70
Davis, John G., 72–73, 78, 82
Declaration of Independence, racial essentialism and, 155–56
degradation of white men, 56–67, 71, 74, 77, 79–80, 83, 91–92, 105–6, 154–55
democracy: conservatism from, 5, 9, 10, 33, 62, 179–80, 184n27; Democratic debate over people's power in, 156–69; Democrats' sanctification of, 11, 117; popular sovereignty and, 6–7, 28; as power, 180; racial, 6, 33, 94; radicalism from, 148, 180; stability of, 8, 67; white supremacy vs., 149
Democratic Party (the Democracy): 1854 election losses, 82, 111; 1856 election success of, 120, 142–43, 145; 1860 Charleston convention and, 169–73; conservative shift of, 3–4, 6, 8–10, 33, 35–37, 66–67, 71, 112–13, 117, 179, 184n27; on human nature, 39; Jefferson's legacy and, 91; local democracy and, 6–7, 10, 55, 61–62, 114, 147–49, 152–53, 177; nationalism and diversity of, 51–56, 114, 117, 130–32, 138, 141, 151, 153–56; pamphlet war and, 161–69; political philosophy of, 7, 25, 42–43, 109, 147; popular sovereignty and, 6–7, 11–12, 19–22, 28–33, 146–49, 156–69; postbellum, 176–77; principles of, 13–15, 18, 33, 37, 85–86, 91, 105, 120–21; progressivism in, 1–3, 9, 14–15, 33, 35–39, 66–67, 179, 190n15; radicalism of, 169; toleration and, 44–51, 88, 153–54; Whiggish

Democratic Party (*continued*)
conservatism vs., 109–18; Whig Party's death/dissolution and, 98–104, 112; white male mastery and, 31, 41, 56–67, 84, 133–34, 148–49. *See also* conservatism; fanaticism; individual rights and individualism; Jacksonian Democrats; partisanship and partisan realignment; southern vs. northern Democrats
Democratic Review, 39, 41, 123
Dickinson, Daniel: on Buchanan, 127; partisan realignment and, 68; on popular sovereignty, 19, 26, 28, 30, 32; on women in politics, 62–63
diversity, 51–56, 114, 149, 151, 153–54, 156, 160, 169. *See also* toleration of individual diversity
domestic hierarchies. *See* household, the, and the family
Dorr, Thomas W., 15, 158
Doughfaces: 1856 presidential election and, 122, 137; Buchanan and, 138–43; Democratic Party and, 5, 6; Lincoln on, 146; partisan realignment and, 79, 109; popular sovereignty and, 11–12, 20, 22–24, 157; white men united by, 24
Douglas, Stephen A.: anticlericalism and, 71; antislavery movement and, 18, 123; on black political agency, 64; Brown on, 177; on Cass and sectionalism, 23; on church and state, 49; Cincinnati national convention (1856) and, 120–21; Clay's legacy and, 101; feud with Frederick Douglass, 64, 148–56; intraparty conflict and, 156–73; on Know-Nothings, 61, 94; Lecompton constitution and, 147, 161; liberalism of, 217n31; Lincoln on, 146; on national diversity, 53; pamphlet war and, 161–69, 219nn80–81; popular sovereignty and, 20, 22, 30–31, 39, 78, 146–51, 154–55, 161–69; on Whigs and slavery, 104

Douglass, Frederick: amalgamation and, 64–65; feud with Stephen Douglas, 148–56; on Whig/Democrat alliance, 108–9; white egalitarianism and, 80
Dred Scott decision (1857), 146–47, 155–56, 162, 165, 220n100

Earle, Jonathan H., 5
Edwards, Laura F., 195n134
egalitarianism: conservatism from, 9–10, 62, 109; Democratic Party and, 2, 5, 9, 29, 33, 59; libertarianism vs., 179; popular sovereignty and, 29–30
election of 1856: Buchanan's conservative body and, 123–26; Buchanan's Doughface body and, 138–43; Buchanan's national body and, 130–32; Buchanan's nonpartisan body and, 126–30; Buchanan's southern manhood and, 132–38
election of judges, 114
English, William H., 13–14, 27, 72, 81–82
Enlightenment thought: anticlericalism and, 50; conservative organicism vs., 59; Democrats and, 2–3, 7, 42–43, 116, 179
enslaved insurrection, 60, 87, 88, 107, 133, 135, 136
Etcheson, Nicole, 219n80
Everett, Edward, 95, 97, 108, 115, 128, 129
expansionism. *See* territorial expansion and organization
Eyal, Yonatan, 183n19

family, the. *See* household, the, and the family
fanaticism: 1855 Virginia gubernatorial election and, 83, 84; black political agency and, 106–7, 135; Buchanan's manliness vs., 123–25; conservatism

in opposition to, 56–62, 69, 95, 98, 107, 119; Democratic election losses and, 82; Democratic label of, 18, 24, 36, 39–43, 69, 86–87; as hypocrisy, 47; individualism vs., 39–43; national diversity, denouncement of, 51–56; national politics of, 91–95, 138; as one-idea politics, 16–18; partisan realignment and, 70–77, 97, 101–4; popular sovereignty as, 118, 155, 173; in slavery debate, 18–21, 24, 69, 89–90; toleration vs., 44–51, 88; Whigs/Democrats united by, 101–4, 106–7, 109, 115; women and, 40, 59, 63–64, 65

Faulkner, Charles James, 95
Faust, Drew Gilpin, 104
Federalists, 9, 41, 66, 117, 178
Fehrenbacher, Don E., 219n80, 220n100
Felch, Alpheus, 98
Fillmore, Millard, 97, 120, 122, 127, 136, 138, 142
Fish, Hamilton, 128
Fisher, Sidney George, 159–62, 173
Fitzpatrick, Benjamin, 59, 175
Forney, John W., 60
Forsyth, John, 164
Freeport Doctrine, 165
Free Soilers: Chase and, 32–33; Democrats on, 28, 29; Jacksonian Democrats and, 5; partisan realignment and, 68–71, 96–97; Pierce and, 127; revolt (1848), 21; sectionalism and, 16. *See also* abolitionists and antislavery movement
free states: 1854 elections in, 70, 82; 1856 presidential election and, 142; black codes in, 29; Doughfaces in, 23–24; fanaticism in, 85, 94; the household in, 59; nativist exclusion in, 153; pamphlet war and, 169, 170; partisan realignment in, 75; popular sovereignty and equality of, 22; racial democracy in, 6; sectionalism and, 26–27; shared values of manhood, whiteness, and domesticity with slave states, 7, 59; southern Democrats in, 54; temperance movements in, 17, 69
Frémont, Jessie Benton, 125–26, 141
Frémont, John C., 65–66, 120–22, 125–26, 136–37, 141
fugitive slave law, 40, 78, 105
fusion. *See* amalgamation

Garibaldi, Giuseppe, 8
Garnett, Muscoe R. H., 59
Garrigus, Jeptha, 51, 75, 76, 79
Garrison, William Lloyd, 62, 65
gender and gender inequality: in 1856 presidential election, 125–26, 142; Buchanan and, 138, 143; conservatism and, 104–6; degradation and, 59; Democratic Party ideology on, 3, 5, 7, 9, 10, 35, 56, 117, 121–22, 143, 177; in the household, 57; Jacksonian principles and, 62, 148–49; popular sovereignty and, 6, 148, 158; white democracy and, 62. *See also* white men
German Americans, 79–80, 142. *See also* immigrants
Giddings, Joshua R., 22, 42, 79, 136
Goldbugs, 176
Gorman, Willis A., 18–19
Graham, Sylvester, 123
grassroots conservatism in contemporary politics, 178–79
Greeley, Horace, 65, 113, 162
Grier, Robert C., 147

Hale, John P., 57
Hall, Bolling, 17
Halstead, Murat, 122
Hamilton, Allen, 129
Hamlin, Hannibal, 110–11
Hammond, James Henry, 42
Hardshells vs. Softshells, 68–69, 72, 127

Harlan, James, 112
Haven, Solomon G., 127
Hendricks, Thomas A., 82, 129
Herrenvolk democracy, 29, 31, 59, 79, 92, 152, 156, 169
Herzen, Aleksandr, 8
Hibbard, Harry, 30
Hobbes, Thomas, 25, 67
Holmes, Oliver Wendell, 30
Holt, Joseph, 4
Holzer, Harold, 219n80
household, the, and the family: bachelorhood vs., 124, 130–31; Cass's Nicholson letter and, 31; Democratic norms of, 7, 9, 31, 116, 121–22; southern vs. northern, 122, 210n16; white male mastery of, 35, 57–67, 133–34
Houston, Sam, 138–39
Hughes, John, 48–49
Hume, David, 42–43
Hundley, Daniel R., 171
Hunter, Robert M. T.: 1855 Virginia gubernatorial election and, 83; on abolitionism, 92–93; on individualism, 38, 66; Jefferson compared to, 90, 91; on King, 134; on Massachusetts, 92; on moral reform, 40; nationalism of, 55–56; on one-idea politics, 17; on religious liberty, 92; on religious toleration, 49–50; on slavery, 69; on Whigs and partisan realignment, 102
Huntington, Samuel P., 8

ideology: cultural context vs., 7, 159; Democrats unified by, 4–5; implications for scholarship, 4–5; partisan realignment and, 69; political rhetoric and, 182n12; Whig Party, 9, 15; white supremacy as, 5
immigrants: Cushing on, 154; Democratic diversity and, 48, 54; *Herrenvolk* democracy and, 79–80; Know-Nothings' proscription of, 77; popular sovereignty and, 31–32, 38; religious toleration and, 60; southern slaveholders and, 90–91; in Virginia, 88, 203n135; white equality and, 92, 94
Independent Treasury (subtreasury), 15, 32
Indiana, 1854 realignment election in, 71–82, 107–8
Indian removal and wars, 14, 30, 66
individual rights and individualism: conservatism from, 9–10, 57, 118, 178; in Democratic ideology, 35–39, 52, 55, 61, 66–67, 109, 116–17; fanaticism vs., 39–43, 76–77; libertarianism and, 179; majoritarianism vs., 148, 179; minorities marginalized through, 180; race/gender basis for, 3, 35–37, 57, 59, 67, 179; toleration and, 44–45, 52; as Whig/Democrat distinction, 113, 114, 116–17. *See also* natural rights
insurrection. *See* enslaved insurrection
intolerance. *See* fanaticism; race and racial inequality
Irish Americans, 90. *See also* immigrants

Jackson, Andrew: anticlericalism and, 50; antistatism of, 168; Buchanan and, 129, 133–34; on democracy and self-interest, 62; on power in democracy, 12, 26, 76, 178–80; precedent of, 14, 26–27; on racial minorities, 30; toleration and, 44
Jacksonian Democrats: American Revolutionary principles and, 25–26; antislavery and, 32–33; Buchanan and, 127–30; classical liberalism of, 2, 12; conservatism from, 9–10; Democratic Party principles from, 5, 9, 12, 18, 24–28, 82, 92, 112–13, 168–69; partisan realignment and, 109–10, 112, 115; popular participation and, 2; popular sovereignty and, 24–28, 148, 156,

157, 168; on power, 14; race/gender marginalization and, 62, 148–49; Republican Party and, 109, 110; white supremacy and, 5, 28–29, 112
Jaffa, Harry V., 219n80
Jefferson, Thomas, 11, 30, 76, 90, 91, 168
Johannsen, Robert, 219n80
Johnson, Herschel V., 23
Johnson, Reverdy, 55, 114, 159–60, 162, 164–65, 168, 172–73
Johnson, Richard Mentor, 133
Jones, George W., 95, 119
Jones, J. O., 78
judges, election of, 114

Kansas, slave-statehood of, 143, 147
Kansas-Nebraska Act (1854), 20–27; 1854 Indiana state election and, 72–74; Blair on, 109; conservatives on, 157–58; nativism and, 31; opposition to, 50; partisan realignment around, 68–69, 74–76, 78–81, 110; popular sovereignty and, 30, 218n54; sectional flexibility of, 138; Whig/Democrat alliance to pass, 97
Kelly, John, 49, 175
Kemper, James Lawson, 92, 101
King, William R., 18, 100, 133–35, 213–14n81
Know-Nothing Party: 1854 Indiana state election and, 72, 77; 1855 Virginia gubernatorial election and, 82, 84–91; 1856 presidential election and, 120–22, 127–29, 136–39; Clay's legacy and, 101; on Democratic hypocrisy, 153; Democrats on, 17, 61, 79–80, 91–92, 106, 160; household mastery and, 58; national politics and, 91–95; partisan realignment and, 69, 70, 75–76, 97, 102, 120; racial amalgamation and, 84–86, 107; sectionalism and, 53
Kossuth, Lajos, 8–9
Kyle, Robert, 13

labor, Hunter's appeal to, 92–93
Lane, Harriet, 134
Lecompton constitution (1857), 143–44, 147, 161, 171–72
Leggett, William, 113
legislatures, sovereignty of, 165–68, 172
liberalism. *See* classical liberalism
libertarianism, 178, 179
Lincoln, Abraham: on Democratic conspiracy to spread slavery, 146; Douglas on, 101; Douglass's endorsement of, 150–51; Gettysburg Address (1863), 176; on Unionism and slavery, 151
Linder, Usher F., 107–8
Little Giant (nickname). *See* Douglas, Stephen A.
local democracy, 6–7, 10, 55, 61–62, 114, 147–49, 152–53, 177
Locke, John, 25, 49, 67
Loco-Focos: individual rights and, 113, 114, 176; political rhetoric and, 3–4; socioeconomic equality and, 2
Lomax, Tennent, 136
Longstreet, Augustus Baldwin, 89

Macon, Nathaniel, 41
Madison, James, 52
Maine, 1851 prohibitory statute in, 46–47, 71
majoritarianism: antistatism and, 168; conservatism and, 118, 148–50; Douglass on, 150; individualism and, 178–79; Jacksonian Democrats and, 2, 67, 109; Whig Party and, 114
manhood. *See* masculinity
Mann, A. Dudley, 95
Marcy, William L., 68
marginalized groups. *See* African Americans; immigrants; women
Market Revolution, 59, 122, 185n10
market/state divide, 11, 13–15
Marshall, Samuel S., 40

masculinity, 57–58, 62, 77, 117, 121–23, 133, 139–42, 154. *See also* gender and gender inequality
Mason, John Y., 39
Massachusetts, fanaticism in, 85, 92, 95–97
mastery of white men, 31, 41, 56–67, 133–34, 148–49
Mazzini, Giuseppe, 8
McConnel, Murray, 25
McLane, Robert, 24
Meade, Richard K., 94
meritocracy, 179
Methodists, 71, 74, 77
Mexican Cession (1848), 18
Mexican War, 14–15
militia, 38
Minnesota Territory, 27
Missouri Compromise (1820), 18, 20, 75, 146
monopolies, 12, 14–15, 177
Moore, Sydenham, 47
moral reform: as bigotry, 44–47; Democrats' "fanaticism" label for, 36, 38–43, 76–77, 88; Jacksonian antagonism toward, 12, 16–17, 115; as threat to white mastery, 60–61; Whigs and, 115
moral suasion, 44–47
Mormons and Church of Jesus Christ of Latter-day Saints, 50, 126, 159

Nantz, Charlotte, 63
national bank, Jacksonian antagonism toward, 12, 13, 15, 26, 29
nationalism: Buchanan and, 130–32; Whig vs. Democratic, 113, 114, 117; white male diversity and, 36, 51–56, 114. *See also* Unionism
Native Americans, 14, 28–30, 66, 152, 154. *See also* Indian removal and wars
nativism: 1854 Indiana state election and, 71–72; 1855 Virginia gubernatorial election and, 84; 1856 presidential election and, 129; Democratic toleration vs., 44, 49, 87–88, 111; fanaticism and, 40; individual rights and, 153; local democracy and, 6, 148; partisan realignment and, 17–18, 69, 71; Philadelphia riots (1844) and, 42; white male equality vs., 31–32, 152
natural rights, 7, 9, 117, 148, 153, 162–63, 179
Nebraska. *See* Kansas-Nebraska Act (1854)
New Hampshire's charter, 48
New Right, 178, 179
Nicholas, S. S., 113
Nichols, Roy F., 4–5
Nofsinger, William R., 72, 78
northern Democrats. *See* southern vs. northern Democrats
Northwest Ordinance (1787), 18

Oakeshott, Michael, 8
O'Conor, Charles, 46
Old Buck (nickname). *See* Buchanan, James
Old Whigs. *See* Whig Party
one-idea politics, 16–18. *See also* fanaticism
Oregon Territory, 14, 27
organic society, 2, 117, 153, 178
Orr, James L., 35–36, 38, 138
O'Sullivan, John L., 39

Paine, Thomas, 25
pamphlet war on popular sovereignty, 161–69, 171, 173, 219nn80–81
parallelism, 52
partisanship and partisan realignment: 1854 Indiana election and, 70–74; 1855 Virginia election and, 81–84; 1856 presidential election and, 120; Democratic ideology clarified through, 109–18, 169; Democrat/Whig alliance, 104–8; disarray of mid-1850s, 68–70;

fanaticism and, 70–77, 97, 101–4;
politics of slavery and, 77–81, 84–87;
racial amalgamation and, 80–81,
105–7; religious liberty and, 87–91;
sectionalism and, 13; Whig Party's
death/dissolution and, 96–104
paternalism, 41, 58, 131–37
patriarchy. *See* household, the, and the
family
Pearce, James, 105
Peaslee, J. W., 78
Peckham, Rufus W., 45–46, 60
Pennsylvania, Democratic intersectionalism through, 130
People's Party, 75
Perkins, John, 23
Pettit, John, 91
philanthropy, 41, 42, 50, 58, 59, 105
Phillips, Philip, 20, 26, 88–89, 152–54
Pierce, Franklin: on 1855 Virginia
gubernatorial election, 95; Doughface
and Whig criticism of, 22, 105; Free
Soilers appointed by, 79; Kansas-Nebraska Act and, 20; Lincoln on,
146; national diversity and, 51; nationalism defined by, 56; partisan realignment and, 68; religious toleration
and, 49; on slavery, 45; state growth
and, 41; Whig Party's death/dissolution and, 99, 100; Wise and, 120, 175
political rhetoric: of "Black Republican
party," 151; of Buchanan's conservative body, 123–26; of Buchanan's
Doughface body, 138–43; of
Buchanan's national body, 130–32; of
Buchanan's nonpartisan body, 126–30; of Buchanan's southern manhood,
132–38; of death and decay, 100–101,
104, 165; Democrats' pioneering
use of, 179; fanaticism as, 18, 24,
36, 39–43, 69; ideology and, 182n12;
regionalism of, 120; role of, 3–4; slavery and, 32; Whigs' legacy exploited
through, 100–101, 111. *See also specific
nicknames*
Polk, James K., 11, 14–16, 19, 21–23, 100
polygamy, 158–59
popular sovereignty: 1854 Indiana state
election and, 73–75; anticlericalism
and, 77; Buchanan and, 131–32,
143–45; church and state vs., 49;
conservatism and, 20–22, 113–14,
143, 148, 156–59, 164; as Democratic
Party doctrine, 6–7, 20–24, 38–39,
41, 73, 78, 111, 117, 121; fanaticism vs.,
60–61, 94, 118; federal intervention
vs., 19–20, 53, 162, 170; Hamlin and,
110; intraparty feud over, 156–73;
Jacksonian principles and, 24–28;
Lecompton constitution and, 143–44,
147; racial boundaries of, 148–56; as
sectionally neutral, 138, 147; territorial, 150–51; theory of, 25–26; white
men's political power and, 11–12, 24,
28–33, 80, 132, 148–49
populism, 10, 178–79
Potter, David M., 54
Pratt, Thomas G., 111
presidential election of 1856. *See* election
of 1856
prohibition. *See* temperance
Protestants and Protestantism: fanaticism and, 90; Know-Nothings and,
72, 88; toleration and, 49–50
Pugh, George, 39–40, 175

race and racial inequality: bigotry, 44–
51; color-blindness vs., 179; degradation and, 58, 59; Democratic Party
ideology on, 5, 7, 9, 10, 28, 35, 56,
80–81, 117, 177; *Herrenvolk* democracy and, 92; in the household, 57;
Jacksonian principles and, 14, 29, 62;
Know-Nothings and, 85–87; partisan
realignment around, 70, 108; politics
of, 77–81, 91–95, 104–5, 137–38;

race and racial inequality (*continued*)
popular sovereignty and, 6, 12, 28–33, 143, 148–56; as social hierarchy, 2; white democracy and, 33, 62, 179. *See also* amalgamation; white supremacy
Randolph, John, 22
Rayner, Kenneth, 93
Reed, William B., 127–28
reformism. *See* fanaticism
religion: Democratic toleration and, 44, 45, 48–51, 67, 153–54; partisan realignment and, 69, 87–91. *See also specific religions*
Republican Party: 1856 presidential election and, 120, 128–29, 133, 136–37, 142; African American political agency and, 107, 108, 151; on Buchanan, 139; creation of (1854), 21, 75; Democrats on, 28, 32, 47, 53, 60, 64–66, 102; Doughfaces and, 23; on Douglas, 169; on *Dred Scott*, 165; Jacksonian Democrats and, 5, 109–10; Kansas-Nebraska Act and, 69; on Mormon polygamy, 126; partisan realignment and, 69, 75, 96, 97, 103, 105, 109–10; racial amalgamation and, 105–6; white man's degradation and, 57–58, 105–6; women's political engagement and, 63
Revolutions of 1848, 8
rhetoric. *See* political rhetoric
Ridge, John R., 154
Right, the, in contemporary politics, 178–79
Ritchey, James, 78
Ross, William H., 39
Rust, Albert, 171

Samford, William F., 157
Sanford, John W. A., 136
Sappenfield, Absalom, 72
Schlesinger, Arthur M., Jr., 5, 48
Scott, Winfield, 42, 44, 97, 99
Second Bank of the United States, 14

second party system of Democrats vs. Whigs, 6, 12, 15; Buchanan and, 126, 127; demise of, 98–104, 120, 127, 129, 176; in Indiana politics, 70, 72; in Virginia politics, 82
sectionalism: Buchanan and, 130–32, 134–35, 138, 141–43; Democratic Party endurance through, 6, 15–16, 23–24, 51, 95; Jacksonians on, 26; Kansas-Nebraska Act and, 21; Know-Nothings and, 89; nationalism vs., 51–56; partisan realignment around, 97, 103, 109; Republicans and, 103, 142; in slavery debate, 16–24; Wise and, 83
self-government: church and state vs., 49, 77, 159; conservatism and, 5, 10, 156–57; as Democratic ideology, 7, 38, 177; Douglas on, 163, 164; fanaticism vs., 40–41, 52–53, 61, 71, 74, 79, 94; Jacksonian precedent and, 26, 27; Kansas-Nebraska Act and, 76; reformism vs., 39–43, 180; territorial expansion and, 29–32; theory vs. practice of, 161; as Whig/Democrat distinction, 113, 114; white male supremacy and, 5, 28, 147, 179. *See also* popular sovereignty
separation of church and state. *See* church and state
servile insurrection. *See* enslaved insurrection
Seward, William H., 106
sexualization of politics and race, 64–66, 70, 77, 81, 107, 122–26, 136–37. *See also* amalgamation
Seymour, Horatio, 61
Shields, James, 12, 27–28, 38–39
Simpson, Craig M., 93
slave codes, 170–71
Slave Power: Chase on, 32–33; Democratic Party and, 3, 5, 6; Doughfaces and, 139–40; Jacksonians and, 109

slavery: abolitionism and, 42; Buchanan on, 135, 136; Democratic Party and, 5–7, 15–16, 32–33, 45–46, 53, 83, 177; the household and, 59–60, 133; Jefferson's legacy and, 91; Lincoln on, 151; local democracy and, 10; partisan realignment and, 6, 18–20, 69, 74–76, 83, 101, 103, 108; politics of, 77–81, 84–87, 91–95, 97, 102, 104–5, 136–38; popular sovereignty and, 20–24, 26, 28, 31–33, 39, 150, 162; religious reform threatening, 89–90; territorial acquisition and, 6, 21, 27; white supremacy threatened by disputes over, 11–12; Wilmot Proviso, 16–19

slave states: 1854 elections in, 70, 82; Buchanan and, 130; Calhoun and, 56, 116; Douglas as candidate to appeal to, 23, 94, 171; fanaticism in reaction to antislavery absolutism, 18, 47; Know-Nothingism in, 89, 95; Midwestern ties to, 73; nativist exclusion in, 153; politics of slavery as cultural standard-bearer of, 77; popular sovereignty and equality of, 22; religious freedom in, 90; shared values of manhood, whiteness, and domesticity with free states, 7, 59; southern manhood tied to political legitimacy in, 133; Taylor's presidency, dissatisfaction with, 97; Wise's nomination and, 83

Slicer, Henry, 49
Smith, Al, 177
social contract theory, 67, 159–61, 179
social order: conservatism and, 9–10, 117; democratic excesses vs., 158, 160; from Democratic principles, 33, 35, 116, 117, 178; fanaticism vs., 43; government role in, 40–41; nationalism and, 55; natural rights and, 2; from Whiggish principles, 115–16; white supremacy and, 179

socioeconomic disparity, 2, 7, 52. *See also* race and racial inequality

Softshells vs. Hardshells, 68–69, 72

southern vs. northern Democrats: 1855 Virginia gubernatorial election and, 83; on Buchanan, 122, 137–38, 143–45; common identity across, 5–7, 15–16, 53–54, 94, 166, 175–77; Lecompton constitution and, 147; partisan realignment and, 68–69; popular sovereignty and, 19–20; racism and, 29; slavery and sectional antagonism, 5, 6, 15–20, 23–24, 54, 77–79, 89–90; territorial organization and, 28, 157–58, 170; toleration and, 45–46; Van Buren/Ritchie alliance and, 82, 90–91, 130; Wilmot Proviso and, 16

states of nature, 159–61
states' rights, 26–27, 52, 114, 152, 162, 166–68
Stephens, Alexander H., 26, 133
Stevens, Thaddeus, 139
Stone, Lucy, 62, 155
subtreasury (Independent Treasury), 15
Sumner, Charles, 51, 136
Swain, Peter, 72, 78

Taney, Roger B., 100, 146
Tappan, Benjamin, 16
tariffs, 13–15, 112
Taylor, Zachary, 97, 100
temperance: 1854 Indiana state election and, 74; Democrats on, 46–47; fanaticism and, 40, 44–45, 58; local democracy and, 6; partisan realignment and, 16–18, 69, 71, 74–76; party distinctions disrupted by, 16–18
territorial expansion and organization: Buchanan on, 131–32; conservatism vs., 113–14; Democratic dissolution over, 177; diversity in, 53; "other Douglas debates" and, 146–48;

territorial expansion and organization (*continued*)
  self-government and, 27–32, 161–69; white opportunity and, 14. *See also* Lecompton constitution; popular sovereignty
Tilden, Samuel, 58
Tocqueville, Alexis de, 117
toleration of individual diversity, 44–52, 88, 153–54
Toombs, Robert, 103, 116, 152, 172
two-party system. *See* second party system of Democrats vs. Whigs

Unionism, 26, 73, 99, 103, 127, 130, 137
Utah, popular sovereignty and, 158–59

Van Buren, John, 22
Van Buren, Martin, 30, 34, 82, 105, 129, 130
Virginia: 1855 gubernatorial race in, 82–84, 87, 94–95, 107, 119; partisan realignment in, 81–84; religious liberty in, 87–91; slavery and politics in, 84–87
voting rights: electoral franchise, 152; naturalization of immigrants and, 32; popular sovereignty and, 38; as privilege of white men, 38, 62–63, 177

Walker Tariff (1846), 15
Ward, Aaron, 26
Ward, Elijah, 55
Webster, Daniel, 97, 100
Weller, John B., 158
Welles, Gideon, 111, 208n81
westernism, 73–74
Whig Party: Buchanan and, 126–29; conservatism and, 97–98; death/dissolution of, 98–104; Democratic principles vs., 109–18; fanatics compared to, 18, 24, 41, 70; ideology of, 9, 15; as Jacksonian foil, 12, 101–2; nativism and, 31; partisan realignment and, 75, 84, 96–98, 104–8, 111, 120; sectionalism and, 16–17, 53, 105; women's political engagement and, 63

white men: 1855 Virginia gubernatorial election and, 83, 84, 87, 119; anticlericalism and, 48; degradation of, 56–67, 71, 74, 77, 79–80, 83, 91–92, 105–6, 154–55; democracy vs., 149; Democratic Party ideology and, 5–7, 9, 10, 35–37, 40, 54–56, 154; diversity for, 52, 114; Doughfaces vs., 139–40; immigrants as, 90–91; Jacksonian principles and, 12, 14, 148–49; liberal toleration and, 44–45; mastery of, 31, 41, 56–67, 71, 74, 143, 177; nationalism and, 54–56; natural rights for, 2–3, 116–17, 153; popular sovereignty and, 11–12, 24, 28–32, 132, 149–50, 152–56, 172; temperance and, 47
white slavery, 32, 92–93
white supremacy: Buchanan and, 137; conservatism and, 9; as Democratic ideology, 5, 105, 112, 155, 176–77, 179; fanaticism vs., 24, 70, 79–81; Jacksonian principles and, 28–29; Jefferson's legacy vs., 91; Know-Nothings vs., 86; popular sovereignty vs., 148, 155. *See also* fanaticism; race and racial inequality
Whitman, Walt, 22, 109–10, 175
Wick, W. W., 79–81
Wiebe, Robert H., 52
Wigfall, Louis T., 166–67
Wilcox, Jonathan S., 34–35, 43–44, 46–48
Wilentz, Sean, 5
Wilmot, David, 18
Wilmot Proviso, 16–19
Winthrop, Robert C., 96–97, 105, 128, 160
Wise, Henry A.: 1855 Virginia gubernatorial election and, 83, 95; on bachelorhood, 124, 143–45; Buchanan and, 119–20, 123, 125, 126, 130–33,

135–36, 143–45, 171; on Democratic principles, 13; on fanaticism, 42, 93–94; on the household, 59; on immigrants, 92; on Know-Nothings, 85, 87–89, 137; on nationalism, 51–52, 54–55, 93–94; pamphlet war and, 162, 171–72; partisan realignment and, 107; Pierce and, 120, 175; on popular sovereignty, 23, 158, 163, 165, 171–72; postbellum speculation of, 175–76; on self-government, 161; white democracy and, 93

women: Buchanan on, 135; Democratic norms and, 9; as dependents, 31, 36, 57, 59, 133; fanaticism and, 40, 59, 63, 65; political agency of, 62–64, 123, 125, 148; popular sovereignty and, 31, 152, 155. *See also* gender and gender inequality

Wood, Fernando, 107, 172, 175–76
Woodbury, Levi, 14, 48
Worth, William J., 13, 15
Wright, Joseph A., 55, 72–73, 95, 141

Yancey, William Lowndes, 18, 23, 63, 100, 173
Young, Brigham, 51, 158
Young America movement, 131, 183n19

RECENT BOOKS IN THE SERIES

A NATION DIVIDED: STUDIES IN THE CIVIL WAR ERA

Confederate Visions: Nationalism, Symbolism, and the Imagined South in the Civil War
IAN BINNINGTON

Marching Masters: Slavery, Race, and the Confederate Army during the Civil War
COLIN EDWARD WOODWARD

Slavery and War in the Americas: Race, Citizenship, and State Building in the United States and Brazil, 1861–1870
VITOR IZECKSOHN

Lincoln's Dilemma: Blair, Sumner, and the Republican Struggle over Racism and Equality in the Civil War Era
PAUL D. ESCOTT

Intimate Reconstructions: Children in Postemancipation Virginia
CATHERINE A. JONES

Daydreams and Nightmares: A Virginia Family Faces Secession and War
BRENT TARTER

Gold and Freedom: The Political Economy of Reconstruction
NICOLAS BARREYRE (TRANSLATED BY ARTHUR GOLDHAMMER)

War upon Our Border: Two Ohio Valley Communities Navigate the Civil War
STEPHEN I. ROCKENBACH

The First Republican Army: The Army of Virginia and the Radicalization of the Civil War
JOHN H. MATSUI

A Strife of Tongues: The Compromise of 1850 and the Ideological Foundations of the American Civil War
STEPHEN E. MAIZLISH

American Abolitionism: Its Direct Political Impact from Colonial Times into Reconstruction
STANLEY HARROLD

Preserving the White Man's Republic: Jacksonian Democracy, Race, and the Transformation of American Conservatism
JOSHUA A. LYNN

www.ingramcontent.com/pod-product-compliance
Lightning Source LLC
Chambersburg PA
CBHW021656230426
43668CB00008B/641